THEODORE ROOSEVELT
Hunter-Conservationist

"No one but he who has partaken thereof, can understand the keen delight of hunting in lonely lands. For him is the joy of the horse well ridden and the rifle well held, for him the long days of toil and hardship, resolutely endured, and crowned at the end with triumph. In after-years there shall come forever to his mind the memory of endless prairies shimmering in the bright sun; of vast snow-clad wastes lying desolate under gray skies; of the melancholy marshes; of the rush to mighty rivers; of the breath of the evergreen forest in summer; of the crooning of ice-armored pines at the touch of the winds of winter; of cataracts roaring between hoary mountain masses; of all the innumerable sights and sounds of the wilderness; of its immensity and mystery; and of the silences that brood in all its depths."

— Theodore Roosevelt

There can be no greater issue than that of conservation in this country.

Theodore Roosevelt
Confession of Faith Speech
Progressive National Convention
Chicago, August 6, 1912

Theodore Roosevelt photographed in New York studio, with his favorite
Model 1876 Winchester .45-75 rifle. The sterling silver Bowie-type knife was
custom made on his order, by Tiffany & Co., in 1885.

THEODORE ROOSEVELT
Hunter-Conservationist

By R. L. Wilson

Preface by Archibald B. Roosevelt

Foreword by John Milius

Prologue by Lowell E. Baier

Published by the Boone and Crockett Club
2009

Theodore Roosevelt Hunter-Conservationist

© 1971, 1994, and 2009 by R.L. Wilson

All rights reserved under International and Pan-American Copyright Conventions.
Published in the United States by the Boone and Crockett Club, Missoula, Montana.

Manufactured in Canada

First Edition

Cover and Book Design: Julie T. Houk

Library of Congress Catalog Card Number: 2006924155
ISBN Number hardcover: 978-0-940864-69-X
ISBN Number paperback: 978-0-940864-52-8
Published November 2009

Published by the
Boone and Crockett Club
250 Station Drive
Missoula, MT 59801
406/542-1888
406/542-0784 (fax)
www.booneandcrockettclub.com

To John Allen Gable, Ph.D. (1943-2005)

Executive Director,
Theodore Roosevelt Association (1974-2004)
Whose Encyclopedic Knowledge
And Unexcelled Comprehension of Theodore Roosevelt
And His Times
Are Enthusiastically Hailed
For Their Immense Value and Inspiration
to Scholars, Documentary Filmmakers, Students,
Museum Specialists and the General Public
of His and Future Generations

Table of Contents

Preface by Archibald B. Roosevelt xi

Foreword by John Milius. xiii

Prologue by Lowell E. Baier 2

Introduction. 5

Chapter One: The Young Naturalist 9

Chapter Two: Harvard and the Midwest. 23

Chapter Three: The Young Reformer's Hunts in the Badlands 35

Chapter Four: Hunting and Ranching in the "Wild West" 59

Chapter Five: Back in the East: The Untamed Bureaucrat. 79

Chapter Six: The Honest Politician. 105

Chapter Seven: The Reformer Enters the White House. 125

Chapter Eight: The Hunter-President as Conservationist 145

Chapter Nine: The Great African Adventure 167

Chapter Ten: Farewell to a Bull Moose 197

Appendices:

– Theodore Roosevelt and the Winchester Arms Company 223

– The Cradle of Conservation, Theodore Roosevelt's Elkhorn Ranch,
  an Icon of America's National Identity, by Lowell E. Baier 257

– The Omen of Death in the Moyowosi, by Greg Martin. 269

– TR Recipient of Congressional Medal of Honor, Posthumously. 277

Selected Bibliography. 281

Acknowledgments 288

Index. 291

The Holland & Holland .500/.450 double rifle – Royal Grade. The gift from English friends, among them Boone and Crockett Club member F.C. Selous, N.C. Rothschild, George Otto Trevelyn, The Lord Bishop of London, E.N. Buxton, and the Duke and Duchess of Bedford. The finest rifle ever owned by TR, and used by him and son Kermit on their historic African safari of 1909-1910.

DETAILED PHOTOGRAPHS BY DOUGLAS SANDBERG; COLLAGE BY PETER BEARD; PHOTOGRAPHED BY G. ALLAN BROWN; CASED RIFLE SET COLLECTION OF FRAZIER HISTORICAL ARMS MUSEUM, LOUISVILLE, KENTUCKY

Theodore Roosevelt with his sons, from left, Theodore, Archibald, Quentin, and Kermit.
Undated photograph, soon after the Roosevelt family moved into the White House.

© Bettman/CORBIS

Preface

I am one of those fortunate ones who had a father who took the time and made the effort to instill in his sons a love of the great outdoors. He taught us to accept the discomforts and hardships that attend sport in the open fields and wilderness, and accept them as a challenge to our manhood.

Although he did not know or care about the science of ballistics as applied to the sporting rifle, he could teach his sons how to shoot straight and to handle themselves in the open spaces. Perhaps that is more important than any theory. There were a lot of guns and rifles around the house, and in the summer months at Oyster Bay, we would often go to our rather amateur target range—its extreme length about two hundred yards—and practice several mornings or afternoons every week. We knew that when we got into our teens, we would be sent off, or my father would take us off, on a trip after big game.

As boys, we did very little shotgun shooting, although we had a rusty old clay pigeon trap with which we would occasionally practice. For guns, we had a old double-barreled 12 gauge "pinfire" inherited from my grandfather, two Parker guns, one a 16 gauge 28" double barrel Damascus steel, and one 24" double barrel 20 gauge flint steel— one of the finest guns for ruffed grouse that I have ever shouldered.

When Larry Wilson asked me what theories my father had on, and what studies he had made of, ballistics, I had to confess my ignorance, and had to try to remember if he had any. In my own boyhood, I never realized that there was such a thing as ballistics applicable to our rifles. I had, of course, heard many of my father's conversations with Admiral Sims and other Naval officers, but supposed that ballistics only applied to large caliber Naval guns. For my father's rifles, and our rifles, constant practice at different ranges took the place of science. It seemed, then, and seems to me now, that for work in the field, it's as good a method as any.

TR was a great stickler in getting a stock that fitted him, and would spend a great deal of time and effort in getting a suitable fit. A most amusing—if somewhat acrimonious—correspondence on these lines with the Winchester Company points this up.

Age, crippling wounds, and the expense and difficulty of getting to big game country have now forced me to be one who follows a small dog with a scatter gun. But I am still grateful to my father for giving me such an excellent boyhood training in outdoor life. ❧

BY ARCHIBALD B. ROOSEVELT
Originally printed in
Theodore Roosevelt Outdoorsman
(1971)

Foreword

TR was my first hero. Other boys favored Hopalong Cassidy, Roy Rogers, Mickey Mantle. I admired them too but TR was something special. He was bigger than life and he had glasses. He had teeth—what teeth! His head was always thrust forward into an unseen wind. Indeed, when he had his glasses shot off at Kettle Hill, he said it must have been friendly fire from the 71st New York because TR always was facing forward. Into the wind. He had asthma, like I did. Allergies. No matter, he got outdoors. He was made for the open. Later in life when he is photographed as President with foreign dignitaries sitting in some hall or parlor, TR seemed anxious, bored, not as comfortable as the others. He wants to get some fresh air.

I grew up to become a teller of tales. You do this by listening to good ones. The best are told again and again around campfires, after some strenuous achievements or in the shelter of a storm. TR's tale is one of the best—a primal tale. A young man who builds himself from his weaknesses though sheer enthusiasm. "To Know the Great Enthusiasms." He builds himself into an idealistic young zealot. A champion, righteous! He meets a girl, falls hopelessly in love (TR was forever vulnerable). They marry, he becomes a firebrand reformer—and all is lost in one night—the love of his life, his irreplaceable mate, his innocence and purity itself. She dies in childbirth. TR cannot even bear to see his daughter. This doesn't even mention that his mother dies the same night of yellow fever and he is tarnished with a scandal created by ruthless, lesser men of his own party. He is blamed for all because he _is_ a true reformer, now seen a hypocrite, dishonored.

"There is nothing a bad man relishes more than a good man's failure." TR's tale could have been written by Joseph Conrad or Leo Tolstoy. But it is a tale of the times. Today, a politician would get a new wife, a mistress, attach himself to another party, cause or reinvent himself. TR's method was different. The doctors told him his health was failing, he would probably contract tuberculosis—expect an early demise. Reinvention. TR packed money, rifles, saddles, and went West.

And here the tale takes on the epic nature of the great adventurers. More in fact, because it is something we all want. TR is the classic dude. His dudedom is unassailably authentic. His speech is colorful, "Hasten forward quickly there." He wears ridiculous buckskin outfits, relishes his '76 Winchester with delicate Victorian engraving of elk and bears. He owns a rigid morality and decorum. He pummels a desperado for manhandling a fallen woman. The hapless loser doesn't stand a chance. "Harvard boxing team." The quote, soiled dove, is outraged at him. He takes up the cause of the little ranchers, squatters, proletariats who largely don't care. He's always on the side of the common man, later called "a traitor to his class." What these plutocrats didn't understand about TR was he was never of their class. His constituency were the bears. His district, the cold mountains and vault of the sky. His dudedom was ferocious. He hunts buffalo and grizzly alone. He meets a Sioux renegade war party who keep their distance. They know the nature of the wild as well as he. The vigor and hardship of the chase literally puts meat on his bones. His health and endurance became so unmatched that when the oppressive patrician faction in a potential range war, the bullies, decide to hire killers to do in TR during his solitary travels, the would-be assassins cannot keep up with the dude and are exhausted and ruined by the pursuit. Fair chase, indeed. Roosevelt, oblivious to all, recounts the experience with a tally of game taken and observed while on his way. Naturalist! He has become a free man. Free in the way that few will ever

BY JOHN MILIUS

A newly discovered inscribed copy to Theodore Roosevelt, of the 1901 first edition, _The Art of Revolver Shooting_, by eminent artist, author, marksman and sportsman Walter Winans. The hand-written inscription is on the inside front cover. Published by G.P. Putnam's Sons, on The Knickerbocker Press imprint, the 251-page volume was illustrated with Winans' own drawings and watercolors, and with several photographs. Among the latter, on page 21, is the presentation Smith & Wesson Frontier double action .44 revolver, etched and fitted with relief-embossed sterling silver and carved ivory grips. After exhibition at the World's Columbian Exposition, 1893, the cased revolver was presented by S&W to Winans.

In _The Art of Revolver Shooting_, Winans identifies the S&W Frontier as "The most ornamental revolver I have ever seen…, which was presented to me. It is in silver and carved ivory, decorated by Tiffany, and was the main attraction in the Revolver Section of the Chicago Exhibition; and I think it is the most costly revolver yet made…." One wonders if Theodore Roosevelt himself had seen this revolver. At least it had been brought to his attention, through the gift of this pioneering work.

BOOK AND THE S&W FRONTIER REVOLVER, #8401, FROM THE ROBERT M. LEE TRUST

Also pictured in the background are photographs of the hunter's cabin erected by the Boone and Crockett Club for the World's Columbian Exposition mentioned above.

BOONE AND CROCKETT CLUB
PERMANENT COLLECTION

experience. Free like a mountain man, mastering the harshest of environments, the most pitiless and grand landscapes. He fairly howls like a wolf. He is the product of natural selection—the fittest to survive. He went West ruined, weakened, defeated, and the West, the harsh indifferent West with its cruel winds, cold black skies filled at night with a clear unconcerned universe. The West of the elk, wolves, bears, rattlesnakes, frozen rivers, and blizzards—the West regenerated him, built him into something forever, made him its son. At the end of a sufficient education he was reinvented. He went back East to conquer old foes, take a fine new wife and raise a large family, win a war, become President. Just before this, some desperados—killers actually—had stolen his boat in the dead of winter. TR and his childhood mentor from the Adirondacks—no soft place—hunt the outlaws down. Roosevelt must take two, alone, across frozen prairies, iced rivers, Indian country— take them to justice. He reads *Anna Karenina* to stay awake. Some in Bismarck, North Dakota ask the logical, "Why didn't you just shoot them?" TR answers, "The rule of law." Thus civilization advances another step. When he leaves Bismarck someone says, "You could be president." Four Eyes replies he'd make a good one.

My father first told me this tale before I could remember. Fathers should. He was 58 when he sired me and had been to WW I. A different generation, he was not a great outdoorsman but the male children when old enough were required to camp on the Zuni Reservation in New Mexico. This was an old family tradition. The place still exists, called the Cottonwood Gulch Foundation, a sort of proto-Outward Bound. My own children attended. We were taught woodsmanship and self reliance—to be like Theodore Roosevelt. To "Ride, tell the truth and shoot straight." We were exposed to the wild like he was because this exposure can do nothing but produce awe and wonder. My father was not a hunter but he loved to eat game. Somehow I equated the quail, venison, and wild ducks we were given with apples fresh from the tree. A bounty. If you grew the

tree or hunted the quail, you were getting that bounty fresh, without the middleman. This has deep philosophical implications. You are responsible for your existence and the food tastes better. Self reliance. Hunting makes one briefly and symbolically responsible for one's existence. To embrace TR's ferocity and vitality is to embrace the fact that man is a hunting creature whatever his occupation. Responsibility for life and death. The great cycle. The mystery. The Indians, of course, knew this, worshipped it. TR knew it resolutely—a source of constant affirmation and vitality. Somewhere, I believe out of this and his "wolf rising in the heart," comes his sense of fairness, honesty, and decency. Nature, to him was not wholly indifferent. Fair chase. Once, I heard, when describing a hunt, he said the game was sparse, but the other rewards included solitude, grandeur and a measure of beauty.

My father's heroes were the Rough Riders, those other sons of the West that TR drew upon when he started his own war. He was Assistant Secretary of the Navy. McKinley was president, but it was Roosevelt's war. Like many to follow, it was a war against the bully, the oppressor putting his boot on someone's neck. It led to unforeseen empire and a loss of innocence. TR was forever losing innocence. He resigned his position and went to his war, led his own regiment of cowboys, hunters, miners, outlaws, even one attorney. He won his war, he went up Kettle Hill, the only man on horseback. Not a good career move or photo op. The other side had machine guns. He got the Medal of Honor. We know the rest. Responsibility— it comes with self reliance.

And, if he so loved the wild things and places, if he knew inherently that they were air and water itself—we need exposure to them to live, some of us more than others. Then TR knew his greatest legacy would be the preservation of these places.

It is so ironic that today TR is criticized as a bloodthirsty hunter, a despoiler of ecology. TR! We couldn't have any ecology were it not for TR. It would have all been sold and resold by Wall Street long ago. Perhaps it is the times that makes these

LEFT: John Milius, who wrote and directed "Rough Riders", filmed throughout Texas in 1996, with Tom Berenger. The TNT mini-series set the record for the highest viewership in cable TV history, a statement to TR and the faithful filmmaking.

BELOW: Startling photograph of TR and the Rough Riders cresting the Hill. The body movements and form, the facial expressions, the slight blur, the smoke from TR's Colt, the flat plain way down low in the background—at first glance it seems like a newly found photograph somehow taken in 1898.

STILLS FROM "SAN JUAN HILL" PRODUCTION BY CLIVE MCLEAN, COURTESY OF ERIKA MCLEAN

critics so out of touch. They think that man has risen above such pursuits as hunting or even self reliance. Certainly responsibility. Remember that when Roosevelt was young the earth was still new and many of these places had been seen only by illiterate frontiersmen and Indians. Free men. In his lifetime, like Geronimo, his friend, he saw everything change. Whatever happened it never repressed his vigor, exuberance, and ferocity. If Lincoln belongs to the ages, Roosevelt belongs to the trees. Recall what George Bernard Shaw said upon a visit to the United States in 1903. He was asked what he'd seen that was remarkable. He replied quickly, "Two natural wonders, Niagara Falls, and the President." @

Tiffany & Co. of New York made this superb Bowie-type knife for Theodore Roosevelt, circa 1884. The hilt and scabbard were cast and chased sterling silver, the blade relief engraved with game scenes and floral scrolls. The knife has seen heavy use, though details of the silver decoration remain imposing. TR's is the finest known hunting knife made in the 19th century by the historic New York-based company. The blade measures 7-1/2 inches; the hilt and crossguard are 6 inches. The scabbard is marked, "Tiffany & Co. M. Sterling."

THEODORE ROOSEVELT
Hunter-Conservationist

Prologue

BY LOWELL E. BAIER
President, Boone and Crockett Club

America's continuing fascination with Theodore Roosevelt rediscovers and reinterprets the man and his many legacies with each successive generation, seeking Roosevelt's relevance for their time and place. In his day, Roosevelt seemed larger than life as the locomotive President, statesman, diplomat, soldier, explorer, hunter, rancher, naturalist, conservationist, progressive crusader, social reformer, trust buster, and prolific author. During the 1960s and '70s, Roosevelt the conservationist was embraced by the environmental movement for political sustenance and validation. The originality and continuing vitality of Theodore Roosevelt's concept of the conservation of America's natural resources is what has politically sustained the national policy of conservation from the 19th into the 21st century.

Contemporaneous with the publication of this third updated and revised edition of what was formerly titled *Theodore Roosevelt Outdoorsman* (1971 and 1994), is the release of Ken Burns' spectacular PBS series, *The National Parks, America's Best Idea.* Burns gives Roosevelt due credit for the inspiration to establish and then enlarge the national park system. Dr. Douglas Brinkley's new book, *The Wilderness Warrior, Theodore Roosevelt and the Crusade for America* further chronicles Roosevelt's evolution as the leader of the conservation movement in America and the establishment of the national policy on conservation.

These twin releases memorialize Roosevelt as the inspiration for our national park system, and leader of the American conservation movement as we know it today. Both bear testimony to the originality of the man and his legend, and the legacy of conservation and America's continuing fascination with both as a beacon to the past and future.

Burns' *The National Parks* visually shows the parks as one of the spectacular achievements of the conservation movement. The major historical figures behind the establishment of the national parks, who implemented the conservation movement with Theodore Roosevelt, developed their insight, passion, and original concepts of conservation from their extensive hunting expeditions and wilderness treks. Brinkley's book accurately portrays how Roosevelt's conservation ethic was a direct result of his connection to the natural world from his intense dedication to hunting and collecting all species of birds and animals. That foundation was crucial to his evolution into history's premier conservationist, and that of his many colleagues who with Roosevelt orchestrated the conservation movement in America, among them George Bird Grinnell, Gifford Pinchot, and C. Hart Merriam.

This new edition published by the Boone and Crockett Club reminds us succinctly what the life of America's foremost hunter-conservationist looked like. The vigorous life Roosevelt led afield, his intimate knowledge of birds, animals, and habitats, the raw courage he demonstrated in the wilds, and his keen understanding of firearms and the correct paring thereof with big game. It recalls for America that hunter-conservationists led the charge from which flowed its very foundation and cornerstones: the national parks, refuges, monuments, forest system, wilderness areas, wild and scenic rivers and our uniquely scenic treasures like Yosemite and Yellowstone, and the laws and regulations that protect and govern these riches.

Today the public-at-large controls these treasures utilizing "informed" opinion, without ever having set foot in the wilderness, or gone more than a mile from a parking lot in a state or national park. The general public has lost its connection with the natural world, yet their academic, electronic environmentalists attempt to control the management policies for our wildlands and wildlife. Roosevelt called these sham spokesmen "nature-fakers."

Theodore Roosevelt Hunter-Conservationist will remind America that today's responsible hunting and sporting community remains naturalists and conservationists, and have all-embracing insights to contribute in the continuing dialogue of how our natural resources are to be managed. Like Roosevelt, Grinnell, Pinchot, and their circle, sportsmen today personally witness the wilderness in its absolute brilliance and raw harshness from weeks spent hunting and camping. Sportsmen trek for endless, painful hours with their favorite firearm, backpack, and horses in search of big game through colorful mountain meadows lush with wildflowers, side hilling through miserable boulder and scree fields, through impenetrable areas of blown-down timber, across spongy tundra or through treacherous bogs and quicksand, through snow, ice, and glacial streams, and across hot cactus-covered deserts.

The diversity and beauty of wildlife sportsmen see in the wilderness is overwhelming, and they anguish when watching a pack of wolves kill a beautiful ram too old to run, or coyotes disembowel a pregnant mule deer caught in heavy snow. It is they who know well the game they hunt, their habits, habitat, and anatomy from endless hours studying their quarry through a spotting scope or binoculars.

From a hunter's experiences and observations afield comes reverence for the wilds, and from that grows the soul of a true conservationist. Hunter-conservationists witness firsthand how wildlife and its habitat are reacting to increasing human and animal populations, land fragmentation, climate change, invasive species, management policies, and so many more influences. Who better than a hunter-conservationist can speak to management policy for our wild lands and wildlife?

Today there is more focus on the environment due to climate change than since the 1960s when environmental legislation galvanized the nation's focus on clean air, water, and industrial pollution. Today the dialogue seems to focus on green energy, carbon footprints, sequestration and reduction, biofuels, and international treaties. A national focus on fish, wildlife, and wildlands seems to be lost in today's debates. *Theodore Roosevelt Hunter-Conservationist* has the potential to properly inform public opinion of the role heroic figures like Theodore Roosevelt played to establish and

protect our wildlife, parks, refuges, and forests. By celebrating this honorable past, this book offers a footprint to the vital continuing role today's sportsmen and sportswomen are playing in the contemporary dialogue on how best to manage America's natural treasures. The insight of hunter-conservationists is a beacon to both.

Theodore Roosevelt founded the Boone and Crockett Club in 1887 with fellow sportsmen, all hunter-conservationists, and these members were Roosevelt's brain trust, colleagues, and lieutenants in leading the crusade of the conservation movement. The leadership of the hunter-conservationist community has been the embodiment of the Club's membership, and continues so today with Theodore Roosevelt's legacy in its bloodstream. ✑

Theodore Roosevelt seated on a horse while on a visit to Yellowstone Park. Circa 1903.

© Underwood & Underwood/CORBIS

Introduction

Among the most admired figures of history is Theodore Roosevelt, one of the most distinguished of American Presidents and one of civilization's most versatile and accomplished individuals. His public and private record of achievements during but sixty years of life (1858-1919) is remarkable: social reformer and trust buster, statesman and diplomat, rancher and hunter, naturalist and conservationist, soldier, explorer and prolific author. Roosevelt also held the offices of Vice President of the United States and Governor of New York. Further, he was recipient of the Nobel Peace Prize, co-organizer of the Rough Riders, builder of the Panama Canal, and founder of the Boone and Crockett Club.

Roosevelt's colorful and forceful personality endeared him to the people of his time. To all Americans he was the great exemplar of courage, hardihood and self-reliance. Through his daring exploits in public office and in private pursuits, Americans experienced vicariously a life of excitement, action and adventure. At times he almost seemed larger than life itself. Not only did he beckon all Americans to the "strenuous life," but he set the pace and pointed the way. By precept and by example he taught his countrymen to shirk no responsibility, shun no duty, flinch from no danger. He personified the highest of American ideals and infused the nation with a new consciousness and pride.

Theodore Roosevelt's entire life was filled with serious challenges of all kinds. From childhood to death he was engaged in a continual struggle to overcome physical infirmities, family misfortunes and political crises. But no matter how severe the challenge, he always managed a more than adequate response. The trials and travails of life never got the best of him or caused him to compromise his high principles of personal conduct. Every battle he fought fairly and squarely, every challenge he responded to openly and honestly.

Weak and frail during childhood, he overcame poor health by determination, arduous exercise and a steady diet of outdoor activities. His experiences as a rancher, hunter, and naturalist developed in him an abiding respect for all forms of human life and taught him self-reliance and self-control. In the great outdoors he also found the solace and solitude that helped to mitigate the tensions and conflicts of an often turbulent public career. It would be difficult to overestimate the influence of wilderness life in molding his character and stimulating his zest for action and adventure. The striking qualities of leadership that he displayed in all his various public offices were in no small measure the result of his life in the West. He was indeed a "cowboy in the White House"—strong-willed, independent, fearless, and unpretentious. As President, he was always in the saddle, heading off the outlaw's of corporate greed and self-interest and looking after the needs of the public.

From boyhood onward, Roosevelt had an absorbing interest in firearms, hunting and the outdoors. He was a proficient marksman, a first-rate hunter and a self-taught naturalist. He wrote numerous authoritative books and essays on ranching, hunting and wildlife. He hunted extensively in the United States, Canada, South America, Africa and to some degree, in Europe and shot almost every conceivable kind of big game. His hunting trips were always exhilarating, often dangerous and usually highly successful. Roosevelt's first gun was a 12-gauge French pinfire double barrel, which he used during his youth to shoot birds in

Smith & Wesson New Model No. 3 single action revolver at right, serial #35796, with S&W Safety Hammerless double action, serial #221873. The gold tie clasp was a present to Kermit while on safari in Africa – Christmas 1909. See page 111 for details on these two revolvers.

Private Collections
Photograph courtesy of James Supica

Egypt. While a Harvard undergraduate, he hunted deer and lynx in Maine with a Sharps heavy caliber single-shot rifle. During the 1880s and 1890s, he acquired a large battery of long guns, most of which were Winchesters, including the Models 1873, 1876, 1886, 1892 and 1894. Even as President he continued adding to his arms collection. Roosevelt's preferences in types and calibers of rifles followed the transition from the end of the percussion, "cap and ball" period, to the early cartridge era, from black powder to smokeless, from big-bore single shots, to big-bore (lever-action) repeaters and then to small-bore (bolt- and lever-action) repeaters.

Such a stream of books and articles has been written about Roosevelt that few facets of his extraordinary life have remained unexplored. Both his public career and private life have been thoroughly canvassed. In 1967, when the author undertook a special project on Roosevelt's favorite Colt Single Action revolver, it was difficult to come by published material on that artifact. Further research indicated how little had been written on Roosevelt's firearms and experiences in shooting and hunting. In fact, a major weakness of several biographies was (and continues to be) underestimating, indeed misunderstanding and misinterpreting, TR's love of hunting...sadly all-too-often reflecting the prejudices and inexperience, indeed ignorance, of some in "modern" times on firearms and the shooting sports. A similar challenge confronted Roosevelt in his own time—from the "nature fakers."

This study encompasses an original biography of Theodore Roosevelt, a close examination of his personal firearms and details of his varied experiences and skillful techniques as a hunter, outdoorsman, and consummate conservationist. It is largely based on his voluminous personal correspondence (and that of his family, friends and acquaintances) and on his published writings, augmented by illuminating photographs and prints. Wherever possible, the author has endeavored to let Theodore Roosevelt and his hunting and shooting companions tell this wholly remarkable, inspiring and exemplary story.

Sadly, in our time, there are no themes more subject to misinterpretation and outright dis-information and distortion than firearms and hunting. And none are more subject to abuse by the most outrageous and blatant advocacy journalism, and at the hands of even more deceitful and dishonest, "ends justify the means" opposition. Further, no themes of our time are more threatened by the lowest level of behavior by politicians who must know that gun bans and other so-called "common sense" laws are a scam, and that attacking hunters is destroying the base on which wildlife conservation has been funded—in America, the hunters were the original conservationists.

Theodore Roosevelt set the highest, most lofty example, for the firearms devotee and the hunter-conservationist. There is no more shining example of behavior and decorum in the world of firearms and hunting—and for our own signal role in those worlds—than this giant of a man and exemplary figure on the national and world stage.

Undated photograph taken at the White House. Pictured from Left to Right: Top Row: R. E. Young, Sec. Robert Bacon (B&C Club member), Mr. Pinchot (B&C Club member), Sen. Cullum, Sec. Garfield, Ambassador Bryce, Mr. Shipp, Sen. Knox. Seated: Hon. Beland, Hon. Sifton, Hon. Fisher (B&C Club member), President Roosevelt (B&C Club founder), Hon. Escobar, Hon. Lellenier, Hon. De. Quienedo.

© UNDERWOOD & UNDERWOOD/CORBIS

CHAPTER 1

The Young Naturalist

The time was the afternoon of January 17, 1870, the place the Pincio in Rome, Italy. A huge snarling mongrel dog snapped his teeth. He was at bay. Facing him was a *frail* asthmatic boy of 12, armed with a toy gun and backed up by two companions and his own fierce determination. As the dog charged, the 12-year-old coolly thrust his gun into the beast's ear and fired. The dog retreated, but when he later saw the boy he made after him again: "growling furiously he charged me," the boy wrote in his diary that evening, "and would have bit but for the gun which I thrust in to his face."

Theodore Roosevelt had met his first "dangerous" beast and had acquitted himself admirably. He had demonstrated the aggressiveness and resourcefulness that in time would take him far in life as well as ensure that his would be a life of adventure and daring. Theodore's parents had sensed his precociousness and anticipated a bright future for him, though exactly in what field they were uncertain, so varied and wide-ranging were his interests. In any event, it was clear that his life would be intimately associated with guns, animals, and hunting.

The Roosevelts

The Roosevelts came from hardy Dutch stock. The first of the family to settle in America was Klaes Martensen van Roosevelt, who came to Manhattan in 1644, 18 years after Peter Minuit had bought the island from the Indians. As merchants, bankers, and importers, the family left its mark on America's colonial history. James Roosevelt fought in the

Cased Lefaucheux side-by-side shotgun, custom made for Cornelius Van Schaack Roosevelt (1794-1871), the grandfather of Theodore. Bearing serial no. 1866, the gun is a 12-gauge pinfire, with 28 5/8-inch Damascus barrels engraved in olde English letters on breech of the solid rib, "Lefaucheux a Paris." Barrel release lever with relief gold inlaid intertwined monogram CVSR within gold-bordered shield motif. Gray-finished steel. Profuse, elegant and often intertwined foliate scroll engraving, detailing often in low relief. Extensive and finely engraved game scenes. Oil-finished select walnut stock. Elegantly blind-tooled leather case, lined in red felt, the lid with leather trim. Brass plaque on case lid with CVSR engraved intertwined monogram; exterior with steamship stickers, indication of travels to Cologne, to England, and other European destinations. "C.V.S.", as he was known, was the sixth generation of the Roosevelt line in America. He was a founder of the Chemical Bank, a benefactor of the Roosevelt Hospital (founded 1871), and was president of the investment firm of Roosevelt & Son, all of New York. The fact that C.V.S. owned this gun, and that TR's uncle Robert had highly recommended the type, would have impacted Roosevelt's father's choice of a gun for his precocious and outdoor-loving son.

GREG MARTIN AUCTIONS;
PHOTOGRAPH BY DOUGLAS SANDBERG

Continental Army during the Revolution and later opened up a hardware store in New York under the name "James Roosevelt and Sons." His son, Cornelius Van Schaack Roosevelt, born in 1794, greatly augmented the family fortune through sizable investments in real estate. Cornelius was one of the founders the Chemical Bank of New York, and late in life devoted a large portion of his fortune to charity. His youngest son, Theodore, born in September of 1831, became the father of the 26th President of the United States.

Theodore Sr. was 24 years old when he married Martha, the 19-year-old daughter of James Stephens Bulloch. They were married at her home in Roswell, Georgia, in 1855, and their first residence was a brownstone (the wedding gift of Cornelius) at 28 East 20th Street, New York City. A year later Martha gave birth to their first child, Anna; four years later, on October 27,1858, their second child, Theodore, was born. The third child, Elliott, was born in 1860, and the fourth, Corinne, was born in 1861.

Martha Roosevelt's family, the Bullochs, were wealthy slave-owners, but when Martha, known as "Mittie," came to New York, she gave up many of her aristocratic ways. She was a delicate woman, poor in health but of striking beauty. Cultured and accomplished, she was "a delightful companion" to her children and an unfailing source of direction and compassion. As young Theodore remembered, she was "given to a hospitality that... was associated more commonly with Southern than Northern households."

Theodore Sr. worked in the family hardware business his grandfather had begun. Theodore Jr. later described his father as "a big, powerful man" who "combined strength and courage with gentleness, tenderness, and great unselfishness." During the Civil War, he refused to bear arms against the South because of his wife's family ties. His sense of obligation, however, did not prevent him from raising funds to equip regiments or from working with the Union League Club. He was active in relief projects for Union soldiers and was appointed a federal-commissioner of allotments by President Abraham Lincoln. He assisted in the organization of the Protective War Claims Association and organized, in his own home, the Soldiers Employment Bureau. After the Civil War, he became the founder of the Orthopedic Hospital in New York, a trustee of the Children's Aid Society, and a founder of the Metropolitan Museum of Art and the American Museum of Natural History.

Theodore's Childhood

The Roosevelt family was warm, gregarious, and outgoing. There was much love and respect among all family members. Martha's sister, Anna Bulloch, was an integral part of the household. Toward the children she was "distinctly overindulgent" and succumbed to their every whim. "She was as devoted to us children as was my mother herself," wrote Theodore, "and we were equally devoted in return.... She knew all of the 'Br'er Rabbit' stories and I was brought up on them." Anna would hold the children spellbound as she related endless tales and anecdotes about plantation life in Georgia and regaled them with vivid hunting stories.

In the summers, the family eagerly abandoned city life for the pleasures of the country. Young Theodore relished those excursions to the countryside:

> In the country we children ran barefoot much of the time, and the seasons went by in a round of uninterrupted and enthralling pleasures—supervising the haying and harvesting, picking apples, hunting frogs successfully and woodchucks unsuccessfully, gathering hickorynuts and chestnuts for sale to patient parents, building wigwams in the woods, and sometimes playing Indians in too realistic manner by staining ourselves (and incidentally our clothes) in liberal fashion with poke-cherry juice.

Throughout most of his childhood Theodore was afflicted by a severe asthmatic condition.

That he survived at all was due largely to the devoted care of his parents. "One of my memories," he wrote, "is of my father walking up and down the room with me in his arms at night when I was a very small person, and of sitting up in bed gasping, with my father and mother trying to help me." His sickly nature made it impossible for him to attend public schools. Though he had plenty of tutors and occasionally went to private schools, he failed, as he frankly admitted, to receive as well-rounded and extensive an education as other children of comparable age and background. This was especially true with respect to his spelling, which during his youth was erratic in the extreme.

Theodore deeply loved and admired his father: "My father was the best man I ever knew. He combined strength and courage with gentleness, tenderness, and great unselfishness. He would not tolerate in us children selfishness or cruelty, idleness, cowardice or untruthfulness... He never physically punished me but once, but he was the only man of whom I was ever really afraid." The father combined a keen "joy out of living" with a high-minded sense of "performance of duty," and expected likewise of his children. Very affluent, he nevertheless continued to work hard at his business, so hard, in fact, that it contributed to his premature death. There is no mistaking the indelible imprint that his sensitive public and private virtues cast upon the character of young Theodore.

Though interested in wildlife, Theodore Sr. was not an active hunter or sportsman. His favorite sport was riding. He hunted with Theodore Jr. in Egypt (1872-78) and shot some game with his sons in Oyster Bay and on family outings. But

today the only existing firearms that can be associated directly with the senior Roosevelt are a cased set of W.W. Greener, Birmingham, percussion pistols and a pinfire 12 gauge Lefaucheux shotgun presented to son Theodore in 1872. The Greener pistols (one of which is now missing) reveal his discriminating tastes: fine gold mounts on the neatly checkered stocks, gold plating on the buttcaps, gold inlaid eagle and W GREENER LONDON on the 50 caliber barrel, fine scroll engraving on most of the metal parts and a superb gold inlaid escutcheon on the back of the grip, engraved with a TR monogram. The pistols, their mahogany case, and sundry accessories must have drawn some degree of interest and fascination from the Roosevelt boys. The TR monogram was later adopted by Theodore Jr. and engraved on some of his own firearms. Young Roosevelt, as subsequent chapters will demonstrate, shared his father's natural liking for fine and elegant shooting and sporting arms.

"An Interest in Natural History"

Theodore's interest in hunting grew out of his early fascination with natural history. He remembered "distinctly the first day that I started on my

LEFT: Theodore Roosevelt, Jr., at age five years.
INSET: Theodore Roosevelt, Jr. at age 18 months.

THEODORE ROOSEVELT COLLECTION, HARVARD COLLEGE LIBRARY

career as zoologist." While walking up Broadway, he passed a store that had in front a dead seal laid out on a slab of wood. "The seal filled me with every possible feeling of romance and adventure," he said. Daily he haunted the neighborhood of the market, scrutinizing every facet of the lifeless seal. Using a "folding pocket foot-rule," he made meticulous but "utterly useless measurements" of the seal. He then wrote a natural history "on the strength of that seal." Eventually he came into possession of the seal's skull; it became the first exhibit in his newly established "Roosevelt Museum of Natural History," located in his bedroom.

His instinctive enthusiasm for natural history was nurtured by the adventure stories of Mayne Reid, and by his uncle, Robert Barnwell Roosevelt, an accomplished and prominent hunter, fisherman, and conservationist, who lived in the adjoining house. Uncle Robert built a piazza in his backyard adjacent to the piazza his brother had built earlier. Both piazzas, when "opened into one another, made a wonderful playground," which was quickly converted into a kind of animal farm. Robert's wife, an animal enthusiast herself, kept a menagerie of guinea pigs, chickens, a monkey, and even a cow. How kindly the neighbors took to this microcosm of animal life is not known, but the Roosevelt children were both delighted and ever insistent upon increasing the stock.

Uncle Robert was a dedicated conservationist and sportsman. He was responsible for the bill creating the New York Fish and Game Commission and was its commissioner for almost twenty years. Politically he was very active: he fought against the notorious Tweed Ring in New York City, was one of the founders of the Union League Club, a commissioner of the Brooklyn Bridge, a minister to the Netherlands, a Congressman and, finally, a treasurer of the Democratic National Committee. Despite his large commitment to politics and business, Robert maintained an abiding concern for wildlife and hunting. He wrote many authoritative books on natural history, hunting and fishing:

Game Fish of the Northern States, Game Birds of the Coasts, Superior Fishing, Fish Hatching, Fish Catching, Florida and the Game Water Birds and *Five Acres Too Much*. He also wrote several appealing adventure stories for the young. Robert doubtless animated young Theodore's ardor for hunting and the outdoor life and perhaps also inspired the boy's later writings on wildlife adventure. Theodore's father added to his son's education in natural history by supplying him with a great many relevant books.

Weapons and Adventure

In 1869 and early 1870, the Roosevelt family made the "grand tour," of Europe. TR's diaries for these years reveal many amusing incidents that might be expected to happen to an inquisitive, venturesome boy of 12, yet they plainly point up his serious side, inquiring mind and unusually mature thoughts. In Europe he visited many of the leading museums and inspected major zoological collections, not all of which impressed him, however: "1869 June 22, London. I went to the zoological gardens. We saw a great maney animals, zebras, lions, camels, Elephants, monkeys, bears, etc. etc. all common to other menageries but we also saw various kinds of wild asses etc. not common. I was a little disappointed." The next day, while at the zoological gardens, he "saw two she bars and a wild cat and a caracal [lynx] fight."

Touring the Tower of London early in July, he saw a "man dressed like an ancient warden...,

Theodore Roosevelt's birthplace as it appeared after reconstruction.

Theodore Sr.'s cased Greener percussion pistol, c. 1865, .50 caliber, finely engraved, with gold mounted varnished and checkered stock. W. GREENER LONDON gold inlaid on the barrel; TR monogram on a gold stock escutcheon and on inlaid brass plaque on the case lid. The only firearm of Theodore Sr. known today.

SAGAMORE HILL NATIONAL HISTORIC SITE, NATIONAL PARK SERVICE

and...a shield made of crocidiles back, all the prisons, and Saxon, Norman, Irish, Roman, greek, welsh, and even Chinese armour and weapons. We saw horse armour and foot armour, pike men and archers and I put my head on the block where so maney had been beheaded..." At Antwerp he "went to the botanic gardens and played at wild bears and hunting and being hunted..."

At the home of Sir Walter Scott in Abbotsford, Scotland, Theodore was thrilled by the "manny curious [things]...among which were Napolyan [Napoleon] pistols, Bob Rodys gun, an Indian neclace of human bones, squlls, sir walter Scots gun, a robbers purse, an Italian shield and numerous others." He felt competent enough to venture a comparative appraisal of collections: The Natural History Museum in Dresden, Germany, he remarked, "has a good collection of reptiles and fish but birds are the chief thing and it has the best collection of nests I have ever seen. I have two of the reptiles and 1 nest and 3 birds in my Museum at home and I have seen severel birds and nests wild at home..."

Theodore was partial to toy guns. In Paris he and brother Elliott "played in among the trees shooting at each other. I took and bought a pop gun." In Rome, he expressed in unambiguous terms his irritation over missing a hunt: "We all went to the meet (chase). It rained most of the while and our ass of a driver would not drive us so as to see the hunt but we saw the ex-king of Naples, ex-queen, and the Empres of Austria..." It was a few days later that he faced in Rome his first charge from the distempered dog mentioned before. He related the episode with customary pungency:

We 3 went out on the Pinchen [Pincio] with George Cromwell. Conie and I played ball with the valet having great fun... We then began to chase with gun and sword dogs. We saw 2. We charged rat a tat, rat a tat went our feet, bang, bang went the two guns, clash, crash went the swords, bow wow went the dogs and

ran and we also. We chased 3 dogs and as we hurried home saw some more. After dinner the two Cromwells and we two boys went out again. We came upon a dog who troted slowly away. His trot be came slower and he showed his teeth. He turned at bay and snapped at and charged us. With my gun to his ear I fired and he started back and stood at bay by the wall and the guard dispersed us. I came on him afterward by a fountain and growling furiously he charged me and would have bit but for the gun which I thrust into his face. We chased another huge dog and tumbled a small one over nearly and then went home.

Shortly after his encounter with the dog, Theodore nonchalantly noted in his diary: "The valet engraved my name on my gun"—a practice to be repeated many times in the future, with initials, monograms and the full name, by Winchester and other gunmakers.

In Turin, Theodore marveled at the Armeria Reale, one of the richest collections of arms and armor in Europe, with a profusion of decorated armor, and exquisite arms for the chase and for war. Having a sharp eye for detail and a remarkable memory, he recorded minutely what he had seen:

We all went to the Armourry where we saw the Horse that had carried king Charles Alberto through maney battles. A most beautiful

The novels of Mayne Reid "enthralled me." Young Theodore's imagination must have been inspired by these illustrations from Reid's adventure books.

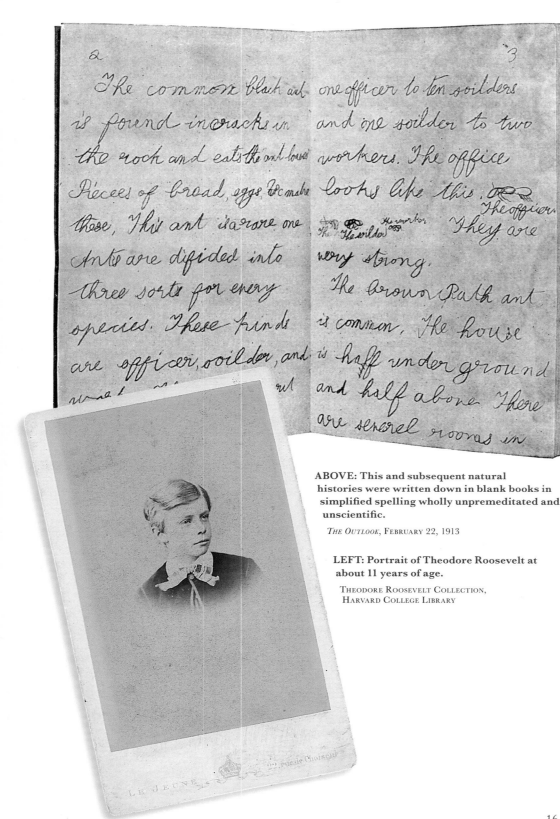

ABOVE: This and subsequent natural histories were written down in blank books in simplified spelling wholly unpremeditated and unscientific.

THE OUTLOOK, FEBRUARY 22, 1913

LEFT: Portrait of Theodore Roosevelt at about 11 years of age.

THEODORE ROOSEVELT COLLECTION,
HARVARD COLLEGE LIBRARY

sword with its handle ornamented with Diamonds, topazes, ruby, etc. This is most beautiful workmanship. Also a most beautiful one presented to the present king by Castelane at Rome. A sword with beautiful carving on it. we saw a great maney turkish weapons and Indian bows and arrows and also severel verry old muskets beautifully carved and of ivorry etc etc but verry heavy. We then went in to the second room where we saw a swiss guard of the Pope. A musketeer of Louis the 14th. We now saw several splendid knights of horse back and maney on foot. Several of the house of Mona and one old Giant one about 7 feet high. We then saw a chines warriour on horseback on a active little horse in queer armour.

We then saw the curuis of Pins Eujean of Savrry [Savoy] worn by him at the battle of Turin and with the dents of three bullets in it. Also his pistol and sword We saw a most beautiful sheald made by Benvenuto. We then saw severel knights Then a Sarecen in armour on horseback A Tategen with the end severed to inflict a severe gash. A hindoo in armour on foot. The sword of Tippo Sabe. Some little Princes armour which I would have liked.

We saw a knight on horse back whos armour was considered the verry finest of all in the collection and another whos horses armour was made of the hide of the Rhimoserous. Severel Pistols of beautiful workmanship with locks of precious stones and barels of silver...

In May, 1870, the family returned to New York. Despite Theodore's overall disappointment with the protracted trip, his diaries show that he had learned a lot about birds and animals and had developed a predilection for the fine and the fancy in weaponry.

In the Adirondacks and the White Mountains

Theodore's Adirondacks and White Mountains trip (August, 1871) afforded him ample opportunity for shooting, fishing, camping out, and writing. He was 13 at the time, old enough to derive almost a man-sized experience from the journey. At Lake George he and cousin West Roosevelt, using an air gun, "had shooting matches with variable success." The following day they "indulged in a few shots on the air gun" before breakfast. Most enjoyable was the camping trip of the Roosevelt party:

> Today we went into the woods… We first rode through the lower St. Regis for about three miles and then put our boats on sleds drawn by horses and made a portage of 5 miles through woods. We finnally arrived at a small stream where we were about to launch our boats, when a thunder shower coming up, forced us to turn them upside down and get under them. While in the lake St. Regis we saw other kinds of wild ducks… loons… and a great blue heron (Ardea herodiss). While going down stream we saw numerous tracks of deer and occasionally of wolves and bears. I also saw a kingfisher… dive for a fish and a mink…swam across the stream while covys of quail…and grouse (Bonasa umbellus) rose from the banks. We had to pass through two small rapids and after the last of these we pitched our tents by another and much larger one, down which only one of our guides attempted to go and he sprung a leak in his boat. On the way we had caught eight trout which we had for supper. After supper Father read aloud to us from "The Last of the Mohicans." In the middle of the reading I fell asleep. Father read by the light of the campfire.

Along with two companions, Theodore "rowed through lower St. Regis Spitfire and then made a portage into big clear pond." Passing through Big Clear Pond the party portaged to a narrow stream. "In descending this stream we saw many muskrats (Fiber zibethicus) and once a deer jumped through the bushes but a few yards from us." That afternoon they "went down a narrow stream and shot the Saranac rapids…" and finally reached lower Lake Saranac.

The Adirondacks and White Mountains trip added appreciably to Theodore's rapidly maturing interest in nature. His diaries manifest an indepth knowledge of animals, whose scientific names seemed to roll off his tongue—though not always spelled correctly when they flowed from his pen. His strong bent for adventure was obvious. He had advanced from pop guns to air rifles and was at last ready to become the proud owner of his first real shooting gun.

Theodore's First Gun— and Spectacles

In the summer of 1872 Theodore, received his first gun, a 12 gauge double barrel French pinfire by Lefaucheux. It was, as he put it, "an excellent gun for a clumsy and often absent-minded boy." It lacked a spring to open it, and if the mechanism became rusty it could be opened with a brick without serious damage. Quite frequently the "cartridges stuck;" even when properly loaded "the result was not always happy and I tattooed myself with partially unburned grains of powder more than once."

Though the gun was a gift from his father, Uncle Robert seems to have determined its type. In his *Game Birds of the North* (1866) he wrote expertly on the merits of the Lefaucheux:

> The best and most generally adopted of the various kinds [of breechloaders] is the *Lefaucheux*, or some slight modification of it; and to that the attention will be principally directed. In this gun the breech, which in the muzzle-loader screws into the barrel, is omitted, and the barrels are open at both ends; they are fastened to the stock by a pin and joint a few inches beyond the guard. When free, the muzzle hangs down, and the breech end presents itself several inches above the stock, so that the cartridge can be readily inserted… When the bolt is withdrawn

After being fitted for a pair of spectacles, he confessed that he "had no idea how beautiful the world was." He realized for the first time that at least some of his clumsiness and awkwardness "was due to the fact that I could not see and yet was wholly ignorant that I was not seeing."

and the barrels are allowed to fall so as to bring the open breech fairly into view, the loaded cartridge is inserted, the barrels are sprung back to their place with a sharp snap that sends them home at once, and are ready to be discharged.… The entire mechanism is so simple that it can hardly become deranged, and will last as long as the barrels. The greatest care is necessary in making the chamber that receives the cartridge of a proper shape, for if this is faulty the cartridges are apt to stick after explosion.

For years displayed at Sagamore Hill National Historic Site, the gun still retains a rich patina from constant use. Although not custom-made, the Lefaucheux's select engraving and quality construction is suggestive of the refined taste noticeable in all of Roosevelt's favorite firearms.

Theodore's excitement over his first gun was dampened by his unaccountably poor marksmanship. His hunting companions were able to shoot at things that he could not even see. Not until one day they read aloud from a faraway billboard did

The Lefaucheux pinfire 12 gauge double barrel shotgun, "an excellent gun for a clumsy and often absent-minded boy." 20/1872 and LEFAUCHEUX BREVETTE are marked on the water table and "Lefaucheux Inventeur 57, rue Vivienne. Paris" is hand engraved on the barrel rib.

SAGAMORE HILL NATIONAL HISTORIC SITE,
NATIONAL PARK SERVICE

Roosevelt suspect the nature of his problem. He was extremely near-sighted and therefore could see "only the things… I ran against or stumbled over." After being fitted for a pair of spectacles, he confessed that he "had no idea how beautiful the world was." He realized for the first time that at least some of his clumsiness and awkwardness "was due to the fact that I could not see and yet was wholly ignorant that I was not seeing."

The Budding Naturalist

Theodore's first formal training in natural history began in the summer of 1872, when he took lessons in taxidermy from John G. Bell, a former companion of John James Audubon. Bell had traveled to the West with the famed naturalist, and stories of these expeditions fired the imagination of his young student. Bell's instruction, wrote Roosevelt, "spurred and directed my interest in collecting specimens for mounting and preservation." He began "an industrious book-study of the subject."

In the winter of 1872-73, the Roosevelts made a second trip abroad. They went to Egypt and journeyed up the Nile River, traveled through the Holy Land and visited Syria and Greece. Throughout the trip, Theodore collected a wide assortment of specimens for his improbable "museum" in New York. His initial acquaintance with Latin came through "learning the scientific names of the birds and mammals which I collected and classified." Bird collecting provided "the chief zest" to his journey along the Nile. Preparing his specimens was a fascinating but filthy task. "I suppose," he wrote half-humorously, "that all growing boys tend to be grubby; but the ornithological small boy, or indeed the boy with the taste for natural history of any kind, is generally the very grubbiest of all."

The months spent in Egypt and the Middle East were a vital link in Roosevelt's ever-expanding chain of experiences as a naturalist and hunter. Apart from his day-to-day study of birds, he hunted consistently and with increasing skill. Generally hunting alone, he relied on his trusty Lefaucheux pinfire and a second double barrel of unknown make. He hunted mostly birds, particularly those

he was anxious to add to his collection. His "Zoological Record" testifies to frequent success:

Saxicola moesta. I shot one specimen of this chat from a column of the Ramaseum at Thebes.

Passer salicicola. Very abundant in Egypt, where it is often found associating with the [Passer domesticus], so that I have not infrequently killed a bird of each kind at a single discharge...on one occasion I stationed myself by a corn field at dusk and as the flights of sparrows passed over me I shot specimens from each flock...

Sturmus vulgaris... Once I saw a very large flock of [these] in the top of a palm, who were making a most extraordinary chattering, and I killed half a dozen with one shot.

Metrops viridis. Abundant in Upper Egypt, being found singly or in small flocks... Once at dusk I fired at a small bird in one of these trees, and to my astonishment—and regret, for from their beatuy, trustfullness

"I suppose," he wrote half-humorously, "that all growing boys tend to be grubby; but the ornithological small boy, or indeed the boy with the taste for natural history of any kind, is generally the very grubbiest of all."

and harmlessness these little birds were great favourites of mine—shot about a dozen green bee eaters…

Theodore's gunning in the "Zoological Record" was for specimens, and, therefore, the majority of species shot were not game birds. Later in life he would express his sincere regret over what he considered some excesses in his zealous boyhood collecting of birdlife.

Occasionally Theodore's father accompanied him on his quest for birds:

Near Cairo. December 14th Saturday
In the morning Father and I went shooting and I shot a white wagtail. In the afternoon I went out walking and I have rarely seen such a quantity of birds before. I distinguished no less than fifteen species (all very tame), each in great numbers in an hours walk. I had an excellent opportunity of observing their habits.

Near Cairo. December 18th 1872. Wednesday…
At about four oclock Father and I sallied out with our guns. we reached a marshy ground, and then suddenly observed a white tailed plover! This is one of the rarest and best marked of Egyptian birds and I immediately recognised it… Although we did not shoot anything we went home well satisfied with having procured a glimpse of this rare and curious bird.

Theodore's proficiency with firearms steadily improved the more he practiced and hunted. He was the first to admit that as a boy his marksmanship had been erratic, and that even after years of hunting he was by no means a perfect marksman. Poor eyesight was partially responsible for these inconsistencies. At the very least, however, he was a better-than-average shot. But he was too honest with himself to try to cloak a bad shooting performance. In Egypt in 1872, he "went out shooting, and after *five shots* procured—a yellow wagtail!!! It was doubtful whether the bird paid for the powder."

A Christmas Gun in Egypt

On Christmas day Theodore was in a state of euphoria after his father presented him with "a beautiful breechloading double barrelled shot gun." In the afternoon, shotgun in hand, he "visited a palm grove and shot four doves…" His father shared Theodore's buoyancy over the new gun. "Teedie took his gun," he wrote to his daughter Corinne,

and shot an ibis and one or two other specimens this morning while the crew were taking breakfast. Imagine seeing not only flocks of these birds, regarded as so rare by us in days gone by as to be selected as a subject for our game of "twenty questions," but also of storks, hawks, owls, pelicans, and, above all, doves innumerable. I presented Teedie with a breech-loader at Christmas, and he was perfectly delighted… He is a most enthusiastic sportsman and has infused some of his spirit into me. Yesterday I walked through the bogs with him at the risk of sinking hopelessly and helplessly, for hours, and carried the dragonman's gun, which is a muzzle-loader, with which I only shot several birds quietly resting upon distant limbs and fallen trees; *but I felt I must keep up with Teedie.*

Hardly a day passed during the following month when Theodore was without his prized gun. He shot doves, plover, pigeon, ibis, and might have bagged a "vinous grosbeak, but my gun missed fire." Early in February he "went off on a shooting expedition and killed a crane, several snipe and some pigeons…" Triumphantly, he wrote his Aunt Anna of his "great enjoyment from the shooting here… I have procured between one and two hundred skins. I expect to procure some more in Syria…" He made good his prediction on the next day by shooting a "peeweet, ziczac, two snipes and eleven pigeons (six at a shot)…" He had his inglorious moments, too. While out riding and studying wildlife he "shot a cat in mistake for a rabbit..."

In March the Roosevelts traveled on horseback to the Dead Sea. No sooner had they reached Jericho than Theodore "went out shooting immediately... Quails and partridges rose from the short grass, bulbuls and warblers hopped among the bushes, while doves, hawks, flinches, jays, and verdons flew among the trees, but I happened to shoot very badly and only procured a quail, a bulbul, and a warbler..." His marksmanship may not have improved, but his writing was getting better, and his truthfulness remained uncompromised.

Theodore was as prolific with his pen as he was with his gun. He dashed off a raft of letters to his friends and relatives back home, giving a blow-by-blow account of his varied experiences. To Edith Carow, whom one day he would take as his second wife, he effervesced:

> I think I have enjoyed myself more this winter than I ever did before. Much to add to my enjoyment Father gave me a gun at Christmas, which rendered me happy and the rest of the family miserable.
>
> I killed several hundred birds with it, and then went and lost it! I think I enjoyed the time in Egypt most, and after that I had the most fun while camping out in Syria.
>
> While camping out we were on horseback for several hours of each day, and as I like riding ever so much, and as the Syrian horses are very good, we had a splendid time. While riding I bothered the family somewhat by carrying the gun over my shoulder, and on the journey to the Jordan, when I was on the most spirited horse I ever rode, I bothered the horse too, as was evidenced by his running away several times when the gun struck him too hard...

Returning to New York in the fall of 1873, Theodore seemed a little bit different. He was only 15,

but he had already been exposed to a large slice of life and had responded with the gusto that would continue to be the distinguishing mark of his character. He was uncommonly mature for his years and was bent on making his entire life one of discovery, adventure, and action. The "vigor of life" (one of his favorite phrases) had become his personal creed. Those who knew him well envisaged a remarkable career, even though his many-sided talents obscured predictions as to just exactly what career he would choose. Of course he was blessed with the advantages of wealth and devoted parents. But that in itself was no guarantee for greatness. He had an inner drive, a relentless and restless ambition that would not allow him to be content with the insipid social existence that the family fortune could easily have provided him. He had "a great admiration for men who were fearless and who could hold their own in the world, and I had a great desire to be like them."

A sound mind and body were prerequisites for "the strenuous life" of which he was so fond. Alas, in youth, he was long on mind but short on body "Theodore," his father admonished, "you have the mind but you have not the body, and without the help of the body the mind cannot go as far as it should. You must *make* your body. It is hard drudgery to make one's body, but I know you will do it." To this paternal advice Theodore had replied resolutely, *"I'll make my body."* And he did.

Theodore turned to many activities in an all-out effort to strengthen his body, but none proved more salubrious than hunting, ranching, and roughing it in the formidable outdoors. The wilderness challenged his stamina, dangerous animals challenged his courage. He would not only survive both, but he would come away with a reverence for the beauty and awesome majesty of the wilderness and a respect for and deep knowledge of animals of all kinds. ☙

...nt the day with old Jack. Our
...g is as follows.

	S	E	Total
...rp tail grouse	26	44	70
...nated grouse	69	119	188
...ail	5		5
...ove	8		8
...nipe		1	1
...lover	16	9	25
...hore Snipe	51		51
...ail	1		1
...oot	1		1
Goose	1	1	2
Duck	17	25	42
Grebe	4	1	5
Bittern	2		2
Hare	1	1	2
Rabbit	1		1
	203	201	404

Left for
trip has
but how
is over and
Alice!

...

CHAPTER 2

Harvard and the Midwest

When the Roosevelts returned to the United States in 1873, Theodore was 16 years old. His continental travels had broadened his outlook and enriched his knowledge, but his formal schooling still left much to be desired. Irregular health had left no alternative save reliance on occasional tutors and on Aunt Anna for academic instruction. As a result, he was "lamentably weak" in Latin, Greek, and mathematics. His father, wanting Theodore to qualify for Harvard, arranged for him to receive a thoroughgoing education under the tutelage of Arthur Cutler. For two years Theodore followed the rigorous academic regimen that Cutler prescribed, and he succeeded in filling all the big gaps in his education.

As TR diligently prepared himself for Harvard, he pursued his private study of natural history. Arthur Cutler later recalled that his pupil "had an unusual collection of birds and small animal; shot and mounted by himself, and ranging in habitat from Egypt to the woods of Pennsylvania. In his excursions outside the city, his rifle [or shotgun] was always with him, and the outfit of a taxidermist was in use on every camping trip." While Theodore crammed his mind with book knowledge and indulged his interest in natural history, he worked hard to build up his body, regularly going to a gymnasium where he put himself through a vigorous calisthenics program.

Roosevelt's field book for 1874 and 1875 detailed pleasurable trips to the Adirondacks, Vermont, New Jersey, and Oyster Bay, where he hunted, studied bird; and took marathon walks.

BACKGROUND: Game tally of Theodore and Elliott on their Midwestern hunt of August-September 1880, from TR's diary of the same year. Note the touch of homesickness: "The trip has been great fun; but how glad I am it is over and I am to see Alice."

LIBRARY OF CONGRESS

INSET: One of two studio photographs made by H. Rocher, a Chicago photographer, while TR and Elliott were hunting in the Midwest in 1880.

THEODORE ROOSEVELT COLLECTION, HARVARD COLLEGE LIBRARY

The Sharps "Old Reliable" mid-range Borchardt 40-2 5/8, one of Theodore's first rifles. Fitted with special Freund sights. Alterations made to the buttstock. The 28" barrel was marked "Old Reliable" and SHARPS RIFLE CO. BRIDGEPORT, CONN. Serial #17130. Manufactured c. 1878-79.

THEODORE ROOSEVELT BIRTHPLACE

Theodore Roosevelt (left) at about 17 years of age, with his brother, Elliott, his sister Corinne (bottom left), and a friend and future wife, Edith Carow.

THEODORE ROOSEVELT COLLECTION, HARVARD COLLEGE LIBRARY

"At present I am writing in a rather smelly room," he wrote to sister Anna, "as the fresh skins of six night herons are reposing on the table beside me..." Early in August he wrote from Oyster Bay:

I spent the early part of this week at the Osborne; and had a lovely time, the days being full of 'ornithological enjoyment and reptilian rapture.' I came home with a jar of pickled toads and salamanders. To offset this acquisition I left my gun case in a barn where we had hitched our horses. Not wishing to make an animated arsenal of myself, I put the gun stock in my trunk, and made the barrels do duty as a fishing rod, in a case rightfully belonging to that article. It is a curious fact that while the ownership of a fishing rod tends to produce a feeling of respectability no such effect is brought about by a gun, especially if said gun be rusty...

In the fall of 1876, Theodore entered Harvard, where he proved himself a good, if not brilliant student. Through conscientious study, he managed to remain generally in the upper tenth of his class and eventually received a Phi Beta Kappa key. He was a voluble and combative student, asking many questions and frequently challenging the remarks of his professors. His ebullience and excitability stood in marked contrast to the staid demeanor and studied air of indifference characteristic of Harvard students of that day.

Practically every student on campus knew Theodore through his prodigious participation in clubs, organizations, and athletics. Further, his bumptious personality and inborn sense of noblesse oblige made him a kind of self-appointed guardian of student morals. Habitually, he would stop students "in the Yard, or call them to him," a classmate later reminisced, "then he would block the narrow gravel path and soon make sparks from an argument fly."

Theodore's father had told the young college freshman that he could devote his life to a scientific career "and do non-remunerative work of value," but if he chose to do so he would have to be prepared to make certain financial sacrifices. But it did not take long for Theodore to realize that science would not be his life's work. He was disillusioned to find that Harvard "utterly ignored the possibilities of the faunal naturalist, the outdoor naturalist and observer of nature." Biology, for example, was treated as "purely a science of the laboratory and the microscope..." Accordingly he "abandoned all thought of becoming a scientist."

Theodore continued field work on his own, but hunting now rivaled his interest in nature study. Late in June he left on a trip to the Adirondacks where on July 5 he "shot my 1st deer, a buck. Also a couple of black ducks and three ruffed grouse." The first deer was shot with a .38 caliber Ballard Sporting Rifle:

a very accurate, handy little weapon; it belonged to me, and was the first rifle I ever owned or used. With it I…once killed a deer, the only specimen of large game I had then shot; and I presented the rifle to my brother when he went to Texas[1]. In our happy ignorance we deemed it quite good enough for buffalo or anything else; but out on the plains my brother soon found himself forced to procure a heavier and more deadly weapon.

During his sophomore year Theodore received a "double-barreled shotgun" for Christmas, a gun of unknown make that has long since vanished. With it and other guns he shot in 1877, "1 buck 10 duck 12 snipe (shore snipe) 3 grouse 6 plover 4 gray squirrel 10 herons." All told, his zoological collection for that year was increased by 16 mammals, 68 birds, 17 reptiles, 61 Batrachian, and 10 fishes. Most of the mammals and birds were taken with the Lefaucheux.

The Maine Wilderness

While an undergraduate, Theodore made three trips to the Maine woods where he had his first rugged wilderness experience. On each trip he was guided by Wilmot Dow and William W. Sewall, both of whom became his "life friends" and were thoroughly experienced outdoorsmen and hunters. "I canoed with them," Theodore wrote in his *Autobiography* "and tramped through the woods with them, visiting the winter logging camps on snow shoes." Thanks to their instruction and to his desire "to keep up," Theodore became reasonably adept in the techniques of the outdoorsman before he graduated from Harvard. It stood him in good stead for his subsequent hunting and ranching trips in the West.

Theodore's first trip to Maine was from September 7 to 26, 1878. Arthur Cutler, his former tutor, accompanied him. Bill Sewall remembered distinctly his initial meeting with Roosevelt and Cutler:

[The party] had come by way of Lake Mattawamkeag, and it was about dark when they got there. Cutler took me off to one side. He said: "I want you to take that young fellow, Theodore, I brought down, under your special care. Be careful of him, see that he don't take too hard jaunts and does not do too much. He is not very strong and he has got a great deal of ambition and grit, and if you should take such a tramp as you are in the habit of taking sometimes, and take him with you, you never would know that anything ailed him. If you should ask him if he was having a good time he would tell you he was having a very good time; and even if he was tired he would not tell you so. The first thing you knew he would be down, because he would go until he fell."

I took him and I found that that was his disposition right away, but he wasn't such a weakling as Cutler tried to make out. We traveled twenty-five miles afoot one day on that first visit of his, which I maintain was a good fair walk for any common man. We hitched well, somehow or other, from the start. He was different from anybody that I had ever met; especially, he was fair-minded. He and I agreed in our ideas of fair play and right and wrong. Besides, he was always good-natured and full of fun. I do not think I ever remember him being "out of sorts." He did not feel well sometimes, but he never would admit it.

I could see not a single thing that wasn't fine in Theodore, no qualities that I didn't like.…I found that he was willing at any time to give every man a fair hearing, but he insisted even then on making his own conclusions. He had strong convictions and was willing to stand up for them…

Theodore was about eighteen when he first came to Maine. He had an idea that he was going to be a naturalist and used to carry with him a little bottle of arsenic and go around picking up bugs. He didn't shoot any

> "Not wishing to make an animated arsenal of myself, I put the gun stock in my trunk, and made the barrels do duty as a fishing rod, in a case rightfully belonging to that article. It is a curious fact that while the ownership of a fishing rod tends to produce a feeling of respectability no such effect is brought about by a gun, especially if said gun be rusty…"

big game, just ducks and partridges. We did a bit of trout-fishing. Theodore was never very fond of that. Somehow he didn't like to sit still so long.

That fall I had engaged another guide, so that the party would be a little better provided for. Wilmot Dow was his name. He was a nephew of mine, a better guide than I was, better hunter, better fisherman, and the best shot of any man in the country. He took care of the rest of the party himself mostly. I was with Theodore all of the time. At the end of the week I told Dow that I had got a different fellow to guide from what I had ever seen before. I had never seen anybody that was like him, and I have held that opinion ever since.

Out of his Maine experiences came one of Theodore Roosevelt's favorite hunting stories. He was out with Bill Sewall when they spotted a stag. "Shoot!" shouted Sewall, and Theodore let go. The stag ran a little way and dropped. "You've got him! You've got him!' said Sewall as he ran forward to investigate. "How did it happen?"

"Why," replied the proud young hunter, "I aimed for his breast."

"You done well," said Sewall. "You done well. You hit him in the eye."

The Sharps Borchardt

Fresh from three rugged weeks in Maine, at the beginning of his junior year at Harvard, Theodore wrote his mother: "...For exercise I have hitherto relied chiefly on walking, but today I have regularly begun sparring [he developed into a skilled boxer]. I have practised a good deal with my rifle, walking to and from the range, which is nearly three miles off; my scores have been fair, although not very good... Have my gun sent in town and cleaned; don't take the cartridges in yet..." The rifle was probably a .40-2 5/8 caliber Sharps Borchardt single shot, and the "gun" a double-barrel shotgun of unknown make. The dealership of

Schuyler, Hartley and Graham on Maiden Lane, New York—conveniently located a few doors from the family business of Roosevelt and Son—perhaps would do the cleaning. Schuyler, Hartley and Graham was a leading supplier of arms and equipment for hunters and shooters, and a firm that sold Theodore guns when he went to the Badlands in the mid-1880s.

Theodore's Sharps "Old Reliable" Mid-Range .40-2 5/8 Borchardt, serial number 17130, was one of his first rifles. Manufactured in 1878 or 1879, it proves the young hunter was already somewhat fastidious in the matter of weaponry. Sights and stocks would regularly be his chief concern on most of his future arms, as the Borchardt clearly shows. Both rear and front sights are marked F. W. FREUND/PATENTED, and they are special to the gun. The rear sight is of the buckhorn type, with an adjustable sighting plate of Freund's own design. The front sight is a steel blade with a short copper strip on the top. Frank and George Freund were renowned frontier gunsmiths and gunmakers, and their patented sights would become favorites of Theodore Roosevelt.

Poor eyesight required Theodore to take extra care in his aim. By ensuring that stock fit and size were just right, he could shoot faster and more accurately. The Borchardt's buttstock was especially adapted to this need. The butt was built up by adding extra wood of about 7/8 of an inch thickness at the heel and 1-1/2 inches at the toe. On most later rifles he would order custom crescent-shaped cheekpieces as a standard feature, and the shotgun style of buttplate would also be repeatedly specified.

The Borchardt, chambered for the .40-2 5/8 cartridge, suggests an early interest in big calibers. With a .40-2 5/8 he could be sure of enough velocity and striking power for a one-shot kill of anything in the woods of Maine excepting moose. Heavy calibers, custom stocks, special sights—all these features would be standard TR criteria for his big game rifles.

OPPOSITE: *The Summer Birds of the Adirondacks in Franklin County, N.Y.*, 1877, was Theodore Roosevelt's first separate publication (shown in background on left), published when the author was 19 years old. Estimates are that the pamphlet was in an edition of 100 copies. Also shown in the background on the right is a facsimile edition of a later publication (1925) that also included notes on birds of Oyster Bay.

BOONE AND CROCKETT CLUB PERMANENT COLLECTION

INSET PHOTOGRAPH: Theodore ready for bird shooting. His double barrel shotgun is a breech loading side-lever type of undetermined make.

THEODORE ROOSEVELT COLLECTION, HARVARD COLLEGE LIBRARY

THE SUMMER BIRDS

OF THE ADIRONDACKS IN FRANKLIN COUNTY, N. Y.

BY THEODORE ROOSEVELT, JR., AND H. D. MINOT.

The following catalogue (written in the mountains) is based upon observations made in August, 1874, August, 1875, and June 22d to July 9th, 1877, especially about the Saint Regis Lakes, Mr. Minot having been with me, only during the last week of June. Each of us has used his initials in making a statement which the other has not verified.

THEODORE ROOSEVELT, Jr.

The general features of the Adirondacks, in those parts which we have examined, are the many lakes, the absence of *mountain*-brooks, the luxuriant forest-growth (the taller deciduous trees often reaching the height of a hundred feet, and the White Pines even that of a hundred and thirty), the sandy soil, the cool, invigorating air, and both a decided wildness and levelness of country as compared with the diversity of the White Mountain region.

The *avifauna* is not so rich as that of the latter country, because wanting in certain "Alleghanian" birds found there, and also in species belonging especially to the Eastern or North-eastern Canadian fauna. Nests, moreover, seem to be more commonly inaccessible, and rarely built beside roads or wood-paths, as they often are in the White Mountains. M.

1. **Robin.** *Turdus migratorius* (Linnæus). Moderately common. Sometimes found in the woods.
2. **Hermit Thrush.** *Turdus Pallasi* (Cabanis). Common. Sings until the middle of August (R.).
3. **Swainson's Thrush.** *Turdus Swainsoni* (Cabanis). The commonest thrush.
4. **Cat-bird.** *Mimus Carolinensis* (Linnæus). Observed beyond the mountains to the northward, near Malone.
5. **Blue Bird.** *Sialia sialis* (Linnæus). Common near Malone.
6. **Golden-crowned "Wren."** *Regulus satrapa* (Lichten.). Quite common; often heard singing in June.
7. **Chickadee.** *Parus atricapillus* (Linnæus). Rather scarce June. Abundant in August (R.).
8. **Hudsonian Chickadee.** *Parus Hudsonicus* (Forster). Found in small flocks at Bay Pond in the early part of August (R.).
9. **Red-bellied Nuthatch.** *Sitta Canadensis* (Linnæus). Common. The White-bellied Nuthatch has not been observed here by us.
10. **Brown Creeper.** *Certhia familiaris* (Linnæus). Common.
11. **Winter Wren.** *Troglodytes hyemalis* (Vieillot). Moderately common.

The
Summer Birds o.
Adirondacks
in Franklin County, N. Y.
By
THEODORE ROOSEVELT, J
and
NOT
ne of th
ster Bay
OSEVELT

More Maine Adventures

Theodore's second trip to Maine, in March 1879, was "a success in every way:"

…I never have passed a pleasanter two weeks than those just gone by; I enjoyed every moment. The first two or three days I had asthma, but, funnily enough, this left me entirely as soon as I went into camp. The thermometer was below zero pretty often, but I was not bothered by the cold at all, except one night when I camped out on the trail of a caribou (which we followed two days without getting more than a glimpse of the animal). Out in the opens when there was any wind it was very disagreable but in the woods the wind never blows and as long as we were moving about it made little difference how low the temperature was, but sitting still for lunch we felt it immediately. I learned how to manage snowshoes very quickly, and enjoyed going on them greatly. I have never seen a grander or more beautiful sight than the northern woods in winter. The evergreens laden with snow make the most beautiful contrast of green and white, and when it freezes after a rain all the trees look as though they were made of crystal. The snow under foot being about three feet deep, and drifting to twice that depth in places,

LEFT: Island Falls, Maine – March 1879. Theodore, at right, armed with the Sharps Borchardt and a small Bowie-type knife. At center, guide Wilmot Dow, and at left, guide William Sewall. Dow's rifle was a muzzleloader.

THEODORE ROOSEVELT COLLECTION, HARVARD COLLEGE LIBRARY

Theodore in 1880 as a member of the senior class at Harvard College. He weighed about 125 to 135 pounds, and his full grown height was 5'9".

BOONE AND CROCKETT CLUB PERMANENT COLLECTION

completely changes the aspect of things. I visited two lumber camps, staying at one four days; it was great fun to see such a perfectly unique type of life. I shot a buck, a coon and some rabbits and partridges and trapped a lynx and a fox—so my trip was a success in every way…

Later in the year Theodore told a Harvard classmate and fellow amateur naturalist, Henry Minot, of not having "done much collecting this summer, for, as you know, I don't approve of too much slaughter." This was an understandable statement coming from a sensitive young man who had a deep love for wildlife. He did not believe in shooting animals indiscriminately. Even then he was an advocate of what he afterward was to call the "fair chase"—a chase in which the hunter did not stack the deal against hunted game by using traps and similarly artificial contrivances. There were times when he did take more game than he should have, at least in terms of his own rules of the hunt, but these exceptions were in moments when the thrill of the chase got the best of him.

Theodore thoroughly planned all his outings and gave meticulous attention to every detail. On his third Maine hunt, from August 28 to September 24, 1879, he took along a rifle, shotgun, duck trousers, heavy underflannels, heavy jacket, and "2 complete changes of clothes, and plenty of handkerchiefs and woolen socks." Judging from a letter to his sister Corinne in mid-September, the supplies had been well chosen:

> …I have just returned from my Munsungun trip, coming back a week earlier than I expected, as I found absolutely no large game. I enjoyed the trip exceedingly, but I think it was the roughest work I have yet had in the way of camping out; our trip to Katahdin was absolute luxury compared to it. "Bill" and I went alone in a pirogue or dugout, in which we spent six days; but besides this we spent four days walking to and from the Aroostook River, where we embarked.

Of the six days we spent on the river, three were entirely occupied with wading; the river was too shoal to carry the boat, and we had to wade up steam all day long, the foaming water (for it was a regular mountain torrent) now up to our waist, now only reaching our ankles: and when night came we would lie down, drenched through, too tired to care much one way or the other Moreover it rained steadily most of the time; and altogether I doubt if I have ever had much harder work. You can have no idea what severe labour dragging a boat up a swift mountain stream is: to be in the water up to your hips ten hours at a stretch is in itself hard enough, and this only represents the least part of it. At seven we would start, one holding the bow of the canoe and the other the stern, and would plod on, stumbling on the smooth, slippery stones, over which the water ran like a mill race, cutting our shoes and feet on the sharp edges of the rocks; now by main strength dragging the heavy dugout up rapids or over shoals, now being forced to unload and carry everything round some waterfall up which it was impossible to wade: at one time having to cut our way through a beaver dam with our axes, and again spending half an hour in hewing out a passage for our boat through a great jam of drift logs. But, oh how we slept at night! And how we enjoyed the salt pork, hardtack and tea which constituted our food!

The rougher the going, the more aroused he became. Theodore's cascading energy caused guide Bill Sewall to exclaim: "I never seen anybody that was like him…"

At Harvard, Theodore constantly exercised his body and followed his father's advice to first take care of morals then health, and finally studies. He neither smoked nor drank hard liquor, and he taught Sunday School in the Cambridge Episcopal Church. He received his best grades in German, rhetoric, and natural history. He became a member of Harvard's most exclusive club, the

At Harvard, Theodore constantly exercised his body and followed his father's advice to first take care of morals then health, and finally studies. He neither smoked nor drank hard liquor, and he taught Sunday School in the Cambridge Episcopal Church.

Porcellian, and also belonged to the Hasty Pudding Club, Alpha Delta Phi, the OK Club, D.K.E., and the Natural History Society. He also served as editor of the Harvard *Advocate* and was selected a member of the Class Committee. In 1880 Theodore graduated twenty-first in a class of 161.

Hunting in the Midwest

College undergraduate work was now completed, and the fall hunting season was not far off. Matters of marriage, graduate study, and a career all held Theodore's attention, but hunting and the call of the wild eased them into the background. On August 16, 1880, Theodore and Elliott headed west for six weeks of bird-shooting on the prairies of Illinois, Iowa, and Minnesota.

Elliott loved hunting and was an expert shot and outdoorsman. He was perhaps more talented and more broadly experienced as a hunter than Theodore, at least until the 1890s. The brothers were very close, and their strongest mutual interest was the outdoors. Elliott's worldwide hunting adventures fired the imagination of Theodore and whetted his initial interest to hunt in the Badlands. Elliott hunted big game in India, Ceylon, and America, and wrote of his trip to the Orient in the Boone and Crockett Club's *Hunting in Many Lands.* Elliott shot bear, goral, tahr, deer, ibex, boar, elephant, and tiger during his adventures in India and Ceylon, in 1881. While bird hunting in Florida from February-March of 1875, he shot 170 quail, duck, geese, and other fowl; in Texas, January through March of 1876, he took a large bag of quail (over 175), plus snipe, curlew, pigeon, dove, duck, turkey grouse, hawk, rabbit, and antelope; back in Texas from mid-December 1876, through early March 1877, he brought down buffalo, antelope, and other game; in Texas during the winter of 1878-79, he shot quail, turkey duck, dove, grouse, deer, javelina, antelope, buffalo, rabbit, and mountain lion. Elliott also hunted with TR in the Badlands, impressing the cowboys with his shooting and riding mastery.

Photographs taken of the two young hunters when they reached Chicago show Theodore holding his boyhood 12-gauge pinfire Lefaucheux double barrel, while Elliott's gun, a cartridge double of unknown make, at least has the look of quality. These were the bird guns they had brought along. Theodore's Lefaucheux, true to the confidence placed in it by Robert Barnwell Roosevelt, was now eight years old, but still as effective as when Theodore first received it.

Regrettably, Elliott's diary for this trip is exceedingly skimpy. Perhaps the young hunters were too preoccupied with hunting to keep detailed records. The following typical excerpts from Elliott's diary point out its terseness:

> *Aug 16 – 1880*
> Theodore & Elliott …
> Thro' sleeper to Chicago –
> *Aug 17*
> breakfast Abula – dinner Pittsburg
> Supper Alliance –
> *Aug 18*
> Chicago… Dr R [N. Isham] – Hotel
>   Clarendon
> Knights Templas – Bruce Wilcox
> *Aug 19*
> Hunting – Wilcox Farm – 450 acres [Illinois]
> 60 cows – Potatoes, pork, corn milk bread
> *Aug 20*
> Tramped, Shot – all day
> *Aug 21*
> Shot – over Sam & Frank [dogs] – 7 hours –
> *Aug 22*
> Sunday read & wrote

Luckily, a letter from Theodore to his sister Corinne provides a more ample account of the trip:

> We have been having a lovely time so far, have shot fair quantities of game, are in good health, though our fare and accommodations are of the roughest. The shooting is great fun; you would

SEPTEMBER, FRIDAY 24. 1880.

Spent the day with old Jack. Our
bag is as follows.

	S	E	Total
Sharp tail grouse	26	44	70
Pinnated grouse	69	119	188
Quail	5		5
Dove	8		8
Snipe		1	1
Plover	16	9	25
Shore snipe	51		51
Rail	1		1
Coot	1		1
Goose	1	1	2
Duck	17	25	42
Grebe	4	1	5
Bittern	2		2
Hare	1	1	2
Rabbit	1		1
	203	201	404

17 duck = 4 mallard 1 wood duck 1 green teal 2 blue
teal 2 blue bill 2 diffm. 1 widgeon 1 sprigtail
2 gadwall 1 hooded merganser   [red head]
16 plover = 3 upland 5 golden 2 black breast 6 others
51 shore snipe = 33 winter yellowlegs 12 summer yellowlegs
6 sandsnipe.

SEPTEMBER, SATURDAY 25. 1880.

Left for St Pauls. The
trip has been great fun;
but how glad I am it
is over and I am to see
Alice!

H. ROCHER   CHICAGO.

ABOVE: Game tally of Theodore and Elliott on their Midwestern hunt of August–September
1880, from TR's diary of the same year.

RIGHT: The second of two studio photographs made by H. Rocher while TR and Elliott were
hunting in the Midwest in 1880. Twenty-one-year-old Theodore, in the light shirt, was holding
his Lefaucheux pinfire shotgun, while brother Elliott, twenty-years old, had a fine-quality side-
by-side breech-loader.

The E. Thomas, Jr., 10-gauge shotgun, bought by Theodore while hunting the Midwest in August and September 1880. The shotgun featured 32" barrels, each barrel marked on the bottom, T. KILBY. Hand engraved on the barrel rib: E. THOMAS JR. MAKER. CHICAGO ILLS, and on each lock plate: E. THOMAS, JR. A deluxe piece of British gun work, sold in Chicago by Thomas. Carved on the inside of the forestock are the initials TR, most likely cut by Theodore himself.

SAGAMORE HILL NATIONAL HISTORIC SITE, NATIONAL PARK SERVICE

laugh to see us start off in a wagon, in our rough, dirty, hunting-suits, not looking very different from our driver; a stub-tailed, melancholy looking pointer under the front seat, and a yellow, fool idea of a setter under the back one, which last is always getting walked on and howling dismally. We enjoy the long drives very much: the roads are smooth and lovely, and the country, a vast undulating prairie, cut up by great fields of corn and wheat with few trees. The birds are not very plentiful, but of great variety; we get prairie chickens in the stubble fields, plover in the pastures, snipe in the 'slews,' and ducks in the ponds. We hunt about an hour or two in a place, then get into our wagon and drive on, so that, though we cover a very large tract of country we are not very tired at the end of the day, only enough to wake us sleep well. The climate is simply superb, and though the scenery is not very varied, yet there is something very attractive to me in these great treeless, rolling plains, and Nellie [Elliott] and I are great chums, and in the evening, sit and compare our adventures in "other lands" until bedtime which is pretty early…

On the same day he wrote Anna:

…We have had three days good shooting, and I feel twice the man for it already. As today is Sunday we are lying off, and, there not being any church near us, have been writing letters, reading & c. The farm people are pretty rough, but I like them very much; like all rural Americans they are intensely independent, and indeed I do'nt wonder at their thinkking us their equals, for we are dressed about as badly as mortals could be, with our cropped heads, unshaven faces, dirty gray shirts, still dirtier yellow trousers and cowhide boots; moreover we can shoot as well as they can (or at least Elliott can) and can stand as much fatigue. I enjoy being with the old boy very much; we care to do exactly the same things. The flies here are a perfect plague of Egypt; and things are not very clean; in fact the reverse; but we are having a lovely time.

On September 11, Theodore and Elliott made a return trip to Chicago "to buy new guns if for nothing else." Apparently the new gun Theodore bought was a double barrel 10 gauge by E. Thomas, Jr. The quality of this piece was excellent, and the manufacture had been done for Thomas in England. For years displayed at Sagamore Hill, the Thomas is finely and profusely engraved, with a skeleton buttplate, rich select walnut and checkered stocks, and the unusual feature of a thumb lever barrel-release just forward of the divided trigger guard. Each barrel was marked on the bottom with the name T. Kilby and with several British proofmarks. On the inside of the forestock, carved in the cutout for the right barrel, are the initials TR. It was undoubtedly Theodore himself who inscribed the gun.

On September 12, Theodore wrote Corinne with tongue-in-cheek:

We have come back here after a weeks hunting in Iowa. Elliott revels in the change to civilization—and epicurean pleasures. As soon as we got here he took some ale to get the dust out of his throat, then a milkpunch because he was thirsty; a mint julep because he was hot; a brandy smash "to keep the cold out of his stomach"; and then sherry and bitters to give him an appetite. He took a very simple dinner—soup, fish, salmi de grouse, sweetbread, mutton, venison, corn, maccaroni, various vegetables and some puddings and pies, together with beer, later claret and in the evening shandi-gaff. I confined myself to roast beef and potatoes; when I took a second help he marvelled at my appetite—and at bed time wondered why in thunder *he* felt "stuffy" and I didn't. The good living also reached his brain, and he tried to lure me into a discussion about the intellectual development of the Hindoos, coupled with some rather discursive and scarcely logical digressions about the Infinity of the Infinate, the Sunday School system and the planet Mars—together with some irrelevant remark about Texas "Jack Rabbits" which are apparently about as large as good sized cows. Elliott says that these remarks are incorrect and malevolent, but I say they pay him off for his last letter about my eating manners.

We have had very good fun so far, in spite of a succession of untoward accidents and delays. I broke both my guns, Elliott dented his, and the shooting was not as good as we had expected; I got bitten by a snake and chucked headforemost out of the wagon.
Your Seedy Brother.

On September 30, Theodore and Elliott returned to Oyster Bay, tired but otherwise wholly satisfied with their trip. All told, Elliott had shot 119 grouse, 44 sharptail, *25* duck, 9 plover, plus a few other birds and game, while Theodore took *95* grouse, 51 snipe, 16 plover, 17 duck, and 25 other game. Their expenses were $500 for the trip itself, and $525 for both the gun Elliott had bought and the E. Thomas double barrel purchased by Theodore.

The 1880 hunting trip, Theodore's first direct exposure to America west of Pennsylvania, had been made against the recommendation of his physician, who, after examining him in the spring of 1880, discovered that he had a bad heart and hence urged him to refrain from physical exertions. The warning was wasted. Theodore threw caution aside and carried on as if the report had pronounced him "as fit as a bull moose."

At this point in life young Roosevelt could think back on undeniably varied and satisfying hunting experiences. He had shot game and wild birds by the hundreds in the Middle East, in New York, New England and Pennsylvania, and in Minnesota, Iowa, and Illinois, had camped in the challenging Maine wilderness, and, from Fargo in the Dakota Territory, had caught glimpses of life in the untamed West. He had owned four shotguns, three of them gifts and one of his own selection. He also had a Sharps Borchardt rifle and his father's Greener pistols. He undoubtedly owned a revolver of some kind in the event of an encounter in which his fists might not be adequate in self-defense. Over the years this impressive array of firearms would be greatly enlarged. All of his future purchases would be, with few exceptions, custom-made to his personal tastes. Guns bought off the rack, particularly rifles, never quite measured up to his exacting wants. 🐚

CHAPTER 3

The Young Reformer's Hunts in the Badlands

Theodore Roosevelt met Alice Hathaway Lee, "a very sweet, pretty girl," while a junior at Harvard. After a persistent courtship, they were married on TR's twenty-second birthday, October 27, 1880. The couple moved to New York, where Theodore enrolled as a law student at Columbia University. His father had died in 1878, leaving him $125,000, "enough to get bread," but requiring him "to provide the butter and jam."

In the summer of 1881, Roosevelt completed most of his first book, *The Naval War of 1812*, which he had begun writing at Harvard and toured Europe with Alice. During the previous year, he had joined the Twenty-first District Republican Club of New York City, because he had already decided "to be one of the governing class." And, as he wrote in his *Autobiography*, "a young man of my bringing-up and convictions could join only the Republican party." Within a year Roosevelt was nominated as candidate for the State Assembly from the Twenty-first District. He was elected by a substantial margin, and thus embarked upon what would become one of the most successful political careers in American history.

The impulsive and self-assured Roosevelt took a commanding role in the debates and introduced bills of a progressive character. He impressed high-ranking Republican legislators with his informed judgments, his courage and, above all, his political tenacity. Almost single-handed, he forced the investigation of State Supreme Court Justice

"Sage-Fowl Shooting," drawn by A.B. Frost appeared in the first edition of *Hunting Trips of a Ranchman*. Theodore was not an avid bird hunter, and most "of the sage-fowl I have killed have been shot with the rifle when I happened to run across a covey while out riding, and wished to take two or three of them back for dinner."

BOONE AND CROCKETT CLUB
PERMANENT COLLECTION

T.R. Westbrook for gross judicial irregularities concerning a business struggle for control of the Manhattan Elevated Railway. Roosevelt gained wide public acclaim for his efforts on behalf of the public interest, even though Judge Westbrook was eventually exonerated.

New York newspapers saluted Roosevelt's political temerity and predicted a brilliant future for the fearless young legislator. *The New York Evening Post* declared that he had "accomplished more good than any man his age." *The Union* emphasized how he was "always at his post, following proceedings of even trifling importance." The *Harlem Record* lauded his "magnificent record" and remarked that "he

has such standing socially and civilly that it will be barefaced imprudence for anyone high to oppose him." Not a few state Republican leaders, however, looked upon Roosevelt as rather a mixed blessing. True, he brought favorable publicity and added luster to the party, but at the same time he seemed too strong-willed and independent to become a faithful party regular for better or for worse.

In the fall of 1882, Roosevelt was re-elected to the assembly by a two-to-one majority. His political career was now in high gear. His unswerving commitment to public morality and his shrill opposition to corruption in government heightened his popularity with the voters. As the epitome of the political moralist, Roosevelt's stature grew by leaps and bounds. His second term as lawmaker came at a time when Grover Cleveland, a Democrat, was governor of New York. Since both Roosevelt and Cleveland opposed machine politics, they were frequently on the same side on various issues, particularly those involving civil service reforms and the denial of special privileges to business corporations. By the end of his second term Roosevelt's name had become synonymous with political reform. A political leader of the first rank had emerged out of the crucible of New York politics.

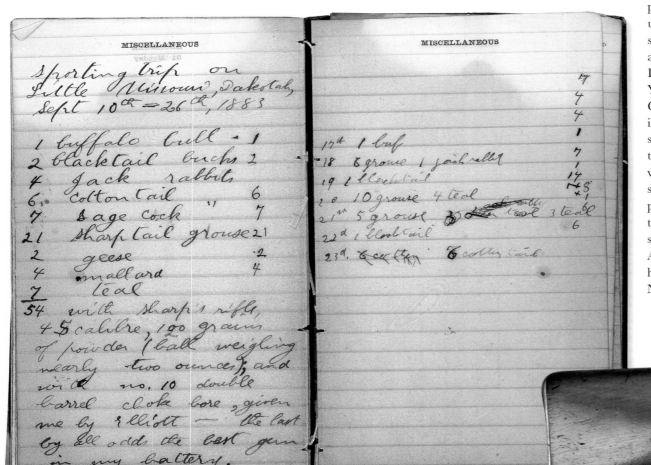

Roosevelt had a busy summer in 1883: besides working on his campaign for the coming fall elections, he was also making plans for a trip to the Dakota Badlands.

Hunting Buffalo in the Badlands

His decision to visit the Dakota Territory was inspired by a chance meeting late in May of 1883 with a former US naval officer, H.H. Gorringe, when Gorringe was in New York promoting the Little Missouri River area as a hunting and ranching paradise. The two men discussed the territory at length. In the summer of 1883, recurring bad health (asthma and "cholera morbus"), the frustrations of a crusading state assemblyman, and his inveterate hankering for hunting adventure and vigorous exercise induced Roosevelt to take a trip West with Gorringe. He wrote Gorringe that:

...I am now being forced to make my plans in regard to the political campaign this Autumn, and so I am anxious to fix, as nearly as is convenient to you, what will be about the dates of our departure and return. I am fond of politics, but fonder still of a little big game hunting. If not too much trouble, could you write me... either telling me about what your plans are, or, better still, appointing a day next week, if possible after Wednesday, when I can see you in person, as I will then be in New York, and am anxious to get your advice as to what to take

out west. I have a heavy 45 calibre Sharps rifle, and a double barrel No. 10, which ought to be enough of a battery.

Gorringe, however, did not go on the trip.

When Theodore Roosevelt stepped off the train in Little Missouri, Dakota Territory, on September 7, 1883, he stepped onto a stage where the Wild West was playing its final act. Nevertheless, as he wrote in his *Autobiography:*

It was still the Wild West in those days, the far West, the West of Owen Wister's stories and Frederic Remington's drawings, the West of the Indian and the buffalo-hunter, the soldier and the cow-puncher...I do not believe there ever was any life more attractive to a vigorous young fellow than life on a cattle-ranch in those days. It was a fine, healthy life, too; it taught a man self-reliance, hardihood, and the value of instant decision—in short, the virtues that ought to come from life in the open country I enjoyed the life to the full...

Little Missouri (later called Medora) was a forbidding frontier town in which there "was no court, no officer of the law, no county organization. Each man was a law unto himself. Each settled his own quarrels and on the spot...Personal responsibility was the curb-bit on the lawless and the law-abiding."

A bona fide buffalo gun, TR's Sharps Model 1874 Sporting Rifle had a 29-7/8" barrel. Note two sets of sights, one set added at a later date. The rifle was a .45 caliber with serial #162276 and included a scarce ramrod accessory beneath the barrel. The original Sharps records show this rifle to have been shipped to George Bird Grinnell, July 20, 1878. Roosevelt and Grinnell were friends, fellow naturalists, and were among the founding members of the Boone and Crockett Club.

FAR LEFT: TR's 1883 diary from his first hunting trip in the Dakota Badlands noting their total game bag was fifty-four.

Posing for a New York photographer, late in 1884, Theodore was wearing his tailor-made buckskin shirt, one of his fancy Colt six-shooters, and the hand-tooled holster, a cartridge belt loaded with .45-75 ammunition, the deluxe chaps, and a set of custom-made spurs.

THEODORE ROOSEVELT COLLECTION, HARVARD COLLEGE LIBRARY

On the afternoon of his arrival, Theodore chatted briefly with William Dantz, who later described the scene to biographer Hermann Hagedorn, author of *Roosevelt in the Badlands*. According to Dantz, the young tenderfoot was "slender, blue-eyed, modishly dressed," wearing glasses that gave him the "appearance of [a] student out on a vacation or a young professor attached to [a geographic] expedition." Dantz recalled that Roosevelt had brought "a number of guns" with him, and among these was a "magnificent Winchester.... Beautifully ornamented with solid gold plates inlaid in [the] stock...[the] side plates...exquisitely engraved." Dantz talked to Roosevelt about the rifle and about hunting; he later informed Hagedorn that the gun was a "1 of 1,000" model: "It was [the] custom of [Winchester] to make every thousandth gun specially carefully. Those guns [were] much prized [and] Roosevelt had secured one." Dantz was mistaken in identifying the rifle as a Winchester. Roosevelt's guns when he first arrived in the Dakotas included only a .45-120 caliber Sharps and a .50-150 double barrel Webley rifle. The first of his Winchester rifles with gold plate inlays and fancy engraving was not shipped from the factory until 1884. And at no time did he own a 1 of 1000. Several biographies of TR have perpetuated this myth, but Dantz had simply erred.

The hunting books that Roosevelt wrote generally contained detailed descriptions of the merits and demerits of various kinds of firearms. In *Hunting Trips of a Ranchman*, his first outdoors book, he graphically assessed the Sharps and Webley rifles.

...When I first came to the plains I had a heavy Sharps rifle, 45-120, shooting an ounce and a quarter of lead and a 50[-150] calibre, double-barreled English express [by Webley]. Both of these, especially the latter, had a vicious recoil; the former was very clumsy; and above all they were neither of them repeaters; for a repeater or magazine gun is as much superior to a single- or

double-barreled breech-loader as the latter is to a muzzle-loader. I threw them both aside...

What is believed to be the Sharps .45-120 is now displayed in the gun room at Sagamore Hill. A Model 1874 Sporting rifle, serial #162276, it was originally shipped to the naturalist George Bird Grinnell. The gun has a few features that reflect Roosevelt's tastes in rifles: special sights (both a fixed leaf and a folding graduated rear), a shotgun style buttplate, a heavy caliber and altered configuration of the forestock. The rare set of rear sights, and the forestock alterations[2] are examples of changes Roosevelt might make on any of his firearms. Yet, no matter how fine or fancy the weapon, Roosevelt was primarily concerned that it shoot straight. If it did not, he simply discarded it.

The .50-150 Webley, a rarity in double rifles, has long since vanished. No details on it are known today, other than brief references in Roosevelt's diaries and in *Hunting Trips of a Ranchman*. Given the quality of the Webley product and Roosevelt's taste in firearms, it was probably a deluxe piece of craftsmanship, perhaps even engraved with a TR monogram or a family crest.

On his first Badlands hunt, Roosevelt's guide was Joe Ferris, who was later a hand on TR's Maltese Cross ranch. Armed with the cumbersome but heavy-hitting .45-120 Sharps, Roosevelt and Ferris daily went off in search of buffalo. Ferris remembered:

Well we left the camp and went up to Lang's[3] and stayed all night. The next morning we started on the buffalo hunt. They used to be pretty thick and we hadn't travelled long, by George, we sighted a big buffalo.

Well, I can't describe it. Its the Bad Lands. After you get away from river for five or ten miles then you strike the rolling prairie. We lost that buffalo. We tried to sight him again, but he got away from us...We started out along about two or three o'clock up one [of] these little dry creeks when long toward

A few days later Roosevelt was on a train headed for New York City. His hunt had been rugged and taxing, even by Western standards, but Roosevelt enjoyed every bit of it. Ferris later reported having heard the "tenderfoot" say to himself at night, while wrapped in blankets, "By Godfrey, but this is fun!"

"I have been playing at frontier hunter in good earnest, having been off entirely alone, with my horse and rifle on the prairie. I wanted to see if I could do perfectly well without a guide, and I succeeded beyond my expectations. I shot a couple of antelope and a deer, and missed a great many more. I felt as absolutely free as a man could feel; as you know I do not mind loneliness; and I enjoyed the trip to the utmost."

night I spied some buffalo. There were three lying down. We could not get within a quarter of a mile of them, and that was an awful long ways to crawl. We left our horses and kept crawling and crawling to get as close as I could to them. They got up, of course, we had no show of getting any closer because [they] had heard us. I said to Roosevelt, you hit him right back of the shoulders. I talked to him so that he wouldn't get excited. He fired, by Jove! he missed, finally he hit one, we jumped on our horses and we ran after him until long after dark. That's the time he tells in his book about the horse throwing back her head and knocking the gun against his head [*Hunting Trips of a Ranchman*, chapter VIII, 'The Lordly Buffalo"; the wounded bull had charged]. Well, I'm telling you that I was scared all right. He bled like a stuck pig and I was afraid that he was hurt more than he let on he was. But he didn't say a word. He didn't pay any attention. He just tried to get this buffalo, but we didn't. Finally it got so dark that we could not see. I remember seeing a little pool and so I started for that water. We camped there. Took our saddles off and got a drink and he had a bottle of Jamaica ginger. I don't know whether he drank any of it or not, but I know I did. I went down to the edge of the pool. He said, don't drink that, he said, I have something here that'll make that water taste better and he pulled out of his pocket a little bottle and poured out a few drops and I filled the glass up with water and drank it, and I said it certainly does taste better.

So long in the night, by George, something came along there. I guess for water. We had our horses staked. We tied the ropes to the horns of the saddles, and those horses got scared at this thing I suppose it was a coyote or something like that that came down to the pool to get a drink, and our horses got scared and jerked the saddles out from under our heads and ran away in the dark, dragging the saddles after them. Well we

ran into the dark and finally found them, as we knew they couldn't go very far with those saddles dragging along after them.

Well we got the horses and brought them back. We used double cinch saddles, and we took the blankets that we used under them and spread them right down and we laid down. I remember that long toward morning it began to rain and it rained quite a bit. Finally I woke up and we were in water about [ankle] deep.... He was plucky. Next morning I never heard a murmur from Roosevelt. We had some of that Scotchman's biscuits and we ate some of them.... We drank a little more water with Jamaica ginger in it and it made them taste a little better. I never heard him murmur up to that time or later. We were there pretty nearly a week before we got a buffalo. Once or twice we got pretty near up to some…

One morning we started up Little Cannon Ball Creek. We got, I guess two or three miles, when I spied a buffalo. Of course we slid off our horses. They stood right there. We didn't have to tie them and he pulled down pretty close. It was from twenty-five to forty yards to the extreme outside we shot at the buffalo and he made a dandy shot. I told him to take aim at the yellow spot, a brownish coat back of the shoulder and he would hit it right through the heart. That buffalo came out of that creek bottom almost straight up twelve feet and almost straight up and down bank. At first I thought he had missed him. However he had taken only a few jumps and the blood squirted. I knew he had him. That shot went right through the front lungs. We followed on the trail a little ways, probably twenty-five or thirty yards we came on him. Roosevelt was like a boy just out of school and so was I. I never saw any one so enthused in all my life and by golly, I was enthused for more reasons than one. I was plumb tired out and he was so eager to shoot his first buffalo that it somehow got into my blood and I wanted

Frederic Remington made these sketches of the Elkhorn ranch house and outbuilding. They were published in TR's *Ranch Life and the Hunting Trail*. While living in the Badlands, Theodore's home was here, more than at the Maltese Cross.

to see him kill his first one as badly as he wanted to kill it.

Roosevelt was so elated that he improvised an Indian war dance around the hulk and then gave a flabbergasted Joe Ferris one hundred dollars in cash!

A few days later Roosevelt was on a train headed for New York City. His hunt had been rugged and taxing, even by Western standards, but Roosevelt enjoyed every bit of it. Ferris later reported having heard the "tenderfoot" say to himself at night, while wrapped in blankets, "By Godfrey, but this is fun!"

Before his departure for New York, Roosevelt decided to invest in a cattle venture of his own. He hired William Merrifield and Joe Ferris' brother Sylvane as his ranch managers, giving them a check for $14,000 with which to buy some beef stock and get things under way. The enterprise was to be known as the Maltese Cross. For fleeting moments Roosevelt even contemplated devoting

The Maltese Cross ranch house, Dakota Territory, c. 1883-84, as it was when TR ranched there. Driven into one log, at its end, was a Maltese Cross brand made from empty cartridge casings—believed driven by TR himself. The structure was small and primitive in comparison to the Elkhorn.

himself full time to ranching, hunting, and writing. His inner sense of public service, however, was enough to dispel such a notion. At any rate his new ranch represented a kind of sanctuary to which he could retreat from the pressing pace of political life and there enjoy the fullness of life in the great outdoors. Many years later Roosevelt would look back on the frontier with nostalgia: "Here," he would say," the romance of my life began."

A Family Tragedy

Roosevelt returned to New York and began an active campaign for a third term in the legislature. Re-elected by a substantial margin, he entered the Assembly with great confidence in his own ability and powers of leadership. As he wrote his wife, "I feel much more at ease in my mind and better able to enjoy things since we have gotten under way; I feel now as though I had the reins in my hand."

But young Roosevelt lost his tight grip when two telegrams reached him in Albany on Wednesday, February 13. The first announced the birth of his daughter and the second bore the shocking news that his wife was critically ill. He rushed to New York, arriving home at midnight to be told by Elliott: "There is a curse on this house. Mother is dying and Alice is dying too." His mother died three hours later and his wife died that afternoon. The double tragedy filled him with inexpressible grief and remorse. Many of his friends believed the shattering experience would cause him to withdraw from public life. Even though such thoughts must have crossed his mind, Roosevelt had other ideas.

"I shall come back to my work at once," he wrote a fellow assemblyman; "there is nothing left for me except to try to so live as not to dishonor the memory of those I loved who have gone before me." Within a week Roosevelt was back in the Assembly full swing. He hid his sorrow behind a facade of hard work and vitality; inwardly, he was depressed. "I have very little expectation of being able to keep on in politics, my success so far has only been won by absolute indifference to my future career." Through the long and lonely spring, as he drafted many reform measures, he thought more and more of the rugged beauty of the Dakotas and of the unsurpassed happiness he had found there "I feel both tired and restless," he wrote on April 30; "for the next few months I shall probably be in Dakota, and I think I shall spend the next two or three years in making shooting trips, either in the far West or in the Northern Woods…"

Back to the Badlands

Immediately after the 1884 Republican National Convention in Chicago, he headed for the Dakotas. Now more than ever he needed to return to a life of challenge and action, of ranching and hunting. The Dakotas would be a source of great solace to him and would help somewhat to assuage the deep grief within him.

No sooner had Roosevelt arrived in the Badlands than he told his friend and guide Lincoln Lang: "There are two things I want to do. I want to get a buckskin suit and I want to get an antelope." Lang was at his service: "I think we can fix you up for both….Mrs. Maddox is the best buckskin-suitmaker around here, and I feel quite sure we will get an antelope on the way over."

We saddled up one morning and we started out for Mrs. Maddox. Mrs. Maddox was the strongest character of all the women we had in the West. She was a dead shot and she was not afraid to shoot, and she was a tarter, let me tell you, and she was a good one to let alone. She was well able to take care of herself.

We started over there that day and we went into the old lady and she said she would make him a suit and she took his measurements and then she invited us to lunch. She gave us a very nice dinner. After that we started out. I was well acquainted with deer and antelope by this time and on the way back we saw a good many antelopes. I spotted two away down in the valley.

If we could go around that way I told him that I believed we could get a shot. So we went and put our horses out of sight.

We came near where they were, and finally we worked over the top of the hill, and there were the two of them. They were about 75 yards off. Most tenderfeet why of course would have got excited. Not him. He did not show any excitement at all. He simply raised up over the hill, and he took aim like that, and the antelope dropped just like that. It dropped where it stood. The funny part of it is, he had not got excited before, but then he did. He dropped his gun and let a yell out of him when he saw that antelope drop and he commenced to wave his hands around his head and he said, "I got him." The other antelope kept running around in a circle and actually came within twenty-five yards, and he could not pick up his gun to kill the other antelope to save his life. I yelled at him to shoot. He could not, he was so excited. He told me afterwards if it was to save his life he could not have killed that one. "Well," he said, "Lincoln, I am delighted." He said, "This would not have seemed nearly so good if somebody had not been here to see it. Do you know what I am going to do? I am going to make you a present of my shot-gun." Right here I think I made one of the mistakes of my life. The reason was I felt he was doing it in his excitement, and I felt he was giving me something of very high value and I said I could not accept it. I should have taken it. I did not care to simply for the reason that I tell you. I have always regretted it since that I did not, because I think I hurt him in not doing so.

After you kill an antelope, the question of dressing is an important matter. Ninety-nine men out of a hundred don't like to get their hands at it. Not him. He insisted upon dressing that animal. He got me to show him just how to do it. It is a disagreeable job. He did not care, that was the kind he was.

Cowpunching and hunting revitalized Roosevelt and helped restore his old thirst for life. He was bullish about the life of a cattleman and hunter. "Well, I have been having a glorious time here," he wrote Anna:

and am well hardened now.…For every day I have been here I have had my hands full. First and foremost, the cattle have done well, and I regard the outlook for making the business a success as being *very* hopeful.…I shall put on a thousand more cattle and shall make it my regular business. In the autumn I shall bring out Seawall [*sic*.] and Dow and put them on a ranche with very few cattle to start with, and in the course of a couple of years give them quite a little herd also.

I have never been in better health than on this trip. I am in the saddle all day long either taking part *in* the round up of the cattle, or else hunting antelope (I got one the other day; another good head for our famous hall at Lee-holm). I am really attached to my two "factors," Ferris and Merrifield; they are very fine men.

The country is growing on me, more and more; it has a curious, fantastic beauty of its own.…How sound I do sleep at night now!… I have shot a few jackrabbits and curlews, with the rifle, and I also killed eight rattlesnakes.…

In a few days Roosevelt ventured out alone on the prairie for a week's hunt, an exhilarating experience which fulfilled:

a boyish ambition of mine—that is, I have been playing at frontier hunter in good earnest, having been off entirely alone, with my horse and rifle on the prairie. I wanted to see if I could do perfectly well without a guide, and I succeeded beyond my expectations. I shot a couple of antelope and a deer, and missed a great many more. I felt as absolutely free as a man could feel; as you know I do not mind loneliness; and

Cowpunching and hunting revitalized Roosevelt and helped restore his old thirst for life. He was bullish about the life of a cattleman and hunter. "Well, I have been having a glorious time here," he wrote Anna.

> Altogether the hunters had shot 6 elk, 3 grizzly bear, 7 deer, and 109 "small game." Roosevelt had been "more anxious for the quality than for the quantity of [the] bag." But what made the expedition so richly rewarding was the challenge of the fair chase and camping out in the uninviting environs for seven weeks. As hunter and outdoorsman, Roosevelt was truly coming of age.

I enjoyed the trip to the utmost. The only disagreeable incident was one day when it rained. Otherwise the weather was lovely, and every night I would lie wrapped up in my blanket looking at the stars till I fell asleep, in the cool air. The country has widely different aspects in different places; one day I would canter hour after hour over the level green grass, or through miles of wild rose thickets, all in bloom, on the next I would be amidst the savage desolation of the Bad Lands, with their dreary plateaus, fantastically shaped buttes and deep, winding canyons. I enjoyed the trip greatly and have never been in better health…

Meanwhile Roosevelt had bought another ranch, the Elkhorn, on the Little Missouri River and stocked it with a thousand head of cattle. Bill Sewall and Will Dow, his former Maine guides, consented to manage the ranch on a profit-sharing basis. They pitched in and built the log ranch house at the Elkhorn. Roosevelt had "no neighbor for ten or fifteen miles on either side," which certainly did not displease him. The Elkhorn ranch and cattle represented an additional investment of $26,000.

Among the ranchers and cowboys of the Dakotas, Roosevelt was conspicuous because of his patrician background, Harvard education, dandy buckskin suit, and imperious manner of speech. On one occasion during a roundup Roosevelt exhorted a cowhand, "Hasten forward quickly there!" On another, he knocked out in the local saloon a drunk who had contemptuously called him "four eyes" and had waved two cocked pistols in his face, ordering him to set up drinks. Moreover, Roosevelt's reading tastes (he spent many evenings in the Dakotas poring over Tolstoy's *Anna Karenina)* were scarcely akin to those of the typical Westerner. With his Dakota friends he was plainly a general among privates. They admired Roosevelt for his authentic love of the open country and for his courage and resoluteness. But always they felt him to be a man apart.

In August, TR wrote Anna that everything was going well; the herds now totaled over 1,600 head, Sewall and Dow were breaking into cowboy life in good humor ("I had great fun," TR noted, "in bringing my two backwoods babies out here"), and Roosevelt was about to start on an extended hunt:

In two or three days I start across country for the Bighorn Mountains, and then you will probably not hear from me for a couple of months. I take a wagon and six ponies, riding one of the latter. I now look like a regular cowboy dandy, with all my equipments finished in the most expensive style…

Guns for the Badlands

The "equipments finished in the most expensive style" were two engraved Colt six-shooters, the fancy tooled-leather belt and holster, a pair of silver-mounted California spurs marked "H. Messing & Son Makers/San Jose Cal." and engraved with the TR monogram, the buckskin shirt and trousers, alligator boots, sealskin chaps, deluxe tooled saddle, a silver-mounted Tiffany & Company Bowie-type knife, and a silver belt buckle engraved with floral scrolls and the head of a bear!

The two Colts were Frontier Single Actions in .44-40 caliber, with 7 1/2 barrels; both pistols highly engraved and specially plated. One of these, serial #92248, had been sent by Colt's to New York dealer Hartley and Graham in May of 1883. Colt factory ledgers reveal that shipment had been "in the white" and without grips, the customary means of supplying a revolver intended for special engraving Hartley and Graham's house engraver at that time was the celebrated L.D. Nimschke, and it was he who was commissioned to embellish the Colt Frontier #92248 for Roosevelt.

Nimschke's design, incorporating a few suggestions by Roosevelt, was superb. On the right ivory grip and on the left recoil shield were relief carved the classic TR monogram, in the identical pattern engraved on Theodore Sr.'s Greener pistols.

The deluxe Nimschke-engraved Colt Single Action serial #92248 was TR's fanciest cowboy six-shooter. It was originally shipped "in-the-white" by the Colt factory in May 1883. The .44-40 caliber pistol had a grip of relief-carved elephant ivory and was gold- and nickel-plated. The revolver was subject to hard use while on the frontier.

AUTRY NATIONAL CENTER
PHOTOGRAPH BY BRUCE PENDLETON WHEN THE
REVOLVER WAS IN THE PRIVATE COLLECTION OF
RICHARD PROSSER MELLON

BACKGROUND IMAGE PROVIDED BY
THEODORE ROOSEVELT COLLECTION,
HARVARD COLLEGE LIBRARY

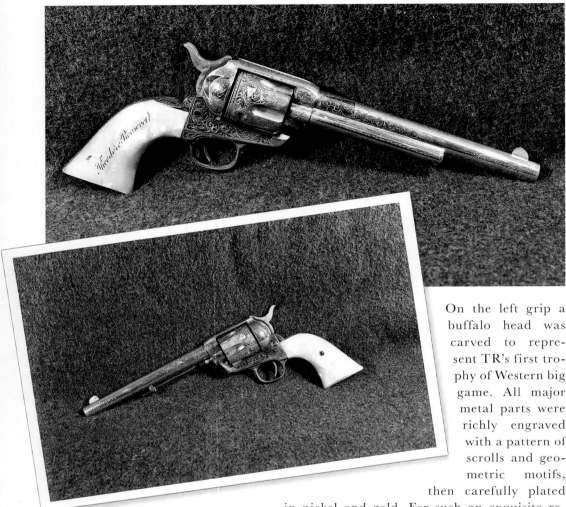

One of TR's fancy Colt Single Action revolvers, distinguished by its mother-of-pearl grips, engraved "Theodore Roosevelt." Serial #92267. Hunter and guide William Merrifield remembered this pistol from the Bighorn Mountains hunt of 1884, "We struck the N-Bar-N cattle.... An Englishman by the name of Wallop owned this outfit. He saw Mr. Roosevelt's name on the end of his six shooter and he remembered his name as being connected with politics in the East."

THEODORE ROOSEVELT BIRTHPLACE

On the left grip a buffalo head was carved to represent TR's first trophy of Western big game. All major metal parts were richly engraved with a pattern of scrolls and geometric motifs, then carefully plated in nickel and gold. For such an exquisite revolver, Roosevelt bought a richly tooled belt and holster, neatly lined with chamois. The companion Single Action, serial #92267, was shipped by Colt's to Hartley and Graham in June 1883. Tastefully engraved, but without monograms or buffalo heads, the pistol's lone identifying feature was the name *Theodore Roosevelt* carved in script on the right pearl grip. TR apparently carried alternately each pistol, using the same hand-tooled belt and holster. He never sported a pair of revolvers, and Colt Single Action #92267 must be considered as a spare to the deluxe, TR monogrammed Colt #92248.

Records of the Winchester factory show that two special lever-action rifles had been shipped

(destination not recorded) on July 31; both had been custom-made for the young Badlands rancher. At least one of these reached Roosevelt in time for the Bighorn Mountains hunt, which began on August 18.

TR's Bighorn Winchester was a Model 1876 .45-75 rifle, serial #38647, dispatched by the factory with his personal selection of features:

.45-75 caliber; 1/2 round, 1/2 octagon barrel; 1/2 magazine; case hardened; pistol grip stock; forearm checkered; barrel without sight.

The other was an equally deluxe Model 1873 rifle, serial #156253:

.32-20 caliber; 1/2 round, 1/2 octagon barrel; 1/2 magazine; case hardened; pistol grip stock (in the rough); forearm checkered; barrel without sight seats cut; plain trigger.

Both rifles were probably shipped to Hartley and Graham, for fitting of folding leaf open sights (the rear sight on the 1876 is marked FREUND), which were a favorite of Roosevelt. The stock on the 1873 model was finished after shipment from the factory.

Roosevelt knew precisely what he wanted in stocks: shotgun buttplates, large crescent cheekpieces, and deluxe checkered wood. On both of his first Winchesters, he went a step further and ordered engraved gold oval plaques inlaid on the right sides of the butts. The large-caliber Model 1876 has a grizzly bear motif on its gold oval, while the Model 1873, shooting the mild .32-20 cartridge, has a rabbit motif. No other decorative engraving is on the Model 1873, other than the later addition of a small gold stock escutcheon with the initials TR.

The Model 1876 #38647 is a spectacular gun, one of the finest Model 1876 Winchesters known— and certainly the most historic. This was the rifle held by Roosevelt in posing for the frontispiece

to his first big game book *Hunting Trips of a Ranchman*, and it also appears in several original photographs, drawings, and prints from the mid 1880's. Beneath the lever is the stamp of the craftsman, J. ULRICH, who embellished the frame with beautifully engraved elk, whitetail deer, buffalo, and antelope motifs and rich scrollwork.

These deluxe Winchesters are the earliest known fully custom-made Roosevelt rifles. Both were probably ordered through Hartley and Graham when TR returned to New York after his first trip West in 1883. In the 1880's, custom rifles could be built rather quickly without impairing their quality. These first Winchesters ordered by Roosevelt were constructed in just thirty days.

"The Winchester [Model 1876 .45-75]," TR wrote in *Hunting Trips of a Ranchman:*

> stocked and sighted to suit myself, is by all odds the best weapon I ever had, and I now use it almost exclusively, having killed every kind of game with it, from a grizzly bear to a bighorn. It is as handy to carry, whether on foot or on horseback, and comes up to the shoulder as readily as a shot-gun; it is absolutely sure, and there is no recoil to jar and disturb the aim, while it carries accurately quite as far as a man can aim with any degree of certainty; and the bullet, weighing three quarters of an ounce, is plenty large enough for any thing on this continent. For shooting the very large game (buffalo, elephants, etc.) of India and South Africa, much heavier rifles are undoubtedly necessary;

but the Winchester is the best gun for any game to be found in the United States, for it is deadly, accurate, and handy as any, stands very rough usage, and is unapproachable for the rapidity of its fire and the facility with which it is loaded.

These welcome words to Winchester executives signaled the beginning of a long and cordial association that would continue for over thirty years. By the time of the great Roosevelt safari of 1909-10, TR had bought and used more than twenty Winchesters, in all models of the lever-action rifle from the 1873 through the 1895. Most of these, like the .45-75, were "stocked and sighted to suit" himself.

In the summer or fall of 1884, Roosevelt bought three more guns: An L.C. Smith "ranch gun," a Bullard repeating rifle, and a Kennedy shotgun. The 'ranch gun' was a "double-barrel No. [12 gauge], with a .40-70 rifle underneath the shotgun barrels." Its center rib was marked: L.C. SMITH MAKER OF BAKER GUN, SYRACUSE. N.Y. DAMASCUS STEEL. A setter dog was engraved on the trigger guard, and the breech, trigger guard, and hammers were lightly scroll-engraved in a pattern commonly seen on fine quality British sporting arms. A thick buttplate was also added. In other respects the "ranch gun" was standard for its type. Roosevelt wanted it along "in riding around near home, where a man may see a deer and is sure to come across ducks and grouse...."

The Bullard rifle was a "50-115 6-shot...express [with] the velocity, shock, and low trajectory of [an

On July 31, 1884, TR's first Winchester rifles were shipped by the factory including this Model 1873 .32-20 (serial #156253). It had virtually every deluxe feature possible excepting profuse engraving. It was presented by Roosevelt to his valet James Amos, in 1906.

THEODORE ROOSEVELT BIRTHPLACE

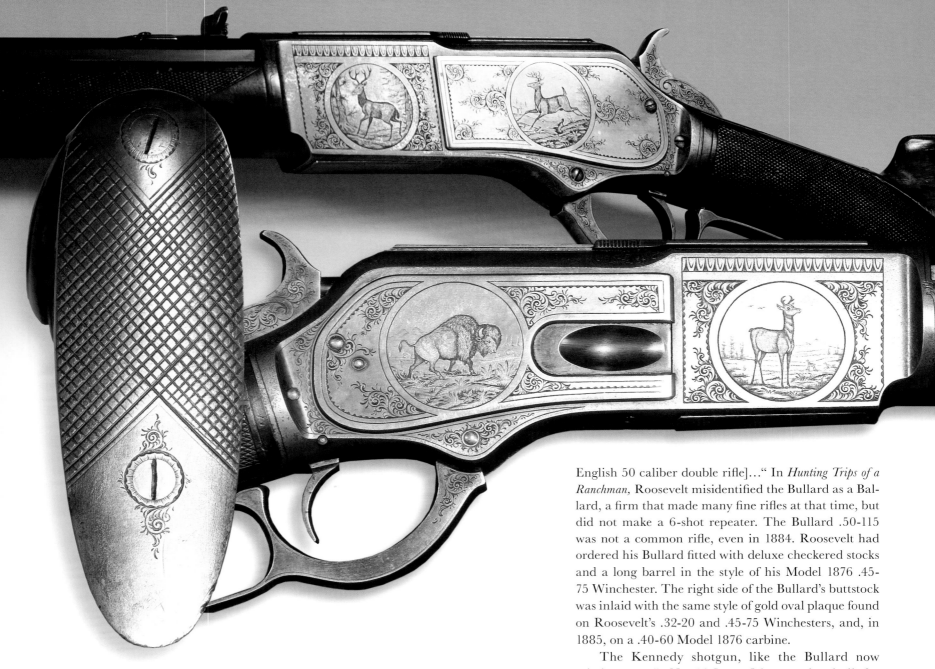

The deluxe .45-75 Winchester Model 1876 rifle serial #38647 had deer and scroll motifs engraved on the left side, with buffalo and antelope and scroll motifs on the right. A gold plaque with a grizzly bear motif was inlaid into the right side of the buttstock (not shown), matching the gold oval rabbit motif inlaid on the model 1873 rifle bought at the same time. Engraving by John Ulrich.

English 50 caliber double rifle]…" In *Hunting Trips of a Ranchman*, Roosevelt misidentified the Bullard as a Ballard, a firm that made many fine rifles at that time, but did not make a 6-shot repeater. The Bullard .50-115 was not a common rifle, even in 1884. Roosevelt had ordered his Bullard fitted with deluxe checkered stocks and a long barrel in the style of his Model 1876 .45-75 Winchester. The right side of the Bullard's buttstock was inlaid with the same style of gold oval plaque found on Roosevelt's .32-20 and .45-75 Winchesters, and, in 1885, on a .40-60 Model 1876 carbine.

The Kennedy shotgun, like the Bullard now missing, was "a No. 16 [gauge] hammerless built for me by Kennedy of St. Paul, for grouse and plover." No other identifying facts are known on the Kennedy, a gun that must have been done up handsomely. Custom-made on individual order, the possibility exists that somewhere on this piece was a TR monogram. Only a handful of shotguns were owned and used by Roosevelt—during his lifetime he had fewer than ten. He owned many rifles, of course, at least nine are known from the ranching days of the 1880's, most of which were Winchesters.

Another Badlands gun that has long since vanished was "a 50 [-150] caliber double barrel English express" by Webley of Birmingham. TR's diary for 1884 identified the make, but it was a rifle he "threw…aside" when the young rancher switched to the Winchester 45-75 repeater. Like the Kennedy shotgun and the .50-115 Bullard, the Webley double rifle is considered to have been of excellent craftsmanship, with a rich stock and tastefully engraved metal parts.

The Bighorn Expedition

The Bighorn Mountains trip, which had begun to take on the proportions of a safari, was the subject of Roosevelt's diary log for August 16:

My companions are my foreman, William Merrifield, who is to hunt with me, and an old French half-breed named Lebo, who is to drive the team and to cook, etc. I take a light "prairie schooner" with a canvas cover, drawn by two stout horses, to carry our goods, and ten riding ponies for Merrifield and myself to ride. One of these is Blackie, a stout, swift rather vicious pony; Splitear, very enduring; Brownie, willing and swift, but very nervous; and Roachie, quiet and rather small. I carry a buckskin suit, sealskin chaparajos, coon skin overcoat, otter fur robe to sleep in (buttonning into a bag form), oil slicker, boots and moccasins, sombrero overalls, jersey 2 flannel shirts, 3 suits of light, and 3 of heavy underclothing, heavy socks, plenty of handkerchiefs, soap, towels, washing and shaving things, rubber blankets, flour, bacon, beans and coffee, sugar and salt. A little brandy and cholera mixture. My battery consists of a long 45 [believed entered in error, caliber correctly would have been .44-40] colt revolver, 150 cartridges, a No. 10 choke bore [by E. Thomas, Jr., Chicago], 300 cartridges,

shotgun a .45-75 Winchester Repeater [Model 1876 #38647], with 1,000 cartridges; a .40-90 Sharps [the Borchardt #17130], 150 cartridges; a .50-150 double barrelled Webly express, 100 cartridges.

Roosevelt engagingly described to Anna the party's departure for the Bighorns:

…I wear a sombrero, silk neckerchief, fringed buckskin shirt, sealskin chaparajos or riding trowsers; alligator hide boots; and with my pearl hilted revolver and beautifully finished Winchester rifle, I shall feel able to face anything. How long I will be gone I can not say; we will go in all nearly a thousand miles. If game is plenty and my success is good, I may return in six weeks; more probably I shall be out a couple of months; and if game is so scarce that we have to travel very far to get to it, or if our horses give out or run away, or we get caught by the snow, we may be out very much longer—till towards Xmas; though I will try to be back to vote.

A.B. Frost drawing from TR's *Hunting Trips of a Ranchman,* **Chapter VI. The work is titled, "Cutting Off a Band of Prong-Horn."**
Boone and Crockett Club
Permanent Collection

Posed on a Western saddle are two firearms believed purchased for Bill Sewall by TR at the time Sewall and Will Dow set up the Elkhorn Ranch. The Colt is a Single Action Army serial #87526, a .44-40 with blued finish, shipped March 15, 1883 (one of 50 like revolvers) to Hartley & Graham, New York. The rifle is a Sharps Borchardt, serial #9616, the heavyweight 28-inch barrel marked "Old Reliable" on top (made in Bridgeport, Connecticut). Saddle bags marked by J.S. Collins and Co., Miles City, Montana Territory.

DAVID SEWALL COLLECTION;
PHOTOGRAPH BY LOUISE PEMBERTON

The Bighorn trip lasted seven weeks—TR's longest hunting expedition until his African safari of 1909-10. From Fort McKinney, Wyoming Territory, on the way back to Medora, the hardy frontiersman sent Anna a thumbnail sketch of "a very successful hunting trip":

For once I have made a very successful hunting trip; I have just come out of the mountains and will start at once for the Little Missouri, which I expect to reach in a fortnight, and a week afterwards will be on my way home, I hope to hear from you there.

It took sixteen days travelling (during which I only killed a few bucks) before I reached the foot of the snow capped Bighorn range; we then wagon and went into the mountains with pack ponies, and as I soon shot all kinds of game the mountains afforded, I came out after two weeks, during which time I killed three grizzly bear, six elk (three of them have magnificent heads and will look well in the "house on the hill[6]") and as many deer, grouse and trout as we needed for the table; after the first day I did not shoot any cow or calf elk, or any deer at all, except one buck that had unusual antlers;—for

I was more anxious for the quality than for the quantity of my bag. I have now a dozen good heads for the hall. Merrifield killed two bears and three elk; he has been an invaluable guide for game, and of course the real credit for the bag rests with him, for he found most of the animals. But I really shot well this time.

He then arrestingly related his first encounter with the deadly grizzly bear:

I shall not soon forget the first [grizzly] I killed. We had found where he had been feeding on the carcass of an elk; and followed his trail into a dense pine forest, fairly choked with fallen timber. While noiselessly and slowly threading our way through the thickest part of it I saw Merrifield, who was directly ahead of me, sink suddenly to his knees and turn half round, his face fairly ablaze with excitement. Cocking my rifle and stepping quickly forward, I found myself face to face with the great bear, who was less than twenty five feet off—not eight steps. He had been roused from his sleep by our approach, he sat up in his lair and turned his huge head slowly towards us. At that distance and in such a place it was very necessary to kill or disable him at the first fire, doubtless my face was pretty white, but the blue barrel was as steady as a rock as I glanced along it until I could see the top of the bead fairly between his two sinister looking eyes; as I pulled the trigger I jumped aside out of the smoke, to be ready if he charged; but it was needless, for the great brute was struggling in the death agony, and, as you will see when I bring home his skin, the bullet hole in his skull was as exactly between his eyes

"Close Quarters with Old Ephraim," a drawing by A.B. Frost from *Hunting Trips of a Ranchman*. TR sighting down the barrel of his Winchester Model 1876 with William Merrifield ready to back him up. TR respected the grizzly bear as awesome prey for any hunter.

as if I had measured the distance with a carpenters rule. This bear was nearly nine feet long and weighed over a thousand pounds. Each of my other bears, which were smaller, needed two bullets apiece; Merrifield killed each of his with a single shot.

The hunting foray proved successful in every way. Altogether the hunters had shot 6 elk, *3* grizzly bear, 7 deer, and 109 "small game." Roosevelt had been "more anxious for the quality than for the quantity of [the] bag." But what made the expedition so richly rewarding was the challenge of the fair chase and camping out in the uninviting environs for seven weeks. As hunter and outdoorsman, Roosevelt was truly coming of age. Though perhaps never outstanding in any single facet of ranching, riding, or hunting, he was capable in everything he did. What he might have lacked in experience or dexterity he made up for in determination and sheer spirit.

From 1883 to 1886, Roosevelt spent only about fourteen months in the Badlands. In other words, he was always an Easterner who only commuted to the West because of the limitless joy it gave him. It is doubtful that he could have settled there permanently much as he loved it. After all, he was a Roosevelt, to whom power and responsibility were essential parts of the family inheritance. His heart belonged to the West, his mind to the East.

Because Roosevelt felt so deeply about the West, he was able to write about it movingly and powerfully. His writings on ranching and hunting were instant successes, especially the trilogy—*Hunting Trips of a Ranchman* (1885), *Ranch Life and the Hunting Trail* (1888), and *The Wilderness Hunter* (1893). *The Saturday Review* characterized *Hunting Trips of a Ranchman* "one of the rare books which sportsmen will be glad to add to their libraries." *Ranch Life and the Hunting Trail,* perhaps the best of the three, was hailed with enthusiasm. *The Field* magazine, published in London welcomed *The Wilderness Hunter* as "a noteworthy and valuable addition to the very brief list of good books on American big game hunting...."

Colt Single Action and Sharps of Bill Sewall, accompanied by a selection of various invitations to the White House and the Inauguration of the President, correspondence, and related memorabilia—all documenting a long and deep friendship.

DAVID SEWALL COLLECTION;
PHOTOGRAPHS BY LOUISE PEMBERTON

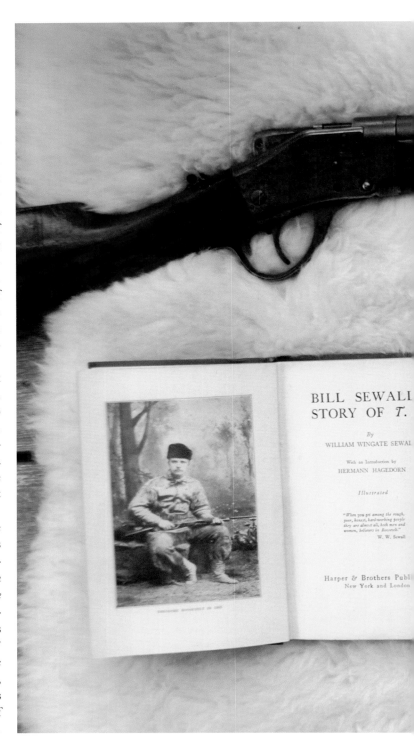

BILL SEWALL
STORY OF *T.*

By
WILLIAM WINGATE SEWALL

With an Introduction by
HERMANN HAGEDORN

Illustrated

Harper & Brothers Publi
New York and London

INAUGURAL DAY, 1905.

THE WHITE HOUSE,

WASHINGTON, March 4, 1905.

The Bearer *Mr. Fred S Sewall*
is a member of the President's immediate party, and as such
is commended to the courtesy of those in charge of the various
inaugural ceremonies.

THE WHITE HOUSE
WASHINGTON

Oyster Bay, N.Y.,
September 3, 1908.

Friend William:

I have your letter of the 2d. If I was going to
take out any man your son would be the very man I would
take, for I believe in the blood. But I shall take no
one excepting my son Kermit and two professional naturalists and field taxidermists, both of the men being high
up in their profession. Out in that country the
actual physical work is done by the natives, and every
white man means an additional expense with no return.
There would not be anything for anyone, in addition to
those I have named, to do. I am really sorry I can not
say yes.

Give my warm regards to all.

Faithfully yours,

Theodore Roosevelt

Mr. W W. Sewall,
Island Falls, Maine.

The President and Mrs. Roosevelt
request the pleasure of the company of
Mr. Sewall
at luncheon on Saturday
March the fourth at two o'clock.
1905.

The President and Mrs. Roose...
request the pleasure of the compan...
Mr. Sewall
at a reception to be held at the
White House
Thursday evening, February the ff...
nineteen hundred and three.
from nine to half after ten o'clock.

Mr. Roosevelt is sufficiently known by his earlier writings as a keen sportsman, and one who looks at sport of whatever description from the best standpoint."

Roosevelt was a disciplined and lucid writer who had mastered the narrative form of writing. His books were exceptionally well organized and balanced. He had uncanny powers of observation and a facility for describing ordinary sights and episodes in a compelling fashion. Even when in some parts of books or articles his writing was not good, it was never prosaic. A passage from *Ranch Life and the Hunting Trail* illustrates his unlabored style:

A ranchman's life is certainly a very pleasant one, albeit generally varied with plenty of hardship and anxiety. Although occasionally he passes days of severe toil,—for example, if he goes on the round-up he works as hard as any of his men,—yet he no longer has to undergo the monotonous drudgery attendant upon the tasks of the cowboy or of the apprentice in the business. His fare is simple, but, if he chooses, it is good enough. Many ranches are provided with nothing at all but salt pork, canned goods, and bread; indeed, it is a curious fact that in traveling through the cow country it is often impossible to get any milk or butter; but this is only because the owners or managers are too lazy to take enough trouble to insure their own comfort. We ourselves always keep up two or three cows, choosing such as are naturally tame, and so we invariably have plenty of milk

Cowboy spurs worn by TR in the Dakota Territory circa 1884-1886. The spurs at top are silver inlaid and engraved marked H. MESSING & SON MAKERS/SAN JOSE CAL. The straps were hand-tooled and each was fitted with sterling silver conches engraved with an elaborate TR monogram. Straps were inverted by error when original photograph was made in the 1920s. The other custom-made pair shown are now in the Smithsonian Institution Collection. One conch was decorated with the Maltese Cross ranch brand, and the other with the Elkhorn brand.

THEODORE ROOSEVELT COLLECTION, HARVARD COLLEGE LIBRARY

OPPOSITE: One of the most fascinating of discoveries in researching TR and his arms interests was the Merwin Hulbert & Co. engraved, inscribed, nickel-plated and pearl-gripped Single Action presentation revolver. In script on its backstrap: William Merrifield. The revolver is engraved on the frame, cylinder, and barrel. The leather cartridge belt and holster, marked by J.S. Collins, Cheyenne, Wyoming. The revolver is serial #21328; a .44-40 caliber with a 7-inch barrel. Merrifield received appointment from President Roosevelt for a four-year term as U.S. Marshal, District of Montana. He was sworn in January 2, 1907.

GREG LAMPE COLLECTION; PHOTOGRAPHS BY RON PAXTON

ARTHUR W. MERRIFIELD
UNITED STATES
MARSHAL
FOR
MONTANA

William Merrifield

A gold Tiffany & Co. pocket watch accompanied the presentation Merwin Hulbert & Co. revolver set, also a TR gift for Merrifield. Inscribed inside the case, "If it's a black bear, I can tree him; if it's a grizzly I can bay him." The watch bears the serial #22910, and its case is of 18 karat gold. TR offered Merrifield a gold watch or $150, in appreciation for taking the first grizzly bear; Merrifield opted for the watch.

GREG LAMPE COLLECTION; PHOTOGRAPHS BY RON PAXTON

and, when there is time for churning, a good deal of butter. We also keep hens, which, in spite of the damaging inroads of hawks, bobcats, and foxes, supply us with eggs, and in time of need, when our rifles have failed to keep us in game, with stewed, roast, or fried chicken also. From our garden we get potatoes, and unless drought, frost, or grasshoppers interfere (which they do about every second year), other vegetables as well. For fresh meat we depend chiefly upon our prowess as hunters.

Just before Christmas, 1884, Roosevelt left the Badlands on the Northern Pacific headed East. The year drew to a close with the young rancher one of the East's most experienced and knowledgeable hunters of Western birds and big game. Only three major species of the West were unknown to his game bag; the mountain goat, the mountain lion, and the javelina. It was only a matter of time before Roosevelt would take these three.

SPECIAL NOTE: Two Winchester Model 1876 deluxe sporting rifles, serial numbers 15106 and 15107, were presented by collector S.P. Stevens to the National Park Service, for display at the Theodore Roosevelt National Park, Medora, North Dakota. The rifles are of .50-95 Express caliber, and boast such special features as half magazines, half round/half octagonal barrels, tang peep sights, and checkered semi-pistol grip select walnut stocks with shotgun style butts. The horn buttplate of #15106 is engraved: FROM [at top, above checkering] TR [an intertwined monogram], the same style monogram as on the Colt Single Action Army revolver, pictured on page 46. Rifle #15106 has a brass oval inlay. The cross is the brand of TR's Maltese Ranch. The date commemorates the day on which TR took his first grizzly bear, accompanied by Merrifield as guide.

Winchester factory ledgers indicate that the rifles were shipped as a pair. Details on the set appear in *Man at Arms* magazine, November/December 1982, in the article, "The Roosevelt-Merrifield Connection," by Richard Rattenbury.

Arthur W. Merrifield and the Roosevelt Memorial Association, Inc.

An intriguing correspondence has been located which reveals the generosity of Theodore Roosevelt, his affection for his hunting guides, and the reverence for the TR legacy of Herman Hagedorn, Director, Roosevelt Memorial Association, Inc., and a pivotal early biographer and admirer. In a two page letter dated September 20, 1921, Hagedorn lists the following "articles mentioned in your letter":

- 3 bbl. Gun made to order for T.R. [the L.C. Smith "ranch gun" of .40-70 caliber with two12 gauge barrels]
- 40-60 Winchester rifle of TR [likely no. 45520 Model 1876]
- T.R.'s first colt 44-6-shooter [no. 92267, with pearl grips, engraved and inscribed on right grip panel, "Theodore Roosevelt"]
- T.R.'s first pair of chaps
- T.R.'s cowboy roundup hat, with cowboy braided horsehair hatband
- T.R.'s riding bridle, cowboy braided of lace leather
- T.R.'s Elkhorn Ranch organ
- Other small relics

Hagedorn proposed purchasing these items for the Association, at a price of $500, stating "Of course, it is impossible to place a value on things of that sort."

Merrifield felt the three-barrel gun to be worth $1,000, and accordingly, kept that item for himself. The balance was sold to the Association, for the $500 figure. Accordingly, on January 24, 1922, Hagedorn confirmed the purchased, and

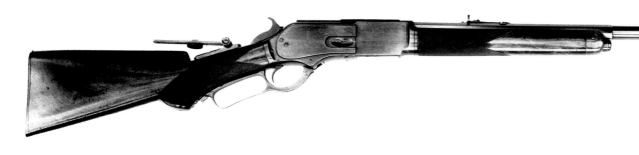

The Bill Merrifield presentation
Winchester Model 1876 half
magazine deluxe rifle, serial #15106,
commemorating the day Merrifield
guided TR to his first grizzly bear.
The rifle is accompanied by serial
#15107, of matching quality and style.

asked "Now will you please write me a brief account of each item, giving me a general declaration of their genuineness? Of course, knowing you, I know that they are absolutely genuine. But I don't want the world to have to take merely my word for the genuineness of your collection…" Merrifield signed a simple statement, and evidently provided additional details, since Hagedorn noted in a February 1, 1922 letter: "The stories you tell are all of the most interesting." In that letter, Hagedorn provides some additional documentation: "Kermit Roosevelt, by the way, has sent us the spurs to which you refer." The signed affidavit requested of Merrifield read:

I, A.W. Merrifield, hereby state under oath that the articles listed below and sent by me to the Roosevelt Memorial Association were the personal property of Theodore Roosevelt, and were used by him during his residence in the Bad Lands of North Dakota during the years 1883 to 1893.

⤺ 40-60 Winchester rifle of TR
⤺ T.R.'s first colt 44-6 shooter
⤺ T.R.'s first pair of chaps
⤺ T.R.'s cowboy roundup hat, with cowboy braided horsehair hatband
⤺ T.R.'s riding bridle, cowboy braided of lace leather
⤺ T.R.'s Elkhorn Ranch organ
⤺ Silver Drinking Cup
⤺ Compass
⤺ Spectacles

Indicating that "we may want to furnish up a room in our new headquarters to look like the sitting-room at Elkhorn ranch.…I am wondering if you have any of the other furniture which was actually used in this sitting-room.…In any case I would be very much pleased if you could send us a description of this room, telling us just what furniture it contained and where the various pieces of furniture stood, together with a description of what pictures, antlers, guns, etc., decorated the four walls, also a description of the fireplace and any other details of construction and furniture that may occur to you. Have you any pictures taken inside the living-room of the ranch-house?…"

In a letter of May 10, 1922, Hagedorn thanked Merrifield for his letter of the 5ᵗʰ "enclosing Mrs. Merrifield's description of the sitting-room of Elkhorn Ranch, and also the bill of lading for the organ.…I guess we will have to write to Bill Sewall about the ranch sitting-room, especially regarding the dimensions of the fireplace.…Can you tell me where any of the pictures, mounted heads, gun-racks or any other objects, such as the chairs, are now located?"

Hagedorn's dedication played a vital role in gathering together TR's firearms and memorabilia from the West, to the extent that the Association and Sagamore Hill maintained the most complete collections of this material for decades. ✤

CHAPTER 4

Hunting and Ranching in the "Wild West"

Roosevelt returned to the Badlands in April 1885, and resumed his tasks at Elkhorn. It was roundup time, and there were plenty of chores facing him. "It was interesting and exciting work," he wrote, "and except for the lack of sleep on the spring and summer roundups, it was not exhausting..." Riding his favorite horse, Manitou, Roosevelt directed the roundup with dispatch and efficiency. He and his cowhands led a Spartan life, on horseback for hours, blistered alternately by the wind and the sun. Seldom did they enjoy the luxury of a change of clothes. Supper consisted of "bacon, Dutch oven bread, and possibly beef." After supper Roosevelt "would roll up in my bedding as soon as possible, and the others would follow suit at their pleasure." At about three in the morning "a yell from the cook" would rouse the hands from their sound sleep. Each cowboy then "came to the fire, where he picked out a tin cup, tin plate, and knife and fork, helped himself to coffee and to whatever food there was, and ate it standing or squatting as best suited him."

Roosevelt found the roundup exacting but altogether satisfying. Writing to a friend in the East, he told how he had

...worked as hard as any of the cowboys; but I have enjoyed it greatly Yesterday I was eighteen hours in the saddle—from 4 A.M. to 10 P.M.—having a half hour each for dinner and tea. I

Thoughtfully documented for posterity, TR is photographed standing guard with a Parker double barrel shotgun over the three boat thieves, their roles portrayed for the camera by others.

© BETTMANN/CORBIS

CHIMNEY BUTTE RANCH.
THEODORE ROOSEVELT, Proprietor.
FERRIS & MERRIFIELD, Managers.

P. O. address,
Little Missouri,
D. T. Range,
Little Missouri,
8 miles south
of railroad,

as in cut
on left
hip and
right
side, both or
either, and

down cut dewlap.
Horse brand, on left hip.

ELKHORN RANCH.
THEODORE ROOSEVELT, Proprietor.
SEAWALL & DOW, Managers.

P. O. address, Lit-
tle Missouri, D. T.
Range, Little Mis-
souri, twenty-five
miles north of rail-
road.

as in cut, on
left side, on right,
or the re-
verse.
Horse brand,
on right or
left should-
er.

**Brands from the Elkhorn and
Maltese Cross (Chimney Butte)
ranches. Reproduced from the
Stockgrowers Journal, Miles City,
Montana, circa 1885.**

THEODORE ROOSEVELT COLLECTION,
HARVARD COLLEGE LIBRARY

can now do cowboy work pretty well.…You are all off about my horsemanship; as you would say if you saw me now. Almost all of our horses on the ranch being young, I had to include in my string three that were but partially broken; and I have had some fine circuses with them. One of them had never been saddled but once before, and he proved vicious, and besides bucking, kept falling over backwards with me; finally he caught me, giving me an awful slam, from which my left arm has by no means recovered. Another bucked me off going down hill; but I think I have cured him, for I put him through a desperate course of sprouts when I got on again. The third I nearly lost in swimming him across a swollen creek, where the flood had carried down a good deal of drift timber. However, I got him through all right in the end, after a regular ducking. Twice one of my old horses turned a somersault while galloping after cattle; once in a prairie dog town, and once while trying to prevent the herd from stampeding in a storm at night…

By the end of the 1885 roundup, Roosevelt was in the prime of health. His body had finally caught up with his mind. A newspaper reporter noted that Roosevelt was "rugged" and "bronzed" and a "thorough Westerner."

There was very little of the whilom dude in his rough and easy costume, with a large handkerchief tied loosely about his neck, but the eye glasses and the flashing eyes behind them, the pleasing smile and the hearty grasp of the hand remained. There was the same eagerness to hear from the world of politics, and the same frank willingness to answer all questions propounded. The slow exasperating drawl and the unique accent that the New Yorker feels he must use when visiting a less blessed portion of civilization have disappeared, and in their place is a nervous, energetic manner of talking with the flat accent of the West…

The Marquis de Morès

The degree to which the Badlands had made a Wild Westerner is well attested by his near-duel with the Marquis de Morès an eccentric French aristocrat who lived extravagantly in a thirty-room mansion and was attended to by no fewer than twenty servants. The Marquis' mansion was not far from Roosevelt's Elkhorn ranch, and the men struck up a friendship of sorts. The Marquis' haughty bearing was not calculated to endear him to the cowboys of Medora, nor did he conceal his contempt for their lack of gentility and refinement.

The Marquis was implicated in the murder of a boisterous cowpuncher named Riley Luffsey, who on several occasions had been overheard to say that someday he would kill de Morès. The Marquis was eventually acquitted of any complicity in the murder of Luffsey, even though testimony of Joe Ferris, a close friend of Roosevelt, proved especially damaging and greatly prolonged the trial.

Angered by Ferris' involvement, de Morès sent Roosevelt a rash letter in which he asked brusquely whether Roosevelt was a "friend" or "enemy":

My principle is to take the bull by the horns. Joe Ferris is very active against me and has been instrumental in getting me indicted by furnishing money to witnesses and hunting them up. The papers also publish very stupid accounts of our quarrelling—I sent you the paper to N.Y. Is this done by your orders? I thought you my friend. If you are my enemy I want to know it. I am always on hand as you know, and between

gentlemen it is easy to settle matters of that sort directly...

Theodore's reaction to the Marquis' thinly veiled threat was quick and decisive. According to Bill Sewall,

Roosevelt read me the [Marquis'] letter and said that he regarded it as a threat that the Marquis would, perhaps, challenge him. If he did, he should accept the challenge, for he would not be bullied. He said that his friends would all be opposed to his fighting a duel, and that he was opposed to dueling himself. But if he was challenged, he should accept. That would give him the choice of weapons. He would choose Winchester rifles, and have the distance arranged at twelve paces. He did not consider himself a very good shot and wanted to be near enough so that he could hit. They would shoot and advance until one or the other was satisfied. He told me that if he was challenged, he wanted me to act as his second. I told him I'd certainly do it, but that I didn't think he would have to fight, that a man who would lay in ambush and shoot at unsuspecting men would not want to fight such a duel as that.

Roosevelt said in his answer to the

The verandah of the Elkhorn ranch house, photographed by Theodore Roosevelt, circa 1885. Leaning against the large elk rack at center is TR's Winchester Model 1876 .45-75 rifle #38647, at bottom right was his fancy saddle, at top right one of his custom-engraved Colt six-shooters in a hand-tooled holster.

Marquis that he had no ill-will toward him, and had furnished no money for the prosecution; but as the closing sentence of the Marquis's letter implied a threat, he felt it a duty to himself to say that at all times and in all places he was ready to answer for his actions. I told him after he read the letter to me that I thought he would get an apology. He said that he did not think he would, the man might ignore the letter, but he did not think he would apologize.

A few days afterward he came to me with a letter in his hands which he read to me. He said, "You were right, Bill," The Marquis had written, that there was "always a way to settle misunderstandings between gentlemen—without trouble." He invited Theodore to his house to dinner. Theodore went and once more everything passed off pleasantly.

Two More Fancy Winchesters

On May 12, 1885, while Roosevelt was on the spring roundup, the Winchester factory shipped another deluxe rifle, a Model 1876, #45520. And on August 15 the company dispatched the fourth in the TR series, a Model 1876 carbine, #45704. Both were fitted up in the finest style, and both were .40-60 caliber. The carbine left the factory incomplete:

.40-60 caliber; 20" round barrel; 1/2 magazine; case hardened; pistol grip, but without forearm, buttstock, or sight swivel band; engraved. [stockwork probably done by Hartley & Graham]

The rifle was complete, but the stocks were not custom-fitted:

.40-60 caliber; 1/2 round, 1/2 octagon barrel; 1/2 magazine, case hardened; checkered pistol grip stock, plain trigger; engraved.

Both guns have unmistakable earmarks of Roosevelt's taste in longarms: engraving both fine

and profuse, 1/2 magazines, pistol grip stocks, case hardening, and large caliber. The rifle's barrel is 1/2 round-1/2 octagon (as was that on the Model 1876 .45-75), and its elaborate game motifs are a grizzly bear, buffalo, elk and big horn sheep. Under the lever, stamped on the lower tang, is the name J. ULRICH, the same craftsman who engraved TR's Model 1876 .45-75. The frame of the carbine is engraved with an identical elk, an identical (but reversed in pose) big horn motif and a unique elk rack and hunting horn design. On the toe of the shotgun style buttplate is a TR monogram. Inlaid on the right side of the buttstock is a gold oval plaque engraved with a raccoon. The carbine's cheekpiece was carved with a large graceful crescent, and special sights were fitted of the folding leaf pattern popular with Roosevelt at the time. This was an exquisite set of .40-60 Winchesters. TR wrote of his carbine in the March 1886 *Outing* magazine:

> A ranchman…with whom hunting is of secondary importance, and who cannot be bothered by carrying a long rifle always round with him on horseback, but who, nevertheless, wishes to have some weapon with which he can kill what game he runs across, usually adopts a short, light saddle-gun, a carbine, weighing but five or six pounds, and of such convenient shape that it can be kept under his thigh alongside the saddle. A 40-60 Winchester is perhaps the best for such a purpose, as it carries far and straight, and hits hard, and is a first-

rate weapon for deer and antelope, and can also be used with effect against sheep, elk, and even bear, although for these last a heavier weapon is of course preferable.

Few sportsmen, East or West, could match Theodore Roosevelt's spectacular collection of four Winchesters and two Colts, his deluxe Bullard, his 10 gauge E. Thomas Jr. double-barrel shotgun, his 16 gauge Kennedy double and the L.C. Smith 12 gauge/.40-70 combination shotgun rifle. His silver-mounted, etched, and relief-engraved Tiffany & Co. hunting knife completed an outdoorsman's equipage *par excellence*.

Standing Off Indians

Whether facing the ostensible challenge of a noble Frenchman or that of a noble "savage," Roosevelt never flinched or cowered. While riding alone up the northeast range in the fall of 1885, Roosevelt unexpectedly came upon four or five Indians "directly in front of me." As soon as they saw him,

> …they whipped their guns out of their slings, started their horses into a run and came on at full tilt, whooping and brandishing their weapons. I instantly reined up and dismounted.…I waited until the Indians were a hundred yards off, and then threw up my rifle and drew a bead on the foremost. The effect was like magic. The whole party scattered out as wild pigeons or teal ducks sometimes do when shot at, and doubled back on their tracks, the men bending over

On August 15th, 1885, Winchester shipped one of TR's deluxe guns, a .40-60 Model 1876 short rifle, serial #45704. Most of the engraving on his Winchesters was taken from standard factory patterns, but the elkhorn and hunting horn motifs on the carbine's frame are unknown on any other Winchester, and are considered to have been executed at the suggestion of TR himself. Used by TR as a "saddle gun for deer and antelope" and carried by him in pursuit of the boat thieves in 1886. In this right side detail, note the gold inlaid stock oval with raccoon motif, rarely engraved on period Winchester arms.

AUTRY NATIONAL CENTER COLLECTION; PHOTOGRAPH BY SUSAN EINSTEIN

"I waited until the Indians were a hundred yards off, and then threw up my rifle and drew a bead on the foremost." Drawing by Frederic Remington for TR's *Ranch Life and the Hunting Trail.*

BOONE AND CROCKETT CLUB
PERMANENT COLLECTION

alongside their horses. When some distance off they halted and gathered together to consult, and after a minute one came forward alone, ostentatiously dropping his rifle and waving a blanket over his head. When he came to within fifty yards I stopped him, and he pulled out a piece of paper—all Indians, when absent from their reservations, are supposed to carry passes—and called out, "How! Me good Indian!" I answered, "How," and assured him most sincerely I was very glad he was a good Indian, but I would not let him come closer; and when his companions began to draw near, I covered him with the rifle and made him move off, which he did with a sudden lapse into the most canonical Anglo-Saxon profanity. I then started to lead my horse out to the prairie, and after hovering round a short time they rode off, while I followed suit, but in the opposite direction. It had all passed too quickly for me to have time to get frightened; but during the rest of my ride I was

exceedingly uneasy, and pushed tough, speedy old Manitou along at a rapid rate, keeping well out on the level…

Towards nightfall I fell in with two old trappers who lived near Killdeer Mountains, and they informed me that my assailants were some young Sioux bucks, at whose hands they themselves had just suffered the loss of two horses.

To New York and the Hounds

Leaving the Badlands in September, Roosevelt returned East to devote his time to politics and writing. His hunting was limited to riding with the hounds at the Meadowbrook Country Club and at Sagamore Hill. In early October he wrote Henry Cabot Lodge "…Last Thursday I hunted, and never knew the old horse go better. I kept in the same field with the hounds almost the whole time, and was second in at the death; ahead of the huntsman and master…"

Later that month, while riding with the hounds, Roosevelt fractured his left arm. With arm dangling and his face spattered with blood, he remounted and rode on to the end:

The weather was glorious, and everything went off without a hitch, the entire neighborhood turned out in drags, tandems, etc. The field was only about 35 in number, mostly in red; but at least 25 were as hard riding men, mounted on as good hunters, as are to be found on either side the Atlantic; every crack rider of the Meadowbrook and Essex clubs was here, each mounted on his very best horse, and each bound to force the pace from start to finish. The country was too stiff for any timid rider to turn out.

We opened over a succession of small fields with fences by actual measurement from 4 feet 6 to five feet, and the fun grew fast and furious very rapidly The run was for ten miles with one check, over the country.…Douglas [Robinson] took my sister's mare out to school her; at the third fence she turned a couple of handsprings

The deluxe Nimschke-engraved Colt Single Action revolver #92248, with its hand-tooled holster, and the Model 1876 .40-60 short rifle.

Artist's sketch of TR's Chimney Butte Ranch from the cover of the *Roosevelt Wild Life Bulletin*: Volume 1, Number 1.

A meet of the Meadowbrook Hunt
Club at TR's home at Oyster Bay,
Long Island.

HARPER'S WEEKLY

and literally "knocked him silly," and took half the skin off his face; he rode along the roads the rest of the way. A great many men had falls, and about half way through I came to grief. Frank [TR's horse] is stiff and the company was altogether too good for him, I had pounded the old fellow along pretty well up with the first rank, but he was nearly done out. Then we came to a five foot fence, stiffer than iron, that staggered the best, my old horse, completely blown, struck the top rail, didn't make an effort to recover, and rolled over on me among a lot of stones. I cut my face to pieces and broke my left arm (which accounts for my super-ordinarily erratic hand writing). After that I fell behind, as with one hand I could not always make Frank take his fences the first time; however three or four miles farther on a turn in the line enabled me again to catch up, and I was in at the death, not a hundred yards behind the first half dozen. I looked pretty gay, with one arm dangling, and my face and clothes like the

walls of a slaughter house. I guess my hunting is over for this season…

"It's a mere trifle," Roosevelt told a *New York Times* reporter, refusing to discuss the matter further! "I am always willing to pay the piper when I have had a good dance; and every now and then I like to drink the wine of life with brandy in it."

Three Thieves and a "Damn Fool"

TR was back at the Elkhorn Ranch again in March 1886. Two days later he hiked with Sewall and Dow to retrieve some deer killed by Dow and hung out for two weeks. Discovering that the deer had been partially devoured by mountain lions, Roosevelt became "very fierce to kill a lion." The lion hunt required the party to board Roosevelt's new boat and row to the opposite bank of the Little Missouri River. But that night the boat was stolen, precipitating one of TR's most perilous Badlands adventures, later published in *Ranch Life and the Hunting Trail*. A rather obscure but interesting account was written by Bill Sewall in a letter to his brother:

I will now give you an account our latest expidition which was a campaign against [three] Thieves.…we have a boat which Mr R bought in St Paul and [it] is the best one on the River and that is what the fuss came from. when the ice breaks up it goes all in a body as thare is no rocks to obstruct it the stream is very crooked and it jams in the turns and floes all the low bottoms and at such times it is impossible to cross without a boat the water is so deep and strong that a raft cant be handled of course this dont last very long but while it does the boat is very much needed.

well when Mr R came Will and I had four Deer on the other side of the river so we went after them and he went with us when we got whare the Deer hung we found the Mountain Lions had torn them down and were eating them [They] had eaten them most all up Mr

R is very fierce to kill a Lion he never has seen one   so it was a good deal of work to get the stuff out by hand we advised him to get Tompkins who is an old hunter and lived on that side of the River to go with him we were going to ferry him and his stud across in the morning and Tompkins was going to meet him with his team and haul him out near the place and they were going to watch for the Lions   well that night we had one of the winds that you hear people tell about out west   it often blows as hard as it did at home in the big blow the other fall when the weather is clear and you cannot see any reason for it or signs of wind but you hear and feel it   well in the night we had a Snorter and pretty early in the morning I went to see if the boat was all right   we had to land some way below the house on account of ice and the Boat was gone suppose I should have thought the wind did it but I found the rope was cut and finally Will found a mitten that had been dropped in their hurry   of course R was dissapointed also mad   the rest of us were not well pleased   so he sent Bill Rowe to town to Telagraph to Mandan to have them arrested if they went thare and I went at it to make a boat   Bill got some nails and in four days I was ready with the boat   Will had helped me what he could and got everything else ready   well that brought it to Saturday so we waited till monday and as it was very cold and ice running we did not start till tuesday   that day and the next passed quietly   we onley shot some [prairie] chickens   the third morning we found the Deer seemed very plenty whare we camped so we made a raid on them the first thing in the morning we started four   Will and I each got one so we had plenty of meat   as we were bringing them in we started four more that were lying about twenty rods from our camp but we had enough so did not shoot at them   we ate our breakfast and went on   Welll along in the afternoon as we came around a bend in the stream I had been looking

sharp all the time and I saw our boat   I said thares your boat   get your guns ready.

I will navigate the boat   so Will and Roosevelt put on their Pistols and got their guns ready   as soon as I got the boat ashore they mounted out   I had my tools handy and as soon as I could hitch the boat [I] was with them   it was rather funny business for one of the men was called a pretty hard ticket   was well armed with a Winchester rifle and a self cocking Smith and Wesson revolver which are considered the most dangerous kind of pistol   all you have to do is to pull the trigger   they will shoot six times as fast as you count nearly   he was also a Shooting man   if he was in the bushes and saw us first he was liable to make it very unhealthy for us   he was a noted thief and had got the idear I guess that he could steal pretty safely [I] don't know as he thought anybody dared to meddle with him   we did not know what the other one was but knew the old German was harmless   well it so happened that he was in the camp [and] the other two were out hunting so we got quiet possesion of the camp   [We] told old Chris [the German] to keep still and build on a fire and it would be all right with him

now I will describe the camp and plan of capture   the camp was simply a fire   it was on the first bank of the river   thare are often two bank whare some very high freshet has washed out wider than usual   well therir camp was on the first bank   it was about fifteen feet wide   then the second was about six feet high with an open space clear of brush about four rods wide.

behind that was thick Bull and Rose bushes that a man could not get through without makeing quite a noise   so I advised [them] to lay behind this bank and when they came   which we knew they would if they had not seen us and when they got in the middle of the open space to hold them up as

"I looked pretty gay, with one arm dangling, and my face and clothes like the walls of a slaughter house. I guess my hunting is over for this season..."

By the end of the 1885 roundup, Roosevelt was in the prime of health. His body had finally caught up with his mind. A newspaper reporter noted that Roosevelt was "rugged" and "bronzed" and a "thorough Westerner."

they call it here   it consists of suddenly aiming a cocked gun or pistol at a man and saying hands up   and if he has any real regard for his life he holds his hands right up   so Will and I kept watch and listened   our eyes are better than R   Will on the right I on the left   R was to rise up and tell them to I hold their] hands up   Will and I both with double barrel guns loaded with Buck shot and we were all three going to shoot if they offered to raise a gun   it is rather savage work but it dont do to fool with such fellows   if thare was killing to be done we meant to do it ourselves.

well in about half an hour one of them came   we heard him a long while when he got just right we rose up and he put his hands up very quick   this was more good luck   we took his gun and gave him a seat under the bank with the cheerful information that if he made any noise or tried to get away we would shoot him

but the hardest one was still to come   Will had found his pistol in the camp but he had his Winchester with him   in about half an hour he came [and] without the least suspision walked into the open space   when R called to him he hesitated as if he had a mind to try it Will was afraid he would try to raise his gun and we would have to shoot him so he snapped out in his shortest and most ugly snap   Damm you drop that gun and he dropped it   so they were taken without danger to ourselves or harm to them   I dont think this fellow who goes by the name of Mike Finnegin was scared at all but mad   if he had had any chance [I] think he would have tried us   but few men would try to fight when they saw three men with cocked guns aimed at them and not more than twenty feet off   Mr R told them if they kept quiet and did not try to get off they would be all right if they tryed anything we would shoot them   we took turns watching them nights   [We] had to keep them a week   the ice was jammed so we could

not get down the river   I watched them days while Mr R and Will hunted   they were perfectly quiet   never made any trouble   we used and fed them as if they were guests but minded to keep a very sharps watch over them and gave them no chance to escape   when the ice moved so we could get down whare we could get a team Mr. R. got one and men with it and took them to Dickenson the nearest town whare they were tried before a justice and bound over [to the court] not getting bail two of them were sent to Mandan to jail   the old German they let go…

Roosevelt himself took the prisoners on into Dickinson:

…I took the three thieves into Dickinson, the nearest town. The going was bad, and the little mares could only drag the wagon at a walk; so, though we drove during the daylight, it took us two days and a night to make the journey. It was a most desolate drive. The prairie had been burned the fall before, and was a mere bleak waste of blackened earth, and a cold, rainy mist lasted throught the two days. The only variety was where the road crossed the shallow headwaters of Knife and Green rivers. Here the ice was high along the banks, and the wagon had to be taken to pieces to get it over. My three captives were unarmed, but as I was alone with them, except for the driver, of whom I knew nothing, I had to be doubly on my guard, and never let them come close to me. The little mares went so slowly and the heavy road rendered any hope of escape by flogging up the horses so entirely out of the question, that I soon found the safest plan was to put the prisoners in the wagon and myself walk behind with the inevitable Winchester [Model 1876 carbine, .40-60 caliber, #45704]. Accordingly I trudged steadily the whole time behind the wagon through the ankle-deep mud. It was a gloomy walk. Hour after hour went by always the same, while I plodded along through

The three captors of the three thieves. At left, Wilmot Dow, at right, William Sewall, and at center, Theodore Roosevelt. TR held a fancy Bullard .50-115 lever-action rifle, which had been made to match the Winchester Model 1873, the Model 1876 .45-75, and the Model 1876 .40-60 carbine—each having deluxe stocks and sights, and gold inlaid oval stock plaques engraved with game scenes.

Dow and Sewall in the boat made to
chase the thieves. Dow was wearing
two Colt Single Action revolvers,
Sewall had one, and on the boat were
a double-barrel shotgun (left), TR's
Model 1876 .40-60 carbine, and at
right the L.C. Smith ranch gun. From
an original photograph by TR.

the dreary landscape—hunger, cold, and fatigue
struggling with a sense of dogged, weary resolution. At night, when we put up at the squalid
hut of a frontier granger, the only habitation on
our road, it was even worse. I did not dare to go
to sleep, but making my three men get into the
upper bunk, from which they could get out only
with difficulty, I sat up with my back against the
cabin-door and kept watch over them all night
long. So, after thirty-six hours' sleeplessness, I
was most heartily glad when we at last jolted
into the long, straggling main street of Dickinson, and I was able to give my unwilling companions into the hands of the sheriff.

Under the laws of Dakota I received my fees
as a deputy sheriff for making the three arrests,
and also mileage for the three hundred odd
miles gone over—a total of some fifty dollars…

After surrendering his prisoners, Roosevelt,
covered with prairie mud, set out to find a doctor
to look after his blistered feet. By coincidence the
first person he asked for directions was the only
physician for miles around, Dr. Victor Hugo Stickney. "By George," he declared to the flabbergasted
Stickney, "you're exactly the man I want to see. I've
just come 40 miles on foot from the Killdeer Mountains, bringing down some horse thieves at the point
of a Winchester and my feet are blistered so badly
that I can hardly walk. I want you to fix me up."

The capture of the three thieves became the
talk of the territory. Theodore Roosevelt had convincingly shown his pluck and courage. As TR's
friend and fellow rancher John Simpson told him:
"Roosevelt, no one but you would have followed
those men with just a couple of cow-hands. You are
the only real damn fool in the country."

"Really, I enjoy this life; with books, guns and horses…"

Late in April 1886, TR hunted antelope for a week in the company of William Merrifield, an experienced hunter and outdoorsman and one of the managers of Maltese Cross Ranch. To Merrifield it seemed that Roosevelt was always in a state of perpetual motion. Many years later he recalled that Roosevelt "used to walk up and down this room [at the Maltese Cross], then sit down awhile, then jump up and grab a gun and go out hunting. Then he would come back in again and start to write… and would work sometimes until early in the morning." Politics was a remote subject when Roosevelt was at his ranch: "It often amuses me when I accidentally hear that I am supposed to be harboring secret and biting regret for my political career; when as a matter of fact I have hardly ever when alone given it two thoughts since it dosed, and have been quite as much wrapped up in hunting, ranching, and bookmaking as I ever was in politics." He was being quite honest with himself when he declared, "Really, I enjoy this life; with books, guns and horses, and this free, open air existence, it would be singular if I did not…"

In August Roosevelt and Merrifield traveled to the Rocky Mountains for a hunting trip that Roosevelt had been planning for some time. The roundup at the ranch was over, and TR was itching for excitement. He chose to hunt in the Rockies because he was especially eager to shoot the white antelope-goat, "the least known and rarest of all American game…not one in ten of the professional hunters has ever killed one; and I know of but one or two Eastern sportsmen who can boast a goat's head as a trophy."

Roosevelt's guide, a Missourian named Jack Willis, had unwittingly sparked TR's interest in the white antelope-goat. In his book *Roosevelt in the Rough*, Willis tellingly relates both the hunt itself and the fortuitous circumstances that prompted the hunting trip:

> …in a taxidermist's store at Medora, Roosevelt's attention was attracted by the head of a white antelope-goat, which was then, as it still is, the rarest and least known of all of America's wild animals.…Roosevelt asked all about the animal and where the head had come from. The taxidermist gave him the information he wanted and told him something about my reputation as a hunter.

> Immediately Roosevelt wrote me this letter:

> "I want to shoot a white antelope goat. I have heard it is the hardest animal in the Rockies to find and the most difficult to kill. I have also heard that you are a great hunter. If I come to Montana, will you act as my guide, and do you think I can kill a white goat?'

> My first impression was that this was another joke from the joke town and I was disposed to ignore it. But there was nothing funny about Roosevelt's chirography. It was the worst I had ever seen, bar none, and deciphering his letter was a much tougher job than stalking a silver-tip. It annoyed me to have to wrestle with his almost illegible note and after I had finally made it out I sent him this message:

> "If you can't shoot any better than you can write, NO."

> I supposed that ended it, but in three days along came a telegram from Roosevelt, [telling me when he would arrive and wanting] me to show him the way to the white goats, in return for which I would be well paid. Curious to see what he looked like, I was at the station when his train arrived.

Corduroy Knickers and a Brewer's Son's Cheeks

> Two men climbed down from the Pullman. One of them had on the corduroy knickers and coat of a tenderfoot. I knew he was Roosevelt, and he looked too much like a dude to make any hit with me. He bad red cheeks, like those of a brewer's son I knew, and that didn't help any. The only thing about him that appealed to me

He chose to hunt in the Rockies because he was especially eager to shoot the white antelope-goat, "the least known and rarest of all American game… not one in ten of the professional hunters has ever killed one; and I know of but one or two Eastern sportsmen who can boast a goat's head as a trophy."

"Stalking Goats" with guide Jack
Willis on the Rocky Mountain white
goat hunt in the fall of 1886. Frederic
Remington drawing from *Ranch Life
and the Hunting Trail*.

at all was his eyes. They were keen and bright and dancing with animation. From them I knew he was honest and had a mind that worked fast and smoothly and was set on a hair-trigger. But in spite of that I didn't like his looks. His companion, who was properly garbed in buckskin coat and pants, was William Merrifield…

"I'm here," shouted Roosevelt, impulsively, as he seized my hand with a grip that I hadn't supposed was in him.

"I see you are," I replied, coldly.

"When do we start?"

"*We* are not going to start at all. You can start whenever you like, so far as I am concerned."

"Why not? What's wrong?" asked Roosevelt, with disappointment and anxiety written all over him. "I'll pay you $25 for every shot you get me at a white goat."

"That's one reason why we are not going anywhere," I explained. "I won't work for anyone on salary. I go where I like and when I like and do as I darned well please."

A Beautiful Winchester

After some further expostulation and argument, which simply took up time, Roosevelt suggested that we sit down and talk things over, so I escorted them to a hotel where they engaged a room and unpacked some of their things.…He proudly showed me his…rifle. It was a 45-75 Winchester [Model 1876, #38647] and a beauty. I made no bones of telling him so, and he was pleased by my admiration of it.

He told me of his ranch and of his hunting trips in Maine, while I carefully explained that shooting "game" that was almost housebroken, in Maine, wasn't real hunting, as we knew it in Montana. He was insistent that I act as his guide and I was just as persistent, and more profane, in my refusal of every proposal he advanced. But the longer I talked with him the better I liked him. There was something of the savor of the West in his manner and his frankness, and,

so long as I could keep my eyes away from his foolish pants, I cottoned to the things he said and the way he said them. In about an hour he had made me forget his knickers and had won me over as far as I would ever go for any man. And that, if I do say it myself, was some conquest, for he sure had bucked up against a hard game. That was the first evidence I had of his great personal magnetism.

"I'll tell you what I'll do," I finally told him, after I had convinced myself that he was a Westerner at heart and had the makings of a real man. "I won't act as guide or wet nurse for any man. As a rule I don't want anyone around to bother me and get in my way. But I am starting out on a hunt in two or three days and if you and Merrifield want to come along, as my guests, I'll be glad to have you."

"That's bully," exclaimed Roosevelt, excitedly "I'll furnish the grub and pay you $25 for every shot you get me at a white goat."

.…I made short work of our preparations and we were soon on our way with two pack horses and our mounts. We went out on Vermilion Creek, west of Thompson Falls, where we established our first camp, left our horses and took to the hills in a wild section of the main range.

The First Goat

It was hard going, for the goats are at home only in rough country. Being accustomed to it, I walked so fast that Roosevelt was forced into a jog trot most of the time to keep up with me. But he never complained, nor did he ever ask me to slacken my speed. Moisture would develop on his glasses, from perspiration, and he would have to pause at intervals to wipe them off, but he kept right on coming. That satisfied me as to his gameness, for which I came to have the highest admiration as we got to know each other better. His muscles were strong and after they became hardened, which took about a week, he

could keep up with me on almost any trail, no matter how hard the going...

In the afternoon of our first day out, we located a salt lick. I knew goats would come here, so we waited for them, above the lick, for a goat always runs uphill when he is attacked. In half an hour a big billy showed up.* After looking carefully around and detecting no sign of danger he descended to the lick and Roosevelt got a beautiful shot at him, at less than two hundred yards.

Perhaps because he was a bit excited over his first shot at one of the animals he wanted so badly, and which he had been told were so hard to get, he missed. As the goat dashed blindly up the hill Roosevelt fired again. I saw a bit of wool fly from the beast's foreleg and from the way he favored that leg in running I knew he had been wounded. We set out after him and followed him for seven miles, by the drops of blood he had left behind. We came to a place where he had rubbed his injured leg in the dust, to stop the flow of blood—which is a way animals have to give themselves first aid— but failed to catch sight of him. Late in the afternoon we gave up the chase and tramped nine miles back to camp.

Roosevelt was all in from the long and hard hike, but he made no complaint about that. Instead of spending the evening coddling himself and talking about his blisters and bruises, he occupied himself entirely with lamentations over his poor marksmanship. He repeatedly assured us he never had missed such an easy shot and his failure worried him considerably I told him the only trouble was that he had been over-anxious, besides which he was in a strange country and shooting at game he never had hunted before. But he refused to be comforted and his smiles were not of the cheerful kind.

He insisted that the slaying of the wounded goat was the only balm that would soothe

*Roosevelt stated that the goat was not sighted until the third or fourth day, and his information is regarded as correct.

his injured pride, so we took up its trail at dawn the next morning. Merrifield stayed in camp to doctor his feet…

Soon after daylight I spotted a goat on top of a butte, about a quarter of a mile away, and pointed it out to Roosevelt. Curiously enough, it proved to be the one he had wounded the previous day, though the blood spots we were following led off in another direction. He started to pull down on it but I told him to save his ammunition, for, besides the long range, there was strong wind blowing at twenty miles an hour or more, and it seemed to be an impossible shot.…

[He fired] and I could hardly believe my eyes when I saw the goat jump up and fall back, almost too dead to skin. The bullet had gone through its heart, as clean as a whistle. It was a lucky shot, of course, but that didn't alter the fact that he got what he shot at, and I took off my hat to him. The yell of delight he let loose could have been heard for two miles in any country.

"If I never kill another thing, this trip has been a great success," he shouted. "I am perfectly satisfied." He quickly opened his wallet and offered me a $100 bill, which I as promptly refused.

When we got up to the goat and found it was the same one he had nicked in the leg the day before he was happier than ever. He rubbed his hands together, in the way he had when he was greatly pleased over anything, and fairly danced around with joy. Nothing would do but he must have a picture of the goat, where it fell, so I walked six miles back to camp after the camera and Merrifield, sore feet and all. Merrifield snapped a photograph, with Roosevelt and me beside the body of his victim, and Roosevelt was full of joy. Merrifield, in his high-heeled boots, was miserable…

"Roosevelt Luck"

The next day Roosevelt learned just how much his beloved "shoe packs" were worth in a man's country and the extent to which they could be relied on in a pinch. We were after another goat and had to cross a narrow ledge of slaty rock, with a high cliff on one side and a perpendicular drop on the other. Properly booted, I crossed it without any trouble and it did not occur to me that Roosevelt might be in any danger until I heard a fall and a grinding of rocks behind me. His smooth and soft-soled shoes had slipped on the slate and he went down, with no chance to save himself.

Too far away to even attempt to reach him, I turned around just in time to see him disappearing, head foremost, over the sharp edge, with his rifle still in his hand. When I saw him fall I wouldn't have given two-bits for his life, for it was easily a sixty-foot fall and the bottom of the precipice, where the hill mushroomed out, was covered with jagged rocks. But, instead of fetching up on any of the stone bayonets, he struck first in the top of a tall pine tree, which broke the worst of his fall. From that he bounded into the outstretched arms of a second tree and then into the branches of a third one, finally landing on a bunch of moss that was as thick as a feather bed and much more comfortable. And he still had his rifle in his hand.

Seeing me peering anxiously over the rim of the cliff, he was quick to relieve my anxiety "Not hurt a bit," he shouted, gaily, as he gathered himself together and shook his legs. "Wait till I find my glasses." He recovered them, undamaged, from the pile of moss.

That was my first experience with what afterward came to be known as "Roosevelt luck."…

When Roosevelt left the Badlands in the fall of 1886, he was not only an accomplished ranchman and hunter, he was also a complete man. The West had transformed him into a healthy, sturdy, strong-

OPPOSITE: The white or mountain goat, an almost legendary trophy that, when TR first hunted it, was "the least known and rarest of all American game." Artist Frederic Remington did not fail to include the gold oval plaque inlay on the butt stock of TR's Winchester .45-75 in this drawing from *Ranch Life and the Hunting Trail*. Pictured with TR is guide Jack Willis.

He was unusually
self-contained
for a young man
of 28, and he
now showed no
outward trace of
the deep grief he
had suffered from
the death of his
wife and mother.
Although he
had faced many
dangers and had
been exposed to
rigorous trials
in the outdoors,
he never quailed
or quit.

willed individual. He was unusually self-contained for a young man of 28, and he now showed no outward trace of the deep grief he had suffered from the death of his wife and mother. Although he had faced many dangers and had been exposed to rigorous trials in the outdoors, he never quailed or quit. Two years in the West, in the words of one of Roosevelt's most perceptive biographers,

had converted Roosevelt's iron resolve to one of steel. They had reinforced his high code of personal morality. They had developed his natural qualities of leadership. And they had encouraged his growing disposition to judge men on their merits.

Roosevelt himself was aware of his debt: "I owe more than I can ever express to the West."

Later in his life, at the request of the magazine *Outdoor America*, Roosevelt summed up his feelings on the fundamental benefits of the outdoor life as he learned it in the West:

You ask me to speak about vigor of body. I believe in it for its own sake. I believe in it still more as an aid to vigor of mind, and above all, to vigor of character. But I do not believe in it at all if it is made an end instead of a means, and especially if play is permitted to become the serious business of life.

High proficiency in sport is not necessary in order to get good out of it, altho, of course, it is in every way bad to show a slipshod indifference to high proficiency, an unwillingness or inability to put one's whole heart into a struggle. Personally, as you know, I am not really good at any games. Perhaps in my time I came nearer to being fairly good as a walker, rider, and rifle-shot than in any other way; but I was never more than an average good man even in these three respects

Whatever success I have had in game-hunting—and it has been by no means

noteworthy—has been due, as well as I can make out, to three causes: first, common sense and good judgment, second, perseverance, which is the only way of allowing one to make good one's own blunders; third, the fact that I shot as well at game as at a target. This does not make me hit difficult shots, but it prevented my missing easy shots, which a good target-shot will often do in the field. Most of my bears, for instance, were killed close up, and the shots were not difficult so long as one did not get rattled. Now, of course, the possession and practise of these three qualities did not make me by any means as successful a hunter as the men who in addition to possessing them were also better shots than I was, or who had greater power of endurance, or who were more skilled in plainscraft and woodcraft. But they did enable me to kill a reasonable quantity of big game and to do it in ways that have made my observations of value to the faunal or outdoor naturalist. Besides, I knew what I wanted, and was willing to work hard to get it.

In short, I am not an athlete; I am simply a good, ordinary out-of-doors man. You speak of my recent hundred-mile ride. Now this was no feat for any young man in condition to regard as worth speaking about; twice out in the cattle country, on the round-up, when I was young, I have myself spent thirty-six hours in the saddle, merely dismounting to eat or change horses; the hundred-mile ride represented what any elderly man in fair trim can do if he chooses. In the summer I often take the smaller boys for what they call a night picnic on the Sound; we row off eight or ten miles, camp out, and row back in the morning. Each of us has a light blanket to sleep in, and the boys are sufficiently deluded to believe that the chicken or beefsteak I fry in bacon fat on these expeditions has a flavor impossible elsewhere to be obtained. Now these expeditions represent just about the kind of thing I do. Instead of rowing, it may be riding, or chopping, or walking, or playing tennis or shooting at a target. But it is always a pastime which any healthy middle-aged man fond of outdoors life, but not an athlete, can indulge in if he chooses.

I think my last sentence covers the whole case-that is, when I say "if he chooses." It has always seemed to me that in life there are two ways of achieving success, or, for the matter of that, of achieving what is commonly called greatness. One is to do that which can only be done by the men of exceptional and extraordinary abilities. Of course this means that only this man can do it, and it is a very rare kind of success or greatness. The other is to do that which many men could do, but which, as a matter of fact, none of them actually does. This is the ordinary kind of success or kind of greatness. Nobody but one of the world's rare geniuses could have written the Gettysburg speech, or the second inaugural or met as Lincoln met the awful crises of the Civil War. But most of us can do the ordinary things, which, however, most of us do not do. My own successes have come within this category Any fairly hardy and healthy man can do what I have done in hunting and ranching if he only really wishes to, and will take the pains and troubles and at the same time use common sense.

Any one that chose could lead the kind of life I have led, and any one who had led that life could if he chose—and by "choosing," I of course mean choosing to exercise in advance the requisite industry, judgment, and foresight, none of them to an extraordinary degree—have raised my regiment or served in positions analogous to those in which I have served in civil life.

Though Roosevelt had greatly underrated his own accomplishments and abilities as a hunter and outdoorsman in the above statement, it was his clearest and most cogent expression on the enormous personal rewards of the wilderness life.

Marriage and the Future

Soon after his return to New York, Roosevelt was frequently seen in the company of Edith Kermit Carow, a former childhood sweetheart. The two had become reacquainted when they met in 1885. He also became the Republican candidate for Mayor of New York. After an active but unsuccessful campaign, he left for London, where he married Edith Carow on December 2nd 1886. They then started out on an extensive European tour, not returning to the United States until March.

Roosevelt received bad news on arrival in New York. The winter of 1886-87 had been so severe in the Dakotas that most of his cattle had died. Inspecting his ranch after the spring thaw, Roosevelt was shocked at the desolation. His losses were so high that he was skeptical about buying more cattle. He was becoming disenchanted with the economics of ranching: for him it had been distinctly enjoyable but financially unprofitable. He went back to New York convinced that he was through as a rancher.

If Roosevelt's ranching career was over, his writing career was now in high gear. He had just published a biography of Thomas Hart Benton and was in the midst of completing one on Gouverneur Morris. He was also researching for a multi-volume study of Westward expansion. The Benton and Morris biographies were good but undistinguished, but the four-volume *Winning of the West* was a jewel of historical scholarship and a narrative of great force and eloquence. Perhaps this historiographical *tour de force* was in part Roosevelt's way of paying back the West for all that it had done for him. Throughout his life Roosevelt would maintain a love affair with Western America. ❦

CHAPTER 5

Back in the East: The Untamed Bureaucrat

During the late 1880s and the 1890s, Theodore Roosevelt's political career and literary productions were burgeoning. Every day was tilled with numberless activities and duties, not the least being those concerning his growing family. TR's interest in hunting and the wilderness remained sharp. From 1887 to 1896, he was able to fit into his tight schedule annual fall hunting trips in the Badlands. He also tackled for the first time the big game of British Columbia and the wily javelina of Texas. Still, owing to his many obligations in the East, Roosevelt's hunting opportunities during those years were relatively few and far between.

The Tennis Match Winchester

There was no hesitancy on Roosevelt's part when asked to expound on his favorite rifle: "The Winchester [1876] stocked and sighted to suit myself." But this faithful, hefty old standby was about to be superseded by a new lever action, the Model 1886, which Winchester had recently developed. Lighter and of superior handling and balance, it was chambered for the big calibers that were TR favorites. Perhaps because of the stiff financial setback he suffered from his cattle losses in the winter of 1886-87, Roosevelt did not immediately order one of the new repeaters. Several months later, however, after capturing first prize in a tennis match, he "turned [in] my share of the cup to a new Winchester rifle that I have been longing for."

Trophies of a successful hunt – TR and fellow Boone and Crockett Club member Robert H. Munro-Ferguson, circa 1891. Both hunters are shown with deluxe Winchester Model 1886 rifles.

BOONE AND CROCKETT CLUB
PERMANENT COLLECTION

Theodore Roosevelt's fifth
Winchester of record, a Model 1886
.45-90 rifle, serial #9205, shipped
from the factory on September 30,
1887. The rifle had no engraving,
but it did have other features TR
favored: 1/2 round, 1/2 octagonal
barrel; 1/2 magazine, deluxe pistol
grip stock, shotgun butt plate, and
crescent cheekpiece.

SAGAMORE HILL NATIONAL HISTORIC SITE,
NATIONAL PARK SERVICE

On September 30th, in time for the fall hunt of 1887, Winchester shipped Theodore Roosevelt's fifth Winchester: A .45-90 deluxe Model, serial #9205. He wrote in *Ranch Life and the Hunting Trail:*

Now that the buffalo have gone, and the Sharps rifle by which they were destroyed is also gone, almost all ranchmen use some form of repeater. Personally I prefer the Winchester, using the new model [1886], with a 45-caliber bullet of grains, backed by *90* grains of powder, or else falling back on my faithful old standby, the *45-75…*

Factory records list the tennis match gun's special features:

.45-90 caliber; 28" round- 1/2 octagonal barrel; 1/2 magazine, checkered pistol grip stock; shotgun buttplate, buttplate checkered; cheekpiece.

The big caliber, the 1/2 round-1/2 octagon barrel shape, the 1/2 magazine, the pistol grip fancy stock with cheekpiece, and the shotgun buttplate were all in keeping with Roosevelt's strict tastes in lever-action rifles. But by now, no doubt partly for the sake of economy, he no longer specified deluxe engraving. For him the days of fancy scrollwork and game motifs were over, and apart from guns presented to him by friends and manufacturers, the only decorative engraving he ordered in the future was a stock plaque engraved simply TR.

The new Winchester served as TR's regular big game rifle from 1887 through 1894. During those years, the number of game taken with this new favorite was over a hundred, including antelope, black and grizzly bear, caribou, blacktail and whitetail deer, elk, moose, mountain goat, and mountain sheep. For ammunition, Roosevelt at first used factory loads, then switched to his own handloads: a hybrid 330 grain hollow point slug backed up by 85 grains of Orange Lightning smokeless powder!

The old .45-75 had been used repeatedly, as the new .45-90 would be. Not surprisingly, Winchester records of these Model 1876 and 1886 rifles reveal that Roosevelt returned the '76 to New Haven for rework four times and the '86 five times. Twice in 1888 the two rifles were sent to the factory together. The condition of both rifles today is so exceptional that it is more than likely that they were refinished. Such refinishing would confirm the reverence Theodore Roosevelt held for his favorite old Winchester hunting rifles.

In the fall of 1887, Roosevelt put his Winchester .45-90 through the first practical test on a hunting trip in the Badlands. Fred Herrig, the guide on that trip and later one of the Rough Riders, recorded how Roosevelt brought down a Big Horn ram:

He had his .45-90 rifle swinging easy over his left arm. I pointed about four hundred yards in front of us a little down the ridge. It was one of the finest rams I ever saw, his long brown hair so much lighter in color than an ewe's that he

stood out tolerably plain even among the bowl-
ders and at that distance. I was just pointing
the critter out when he faced about, lifted his
big horns over a rock he'd been grazing behind, and caught sight of us against the sky-line.
"There he goes," I yelled, for 'twas no use keeping quiet any longer. Maybe that ram didn't
run. But [Mr. Roosevelt] had seen him from
the first jump and had his gun going. "Spat"
went a bullet against the sandstone. "Too far
to the left" I yelled. "Buff," the next one quick-
er than I can tell it, knocked up the dust almost under the ram's feet. "Now's your chance"
said I, for the beast had been running almost
parallel with the crest of the range, and I was
afraid every second he'd plunge down the bluff
and we'd lose him. With that the rifle cracked
once more and that time I didn't see where the
ball struck. But I did see the ram jump into the
air, headed straight down the bluff, and disappear. When we got to where we lost him, fear-
ing to find he'd made one of those gigantic leaps
down a precipice that the big horns are fond of
in an emergency, [Mr. Roosevelt] gave a yell
you could have heard two miles. The ram lay
ten feet down the cliff, on a little shelf of rock,
half over the edge and half propped up against
a dwarf pine....It was after midnight when we
got home that night, and we were happy even if
our ears were frozen. "We can get new skin on
our ears" said [Mr. Roosevelt], "but we'll never
get another ram like that one."

Boone and Crockett Club

The years 1887 and 1888 were on the whole sedentary ones for the normally peripatetic Theodore Roosevelt. He was close to completing *Ranch
Life and the Hunting Trail,* his second book on hunting and was assiduously at work on *The Winning
of the West.* While immersed in his writings, he
ruminated on an idea that had been in his mind
a long time: the establishment of a national association dedicated to outdoor activities and to the
preservation of wildlife. In December 1887, he invited to dinner several friends whom he believed
would be receptive to the idea. Thus was born the
Boone and Crockett Club. Among the eminent
charter members were the naturalist George Bird
Grinnell, the artist Albert Bierstadt, and TR's
brother, Elliott.

The organization's constitution, written by
TR, enunciated broad and varied aims:

> The Boone and Crockett Club is an association
> of men living for the most part in New York, but
> also in other parts of the country, who are in-
> terested in big-game hunting, in big-game and
> forestry preservation, and generally in manly
> out-door sports, and in travel and exploration
> in little-known regions. The objects of the club,
> as set forth in its constitution, are:
>
> 1. To promote manly sport with the rifle.
> 2. To promote travel and exploration in the
>   wild and unknown or but partially known
>   portions of the country.
> 3. To work for the preservation of the large
>   game of this country, and, so far as possible,
>   to further legislation for that purpose, and to
>   assist in enforcing the existing laws.
> 4. To promote inquiry into and to record ob-
>   servations on the habits and natural history
>   of the various wild animals.
> 5. To bring about among the members the in-
>   terchange of opinions and ideas on hunting,
>   travel, and exploration, on the various kinds

2

President

Theodore Roosevelt.

Sagamore Hill, Oyster Bay
Long Island N.Y.

Secretary

Archibald Rogers.

Hyde Park, Duchess Co. N.Y.

Members.

3	Bierstadt Albert	1271 Broadway N.Y. City
4	Bishop Heber R.	15 Broad St "
5	Bristow, Hon Benj F.	37 W. 49 St "
6	Drayton J. Coleman.	374 Ave 5 "
7	Elliott D.G.	147 West 12th St.
		72 Fifth Ave "
8	Grinnell Geo Bird	Broadway
		348 Park Row "
9	"	
10	Hague Arnold	{ Metropolitan club { Washington DC
11	Jones Col James H.	180 to 09 St N.Y. City
12	King Clarence	18 Wall St "

ABOVE AND OPPOSITE: Original minutes from the founding of the Boone and Crockett Club.
BOONE AND CROCKETT CLUB PERMANENT COLLECTION

of hunting-rifles, on the haunts of game, animals, etc.

No one is eligible for membership who has not killed with the rifle in fair chase, by still-hunting or otherwise, at least one individual of one of the various kinds of American large game.

Under the head of American large game the club includes the following animals: bear, buffalo (bison), mountain-sheep, caribou, cougar, musk-ox, white goat, elk (wapiti), wolf (not coyote), prong-horn antelope, moose, and deer.

The club has decided that the term "fair chase" shall not be held to include killing bear, wolf, or cougar in traps, nor "fire-hunting," nor "crusting" moose, elk, or deer in deep snow, nor killing game from a boat while it is swimming in the water.

The club is emphatically an association of men who believe that the hardier and manlier the sport is the more attractive it is, and who do not think that there is any place in the ranks of true sportsmen either for the game-butcher, on the one hand, or, on the other, for the man who wishes to do all his shooting in preserves, and to shirk rough hard work. Most of the members are men who have passed a considerable portion of their lives in wild surroundings, or who have at least made long trips after the big game of the wilderness, whether in the Rocky Mountains, on the great plains, or among the frozen forests of the North. Different members of the club, of course, have had different specialties. One, for instance, has probably done as much grizzly-bear shooting as any living man; another has performed his chief feats in chasing the black bear through the Southern canebrakes with horn and hound, and at one time made a practice of killing the bear, when bayed by his pack, with the knife only; yet another has had more experience than any other living

American in breeding and managing big greyhounds and deer-hounds for the pursuit of such formidable game as wolf and elk, besides deer and antelope; another has devoted his attention very largely to different kinds of hunting-rifles, and the effects of their various projectiles upon game and so on, and so on. The club proposes hereafter to issue an annual volume, consisting of various articles by the members upon big-game hunting, upon the national game and forest preserves, upon travel, exploration, and the like. It has always been the aim of the founders of this club to have it accomplish in the field of American big-game hunting work somewhat akin to that which has been done by the London Alpine Club in mountaineering...

The Boone and Crockett Club was responsible for both influencing and initiating enlightened policies on hunting, wildlife and forest preservation. Club member, John W. Noble, Secretary of the Interior under President Benjamin Harrison helped to establish the first forest preserve in America. In 1897 the Club influenced legislation in New York providing for fair hunting practices and also solidly supported the preservation of Yellowstone Park. The New York Zoological Society, Glacier National Park, and scores of federal game preserves were but a few of the achievements of the Boone and Crockett Club members. Practically all of its members were highly conscientious, but it was Roosevelt who served as the sheet anchor and soul of the association. As founder and first president, his deep personal commitment to the Boone and Crockett Club's high-minded ideals remained right up to his death in 1919.

Roosevelt also held active memberships in the Explorers Club of New York and The Camp Fire Club of America. An interesting autographed letter in the Camp Fire collection, dated February 28, 1911, contains a list of some of Roosevelt's prized trophies from the African safari of 1909-10, and closes with the

The Wilderness Warrior:
Theodore Roosevelt and the Crusade for America

Published in 2009, historian Douglas Brinkley's monumental 940-page *Wilderness Warrior Theodore Roosevelt and the Crusade for America* documents in unprecedented ways and in breathtaking scope the saga of conservation's indisputable champion. This epic tome presents its profoundly consequential subject with the thoroughness and grand scale that has been beyond the grasp of every one of Roosevelt's previous biographers.

The vital role of the Boone and Crockett Club in that epic saga is thoroughly documented, the index alone lists numerous relevant pages, as well as sub-references to some two dozen themes. To quote a few of several key passages:

The overwhelming question weighing on Roosevelt's conscience as he worked on [his book] Ranch Life was simple: how could he be proactive to save big game animals? Although Roosevelt's exact moment of reckoning remains unclear, in early December 1887 he found a conservationist solution to his quandary. Borrowing from the way his elders tackled societal ills, he would create a hunting club devoted to saving big game and its habitats. High-powered sportsmen like himself, he believed, banding together, had to lead a new wildlife protection movement. Posterity had a claim that couldn't be ignored; saving American mammals was an imperative. A "fair chase" doctrine – hunting rules and regulations – had been created. And as far as Roosevelt was concerned, the time for watered-down measures had passed; his club would fight for true solutions, its goal being the creation of wilderness preserves all over the American West for buffalo, antelope, mountain goats, elk, and deer.

By the time Roosevelt left the Badlands for New York, his conservationist resolve had grown firm. What his Uncle Bob had done for fish, he would do for American big game. A day after arriving back in New York, in early December 1887, Roosevelt convened some of the best and brightest wildlife lovers and naturalists in the New York area to dine at his sister's Madison Avenue home. He was ready to make a hard sell. If his father could found the American Museum of Natural History from a parlor in Manhattan, Theodore

saw no reason why this group, meeting in the cramped uptown quarters he shared with Edith, Bamie, and little Alice when not at Sagamore Hill, couldn't save buffalo and elk in the American West.... After all, Hunting Trips of a Ranchman had established him as the authority on big game. Roosevelt now had a sacred responsibility, he believed, to save herds of North American ungulates from extinction.

Roosevelt tapped his brother, Elliott, and his cousin J. West Roosevelt (both childhood veterans of board meetings for Theodore's Roosevelt Museum during the 1870s) to join the Boone and Crockett Club. It was now the turn of their generation, emerging into maturity, to continue the kind of conservation work Robert B. Roosevelt had long championed. Most of the other founders were New York capitalists with deep pockets, like T.R. himself: E.P. Rogers, a yachtsman and financial investor; Archibald Rogers, the rear commodore of the New York Yacht Club; J. Coleman Drayton, who was John Jacob Astor's son-in-law; Thomas Paton, the husband of the heiress Marion Rowle; and Rutherford Stuyvesant, a wealthy real estate investor. From the outset Roosevelt knew that large sums of money would be necessary to lobby effectively in Washington, D.C.... Basically, the founders were from the establishment, easily distinguishable from the plain citizenry of New York even though none was afraid to get mud on his boots.

In early January, 1888, the twelve founders of the Boone and Crockett Club had approved a prescient conservationist constitution at Pinnards Restaurant in Manhattan. Ideas had been allowed to percolate freely. The thought of buffalo once again thundering on the plains aroused the founders' enthusiasm during their inaugural deliberations. A decision was made from the outset that the club would have permanent members of exactly 100 hunters. The bylaws also stipulated that a limited number of associate members (no more than fifty) would also be allowed. Roosevelt—who would remain the club president until 1894—filled the associate memberships with a galaxy of truly talented writers, including Owen Wister and Henry Cabot

Lodge (two outdoorsmen he admired unconditionally). Scientists, military officers, political leaders, explorers, and industrialists were also recruited as members, in hopes that they'd forge innovative solutions to stop the exploitation of America's natural resources. Roosevelt himself brought in the army generals William T. Sherman and Philip H. Sheridan, the artist Albert Bierstadt, the former secretary of the interior (from 1877 to 1881) Carl Schurz, and the geologists Clarence King and Raphael Pulmelly.... "The members of the club, so far as it is developed, are all persons of high social standing," an editorial writer in Grinnell's Forest and Stream said of the club's founding, "and it would seem that an organization of this description, composed of men of intelligence and education might wield a great influence for good in matters relating to game protections."

Many historians now believe that the Boone and Crockett Club—Roosevelt's brainchild—was the first wildlife conservation group to lobby effectively on behalf of big game.... In essence, the club became the most important lobbying group to promote all national parks in the late 1880s....

The club had awakened a national conscience pertaining to the wanton destruction of America's limited natural resources. Like cavalry officers on a mad charge, Roosevelt and Grinnell often went to Washington, D.C., to demand congressional action on behalf of wildlife. Their message was as clear as a bell. Shame fell upon senators who tried to cross words with Roosevelt and company. "Those who used to boast of their slaughter are now ashamed of it," a triumphant Grinnell declared in 1889, referring to the club's success, during its first year, in convincing Americans about the need for regulated hunting and for federal parks; "and it is becoming [a] recognized fact that a man who wastefully destroys big game, whether for the market, or only for heads, has nothing of the true sportsman about him."[1]

In the book's acknowledgements, Brinkley credits the late Dr. John A. Gable, for years Executive Director of the Theodore Roosevelt Association, with being "largely re-

sponsible for my writing this book." Professor Brinkley also notes that in this project he had "five guardian angels," one of them being "Lowell Baier, president of the Boone and Crockett Club." The author further notes that "the Boone and Crockett Club Archive in Missoula, Montana – all 130 boxes – proved indispensable."[2]

As his text flows and covers every possible bit of ground, Brinkley states: "As Stewart Udall, secretary of the interior under both John F. Kennedy and Lyndon Johnson, perceptively noted, "The Boone and Crockett wildlife cree....became national policy when Theodore Roosevelt became president...."[3]

Brinkley also documents Roosevelt's involvement with the New York Zoological Society and the Bronx Zoo, including selection of William Temple Hornaday as the first director and general curator: "In the autumn of 1894, Roosevelt began collaborating with Madison Grant...on the creation of the New York Zoological Society.... In the spring of 1895, a group from the Boone and Crockett Club officially formed the New York Zoological Society.... The 261-acre forested zoo, with a topographical range from granite ridges to natural meadows and glades to forest, was ideal for a wide variety of animals to thrive in the open air.... The creation of the Bronx Zoo, with the help of regiments of planners, was the capstone to Roosevelt's tenure as president of the Boone and Crockett Club."[4]

Publication of *The Wilderness Warrior* could not be more timely, with the national conscience aroused more than ever in the past with concerns of "global warming," the conservation of wildlife, habitats, and natural resources, and passage and increased enforcement of conservation-related laws and regulations. Of further importance is the September 2009 release in of documentary filmmaker Ken Burns' equally monumental "The National parks America's Best Idea." The importance of Roosevelt the hunter and sportsman is a vital theme in advertising for the program. The back cover of the September 2009 Smithsonian magazine features a photograph of TR as president, obviously immersed in thought and ready for action, with the proclamation: "He hunted wild game with his rifle and saved them with a pen. Meet Teddy Roosevelt and the rest of the people behind our national parks."

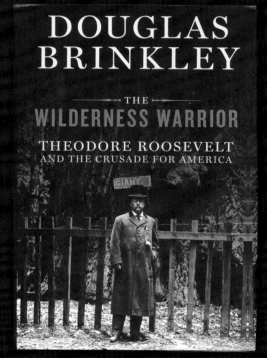

[1] The Wilderness Warrior, *passim.*, pp. 201-207
[2] *Ibid.*, pp. 898-898
[3] *Ibid.* p. 39
[4] *Ibid.* pp. 276-279

"The Winning Theodore Roosevelt, Stick to your saddle and don't be bounced." Drawn by cartoonist Thomas Nast in 1889, and presented to TR in 1896. Inserted into TR's airborne hat was the message, "The commission means business T.R."

statement: "Of course I should greatly appreciate the honor badge…" The Club was about to give Roosevelt an honor award for big game achievement.

Civil Service Commissioner

In the fall of 1888, Roosevelt's political ambitions, dormant during the preceding two years, were aroused by the impending Presidential election. He campaigned hard and faithfully for the Republican Benjamin Harrison, who, when elected President, rewarded him with one of four positions on the Civil Service Commission. Although Roosevelt thought the offer was hardly commensurate with his abilities, he took it and served for six years, four under Harrison and two under President Grover Cleveland.

Roosevelt was a hard-fisted, no-nonsense Commissioner who tried valiantly to help reform a spoils-ridden civil service system. His almost ruthless honesty and impartiality exacerbated Republican leaders. His propensity for political morality prompted President Harrison to remark wryly that Roosevelt "wanted to put an end to all the evil in the world between sunrise and sunset." Notwithstanding the growing conviction among disgruntled Republicans that Roosevelt was a political maverick too honest to be trusted, he plowed ahead unhesitatingly in his efforts to purge the civil service of its most odious corruptions. He instituted many reforms and adopted many practices to this end. All in all, he was unusually effective. More important, he was back in the political saddle again, feeling useful and thinking ahead to the future.

Being a Civil Service Commissioner did not interfere with raising a family or keeping up with his other interests. A "household of children," he wrote, "certainly makes all other forms of success and achievement lose their importance by comparison." Three of Roosevelt's children were born in these Washington years: Theodore, the oldest son, was two when Kermit was born in October 1889; Ethel arrived in August 1891, and Archibald in April 1894; Quentin, the youngest child, would be born in November 1897.

Home and Family

Theodore Roosevelt was as much a private man as he was a public man. Bluff, vigorous, and occasionally impatient as he was on the political stage, at Sagamore Hill or in Washington, he was tender, helpful, a gentle yet demanding mentor. As he said in his *Autobiography:*

> At Sagamore Hill we love a great many things— birds and trees and books, and all things beautiful, and horses and rifles and children and hard work and the joy of life.

TR introduced each of his four sons to hunting and life in the wilderness. Sometimes he relied on help from old hunting companions such as Bill Sewall, John Burroughs, Robert Munro Ferguson. Seth Bullock, and Dr. Alexander Lambert. A Christmas or birthday gift of a rifle was usually anticipated by his sons, and they could always depend on their father's battery as a source of weapons for target shooting or a wilderness holiday. TR took great pleasure in watching his sons develop into enthusiastic hunters and sportsmen.

In his book *All in the Family,* Theodore Jr. nostalgically remembered his own introduction to shooting, a process repeated with variations for each son when the proper age level was reached:

> Father often told us tales of his ranch and the West. Shuddering with delicious excitement, we heard of cattle thieves, grizzly bears, or the battle of the Rosebud. Naturally we boys wished to learn how to shoot. The first rifle given us was a [Flobert]. Father brought it out with him from town one day I was off somewhere about the place on "affairs of Egypt," and did not get back until he was dressing for dinner. At once I made for his room, where I found him just preparing his bath. The rifle was standing in a corner. Of course I fell on it with delight. He was as much excited as I was. I wanted to see it fired to make sure it was a real rifle. That presented a difficulty. It would be too dark to shoot after supper and Father was not dressed to go out at the moment. He took it, slipped a cartridge into the chamber, and making me promise not to tell

Mother, fired it into the ceiling. The report was slight, the smoke hardly noticeable, and the hole made in the ceiling so small that our sin was not detected.

In the same book, young Roosevelt described the Gun Room, which was on the top floor of the three-story mansion at Sagamore Hill. Wall cases and a mammoth closet provided ample space. Gun cases and cleaning equipment were stored in a closet, but there were times when these would be spread all over. The room was also an ideal sanctum where TR could write in relative quiet, and it was often used for this purpose.

> At the top of the house at Oyster Bay was a large room named the Gun Room. Beneath its windows on fine days spread a glorious panorama. Green fields led to greener woods and beyond lay the South with the white sails of boats sprinkling it like stars. On the far horizon the Connecticut shores showed dimly. The Gun Room was a sort of overflow library where odds and ends of all kinds were gathered. Around its walls unglazed shelves full of books were ranged. A couple of very meritorious Arab scimitars in frayed plush scabbards hung on the wall. Next to them was a photograph of the college club to which Father belonged. In it he appeared as a slight, solemn looking young fellow, with most preposterous mutton-chop whiskers. On a cabinet stood two glass-covered groups of birds collected by Father when at the age of eleven he went to the Nile with his family. On a nearby shelf a brace of handsomely inlaid [Greener] dueling pistols reposed in a mahogany box. There were two gorgeous [Colt] six-shooters with carved ivory butts—relics of the time when Father as a young man wished to dress as well as act the part of a dashing young cattleman. In one corner was a gun cabinet where our arms were kept. In early days it contained three shotguns—one ancient

His propensity for political morality prompted President Harrison to remark wryly that Roosevelt "wanted to put an end to all the evil in the world between sunrise and sunset."

12 gauge, a pin-fire, one 10 gauge cannon, and a more or less modern 16. The rifles began with a Sharps, that almost forgotten weapon which helped win the West, followed by a collection of Winchesters ranging from a 45-70 to a 30-30....A weapon that always spelled romance to us was Father's 30-30 Winchester [Model 1894 serial #15659] with the fang marks on its butt where a mountain lion had worried it...

There were two closets—one for some unknown reason containing Mother's dresses, and as such was of small interest to us. The other was very different. It faced the gun case and ran back under the eaves like a robber's cave. Like a robber's cave it was fraught for us with every possibility. There were cartridge boxes, leather cases, ramrods, old pistols, and all the paraphernalia that collects around a sportsman. It had an entrancing musty smell like a shop in an Eastern bazaar.

We children spent many hours in it—though it was stiflingly hot—for we never knew what treasures we might unearth while rooting among its contents.

For decades the room remained essentially as it was when TR died in 1919, maintained by the National Park Service and the Boone and Crockett Club. Roosevelt's Model 1886 .45-90 Winchester, his Springfield Sporter (#6000) rifle, the Lefaucheux pinfire and the E. Thomas shotguns, the San Juan Hill Colt revolver, and a few other TR hunting and antique firearms (once including a Kit Carson Hawken rifle) were on display there. The Sagamore Hill Gun Room exhibited the finest and most representative collection of Theodore Roosevelt firearms in existence.

Kermit, in *The Happy Hunting-Grounds*, remembered his father's advice and coaching on guns and hunting:

...When we were small he would read us incidents from the hunting books of Roualeyn Gordon Cumming, or Samuel Baker, or Drummond, or Baldwin. These we always referred to as "I stories," because they were told in the first person, and when we were sent to bed we would clamor for just one more, a petition that was seldom denied...

Until father sold his ranches in North Dakota he used to go out West each year for a month or so. Unfortunately, we were none of us old enough to be taken along, but we would wait eagerly for his letters, and the recipient of what we called a picture letter gloried in the envy of the rest until another mail placed a substitute upon the pedestal. In these picture letters father would sketch scenes and incidents about the ranch or on his short hunting trips. We read most of them to pieces, unluckily...

By the time we were twelve or thirteen we were encouraged to plan hunting trips in the West. Father never had time to go with us, but we would be sent out to some friend of his, like Captain Seth Bullock, to spend

two or three weeks in the Black Hills, or perhaps we would go after duck and prairie-chicken with Marvin Hewitt. Father would enter into all the plans and go down with us to the range to practise with rifle or shotgun, and when we came back we would go over every detail of the trip with him, revelling in his praise when he felt that we had acquitted ourselves well...

Cousin Nicholas Roosevelt was among the young friends and relatives who shot at the Sagamore Hill range:

As we grew older we were permitted first to watch target practice and then to take part in it. He had a small rifle range in a safe hollow and not only kept up his own skill as a marksman, which was considerable, but also taught us youngsters how to shoot. We began with a 22, and, if I remember rightly, progressed to a 30-30. He gave us detailed instructions about the care and handling of guns, the sighting and aiming, and, above all, the manners of the rifle range. He warned us against ever pointing a gun, whether loaded or not, at anyone, anywhere, any time. Among the few recollections I have of his showing sharpness toward any of us youngsters was if someone was careless with a weapon. I have often thought how right he was to impress on us so deeply the importance of this basic practice.

Each of TR's sons, Theodore Jr., Kermit, Archibald, and Quentin, were skillful huntsmen. Quentin was only 21 years old when killed

NEAR RIGHT: Eland taken by TR's grandson, Kermit Roosevelt, with his sons Jonathan and Kermit, Jr., on safari in Africa, commemorating the fiftieth anniversary of their respective grandfathers' safari.

LIFE MAGAZINE PHOTOGRAPHY BY TERRENCE SPENCER

FAR RIGHT: "[Ted] killed his first buck this year, shooting it with his rifle at a distance of over a hundred yards. It was about a week before his fourteenth birthday and I suppose life in the future will rarely hold such bright moments for him." TR was writing to naturalist John Burroughs, dated October 9, 1901. The rifle was a Savage Model 1899 lever action.

in World War I, but at the time of his death, he had already hunted mountain lion, deer, and small game. Archibald, despite serious wounds in both World War I and II, hunted mountain lion, deer, fox and many other different kinds and varieties of game. TR dedicated *A Book-Lover's Holidays in the Open* to Quentin and Archibald. To Kermit—"my side-partner in our 'great adventure' "— he dedicated *African Game Trails.*

Kermit, who died in Alaska in 1943, hunted in North and South America, in Mexico, Africa, Europe, India, China, Korea, and Central Asia. His hunting experience was actually more varied than his father's, and his bag of big game covered a broad spectrum: Indian and Korean tiger, the Marco Polo sheep of Central Asia, the full range of African game, the desert bighorn sheep of Mexico, jaguar in Brazil and so forth. Kermit summed up the pleasures the Roosevelts derived from hunting:

We get three sorts and periods of enjoyment out of a hunting trip. The first is when the plans are being discussed and the outfit assembled; this is the pleasure of anticipation. The second is the enjoyment of the actual trip itself; and the third is the pleasure of retrospection when we sit round a blazing woodfire and talk over the incidents and adventures of the trip. There is no general rule to know which of the three gives

the keenest joy. I can think of a different expedition in which each sort stands out in pre-eminence. Even if the trip has been exceptionally hard and the luck unusually bad, the pleasures of anticipation and preparation cannot be taken away, and frequently the retrospect is the more satisfactory because of the difficulties and discomforts surmounted.

Theodore Jr. and Kermit were both active members of the Boone and Crockett Club. They held several offices and fulfilled numerous committee assignments in the best tradition of their father. Archibald continued his active membership, and, along with his brother-in-law Richard Derby, was instrumental in creating the Club's Sagamore Hill Medal, an award given for extraordinary trophies of big game. The bronze medal commemorates Theodore Roosevelt, Theodore Jr. and Kermit. Only nine Sagamore Hill awards were presented between 1948 and 1964, carefully selected from the thousands of big game entered in competition by hunters and shot under the Boone and Crockett rules of the fair chase. No more than one medal can be presented in any single year, and some years none are given. The Sagamore Hill Medal is the most prized award in American big game hunting.

The Roosevelt family's hunting record is unrivaled in the history of the pursuit of big game among American sportsmen. This holds true for their contributions to the literature of hunting. The family's all-around achievements are unique: Over 15 books on big-game hunting, countless articles in sundry periodicals, hundreds of specimens in major museums of America and Europe, the creation of the Boone and Crockett Club and the Sagamore Hill Medal, the creation and sponsorship of effective game conservation programs and the successful pursuit of an infinite variety of trophies on six continents. It is an unblemished record of responsible and conscientious accomplishment which has earned the respect and admiration of hunters and conservationists the world over.

Hunting Trips of a Civil Service Commissioner

As a ranchman in the Badlands, Roosevelt had thoroughly spoiled himself. He had hunted far and wide, taking nearly all the best species of big and small game in the West and putting together a first-class battery of shooting and sporting firearms. Now, as Civil Service Commissioner, he was constantly behind a desk piled high with tedious paperwork. It was natural, therefore, that he sought to get in as much hunting and outdoor exercise as he could. He found the time for at least one hunt during every year he sat on the Commission. The first was a hunt in British Columbia. Together with his cousin, West Roosevelt, and his good friend, William Merrifield, he determined:

> to hunt in the Kootenai country; first we will take canoes, and then go on foot, with Indians to pack our goods. My time has been so cut short that I do not expect to do very much in the big game line; it is rather an exploring expedition to prepare for a hunting trip next year...

The results of the "exploring expedition" would satisfy the longings of any modern-day hunter. "I have had a very rough and hard trip, which ended successfully," he wrote in mid-September,

Sagamore Hill Award

The Sagamore Hill Medal is given by the Roosevelt family in memory of Theodore Roosevelt (Founder and first President of the Boone and Crockett Club), Theodore Roosevelt, Jr., and Kermit Roosevelt. It was created in 1948. It may be awarded by the Boone and Crockett Club's Big Game Final Awards Judges Panel, if in their opinion there is an outstanding trophy worthy of great distinction. Only one may be given in any Big Game Awards program. A special award may also be presented to individuals by the Executive Committee of the Boone and Crockett Club for distinguished devotion to the objectives of the Club. The Sagamore Hill Medal is the highest award given by the Boone and Crockett Club.

SPECIAL SAGAMORE HILL AWARDS

1952 - DEFOREST GRANT "For long and distinguished service to conservation."

1968 - RICHARD KING MELLON "For devoted and dedicated service to the conservation of our North American wildlife heritage."

1977 - ROBERT MUNRO-FERGUSON "For unswerving loyalty to his heritage, his principles and his friends."

1987 - C.R. "PINK" GUTERMUTH "For life-long conservation service to the nation and for achievement of the Boone and Crockett Club's goals."

1992 - WILLIAM I. SPENCER "For tenacious focus on the vision of the Club's founders and absolute insistence on the perpetuation of their original mission."

1996 - PHILIP L. WRIGHT "For lifelong commitment to conservation; For dedication to the principles of fair chase and scientific integrity with the records program."

1997 - GEORGE C. HIXON "For steadfast devotion to the preservation of the Club's rich traditions and its historical legacy of wildlife conservation."

SAGAMORE HILL TROPHY AWARDS

1948 - ROBERT C. REEVE AK brown bear	**1965 - MELVIN J. JOHNSON** typical whitetail
1949 - E.C. HAASE Rocky Mountain goat	**1973 - DOUG BURRIS JR.** typical mule deer
1950 - DR. R.C. BENTZEN typical wapiti	**1976 - GARRY BEAUBIEN** mountain caribou
1951 - GEORGE LESSER woodland caribou	**1986 - MICHAEL J. O'HACO JR.** pronghorn
1953 - EDISON PILLMORE typical mule deer	**1989 - GENE C. ALFORD** cougar
1957 - FRANK COOK Dall's sheep	**1992 - CHARLES E. ERICKSON JR.**
1959 - FRED C. MERCER typical wapiti	non-typical Coues' whitetail
1961 - HARRY L. SWANK JR. Dall's sheep	**2001 - GERNOT WOBER** Rocky Mountain goat
1963 - NORMAN BLANK Stone's sheep	

though it opened somewhat discouragingly. The first week was so hard that West became completely done out, and left the mountains, with Merrifield. Then Willis, an Indian, and myself took packs and went in on foot to the snow line. The climbing and walking were fatiguing beyond belief, and of course we had neither shelter, nor extra clothing, nor so much as a jacket among us, and but one blanket apiece, so we had to keep the fires blazing all night. But I was never in better health, nor so well able to walk, the scenery was magnificent, and I killed a bear, a bull caribou…, a deer, grouse, etc. I never enjoyed any dinner more than those I made on the caribou venison and bear meat. Altogether it was the best trip I have taken since the Bighorn days; and now I will go back and fall-to on my book [*The Winning of the West*] with redoubled energy, at the same time holding myself in readiness to take a part in the political campaign if needful.

By the first of October, fresh from taking his first caribou on "the best trip…since the Bighorn days," TR was back at his desk in Washington.

His next major hunt while Civil Service Commissioner came in August 1889, when he journeyed to the Rocky Mountains to hunt bear. "I am so out of training," he declared in July, "that I look forward with acute physical terror to going up the first mountain." With bear on his mind, he wrote humorously to fellow Boone and Crockett Club member, Henry Cabot Lodge:

Today I caught a glimpse of the President, and repeated to him the parable of the backwoodsman and the bear. You remember that the prayer of the backwoodsman was "Oh Lord, help me kill that bar; and if you don't help me, oh Lord, don't help the bar."

On this Rocky Mountains hunt Roosevelt, narrowly escaped being either killed or badly mauled by a wild-charging grizzly. He later recounted the harrowing experience in *Trail and Campfire* (a Boone and Crockett Club book). "On but one occasion was I ever regularly charged by a grizzly," he wrote.

To this animal I had given a mortal wound, and without any effort at retaliation he bolted into a thicket of what, in my hurry, I thought was laurel (it being composed in reality of thick-growing berry bushes). On my following him up and giving him a second wound, he charged very determinedly, taking two bullets without flinching. I just escaped the charge by jumping to one side, and he died almost immediately after striking at me as he rushed by. This bear charged with his mouth open, but made very little noise after the growl or roar with which he greeted my second bullet. I mention the fact of his having kept his mouth open, because one or two of my friends who have been charged have informed me that in their cases they particularly noticed that the bear charged with his mouth shut. Perhaps the fact that my bear was shot through [the] lungs may account for the difference, or it may simply be another example of individual variation.

Despite the matter-of-fact tone of the article, Roosevelt was very pleased with the way he comported himself. He wrote and spoke of that episode on many occasions. "By Jupiter, I feel well," he excitedly wrote Lodge from Montana in late August, "I have had a hard but successful trip—moose, bear, elk, etc.; one bear nearly got me—and never was in better condition. So now for work again…" The Lord had either helped TR, or at least neglected to help the bear!

In 1890, Roosevelt and his wife vacationed in Yellowstone Park and at Medora—from the first week of September until early October. "Edith particularly enjoyed the riding at the ranch…" TR wrote, "and the strange, wild, beautiful scenery, and the loneliness and freedom of the life fascinated and appealed to her as it did to me…" Roosevelt did some hunting with his friend, Robert H. Munro-Ferguson (a fellow member of the Boone and Crockett Club), shot "two or three deer," and spent "eleven hours of darkness in fighting a prairie fire." But the 1890 Badlands trip was otherwise a quiet one. Roosevelt had hunted only sporadically that year and was a bit disappointed that he had acquired so few trophy heads to give to friends or to add to the collection at Sagamore Hill.

The year 1891 was another fast-paced sequence of fighting spoils politics, red tape, and corruption. But the hard-working, outdoors-minded Civil Service Commissioner did manage a concentrated Badlands hunt in the fall. "I am just back from my hunt," he wrote Lodge in mid-October.

I shot nine elk. One of the heads is for you, not an unusual head at all, I am sorry to say; simply an ordinary "stag of twelve," what the old books call a "royal." Bob [R. H. M. Ferguson], whom I left out in the wilds, was having even better luck. When I left he had got on the trail of a bear; I think he will get it I got into splendid trim physically by the end of my hunt.

While in Texas on official business in 1892, TR could not resist the chance to hunt peccary. He wrote friend Cecil Arthur Spring Rice that he:

went down to some ranches in the semi tropical country round the Nueces, and hunted peccaries. I killed two. It was great fun, for we followed them on horseback, with hounds—such hounds!—and the little beasts fought with the usual stupid courage of pigs when brought to bay. They ought to be killed with a spear; the country is so thick, with huge cactus and thorny mesquite trees, that the riding is hard; but they are small, and it would be safe to go at them on foot—at any rate for two men.

In *The Wilderness Hunter,* which was published the following year, TR devoted a chapter to his "Peccary-Hunt on the Nueces." One chase after a band of five pigs in particular gave the Commissioner a hard and invigorating ride. Three of the stubborn and tough beasts charged, one of them gashing a dog with a vicious bite. "The...chase on horseback was great fun, and there was a certain excitement in seeing the fierce little creatures come to bay....They are very active, absolutely fearless, and inflict a most formidable bite."

In the fall of 1892, Roosevelt "passed a very pleasant three weeks on my ranch, and on the trip south to Deadwood." He shot "three or four deer and antelope—one deer from the ranch verandah!" The shot from the verandah had been totally unexpected. "One morning, as I was sitting on the piazza," he wrote Bill Sewall, "I heard a splashing in the river...and there were three deer! They walked

"As [the big bull] stood fronting me with his head down I fired... and he turned a tremendous back somersault." The scene was depicted as a watercolor by artist J. Carter Beard for *The Wilderness Hunter.*

A.B. Frost's "The Death of the
Grizzly" was the frontispiece to TR's
The Wilderness Hunter.

up along the sand to the crossing; and I picked up my rifle, leaned against one of the big cottonwoods and dropped one in its tracks. We were out of meat and the venison tasted first rate. I never expected to shoot a deer from the piazza."

Hunting and Writing

I wanted to make [*The Wilderness Hunter*] a plea for manliness and simplicity and delight in a vigorous outdoor life, as well as to try to sketch the feeling that the wilderness, with its great rivers, great mountains, great forests, and great prairies, leaves on one. The slaughter of the game, though necessary in order to give a needed touch of salt to the affair, is subsidiary after all.

The Wilderness Hunter, one of Theodore Roosevelt's finest writings on hunting, was published in 1893, as was *American Big Game Hunting* the first of three volumes he co-edited as books of the Boone and Crockett Club. Reviews of *The Wilderness Hunter* were uniformly laudatory. The *New York Nation* gave unstinting praise:

Probably no American is better qualified than Mr. Roosevelt to write on such a subject as this, for he has himself hunted and killed every variety of game native to the United States, has lived on our so-called frontier, has known the peculiar life, thought, and action of its people, and, above all, possesses a true appreciation of nature, animate and inanimate, and the literary ability to relate what he has seen. He has studied the habit of the game while hunting it, at the same time he has noted with interest and intelligence all the sights and sounds peculiar to the wilderness, and, having the eye of a naturalist, has not allowed the habits of the smaller birds and animals to escape unnoticed in his pursuit of a larger quarry. So many books on hunting have been written which fail to show anything but the natural Anglo-Saxon bloodthirstiness, that it is refreshing to have a writer

pause to cover his sinister motives with the cloak of a fine cloud effect, or glorify them with the splendor of a flaming sunset. Time and opportunity come to few men, engaged in the active work of life, to see and do what our author has seen and done. Our country still has the unexplored places, the peculiar life, and strange characters, not to be found in the earth's older regions, which belong to a nation's youth and are so dear to romance and adventure, and Mr. Roosevelt has seen and written of these things in a straightforward style, without either coolness or sentimentality, devoting most of his time to action, and leaving the romance to others.

The London *Field* noted Roosevelt's gun preferences in reviewing *American Big Game Hunting*

The editors of this book [Theodore Roosevelt and George Bird Grinnell] preface an interesting series of big game hunting stories in the United States, with an account of the Boone and Crockett Club, and the worthy objects which this body has in view. The stories which follow have all been written by well-known American sportsmen, and are descriptive of the pursuit of every kind of big game to be found in the United States, including the now all but extinct buffalo....That the opinions of American sportsmen differ considerably as to the comparative efficiency of rifles may be gathered from the fact that Mr. Theodore Roosevelt, in his recent work, *The Wilderness Hunter*, informs us that he has discarded an expensive double-barreled .500 Express, by one of the crack English makers, for a Winchester repeater, which he always uses for big game shooting....

An examination of Roosevelt's correspondence for 1893 and 1894 shows that he made regular fall trips to the Badlands in both years but did comparatively little hunting. The success of each hunt was measured more in terms of how rough and

Today I caught a glimpse of the President, and repeated to him the parable of the backwoodsman and the bear. You remember that the prayer of the backwoodsman was "Oh Lord, help me kill that bar; and if you don't help me, oh Lord, don't help the bar."

refreshing it was than in the amount of game he shot. In September 1894 he wrote Lodge that he had "passed a delightful fortnight, all the time in the open; and [I] feel as rugged as a bull moose.... I shot five antelope—only one a doe —and a fine white tail buck, too."

TR wrote a colorful account of this rugged wilderness holiday in a letter to his friend James Brander Matthews:

> ...for my own pleasure this year when I was out on the antelope plains I got into a country where I didn't take my clothes off for ten days. I had two cowpunchers along, and the quilts and bedding, including the pillows which they had, were quite as bad as those Garland [Hamlin Garland, "Only a Lumber Jack," December 8th issue of *Harper's Weekly*] describes in his logging camp; yet they both felt they were off on a holiday and having a lovely time. Our food on this ten days' trip was precisely like that he describes in the logging camp, except that we had venison instead of beef, and we ate it under less comfortable surroundings as a whole, or at least under what my men regarded as less comfortable surroundings. I have worked hard in cow camps for weeks at a time, doing precisely such work as the cowpunchers, and I know what I am talking about. I didn't play; I *worked* while on my ranch. There is a great deal of toil and hardship about the out-of-door life of lumbermen & cowboys, and especially about some phases which he doesn't touch, such as driving logs in the springtime and handling cattle from a line camp in bitter winter weather; but the life as a whole is a decidedly healthy and attractive one to men who do not feel the need of mental recreation and stimulus—and few of them do.

Rifles for Big Game

"I suppose all hunters are continually asked what rifles they use," TR wrote in the Boone and Crockett Club book *Hunting in Many Lands* (1895).

From his own experience and knowledge he was well qualified to discourse at length on technical aspects of sundry types of rifles. The following extended excerpt offers proof of this:

> ...Any good modern rifle is good enough, and, after a certain degree of excellence in the weapon is attained, the difference between it and a somewhat better rifle counts for comparatively little compared to the difference in the skill, nerve and judgment of the men using them. Moreover, there is room for a great deal of individual variation of opinion among experts as to rifles. I personally prefer the Winchester. I used a 45-75 until I broke it in a fall while goat hunting, and since then I have used a 45-90. For my own use I consider either gun much preferable to the 500 and 577 caliber double-barreled Express for use with bears, buffalo, moose and elk, yet my brother, for instance, always preferred the double-barreled Express; Mr. Theodore Van Dyke prefers the large bore, and H.L. Stimson has had built a special 577 Winchester, which he tells me he finds excellent for grizzly bears. There is the same difference of opinion among men who hunt game on other continents than ours. Thus, Mr. Royal Carroll, in shooting rhinoceros, buffalo and the like in South Africa, preferred big, heavy English double-barrels; while Mr. William Chanler, after trying these same double-barrels, finally threw them aside in favor of the 45-90 Winchester for use even against such large and thick-hided beasts as rhinoceros. There was an amusing incident connected with Mr. Chanler's experiences. In a letter to the London *Field* he happened to mention that he preferred, for rhinoceros and other large game, the 45-90 Winchester to the double-barrel 577, so frequently produced by the English gun makers. His letter was followed by a perfect chorus of protests in the shape of other letters by men who preferred the double-barrel. These men had a perfect right to their opinions,

but the comic feature of their letters was that, as a rule, they almost seemed to think that Mr. Chanler's preference of the 45-90 repeater showed some kind of moral delinquency on his part, while the gun maker, whose double-barrel Mr. Chanler had discarded in favor of the Winchester, solemnly produced tests to show that the bullets from his gun had more penetration than those from the Winchester—which had no more to do with the question than the production by the Winchester people of targets to show that this weapon possessed superior accuracy would have had. Of course, the element of penetration is only one of twenty entering into the question, accuracy, handiness, rapidity of fire, penetration, shock—all have to be considered. Penetration is useless after a certain point has been reached. Shock is useless if it is gained at too great expense of penetration or accuracy Flatness of trajectory, though admirable, is not as important as accuracy, and when gained at a great expense of accuracy is simply a disadvantage. All of these points are admirably discussed in Mr. A.C. Gould's "Modern American Rifles." In the right place, a fair-sized bullet is as good as a very big one; in the wrong place, the big one is best, but the medium one will do more good in the right place than the big one away from its right place; and if it is more accurate it is therefore preferable.

Entirely apart from the merit of guns, there is a considerable element of mere fashion in them. For the last twenty years there has been much controversy between the advocates of two styles of rifles—that is, the weapon with a comparatively small bore and long, solid bullet and a moderate charge of powder, and the weapon of comparatively large bore with a very heavy charge of powder and a short bullet, often with a hollow end. The first is the type of rifle that has always been used by ninety-nine out of a hundred American hunters, and indeed it is the only

The four members of the New York Police Commission, from left, Avery D. Andrews, Andrew Parker, TR, and Gen. Fred D. Grant.

FROM *A CARTOON HISTORY OF ROOSEVELT'S CAREER*

kind of rifle that has ever been used to any extent in North America; the second is the favorite weapon of English sportsmen in those grandest of the World's hunting grounds, India and South Africa. When a single-shot rifle is not used, the American usually takes a repeater, the Englishman a double-barrel. Each type has some good qualities that the other lacks, and each has some defects. The personal equation must always be taken into account in dealing with either; excellent sportsmen of equal experience give conflicting accounts of the performances of the two types. Personally, I think that the American type is nearer right. In reading the last book of the great South African hunter, Mr. Selous, I noticed with much interest that in hunting elephants he and many of the Dutch elephant hunters had abandoned the huge four and eight bores championed by that doughty hunter, Sir Samuel Baker, and had adopted precisely the type of rifle which was in almost universal use among the American buffalo hunters from 1870 to 1883—that is, a rifle of 45 caliber, shooting 75 grains of powder and a bullet of 550 grains. The favorite weapon of the American buffalo hunter was a Sharps rifle of 45 caliber, shooting about 550 grains of lead and using ordinarily 90 to 110 grains of powder—which, however, was probably not as strong as the powder used by Mr. Selous; in other words, the types of gun were identically the same. I have elsewhere

stated that by actual experience the big double-barreled English eight and ten bores were found inferior to Sharps rifle for bison-hunting on the Western plains. I know nothing about elephant or rhinoceros shooting; but my own experience with bison, bear, moose and elk has long convinced me that for them and for all similar animals (including, I have no doubt, the lion and tiger) the 45-90 type of repeater is, on the whole, the best of the existing sporting rifles for my own use. I have of late years loaded my cartridges not with ordinary rifle powder, but with 85 grains of Orange lightning, and have used a bullet with 350 grains of lead, and then have bored a small hole, taking out 15 or 20 grains, in the point, but for heavy game I think the solid bullet better. Judging from what I have been told by some of my friends, however, it seems not unlikely that the best sporting rifle will ultimately prove to be the very small caliber repeating rifle now found in various forms in the military service of all countries—a caliber of say 256 or 310, with 40 grains of powder and a 200-grain bullet. These rifles possess marvelous accuracy and a very flat trajectory. The speed of the bullet causes it to mushroom if made of lead, and gives it great penetration if hardened. Certain of my friends have used rifles of this type on bears, caribou and deer; they were said to be far superior to the ordinary sporting rifle. A repeating rifle of this type is really merely a much more perfect form of the repeating rifles that have for so long been favorites with American hunters.

But these are merely my personal opinions; and, as I said before, among the many kinds of excellent sporting rifles turned out by the best modern makers each has its special good points and its special defects; and equally good sportsmen, of equally wide experience, will be found to vary widely in their judgment of the relative worth of the different weapons. Some people can do better with one rifle and some with another, and in the long run it is "the man behind the gun" that counts most.

Roosevelt was meticulous not only in his choice of firearms but in the kind of cartridges he used as well: their shape, weight, make, type, and amount of powder were all carefully considered before he made his selection. He knew enough about ballistics to predict accurately that in due time the small caliber would become the standard sporting rifle cartridge. Given his near-encyclopedic knowledge of sporting firearms and cartridges, it is sometimes difficult to remember that he was, after all, a promising public official who was just about to leave the Civil Service Commission to become Police Commissioner of New York City

Police Commissioner of New York

Out of the soft sereneness
of Civil Service peace
Into a coarse connection
with persons and police
Out of the chaste and classic
Realm of purity
Into the low and common
Title of P.C.!

New York Sun, April, 1895

By 1895, the daily grind of life in Washington had become tiresome to the energetic Roosevelt, and he was ready for a change. When offered the onerous job of New York City Police Commissioner he accepted, mainly because it was different, it certainly did not represent a political stepping stone. Well suited personally and professionally for his new position, TR had not the vaguest notion of the administrative nightmare he would be facing or of the wholesale corruption and delinquency festering in the department. A thorough cleansing was in order, and Roosevelt was just the right purgative.

The 35-year-old Police Commissioner arrived in New York in April to serve under the reform-minded mayor, William Strong. On the Commission with TR were two Democrats, Avery Andrews and Andrew Parker, and a Republican, Franklin Grant, son of the late President. President of the Commission for two years, Roosevelt accepted the appointment "with the distinct understanding that I was to administer the Police Department with entire disregard of partisan politics, and only from the standpoint of a good citizen interested in promoting the welfare of all good citizens..."

Roosevelt had not been in office a month when the *New York Herald* chimed: "Sing heavenly muse, the sad dejection of our poor policeman. We have a real policeman. His name is Theodore Roosevelt. His teeth are big and white, his eyes are small and piercing, his voice is rasping. His heart is full of reform..." And reform he did. He demanded that the police be well mannered and well dressed. He changed their lax attitude toward the Sunday dosing of saloons. He personally inspected his officers and patrolmen both inside and outside the Mulberry Street headquarters. Suspecting that many of his men were remiss in the performance of their duties, he frequently traversed huge sections of the city, looking for abuses. Often he chose an early-morning hour, when the police were inclined to be most slack. Roosevelt's pugnacious attitude and unceasing efforts to curb corruption caused Mayor Strong to remark: "I found the Dutchman I had appointed meant to turn us all into Puritans."

Well versed as he was in firearms, Roosevelt underscored the importance of his men knowing how

Roosevelt had not been in office a month when the *New York Herald* chimed: "Sing heavenly muse, the sad dejection of our poor policeman. We have a real policeman. His name is Theodore Roosevelt. His teeth are big and white, his eyes are small and piercing, his voice is rasping. His heart is full of reform..."

with outbursts of joy. They gave it wide publicity   while out with John Willis, now a prominent

to handle weapons. When he discovered that most of the policemen were inept marksmen, he resolved was there no uniformity in their armament, but officers had never received any real instruction

CHAPTER 6

The Honest Politician

As New York City Police Commissioner Roosevelt had been so effective and incorruptible that many politicians were anxious for his departure. Thomas Platt, the notorious Republican boss of New York, was particularly hostile toward him and tried to have him removed from the Commission. *The New York Times* took up the issue, condemning Platt and his cronies. Roosevelt remained at his post until April 1897, when he resigned to accept an appointment by President William McKinley as Assistant Secretary of the Navy. Henry Cabot Lodge and others had spoken to McKinley about Roosevelt's political availability, but the President offered the position somewhat reluctantly because he considered Roosevelt "too pugnacious...always getting into rows with everybody."

Roosevelt assumed office at a time when the American public was becoming daily more aroused by sensational newspaper accounts of Spanish oppression and atrocities in Cuba. There was a swelling conviction among Americans that Cubans ought to be redeemed from the harsh rule of Spain and that the United States ought to be the instrument of that redemption. There were no economic motives behind the American people's interests in Cuba's fate, despite the considerable trade between the two. Many Americans felt an authentic humanitarian solicitude for the plight of Cubans. To be sure, the yellow press had a field day exaggerating incidents of Spanish cruelty, but the public itself was all too eager to believe the worst of Spain.

Roosevelt was convinced that war with Spain was unavoidable, and he forthwith began making plans

Theodore Roosevelt and his Rough Riders immediately after the Battle of San Juan Hill. The photograph was made on the spot. One of his biographers wrote that "the battle... assumed in Roosevelt's mind the aspects of a pleasantly dangerous sporting event."

THEODORE ROOSEVELT COLLECTION, HARVARD COLLEGE LIBRARY

**Assistant Secretary of the Navy
Theodore Roosevelt, c. 1897-1898**

THEODORE ROOSEVELT COLLECTION,
HARVARD COLLEGE LIBRARY

for the Navy as if he were the Secretary rather than merely the assistant. "I tried to gather from every source," he wrote in his *Autobiography*, "information as to who the best men were to occupy the fighting positions." In a letter to his friend Cecil Spring Rice he confided that "there is a great deal of work to be done here, and though my position is of course an entirely subordinate one, still I can accomplish something." In point of fact, he accomplished much. He was fast coming to believe that the end of Spanish rule in Cuba would be a good thing for the entire Western Hemisphere. In answer to a request for a special problem for the staff and class at the Naval War College Roosevelt devised a timely and rather martial inquiry:

> Special Confidential Problem for War College:
>   Japan makes demands on Hawaiian
>   Islands
>   This country intervenes
>   What force will be necessary to up-
>   hold the intervention, and how shall it be
>   employed?
>   Keeping in mind possible implications
>   with another Power on the Atlantic Coast
>   (Cuba).

As was the case when he was a Police Commissioner, Roosevelt lost no time inquiring into the fighting ability of naval crews, with a view to improving their marksmanship. TR demonstrated that he knew what he was talking about:

> ...in the days of the old smooth-bore guns the ships were very close and in reality hardly any aim was taken. But as they wallowed through the water, fifty yards or so apart, it was found that the shots were more apt to strike the adversary's hull if they were fired when the gun was pointing down than if it was pointing up.
>
> Now the whole truth is exactly as you say, that it is a matter of that kind of skill which we call "knack." In each ship's crew there is a limited number of men who can become first-class gun pointers, and only a limited number. We have tried the experiment of making the petty officers captains of the guns, and it does not work well; and now we are trying to develop gun pointers pure and simple.
>
> I myself have no natural skill with firearms, and indeed very little with any form of pursuit needing physical and manual dexterity and accuracy of eye. I never learned to shoot quick, and the rifle is the only weapon with which I became even fairly skillful. I have been moderately successful with game simply because I got to fire as well at game as at a target, and though this was not very well, yet it was better than what most first-class target shots would do if unused to game shooting.
>
> I did not do any sub-calibre practice myself, but I had great sport on the *Dolphin* with a rapid-fire six-pounder gun; and I found that personally I could do best by shooting when the ship's side was rising, getting the gun in position, and then, just as the front sight touched the target on the way up, pulling trigger. But in trying to fire rapidly it is, of course, impossible to pay heed to the rising or falling of the ship. I think myself that altogether too much is sacrificed to rapidity of fire. The number of *hits* is what counts...

The analogy between his experience with firearms and naval marksmanship was pertinent, especially the injunction to "fire as well at game as at a target." Rapidity of fire should be a secondary consideration: "The number of *hits* is what counts."

A Declaration of War

All through 1897 McKinley sincerely hoped for peace; he wanted Spain to "be given a reasonable chance" to offer home rule to the Cubans. However, on February 15, 1898, the U.S. battleship *Maine,* resting in Havana harbor, mysteriously blew up. Two hundred and sixty American lives were lost.

Henry Cabot Lodge and others had spoken to McKinley about Roosevelt's political availability, but the President offered the position somewhat reluctantly because he considered Roosevelt "too pugnacious... always getting into rows with everybody."

"In all the world there could be no better material for soldiers than that afforded by these grim hunters of the mountains, these wild rough riders of the plains. They were accustomed to handling wild and savage horses; they were accustomed to following the chase with the rifle, both for sport and as a means of livelihood."

McKinley and his cabinet, despite an outraged public and press, were temperate enough to consider the possibility that the sinking was an accident, and therefore ordered a thorough investigation. Roosevelt, however, urged war: "...The *Maine* was sunk by an act of dirty treachery on the part of the Spaniards, I believe, though we shall never find out definitely and officially it will go down as an accident." No war-monger himself, Roosevelt was nevertheless spoiling for a fight. The honor of the nation had to be vindicated. Most Americans agreed.

On February 25th, without checking with his superiors, Roosevelt sent a provocative telegram to Commodore George Dewey:

Order the Squadron, except Monocacy, to Hong Kong. Keep full of coal. In the event of declaration of war Spain, your duty will be to see that the Spanish squadron does not leave the Asiatic coast, and then offensive operations in Philippine Islands. Keep Olympia until further orders.

It required much temerity for Roosevelt to send such a message entirely on his own initiative. In fact, Secretary of the Navy John D. Long, who was away at the time, had ordered his assistant not to make any decision with regard to basic naval policy Though a crucial policy decision, the cable had not been unreasonable. Instead, as subsequent events bore out, it proved to be a brilliant maneuver. Though Long was thunderstruck by Roosevelt's audacity, he was not wholly surprised to see his assistant disregard authority

In March 1898, Congress unanimously voted a defense fund of 50 million dollars. The report of the court of inquiry on the sinking of the *Maine* announced that it had been unable to determine what caused the explosion. On April 9 Spain made an attempt to placate American bellicosity by suspending its military actions against the Cuban rebels. The American Minister in Spain

reported confidently to McKinley that the conflict could be settled by rational negotiations. But war fever in America had reached such a crescendo that McKinley was finding it inordinately difficult to counteract the jingoist clamor.

War with Spain came because, in the final analysis, McKinley could not resist mounting congressional pressure. Roosevelt was ecstatic over the President's war message and Congress' overwhelmingly favorable vote. He resigned from his post with alacrity, accepted a lieutenant colonelcy commission, and began organizing a regiment of volunteer cavalrymen. A good friend and professional military man, Col. Leonard Wood, commanded the regiment. Roosevelt received thousands of applications—many of which were from cowboys and a few even from Indians—and hand-picked every man. In the meantime Commodore Dewey, carrying out the orders Roosevelt had sent him four months earlier, annihilated the Spanish fleet at Manila Bay.

The Rough Rider
Organizing and equipping his cavalry regiment required an almost herculean expenditure of energy on Roosevelt's part. "In trying to get the equipment," he recollected in his *Autobiography*, "I met with checks and rebuffs, and in return was the cause of worry and concern to various bureau chiefs." Cutting red tape and constantly going over the heads of War Department officials, Roosevelt succeeded in amply equipping his men. The regiment assembled in San Antonio, and when Roosevelt reached there, "the men, rifles, and horses, which were the essentials, were coming in fast." TR took charge of drilling the troops and put them through a Spartan routine and discipline. He "speedily made it evident that there was no room and no mercy for any man who shirked any duty." In remarkably short order he turned out a crack outfit.

Many years before, in 1886, Roosevelt had come close to organizing a Rough Rider regiment. The *Bismarck* (Dakota Territory) *Tribune* in August of that year reported:

ABOVE: Frederic Remington's oil painting, "The Charge Up San Juan Hill." TR is on horseback, revolver in hand. "Remington has made a picture of the charge of the Rough Riders... He does not give the individual faces and he portrays me with a decorum of attitude which was foreign to my actual conduct at the time; but it is a good picture."

INSET: The Rough Rider as full colonel, in his hat lining were sewn several extra pairs of spectacles. "...I had served three years as a captain the National Guard; I had been deputy sheriff in the cow county, where the position was not a sinecure; I was accustomed to big game hunting and to work on a cow ranch, so that I was thoroughly familiar with the use both of horses and rifle, and knew how to handle cowboys, hunters, and miners; finally I had studied much in the literature of war..."

tle and more than distinguished themselves. In a hastily written letter to his sister Corinne, TR gave a capsule description of the fighting:

Las Guasimas, June 25th '98

    Yesterday we struck the Spaniards and had a brisk fight for 2 hours before we drove them out of their position. We lost a dozen men killed or mortally wounded, and sixty severely or slightly wounded....One man was killed as he stood beside a tree with me. Another bullet went through a tree behind which I stood and filled my eyes with bark. The last charge I led on the left using a rifle I took from a wounded man; and I kept three of the empty cartridges we got from a dead Spaniard at this point, for the children. Every man behaved well; there was no flinching. The fire was very hot at one or two points where the men around me went down like ninepins. We have been ashore three days and were moved at once to the front without our baggage. I have been sleeping on the ground in the mackintosh, and so drenched with sweat that I haven't been dry a minute, day or night. The marches have been very severe. One of my horses was drowned swimming through the surf....My bag has never turned up, like most of our baggage, and it is very doubtful if it ever does turn up, and I have nothing with me, no soap, toothbrush, razor, brandy, medicine chest, socks or underclothes....Richard Harding Davis [a distinguished war Correspondent] was with me in the fight and behaved capitally. The Spaniards shot well; but they did not stand when we rushed. It was a good fight. I am in good health....

It was in the battle of Santiago that the Rough Riders executed their famous charge on San Juan Hill. Roosevelt led the assault that culminated in a decisive defeat for the Spaniards. For Roosevelt it was "the great day of my life." In truth, it was a key day in the making of a future President.

TR sent Colonel Leonard Wood a detailed and comprehensive report on the military exploits of his Rough Riders:

In obedience to your directions, I herewith report on the operations of my regiment from the 1st to the 17th [July] inst., inclusive.

    ...On the morning of the 1st my regiment was formed at the head of the Second Brigade, by the El Poso sugar mill. When the batteries opened the Spaniards replied to us with shrapnel, which killed and wounded several of the men of my regiment. We then marched toward the right and my regiment crossed the ford before the balloon came down there and attracted the fire of the enemy....My orders had been to march forward until I joined Gen'l Lawton's left wing, but after going about three quarters of a mile I was halted and told to remain in reverse near the creek by a deep lane. The bullets dropped thick among us for the next hour while we lay there and many of my men were killed or wounded...

    You then sent me word to move forward in support of the regular cavalry and I advanced the regiment in columns of companies, each company deployed as skirmishers. We moved through several skirmish lines of the regiment ahead of us, as it seemed to me that our only chance was in rushing the entrenchments in front instead of firing at them from a distance. Accordingly we charged the blockhouse and entrenchments on the hill [Kettle Hill] to our right against a heavy fire. It was taken in good style, the men of my regiment thus being the first to capture any fortified position and to break through the Spanish lines....At the last wire fence up this hill I was obliged to abandon my horse and after that went on foot. After capturing this hill we first of all directed a heavy fire upon the San Juan hill to our left, which was at the time being assailed by the regular infantry and cavalry, supported by Captain Parker's gatling guns. By the time

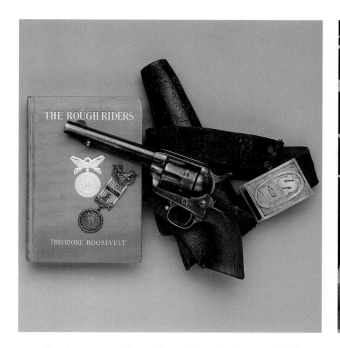

San Juan was taken a large force had assembled on the hill we had previously captured, consisting not only of my own regiment but of the 9th and of portions of other cavalry regiments We then charged forward under a heavy fire across the valley against the Spanish entrenchments on the hill in the rear of the San Juan hill. This we also took, capturing several prisoners. We then formed in what order we could and moved forward driving the Spaniards before us to the crest of the hills in our front which were immediately opposite the city of Santiago itself. Here I received orders to halt and hold the line of hill-crest. I had at that time fragments of the six cavalry regiments and an occasional Infantry man under me—three or four hundred men all told. As I was the highest there, I took command of all of them and so continued until next morning.

The Spanish attempted a counterattack that afternoon, but were easily driven back, and then and until dark we remained under a heavy fire from their rifles and great guns lying flat on our faces, on the gentle slope just behind the crest. Captain Parker's gatling battery was run up to the right of my regiment and did most excellent and gallant service. In order to charge the men had, of course, been obliged to throw away their packs, and we had nothing to sleep in and nothing to eat. We were lucky enough, however, to find in the last blockhouse captured the Spanish dinner still cooking, which we ate with relish. It consisted chiefly of rice and peas, with a big pot containing a stew of fresh meat, probably for the officers. We also distributed the captured Spanish blankets, as far as they would go, among our men, and gathered a good deal of the Mauser ammunition for use in the Colt's rapid-fire guns which were being brought up. That night we dug entrenchments across our front. At *3* o'clock in the morning the Spaniards made another attack upon us, which was easily repelled, and at 4 they opened the day with a heavy rifle and shrapnel fire. All day long we lay under this, replying whenever we got the chance. In the evening at about 8 o'clock the Spaniards fired their guns and then opened a heavy rifle fire, their skirmishers coming well forward. I got all my men down into the trenches, as did the other commands near me, and we opened a heavy return fire. The Spanish advance was at once stopped and after an hour their fire died away. This night we completed

ABOVE LEFT: Historic Rough Rider U.S. Martially marked Colt Single Action Army Artillery Model revolver, serial #115162 on the frame, the balance of numbers mixed; accompanied by leather flap holster, belt and brass buckle, and Spanish-American War medal. Documented as issued to and used by Sergeant John V. Morrison, I Troop, 1st Volunteer Cavalry Regiment – The Rough Riders. Morrison was present at the campaign in Cuba and in the charge up San Juan Hill; he is listed on page 260 of TR's *The Rough Riders*.

ABOVE: U.S. Model 1896 Krag-Jorgensen saddle ring carbine, used by Troop M, 6th U.S. Cavalry Regiment. U.S. Army Adjutant General's office documents that the 6th took part in action against Santiago, Cuba and was involved in the Battle of San Juan Hill. Serial #67201; .30-40 Krag caliber.

COURTESY OF GREG MARTIN

U.S. Volunteer Cavalry: Leonard Roy Metz

Indicative of the intense loyalty, admiration, and affection from volunteers for the Spanish-American War toward Colonel Theodore Roosevelt, Leonard Roy Metz—whose memorabilia is displayed here—expressed that powerful influence and example throughout the remainder of his life. Grandson Gregory Metz Thomas (the little boy at top of the locomotive cab steps, with his grandfather Metz in the window, above 800) to this day remembers his grandfather's reminiscences of meeting and knowing TR.

Metz is recorded as a saddler, Troop G, 2nd U.S. Volunteer Cavalry, in various sources, included records of the Veteran's Administration, Bureau of Pensions. He was mustered into service at Sheridan, Wyoming, enlisting for two years (from May 15, 1898), with the rank of private. And was mustered out October 24, 1898, at Camp Cube Libre, Florida. He became a celebrated locomotive engineer on the Rio Grande, but also served the military in the Philippine Islands. His Colt double action New Army revolver, serial #141581, is marked on the butt, US/ARMY/MODEL/1898, with inspector marking JTT (John Taliaferro Thompson, some years later inventor of the Thompson Submachine Gun). The leather holster includes on flap, MAESTRANZA/DE/MANILA (also on cartridge belt), accompanied by U.S. stamping. The nickel-plated pocket revolver was made by Hopkins & Allen, in .32 caliber; serial #42767. Among Metz' service medals, the Rough Riders (above pocket purse and pencils at lower left) from "Camp Cuba Libre" Jacksonville, Florida, 1898.

INSET: Opposite side view of the revolvers, cartridge belt and holster, as well as service leggings, spurs, gauntlets, campaign medals, and marksmanship awards; plus compass and Roosevelt family book. Sword from Masonic membership. Family images include grandson Gregory M. Thomas in University of California, Berkeley, varsity football photograph, lower left.

GREGORY M. THOMAS, FIREARMS, MEMORABILIA, AND PHOTOGRAPHS; IMAGES TAKEN BY DOUGLAS SANDBERG

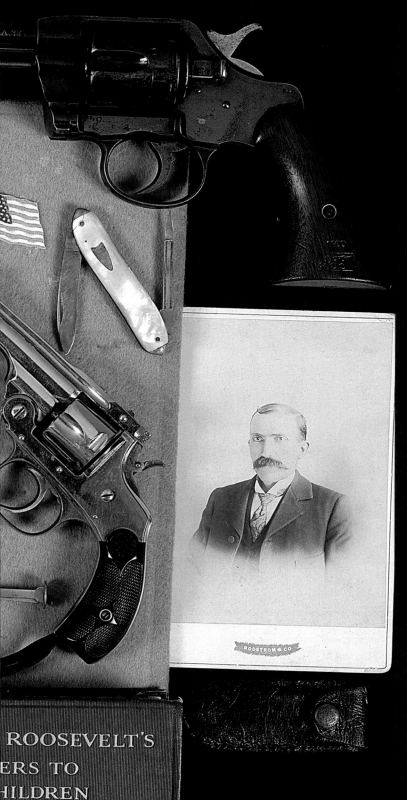

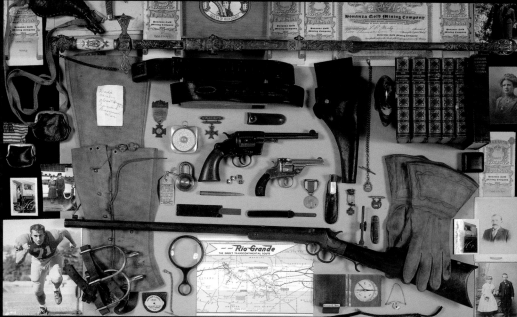

ROOSEVELT'S
ERS TO
HILDREN

RIGHT: Presentation Model 1895 rifle, from TR to his friend and co-commander of the Rough Riders, Colonel Leonard Wood. The rifle is a .30-40 caliber with a 28" barrel, checkered deluxe stock, shotgun butt with metal buttplate, Lyman receiver sight. The factory letter notes: "gold plate in stock, engraved, which they send." Received in the warehouse December 9, 1899, shipped the same day; Order #45199, Serial #23576. Gold plaque on the bottom of buttstock inscribed: Leonard Wood/Gov. of Cuba/12-20-99/ from/T.R. Roosevelt was Governor of New York at the time of presentation.

NATIONAL FIREARMS MUSEUM

INSET: TR with orderly Gordon Johnston at Camp Wikhoff, home from the "splendid little war." Note the holster on TR's right hip, for his Colt New Army and Navy Model double action revolver.

THEODORE ROOSEVELT COLLECTION, HARVARD COLLEGE LIBRARY

them out after these guerillas, of whom they killed 13. They were stationed in trees (as the guerillas were generally) and owing to the density of the foliage and to the use of smokeless powder rifles it was an exceedingly difficult matter to locate them. For the next seven days, until the 10th, we lay in our lines while the truce continued. We had continually to work at additional bomb proofs and at the trenches, and as we had no proper supply of food and utterly inadequate medical facilities the men suffered a good deal. The officers clubbed together to purchase beans, tomatoes and sugar for the men, so that they might have some relief from the bacon and hard tack. With a great deal of difficulty we got them coffee.

As for the sick and wounded they suffered so in the hospitals when sent to the rear from lack of food and attention that we found it best to keep them at the front and give them such care as our own doctors could—thirteen of our wounded men continued to fight through the battle in spite of their wounds, and of those sent to the rear many, both of the sick and wounded, came up to rejoin us as soon as their condition allowed them to walk; most of the worst cases were ultimately sent to the States.

On the 10th the truce was at an end and the bombardment reopened. As far as our lines were concerned, it was on the Spanish part very feeble. We suffered no losses and speedily got the fire from their trenches in our front completely

most of our trenches and began to build bomb proofs. The protection afforded to our men was good and next morning had but one man wounded from the rifle and shell fire until 12 o'clock, when the truce came.

There were numerous Red Cross flags flying in various parts of the city, two of them so arranged that they directly covered batteries in our front and for some time were the cause of our not firing at them. The Spanish guerillas were very active, especially in our rear, where they seemed by preference to attack the wounded men who were being carried on litters, the doctors and medical attendants with Red Cross bandages on their arms and the burial parties. I organized a detail of sharpshooters and sent

under. On the 11th we were moved 3/4 of a mile to the right, the truce again being on. Nothing happened here, except we continued to watch and do our best to get the men, especially the sick, properly fed, and having no transportation and being unable to get hardly any through the regular channels, we used anything we could find—captured Spanish cavalry horses, abandoned mules, which had been shot, but which our men took and cured, diminutive skinny ponies purchased from the Cubans, etc. By these means and by the exertions of the officers we were able from time to time to get supplies of beans, sugar, tomatoes, and even oatmeal, while from the Red Cross people we got one invaluable load of rice, corn meal, etc. All of this was of the utmost consequence, not only for the sick normically [sic.] well, as the lack of proper food was telling terribly on the men. It was utterly impossible to get them clothes and shoes; those they had were, in many cases, literally dropping to pieces.

On the 17th the city surrendered. On the 18th we shifted camp to here [Santiago], the best camp we have had, but the march hither under the noonday sun told very heavily on our men weakened by underfeeding and overwork, and next morning 128 cases were reported to the doctors, and I now have but half of the 600 men with which I landed four weeks ago, fit for duty, and these are not fit to do anything like the work they could do then. As we had but one wagon, the change necessitated leaving much of the stuff behind, with a night of discomfort, with scanty shelter and scanty food, for most of the officers and many of the men. Only the possession of the improvised pack train alluded to above saved this from being worse. Yesterday I sent in a detail of six officers and men to see if they could not purchase or make arrangements for a supply of proper food and proper clothing for the men, even if we had to pay for it out of our own pockets. Our suffering has been due primarily to lack of transportation and of proper food and sufficient clothing and of medical supplies…

The military tactics devised by the high command were not always as sound as Roosevelt thought they should have been. He was very critical of the egregious failures in logistics and of the long delays in the execution of military operations. For his own men, however, he had nothing but unmeasured praise: "The regiment was a wholly exceptional volunteer organization…, they were hardy, self-reliant nothing but the splendid fighting capacity and uncomplaining endurance…carried us through."

On the other side it should be noted that established military leaders were often unhappy with Roosevelt's performance. They found him impetuous, impudent, and virtually impossible to discipline. But the country loved him.

Spanish forces were pitiably unequal to the task before them and lost battle after battle. American troops faced deadlier threats from malarial fever than from enemy guns. By the middle of July the Spanish commander realized his position was untenable and surrendered his army. The war in Cuba was over, but scores of Americans continued to die or become extremely ill with yellow fever. Alarmed by the fatalities, Roosevelt wrote to the Secretary of War and requested an expeditious withdrawal of troops. For his boldness on this count Roosevelt received the plaudits of his men, but President McKinley was incensed when TR's indiscreet letter of request was published in newspapers. The incident made Roosevelt even more popular with the public since it showed his genuine concern for the welfare of American soldiers. He had already become a national hero because of his inspiring and dauntless leadership on the battlefield. The name Theodore Roosevelt was now a kind of household word that connoted all of the supreme virtues of manliness.

Roosevelt wrote to the Secretary of War and requested an expeditious withdrawal of troops. For his boldness on this count Roosevelt received the plaudits of his men, but President McKinley was incensed when TR's indiscreet letter of request was published in newspapers. The incident made Roosevelt even more popular with the public since it showed his genuine concern for the welfare of American soldiers.

Roosevelt wanted badly to serve another term as governor, and he stoutly opposed any plans for his nomination as Vice President. As he told Platt, "I can't help feeling more and more that the Vice Presidency is not an office in which I could do anything and not an office in which a man still vigorous and not past middle life has much chance of doing anything." But the political cards were stacked against him.

Governor of New York

Upon his return to New York on August 15th Roosevelt learned that many Republican newspapers were enthusiastically supporting him for the gubernatorial nomination. He was hardly surprised, for he had expected that his military laurels would earn him high consideration from Republican leaders, who, as it happened, were in a bind. They needed a candidate who exemplified ability and honesty, since the incumbent Republican administration had been marred by corruption and incompetence. Top-ranking Republicans were worried about Roosevelt's uncompromising probity and independence of mind and judgment, but they were realistic enough to know that without him as candidate the party would surely be defeated. Reluctantly, therefore, they secured the nomination for him, convinced that he would win but afraid that he would not prove tractable.

Roosevelt campaigned aggressively and tirelessly, as though he knew that the governorship would serve as a stepping stone to higher office. In one of his first speeches he avowed: "First and foremost, this campaign is a campaign for good government, for good government both in the nation and the State... I shall try to administer the affairs of the State as to make each citizen a little prouder of the State..." Though he won the election by only 18,000 votes, he ran well ahead of the ticket. The Republican Party had been so discredited that only the magic name of Roosevelt could have rescued it from what had promised to be a humiliating defeat.

Roosevelt was a signally effective governor. In the short space of two years he initiated a program of reform and retrenchment that startled conservative party bosses as much as it elated New York taxpayers. He insisted that the canal system be run efficiently and honestly and he strove to tighten up what had always been a slipshod civil service system. He advocated the abolition of all forms of corporate privileges and called for a more equitable tax structure so that corporations would pay a proportionate share of the state's expenses. Whenever

possible, he chose to work within the party machinery since he was, after all, a loyal party man. However, when the interests of the party did not square with those of the public, he invariably supported the latter. For this reason his reform proposals antagonized party bosses who feared the party would lose the support of corporate wealth. Roosevelt himself had no quarrel with wealth as such, so long as it was honestly accumulated. But when, as so often happened, corporate wealth resulted from privilege and fraud, he adamantly opposed it.

As Governor Roosevelt favored the adoption of the State National Guard of the Krag bolt action rifle, so that state and federal armed forces would share a common type and caliber of weapon. In his annual gubernatorial message of 1900, he supported a system of organized rifle practice:

> ...It is very much to be wished that means could be taken to provide the most ample facilities for rifle practice....It would be a good thing if there were a rifle range in every village of this State...Moreover, it should be remembered that target practice proper is the alphabet of the soldier's marksmanship....In a battle the only bullets that count are those that hit.

It is ironic that Roosevelt's most notable single success—the adoption of a fair franchise tax—should have been responsible for his serving only a single term. Party leaders, especially Tom Platt, determined he be replaced by someone more compliant. Roosevelt's record entitled him to renomination, however, and it would have been most awkward for the bosses had they merely dropped him. The shrewd Platt understood that the combative reformer had to be "promoted" to some position outside the state. Owing to the strong influence of New York Republicans in the national party, it was not difficult to get Roosevelt in line for the Vice Presidential nomination on the William McKinley ticket.

Roosevelt wanted badly to serve another term as governor, and he stoutly opposed any plans for his nomination as Vice President. As he told Platt, "I can't help feeling more and more that the Vice Presidency is not an office in which I could do anything and not an office in which a man still vigorous and not past middle life has much chance of doing anything." But the political cards were stacked against him. When the Republican Convention in Philadelphia unanimously nominated him as Vice President, there was little he could do but accept graciously.

In the ensuing campaign between McKinley and the fiery William Jennings Bryan, the President took to his front porch in Canton, Ohio, and Roosevelt took to the stump. He campaigned fiercely and with great effect. In all he traveled over 21,000 miles and delivered a mountain of speeches. The election resulted in a massive victory for McKinley, who was eager for another term, the new Vice President, however, could envision only four lifeless years in an innocuous office. He winced at the thought of the ceremonial services he would be expected to carry out and the policies he would be unable to make. But only one life stood between Roosevelt and the Presidency and that life, McKinley's, was soon to be taken by a deranged anarchist.

Guns and Hunting, 1899-1901

The period from Roosevelt's appointment as Assistant Secretary of the Navy to his election as Vice President was unusually barren from the standpoint of hunting and the outdoors. Politics had become so all-engrossing that he had practically no time even for physical exercise. His body felt debilitated and some of his natural vigor abated. He complained that he could "get no exercise of any kind, and regret to say am becoming a most orthodox middle-aged individual. I could not climb up a butte at any speed to save my neck, and I should regard a bucking horse with unaffected horror…"

Nevertheless, guns and hunting were never far from Roosevelt's thoughts. On April 21, 1899, his seventh Winchester of record was shipped from the factory It was a Model 1894 rifle of the takedown style. The serial number was 61494, the barrel octagonal, the trigger plain, and the caliber

"The Bronco Buster" by Frederic Remington was presented to Colonel Roosevelt by his command when the Rough Riders disbanded in 1898. On the base was inscribed: Colonel Theodore Roosevelt/ From His Regiment at Camp Wikoff/September 15th 1898. "Nothing could possibly happen that would touch and please me as this.…The foundation of the regiment was the cow-puncher, and we have him here in bronze. No gift could have been so appropriate as this bronze.… This is something I shall hand down to my children, and I shall value it more than I do the weapons we carried through the campaign."

.30-30—by then a TR favorite, with its knockdown power like a "sledge hammer." Like many of his rifles, the magazine was 1/2, and the rear sight was a folding-leaf type, but for some reason deluxe stocks, his customary style of buckhorn sights, and the shotgun buttplate were not specified. Winchester factory records show Model 1894 #61494 to have been returned for rework on five occasions. The sedentary political life had not made Roosevelt any less demanding of full performance in his weaponry.

Late in November 1900, at the suggestion of fellow Boone and Crockett Club member, Dr. Alexander Lambert, Governor Roosevelt began to lay plans for a mountain lion hunt in Colorado— his first big game hunt in almost five years. In several letters to hunter Philip B. Stewart, TR covered every contingency, from footgear to sidearms to newspaper interference, seemingly enjoying the anticipation as much as he would the hunt itself:

> I am very anxious to get out for a mountain lion hunt with you, reaching Colorado Springs somewhere about the tenth of January, and spending a month on the hunt or indeed six weeks if necessary…Dr. Lambert says you can arrange for me. If so I shall be very glad. Will you write me the details and also especially what footgear to get. Can I not get it in Colorado? New York is a poor place to get winter footgear for the mountains, and my hunting of course has generally been done in the fall. I am all out of condition and you would have to make up your mind to my not being fit for very much for a week or ten days, but I would get into condition very soon. Shall I bring my thirty-thirty Winchester? Is it worth while bringing a revolver? I am no use with one and hate to carry it unless it is necessary. Shall I bring bedding with me, or had I better get that out in Colorado?…

Early in December Roosevelt was again in touch with Stewart: "I have a fur cap which draws down over the ears.…I gather that will be just the thing for one of those scampering rides." He also needed a leather coat large enough to allow for a 42" chest measurement and for a "sweater, flannel shirts, etc., etc.,…underneath." For mild weather TR planned to wear a corduroy jacket "or a venerable buckskin shirt which does not look well, because I have swelled considerably since I used to wear it seventeen years ago." For his feet he wanted "German socks and articles, to fit a size seven."

"Upon my word," he jubilantly wrote Stewart in December, "I feel like a boy again and am just crazy to get out." He informed Stewart that he had "one good qualification as a hunter. I am willing to work steadily for a limited amount of game. If we have any luck I suppose in time we are sure to get some mountain lion or something, and if so I shall be quite content…"

Mountain Lions in Colorado

Roosevelt arrived in Colorado Springs on January 10th, vibrant and full of excitement. It seemed as if mere presence in the West had restored his spirit and quickened his vigor. He had hunted mountain lion before, but never to his complete satisfaction. This time, perhaps because he was so eager, he shot twelve, plus four bobcats. The biggest lion, eight feet long and weighing 227 pounds, had a 9-5/16 x 6-7/16 skull, the Boone and Crockett World's Record for the species for the next 65 years, which still ranks in the top 15 cougars of all-time. Both Roosevelt and his guide, John B. Goff, published recollections of their Colorado mountain adventure. TR wrote a trenchant chapter on the hunt in his *Outdoor Pastimes of an American Hunter* (1905). It ranks among his finest essays on the pursuit of big game.

Goff's account of the lion hunt was just as incisive, and was full of praise for Roosevelt's hunting skills and courage. Particularly telling was Goff's narration of the first kill. The hounds had forced the lion up a tree:

> …When we got to within thirty or forty yards of where the animal was located he jumped from

OPPOSITE: As Vice President, TR spent three weeks hunting in the company of John Goff. Artist Charles M. Russell is said to have based this 1905 depiction of a Roosevelt hunting experience, "In the Mountains" on a description of an actual hunt.

GIFT OF C.R. SMITH, MONTANA HISTORICAL SOCIETY MUSEUM, HELENA

McKinley-Roosevelt campaign buttons from 1900.

© BETTMAN/CORBIS

the tree and ran about 150 yards, when the fighters (composed of two dogs, each of one-half bull and one-half shepherd extraction, and one dog one-half bloodhound, three in all) overtook the lion. They were having a rough-and-tumble fight, with the honors about even, when we came up. In order to save the dogs—for they were being bitten and scratched up horribly and it was too risky to shoot—the colonel ran into the thick of the fight and stabbed the lion behind the fore-leg. He aimed for the handiest part of the body exposed, although in his subsequent exploits of this nature he usually got the heart.

This act on the part of Colonel Roosevelt drew forth our heartiest admiration, and we considered him a hero at once. This is something which, while I would do myself in a close emergency, yet it is a feature of lion hunting which I would not care to make a practice of. It is dangerous work at best, for in the position in which it is necessary to meet the foe, the latter could easily lift a paw and strike him in the face, or catch him in the leg or arm with its teeth. It is usually kept too busy with the dogs to spring, even if, as would be rare, it were so inclined. There has been much very tiresome stuffy written for the daily press about this stabbing work of the governor's. Of course no sportsman has gulped it

down without making due allowance for the idiots who framed it, or for the editors who passed on it, but, while I have killed over 300 lions myself, and have been among them for nearly twenty years, yet I would not care to tackle them in the off-hand, fearless manner in which the colonel did on this trip.

Roosevelt returned to the East in March, delighted with the results of his lion hunt. He wrote fellow Boone and Crockett Club member, naturalist, and big game hunter Frederick C. Selous about his experience:

I have just returned from five weeks of a delightful holiday in the northwestern part of Colorado after cougar and lynx. The lynx came in incidentally when we picked up their trail at the end of a day in which we had not come across any cougar. The biggest one I got weighed 39 pounds. Of the cougar I killed 12 and measured and weighed them all. My hunter, John God, carried a steel yard instead of a rifle in his scabbard and I had a tape. I measured between uprights—that is, in a straight line from the tip of the nose to the tip of the tail when the beast was stretched out. I did this because I had heard such marvellous tales of the weight and length of these mountain lions (as the beasts are most inappropriately termed). They were very variable in size. Full grown females varied from 80 to 135 pounds in weight and from six feet to seven feet in length. The three big males I shot were from seven feet six to eight feet and from 160 to 227 pounds. The last I think was as big a cougar as can often be found. We hunted on horseback and the great interest (aside from the delight of the long rides through the brilliant winter weather over the snow-clad plains and among the mountains) was to see the dogs work. My part was wholly insignificant. If the animal was treed I shot it. If, as four times happened, the dogs got it on the ground, there was a savage worry and I ended the struggle with the knife as soon as possible to save the pack. They were quite competent to kill the cougar by themselves, but always received a good deal of damage, everyone of them being cut up at some time or other. There were eight hounds and four fighters, two of the latter being killed. The cougar certainly cannot be as formidable an opponent as the jaguar or leopard. It hardly ever charges either man or dog, simply clawing and biting when it is attacked. Preposterous fables are told about it…

By the way, I was in the winter range of the deer and I have never seen them so numerous. They were all black tail. Every day I saw scores and some days hundreds. There were also elk. I did not shoot either deer or elk, of course, but I saw elk antlers shot last fall ranging from 52 to *56* inches in length. I think you were a few years ahead of time (although only a very few years) when you stated that already bigger antlers could be secured in Hungary than in the Rockies…

The lion skulls acquired on that hunt were sent to the Smithsonian Institution. Naturalists considered them a major contribution to scientific knowledge. Roosevelt, a competent naturalist himself, was pleased by such distinguished critical acclaim, but felt even more elated by the overall gratification he derived from the hunt itself. It was just the right combination of outdoor challenge and achievement to break the long hiatus from big game hunting and to precede his inauguration as Vice President.

The Vice Presidency

Inauguration day went smoothly for President McKinley but not for Vice President Roosevelt. He was still disquieted by the contemplation of the four years of inaction and inanition that he thought lay ahead. He had decided to study "law with a view to seeing if I cannot go into practice as a lawyer when my term as Vice President comes to an end." For five days he presided over the Senate, which met to approve McKinley's major appointments. Congress then adjourned until December, and Roosevelt returned home to Oyster Bay He spent the spring and summer with his family, riding, picnicking, and target shooting.

In August, 1901, he was invited to participate in the twenty-fifth anniversary of Colorado statehood. Naturally he couldn't resist the chance for more hunting. "Do you think it would be possible," he wrote his friend Philip B. Stewart, "to get two or three days' coyote and wolf hunting with…greyhounds after the celebration is over or a week of hunting, if we can't get a wolf in three days?…I know the weather will be hot and I suppose it will be a little rough on the dogs, but I may not get another chance to do any wolf coursing, and I am particularly anxious to do it…" From August 5th to 8th TR and Stewart hunted together. Not much could be done in four days, but it was a good holiday, capped by a fishing trip on the White River. A week later the Vice President was again back at Sagamore Hill.

Exactly three weeks later, on September 6, while enjoying the annual outing of the Fish and Game League near Isle laMotte in Lake Champlain, Roosevelt received a shocking message from Buffalo: President McKinley had been shot by an anarchist. The Vice President immediately rushed to Buffalo, where he was informed that McKinley's condition had improved. To prevent a national panic and to reassure the nation there was no danger, TR left Buffalo for the Adirondacks to rejoin his family On the afternoon of September 13th, he climbed Mt. Marcy, and as he descended a messenger met him with the tragic telegram: "The President appears to be dying and members of the Cabinet in Buffalo think you should lose no time in coming." The nearest railroad station was 50 miles from the lodge, so Roosevelt did not arrive there until 5:30 a.m. He was met by his personal secretary, William Loeb, Jr., who apprised him of the situation. McKinley had died at 2 a.m. Theodore Roosevelt was now President of the United States. ❧

CHAPTER 7

The Reformer Enters the White House

President Roosevelt assumed the responsibilities of his office with his accustomed iron determination: He would govern the country judiciously and in the interests of all Americans. He was ever mindful of the tragic and fateful circumstance that had catapulted him into the White House. His first concern was to assure the nation that his administration would carry on the policies of McKinley, and that the assassination, however dreadful, would in no way obstruct the normal functioning of the national government. He also wanted to assure Congress that his legislative proposals would not deviate substantially from those of his predecessor. Thus, his first message to Congress, on December 5, 1901, was conservative, eclectic, and purposely ambiguous.

Despite Roosevelt's concerted efforts to pass himself off as a kind of carbon copy of McKinley, both he and numerous Republican leaders knew otherwise. In his heart he realized that his brand of Republicanism was infinitely more liberal than McKinley's and that of most Republican policy-makers. Ranking party-members were sure from the start of Roosevelt's administration that he had a mind of his own and would not accept the role of a rubber stamp. Industrial titans, bankers, and financiers were worried that the new President would not be as mindful of the interests of big business as McKinley had been. These skeptics had good reason to harbor such fears. Roosevelt was no McKinley. His entire political career had unmistakably

At Yosemite National Park, California, in the spring of 1903. TR is front and center, his secretary William Loeb, Jr. is second from the right, and naturalist John Muir stands to the right of TR.

THEODORE ROOSEVELT COLLECTION, HARVARD COLLEGE LIBRARY

Elk, buffalo, bear, and moose trophies in the White House dining room. The original photograph was reproduced in *Outdoor Pastimes of an American Hunter* in 1905.

THEODORE ROOSEVELT COLLECTION, HARVARD COLLEGE LIBRARY

Admiring cartoon from the *Brooklyn Eagle*, "Two views of the President— As He Isn't and As He Is."

THEODORE ROOSEVELT COLLECTION, HARVARD COLLEGE LIBRARY

demonstrated that he followed his own instincts and judgments.

"When I became President," Roosevelt wrote, "the question as to the method by which the United States government was to control the corporations was not yet important. The absolute vital question was whether the government had power to control them at all." This was an historically solid observation. Mighty corporations had evolved into mammoth trusts so powerful and influential as to be beyond the control of the government itself. In fact, it was industrial and financial capitalism that dictated to government, dominated both major parties and mercilessly exploited the economic system. Farmers and factory workers were grossly underpaid and overworked,

child labor was rampant, labor unions were weak and unrecognized and the legitimate demands of consumers for pure food and drugs were disregarded. Escalating public indignation and the mounting literature of exposure by a host of muckraking journalists created a climate for reform. But this in itself was not enough. Reform required political action, and the latter a bold spokesman and initiator. It fell to Roosevelt to be the political agent for the "forgotten American." And though he was no radical, no Eugene V. Debs, say, his avowed purpose was to give all interests and groups a Square Deal, a fair shake. To do that, he had perforce to strike out against the "malefactors of great wealth."

At the outset of his administration, he pressed for the formation of a Bureau of Corporations within the newly created Department of Commerce and Labor, to provide for the inspection of corporate activity. He also endorsed a new law that increased the Attorney General's power to expedite antitrust proceedings. Joseph Pulitzer, the distinguished journalist, said of TR's early attempts to bring big business under the pale of the law,

> ...if he had done nothing else except to start the great machinery of the government and the most powerful force and majesty of the law in the direction of prosecuting these great offenders, he would have been entitled to the greatest credit for the greatest service to the nation.

As Roosevelt began to battle the trusts, a major strike by the United Mine Workers shut down the entire anthracite coal industry. The strike came in May 1902, when John Mitchell, head of the UMW, launched a new battle for increased wages for his men. Working conditions in the mines were poor, the hours were long, and much of the machinery was antiquated and unsafe. The mine operators, however, led by the arrogant George F. Barr, refused to agree to a raise or to recognize the miners' union. In the early spring, the price of coal began to rise, and by early summer violence was reported in some of the mining areas. By October many schools were forced to close, and in large urban areas, the price of coal had risen to over ten times the prestrike price. The country was beginning to fear the discomforts of a winter without coal.

Roosevelt kept close tabs on the progress of the strike and repeatedly urged the mine operators to negotiate with the union. They refused. Barr in particular infuriated the President by his abrasive personality and his indifference to national needs and to the grievances of the mine workers. With winter approaching and the mine owners opposed to any solution outside of total surrender by the UMW, Roosevelt struck swiftly and dramatically. He avowed that unless the mine owners agreed to arbitration of the dispute, he would seize the mines and run them in receivership. The owners were sufficiently intimidated to accede to arbitration. By boldly threatening governmental intervention and by his subtle use of restraint, Roosevelt prevented a

major disaster. Above all, he had proved to a grateful public that the government could act justly and disinterestedly in disputes between labor and management. In this instance he personally had sided neither with labor nor management. Rather he was on the side of justice and the public interest.

The Teddy Bear

In November 1902, with the coal strike behind him, Roosevelt was ready for a holiday. He decided on a bear hunting trip in Mississippi—for pleasure, of course, but for political reasons as well. He wanted to visit the Southern states to line up delegates in his bid to secure the nomination to the Presidency in 1904. He also wished to reaffirm his position against the political disenfranchisement and segregation of Negroes.

Journeying through the South in mid-November, Roosevelt and several prominent political figures went on a bear hunt in the Mississippi Delta near Smedes. An ex-slave and experienced bear hunter, Holt Collier, served as guide. The Southern politicians were keenly anxious for the President to shoot a bear, and when the hunting did not produce one they were highly upset. Collier was

"Roosevelt's Big Game" published by the *New York Herald*. The rifle was a Winchester lever action; the Herald's cartoonist had done his homework well.

> "There were plenty of bears, and if I had gone alone or with one companion I would have gotten one or two. But my kind hosts, with the best of intentions, insisted upon turning the affair into a cross between a hunt and a picnic, which always results in a failure for the hunt and usually in a failure for the picnic."

so intent on providing the President with a trophy for the White House that he spent one day of the hunt tracking down and capturing an old and lame bear. He brought it into camp bound in ropes and surrounded by snarling dogs. Collier urged the President to shoot it, but Roosevelt bluntly refused. Newspapers circulated the story, and a cartoonist for the Washington *Evening Star* drew a sketch that showed Roosevelt disdainfully declining to shoot a small, helpless cub bound with ropes.

The *Star* cartoon started the fad of associating bears with the President. Postcards, toys, advertisements, and even campaign buttons began featuring the Roosevelt bear. Morris Michtom, a candy store owner in Brooklyn, saw the cartoon and was inspired to create a stuffed bear that he placed in his store with the label, "Teddy's Bear." It was an instant success, and he wrote the President asking permission to sell the toy with his name. A year later Michtom started the Ideal Toy Company, which within a few years became a leading manufacturer of the Teddy Bear and other toys. The German firm of Steiff also got into the act, manufacturing a Teddy Bear late in 1902 and sending its first shipment to America in 1903.

The Mississippi hunt left Roosevelt altogether unsatisfied: "I have just had a most unsatisfactory experience in a bear hunt in Mississippi," he wrote to his friend Philip B. Stewart:

> There were plenty of bears, and if I had gone alone or with one companion I would have gotten one or two. But my kind hosts, with the best of intentions, insisted upon turning the affair into a cross between a hunt and a picnic, which always results in a failure for the hunt and usually in a failure for the picnic. On this occasion, as a picnic it was pleasant enough, but as a hunt simply exasperating, and I never got a shot. Naturally the comic press jumped at the failure and have done a good deal of laughing over it… As it was, I had to compromise on taking three thoroughly reputable newspapermen

to the station from which I got off and letting them occasionally come out to visit the camps; and even under these circumstances it was literally only by the use of guards armed with shotguns that I prevented the yellow journal men from coming along too. These same papers, having in vain tried to get into the camp and accompany us with kodaks, etc., turned around and have been industriously insisting that I had been trying to advertise the hunt and was ostentatiously endeavoring to attract public attention.

Naval Gunnery

Aside from a brief boar hunt in Newport, New Hampshire, on August 29, and the disappointing Mississippi "Teddy Bear" trip of November, the President had no time for hunting in 1902. Yet he did have a few opportunities for target practice at Oyster Bay and even managed to fire some naval guns on board the *Mayflower* early in August.

His interest in naval armament came from both practical and historical standpoints—historical because of his classic *The Naval War of 1812* (1882), and practical because of his former office of Assistant Secretary of the Navy and now as President. As Assistant Secretary Roosevelt had inspected ships, reviewed gunnery practice techniques, and proposed marksmanship competition using the big deck guns. As President he encouraged improved naval armaments and marksmanship, studied and recommended shell sizes for arming certain ships, and thoroughly inspected naval vessels on many occasions. He was fond of battleships, and he favored heavy caliber guns (10-, 12-, and 14-inch) capable of hits at long ranges (three to four miles). Both as Assistant Secretary of the Navy and as President, he exerted every effort to build up the navy and make it a more effective instrument of national power. He subscribed fully to Captain Alfred T. Mahan's opinions on the importance of sea power

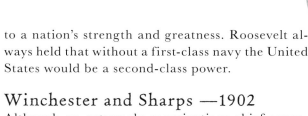

to a nation's strength and greatness. Roosevelt always held that without a first-class navy the United States would be a second-class power.

Winchester and Sharps —1902

Although an extremely conscientious chief executive, Roosevelt did not let his official duties completely shut out his hunting and shooting interests. He carried on a voluminous correspondence with big game hunters, many of whom he knew intimately and had been in touch with since the 1880s. His boyhood passion for hunting books was still strong. Late at night he regularly read books on hunting and adventure. He also, after a fashion, kept up with the latest developments in the field of natural history. And, as President, he added to his already sizable collection of hunting rifles.

Fittingly, the first of these was a Winchester, which no doubt delighted the Company. In March 1902, TR's eighth Winchester was shipped to him from the factory. It was a Model 1886, serial #125422, of the takedown type, custom made, with several special features. The Winchester ledgers noted:

.45- caliber; 22" barrel; 1/2 magazine; fancy pistol grip; shotgun butt carved in style "F"; Lyman rear and front sights, flat top sporting rear sight, not extra light. [Returned for rework eight times]

The big caliber, the 1/2 magazine, the fancy pistol grip stock, the shotgun butt and the special sights were all consistent with the essential characteristics of most of TR's earlier Winchesters. One new feature was an inlaid silver plaque on the left side of the buttstock, with applied in blue enamel (in old English)—TR—an unusual decorative treatment. It is doubtful the President much used

this superb example of gun craftsmanship. Except for the 1909-10 African trip, Roosevelt was about done with shooting the big-bore guns. The .30 caliber, "the ace," had caught his fancy for the big game of North America. And when he hunted bear in Mississippi, his field rifle was the .30-30 Model 1894, serial #15659.

In October 1907, the President ordered from Winchester two exact duplicates of the takedown Model 1886,

…with the exception that on a silver plate on the stock of one I wish the initials "C.M." and on the similar plate on the other, the initials "H.M." Have these two exact duplicates and one ordinary gun of the same model sent to Mr. Clive Metcalf, Wilczinski, Mississippi. Send 200 cartridges, soft-nosed bullets, for the guns at the same time. Let me know when you send them, and be sure that there is no mistake, but that two exact duplicates of my gun,

ABOVE: The Winchester factory shipped this deluxe Model 1886 takedown rifle in March 1902. TR's eighth Winchester of record was a .45-70 caliber, serial #125422, Lyman marked front sight, 22" barrel, and on the left side of the buttstock was an inlaid silver plaque enameled in blue letters – TR.

THEODORE ROOSEVELT
BIRTHPLACE COLLECTION

INSET: Berryman's cartoon from the November 14, 1902, *Washington Evening Star* launched the Teddy Bear fad. The entire affair was the result of the President's sportsmanship as a hunter and outdoorsman.

McILHENNY CO. ARCHIVES

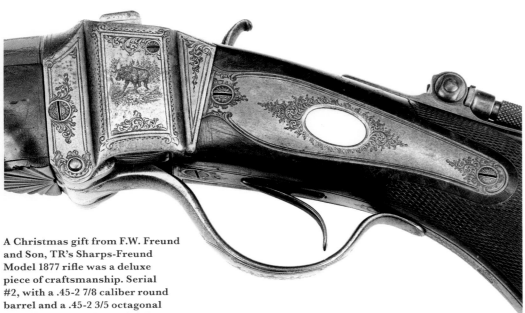

A Christmas gift from F.W. Freund and Son, TR's Sharps-Freund Model 1877 rifle was a deluxe piece of craftsmanship. Serial #2, with a .45-2 7/8 caliber round barrel and a .45-2 3/5 octagonal exchange barrel, Freund sights, select walnut checkered pistol grip stocks, and profuse engraving (by L.D. Nimschke). Inlaid on the left sideplate was a gold oval. Freund's use of a peep sight was a mistake but the President still considered his present "a beauty." A similar deluxe, custom Sharps Model 1877, serial #1, was also presented to TR by Freund.

ROOSEVELT NATIONAL PARK,
MEDORA, NORTH DAKOTA,
GIFT OF HAROLD SCHAFER

save for the initialing on the plate, which is to be as above, and one ordinary stock gun of the same model, are sent...

These rifles, a gift from the President, were shipped by Winchester, as directed a few weeks later. Unfortunately, their serial numbers and whereabouts today are unknown. The Metcalfs had hosted a second Mississippi bear hunt for Roosevelt in 1907, and in appreciation they and guide Holt Collier received the three rifles with the compliments of the President.

In December, 1902, the President was given a spectacular custom-built Sharp rifle by one of his admirers, the crack frontier gunsmith F.W. Freund. The gun was a Model 1877 Sharps single shot of .45-2 7/8 caliber, with an extra barrel chambered for the .45-2 3/5 cartridge. All work was in the finest style, and the serial was number 2. Freund, who then lived in Jersey City, had ordered special embellishments by the renowned Louis D. Nimschke, the same craftsman who had engraved TR's fancy Colt .44-40 six-shooter serial number 92248 some 19 years before.

On White House stationery Roosevelt wrote Freund:

December 26, 1902

My dear Mr. Freund:

I thank you cordially, and your son for the rifle. It is a beauty. Where can I get some cartridges for it? Give my special regards to your son, my comrade of the Spanish War. I am delighted to learn he was on the Iowa. As you know I have always used a slight modification of your sights.

Though not ordered by TR, or made to his exact specifications, the design and construction of the Sharps rifle was in keeping with his preferences in arms, particularly in the fine quality and deluxe workmanship. Sharps collectors consider the rifle as one of the finest ever made, appropriate indeed for a President so expert in the knowledge and use of firearms.

The President's Pistols

Roosevelt's self-sufficiency was perhaps the salient trait of his character. As New York Police Commissioner he sometimes carried a blackjack while out on midnight rounds. As President of the United States, he not only occasionally had a blackjack on his person, he carried his own revolver. Charles W. Eliot, President of Harvard University, related an incident when the President was so armed:

Theodore Roosevelt while he was President of the United States, attended the Harvard Commencement in 1902. He reached my house on the morning of the Commencement, shortly before the academic procession was to form in the College Yard. When I asked him what I could do for him, he replied, "I must clean up before I go down to Massachusetts Hall." I showed him to a chamber and followed him in, that I might tell him where the bathroom was. He hastily threw his coat and waistcoat on the bed, and drew from his hip pocket a good-sized pistol which he laid on the dressing-table. President

McKinley had been assassinated in the previous September. When I asked if he habitually carried a revolver, he replied, "Yes, when I am going into public places. I should have some chance of shooting the assassin before he could shoot me, if he were near me."

TR's valet, James Amos, also remembered the President's readiness for any emergency,

Shortly after Mr. Roosevelt's inauguration he went to Yale University in New Haven, to receive a degree, I think. Of course there was great curiosity to see the new President and a great pressure of crowds everywhere. Mr. George B. Cortelyou, who had been President McKinley's secretary and now held a similar position with Mr. Roosevelt, was very nervous because of the President's apparent lack of thought about exposing himself. He had just had one harrowing experience and he did not want to see it repeated. He then suggested to the President that he refrain from shaking hands at the public reception to be given in his honor in New Haven. President McKinley had been shot by a man offering his hand at such a reception. But Mr. Roosevelt replied that he feared he could not do that, because it might be a great disappointment to the people and might tend to bring him under the charge of cowardice if he carried precaution against attack to such an extent. He added that the official precautions for protecting him were under the direction of William I.

Burns, in whom he had the greatest confidence, and that he believed these sufficient.

But he took one precaution. While President he often went armed. I have in my home now a large revolver which Mr. Roosevelt placed at the side of his bed every night in the White House. It was given me by Mrs. Roosevelt after his death. He had another smaller weapon which he carried with him on his trips.

The "large revolver" mentioned by Amos was a Smith & Wesson Hand Ejector New Century Model, serial number 6640. Records of the S&W factory show this pistol was manufactured and shipped in 1912 to the Remington Arms-UMC Company. Thus the President's bedside protector was not the New Century handgun that was eventually given to Amos. The actual revolver is lost. Roosevelt's "smaller weapon" was probably an S&W Safety Hammerless, which has also disappeared.

A Deluxe Colt Automatic Pistol

From the batch of the first 100 of Colt's Model 1902 Military semi-automatic pistol, President Roosevelt was presented with a custom example, gold inlaid with the initials TR. Bearing serial number 14941 (the series began with 14999, and counted backwards), the TR pistol was a gift from the Colt factory. Factory ledgers note the caliber as .38, with a 6-inch barrel, blued finish, TR initials gold inlaid, stocks not listed, with shipment to Frank Julian Price, address not noted, sent March 1, 1903; one gun in shipment.

A blackjack known to have occasionally been carried by TR while President.

THEODORE ROOSEVELT'S BLACKJACK
CARRIED BY HIM WHILE PRESIDENT
OF THE UNITED STATES 1901 - 1909

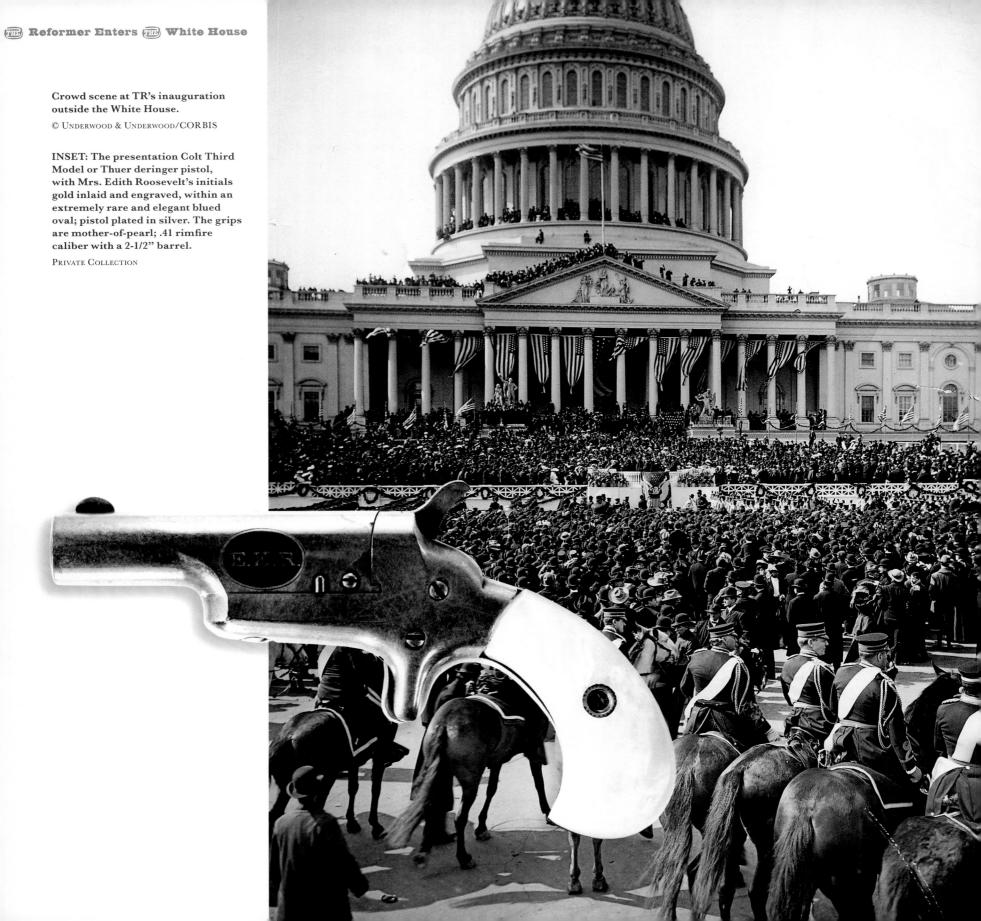

Crowd scene at TR's inauguration outside the White House.

© Underwood & Underwood/CORBIS

INSET: The presentation Colt Third Model or Thuer deringer pistol, with Mrs. Edith Roosevelt's initials gold inlaid and engraved, within an extremely rare and elegant blued oval; pistol plated in silver. The grips are mother-of-pearl; .41 rimfire caliber with a 2-1/2" barrel.

Private Collection

Price was an attorney, who practiced law at an office in New York City, at 33 Pine Street, near Wall Street. A March 4, 1903 letter from TR, to Price, thanks him for the pistol, and asks about the proper cartridge. In his response, on March 8, Attorney Price indicated that the cartridges are "either the 38 calibre Automatic Colt or the 38 calibre Rimless Smokeless."

The Colt Model 1902 was sold at an October 17th-18th, 1993 auction, with an attachable skeleton steel and leather shoulder stock doubling as a holster. Roosevelt's delight in the present was reflected in his March 4th letter: "I shall use it at the first opportunity."

Presentation Arms from TR and His Wife

TR and his wife were uncommonly generous. Amos' revolver is an example of such generosity; he was also presented the Badlands Model 1873 Winchester rifle (in 1906, while TR was in the White House), and at the same time was given the pearl gripped Single Action Colt serial number 92267. John Washburn, son of the rector of the church the Roosevelts attended in Oyster Bay, was presented the Model 1876 Winchester carbine serial number 45704 on his 21st birthday in July 1904. TR had given Sylvane Ferris the Sharps Borchardt .40-2 5/8 rifle sometime in the 1880s, probably when he was replacing the Sharps and Webley rifles with Winchester repeaters. Still another Winchester, a superbly engraved and plated Model 1894 carbine, serial number 53614, was reportedly a gift from Mrs. Roosevelt to an Oyster Bay neighbor. A.W. & C. Scott market gun was a gift to a caretaker on the Sagamore Hill estate. A Colt Third Model or Thuer deringer pistol is deserving of special attention. Marked with serial number 19959, the left side of the barrel is gold inlaid with an EKR monogram, the initials of Edith Kermit Roosevelt. According to a letter from Stanley Bullock, the pistol was presented to him by Mrs. Roosevelt. Quoting a Bullock letter of July 13, 1949:

[President Roosevelt had invited] cattlemen and cowpunchers to ride in the inaugural parade [January 20th 1905]. I was one of 'em. We shipped our saddle horses and outfits from Deadwood [South Dakota] and all went together on a special sleeper to Washington....We were quite an attraction and had a hell of a time. Rode in the parade, roped a policeman and acted like the Easterners expected us to. Teddy had all of us up to the White House for a reception immediately after the parade. A few days later I was a luncheon guest of the Roosevelt family and Mrs. Roosevelt gave me that little gun as a memento of the occasion. The initials, E.K.R., on the gun are hers...

Though more than half of Theodore Roosevelt's firearms remained in the possession of the family at his death, about a dozen had, over the years, been given to friends by TR and his wife.

Trouble and Achievement in the Americas

Roosevelt was as bold and domineering in foreign affairs as he was in domestic. At the time he became President, the United States, thanks in large measure to the Spanish-American War, was a rising world power. The annexation of Hawaii and then of the Philippines had given the nation an economic stake in the Far East. In the Caribbean, American interests and influence were unrivaled. Roosevelt believed that America's international interests would remain intact so long as the nation played a larger role in world affairs. At all costs the nation must be willing to protect what belonged to it and be ready to assert its authority whenever national security seemed in jeopardy.

Because the United States had extensive interests in the Caribbean and the Pacific, many Americans, including Roosevelt, believed that a canal across Central America would materially enhance trade as well as bolster the national defense. The time it took a naval vessel to sail from the Atlantic to

"[President Roosevelt had invited] cattlemen and cowpunchers to ride in the inaugural parade... I was one of 'em. We shipped our saddle horses and outfits from Deadwood and all went together on a special sleeper to Washington.... We were quite an attraction and had a hell of a time... A few days later I was a luncheon guest of the Roosevelt family and Mrs. Roosevelt gave me that little gun as a memento of the occasion. The initials, E.K.R., on the gun are hers..."

200 pages to Congress and the debate would be going on yet, but I took the Canal Zone and let Congress debate; and while the debate goes on the canal does also."

The chronic financial instability of many Caribbean republics caused Roosevelt grave concern that it might invite the intervention of creditor European nations. To forestall this danger, he announced to Congress that the United States would intervene in the internal affairs of those republics in the Caribbean whose policies seemed so reckless or so irresponsible as to invite intervention by some European power. His first opportunity to invoke the so-called Roosevelt Corollary to the Monroe Doctrine came when the Dominican Republic failed to pay its debts to Europe. With the grudging approval of the Dominicans, the United States stepped in, took control over the customs receipts and arranged for the payment of debts through American bankers.

Yosemite and the Yellowstone

Early in 1903 Roosevelt planned a rather unusual hunting trip. He proposed that John Goff and his hunting dogs be allowed in Yellowstone Park "for the business of killing out some of the mountain lions." If the President could find the time, he would try to get "a week with him myself" Roosevelt and Goff would scrupulously "obey...the regulations of the Park and...not a shot shall be fired excepting in the presence of one of the proper government officials." However, TR had some misgivings that the hunt might arouse public protest and adverse newspaper publicity:

> ...I am still wholly at sea as to whether I can take that trip or not. Secretary [of State] Root is afraid that a false impression might get out if I killed anything in the Park, even though it was killed, as of course would be the case, strictly under Park regulations, and though it was only a mountain lion—that is, an animal of the kind you are endeavoring to thin out.

Mrs. Roosevelt presented this Smith & Wesson Hand Ejector New Century Model and holster to TR's valet, James Amos, in 1919. Serial #6640; .44 S&W Special Caliber; 6-1/2" barrel.

THEODORE ROOSEVELT BIRTHPLACE COLLECTION

OPPOSITE: Caricature of TR circa 1902.

© DAVID J. & JANICE L. FRENT COLLECTION/CORBIS

the Pacific, or vice versa, by the long route around South America had kept the idea of an isthmian canal alive for over half a century. Roosevelt began pressing for the canal's realization. The United States in 1903 negotiated with Colombia to build a canal through Panama (which belonged to Colombia) for a cash payment of $10 million and a yearly payment of $250,000. The Colombian government, upon reconsideration, refused to ratify the treaty, sending Roosevelt into a rage. Following a complex and somewhat bizarre chain of intrigue and subterfuge, a revolution broke out in Panama and independence from Colombia was easily achieved. The United States had unofficially but effectively aided the Panamanian rebels, and with unseemly haste, a treaty between the U.S. and the new republic of Panama was signed to build a canal on the same terms that had earlier been extended to Colombia. Roosevelt's role in the whole affair was scarcely above reproach. But, as he put it, "If I had followed traditional conservative methods I should have submitted a dignified state paper of probably

A TRUE AMERICAN ROUGH RIDER.

"Nothing could be more definite and emphatic than Mr. Roosevelt's reaffirmation of the Monroe doctrine   It is, he reminds the world, a declaration that there must be no territorial aggrandizement by a non-American power at the expense of any American power on American soil."—*Dail's paper.*

"If I had followed traditional conservative methods I should have submitted a dignified state paper of probably 200 pages to Congress and the debate would be going on yet, but I took the Canal Zone and let Congress debate; and while the debate goes on the canal does also."

Now I have thought of this: Would it be possible, starting from within the Park, to go just outside the border and kill any mountain lions? Could you send a good man to explore right across the border and see if you could not get some located? Can you have this done at once and let me know what the chances are? If favorable, perhaps I might take a week or two traveling around the Park first, just for the fun of seeing everything — of visiting the canyon in winter and the geysers in winter, and seeing the lake, etc.; and then go off for a week or ten days' hunt in the mountain-lion country just outside. Do let me know about this, Major. I know if anyone can put the thing through you can. If I can fix it all right I will have Johnny Goff and his dogs get in ahead of me, and probably shall send you my rifle in advance so as to avoid any talk of my taking it with me.

The great likelihood of bad publicity and public misunderstanding ultimately caused the President to cancel plans for the Yellowstone hunt. Instead, he camped first at Yosemite with his friend John Muir and undertook an extensive tour of Yellowstone with the noted naturalist, John Burroughs. In mid-April, TR wrote a detailed letter on the Yellowstone vacation to naturalist and fellow Boone and Crockett Club member, Clinton Hart Merriam. It illustrates Roosevelt's acute powers of observation and profound concern for the preservation of wildlife:

I have had a most interesting trip and every opportunity of observing the game, which is certainly more plentiful than when I was last in the Park, twelve years ago. The elk far outnumber all the other animals....The elk in the southern half of the Park winter outside of it to the south, chiefly in Jackson's Hole, and of them I know little but those in the northern half of the Park winter within its borders and I have spent the last eight days among them. From very careful estimates, based for instance on actually counting the individuals in several bands, I am convinced that there are at least fifteen thousand of these elk which stay permanently within the Park. In one day I saw between three and four thousand. But an insignificant number of them are killed by hunters, so as regards them there has been no killing off of the big bulls by sportsmen. There are rather too many for the winter feed, and so it is evident, from the carcasses I have seen, that a somewhat larger proportion than is normal dies, especially among the yearlings.

The cougars are their only enemies, and in many places these big cats, which are quite numerous, are at this season living purely on the elk, killing yearlings and an occasional cow; this does no damage, but around the hot springs the cougars are killing deer, antelope and sheep, and in this neighborhood they should certainly exterminated....The old bulls are now found by themselves in loose parties of from ten to fifty, for the most part high up the mountains. Of course an occasional big bull and more often a two-year-old or three-year-old is found with the great bands of cows and yearlings. Most of the elk we found dead had succumbed to the deep snow, cold, or starvation; two, a bull and a cow, had died from the scab; the others, yearlings with one or two cows, had been killed by cougars...

Evidently the elk had spent the winter in the bottoms of the valleys, in great bands, browsing on the quaking asp, the willows, and the lower limbs of the conifers. They then rarely drank, eating snow instead. Where there was open water, however—as by beaver dams— they drank regularly. Sometimes they would leave the valleys and feed on the side hills nearby during the daytime. At present they have moved high up the mountain side, keeping for the most part above the line of the retreating

FOLLOWING PAGE: TR stands with naturalist John Muir on Glacier Point above Yosemite Valley in California, May 1903. During the trip, Roosevelt was challenged by Muir on hunting. "Mr. Roosevelt," Muir asked, "when are you going to get beyond the boyishness of killing things?" Whatever TR responded is unknown to history.

© BETTMAN/CORBIS

Kermit's Springfield Sporter

Kermit and Theodore Jr. both had custom-built Springfield Sporters for their hunting expeditions. Both rifles were influenced by the design and construction of their father's Sporter, #6000. Although the writer has yet to examine that of TR Jr., Kermit's rifle is pictured, in detail. The only visible serial number is the digit 2 on the left side of the frame. The number 47528 is stamped on the wood, on the grip behind the triggerguard strap and near the case-hardened and engraved pistol grip cap. The steel buttplate is exquisitely checkered, and has a trapdoor at its center.

On the bottom of the triggerguard, likely engraved and gold inlaid by Rudolph J. Kornbrath, is a superb KR monogram with accompanying scrolls. The caliber is .30-06, the barrel length 24", and the top of the barrel is inscribed with the maker's name: R.G. OWEN, SAUQUOIT N.Y. Among the hunters known to the author as Owen clients is Electra Havemeyer Webb, whose .30-06 rifle, used on innumerable hunts in North America, is in the Shelburne Museum, Shelburne, Vermont. Several trophies taken in her hunts are displayed in the Adirondack style lodge at the Museum.

A feature of this rifle is the bracket mounted on each side of the forend, which folds out to engage a convenient tree or other support, to assist in placing the best possible shot.

The floorplate is inscribed:

KERMIT ROOSEVELT'S
Custom Springfield Sporting Rifle, Serial No. 2
With Which He Hunted Marco Polo Sheep, Ibex
The Giant Panda, Whitetail Deer, and other Species
c. 1915 to 1939
East of the Sun and West of the Moon

The hunting experience of Theodore Roosevelt Jr., was revealed in a letter he sent to R.F. Riggs, Western Cartridge Company, East Alton, Illinois, in answer to a query about using a statement from TR Jr. in company advertising. The quotation he sent reads as follows:

> During the trip, the rifle I used was my .375 Hoffmann. It is an excellent weapon, good at all ranges and for all kinds of game. With it I killed a very slightly wounded rhinoceros with one shot. The ammunition I used was made by the Western Cartridge Company. For small game a 235 grain bullet answered the purposes excellently, and for the larger animals I used a 300 grain bullet. These cartridges left the barrel of the rifle in excellent shape and I never had a misfire.

AMONG THE ANIMALS WHICH FELL TO THIS RIFLE WERE:

ovis poli	Siberian roe	sambur
swamp deer	wild boar	Asiatic wapiti
hetal	nilghai	Tibetan antelope
ibex	burhel	Himalayan black
hog deer	tiger	bear
leopard	black buck	

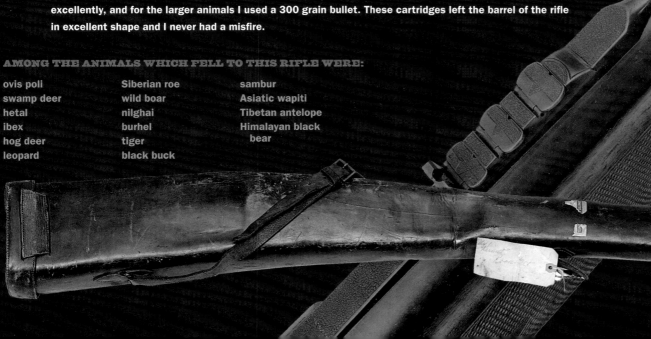

snow. The bands evidently wander very little at this season, staying as I myself saw, for days, and doubtless for weeks, within a radius of two or three miles. They sometimes sleep in the ravines; but some of them pass their entire time on the bare places. Others live chiefly in the snow, feeding on the patches of old grass, left bare as the snow melted. They lie out in the snow in the bleak wind, seeming not to feel the cold at all. At present they are grazing; they are weak and I had no difficulty in running into the herds on horseback—especially if I could make them go up hill. After a short run they open their mouths and pant heavily. They are more timid than the deer, but also more stupid. I saw a golden eagle threaten a band, driving them in their fright directly towards me. It separated a weak yearling from the herd and then hovered around his head—almost striking at it but evidently unable quite to make up its mind to the attack; finally it left and flew away. The coyotes wander about among the sleeping or feeding elk without attracting any attention whatever.

The antelope are quite shy. Their winter range is only the open country near Gardiner.

The deer—which except along the Gardiner are blacktail—are common and tame. They come on the parade ground in troops to pick up the hay. The blacktail is tamer than the whitetail.

Singularly enough the mountain sheep are the tamest of all the creatures. I saw but two bands—one of nineteen near the post, and another of seven in the Yellowstone Canyon. I seated myself within fifteen yards of the former as they grazed, and they paid hardly any heed to me. I walked up to within thirty yards of the latter, right in the open, before they ran. Their mountaineering feats down the cliffs of the Yellowstone Canyon were marvellous.... [PS.] Some of the bears have already come out; they are not feeding on the young green grass, for there isn't any, but on what they find under and in dead logs, and on carcasses...

The trip—and other experiences shared with Theodore Roosevelt impressed John Burroughs, in whose *Camping & Tramping with Roosevelt* is found the following analysis:

...I cannot now recall that I have ever met a man with a keener and more comprehensive interest in the wild life about us—an interest that is at once scientific and thoroughly human.... When I first read his "Wilderness Hunter," many years ago, I was impressed by his rare combination of the sportsman and the naturalist. When I accompanied him on his trip to the Yellowstone Park in April, 1903, I got a fresh impression of the extent of his natural history knowledge and of his trained powers of observation. Nothing escaped him, from bears to mice, from wild geese to chickadees, from elk to red squirrels; he took it all in, and he took it in as only an alert, vigorous mind can take it in. On that occasion I was able to help him identify only one new bird....All the other birds he recognized as quickly as I did...[Born] observers are about as rare as born poets. Plenty of men can see straight and report straight what they see; but the men who see what others miss, who see quickly and surely, who have the detective eye...who "get the drop," so to speak, on every object, who see minutely and who see whole, are rare indeed.

President Roosevelt comes as near fulfilling this ideal as any man I have known. His mind moves with wonderful celerity, and yet as an observer he is very cautious, jumps to no hasty conclusions.

The President unites in himself powers and qualities that rarely go together. Thus, he has both physical and moral courage in a degree rare in history. He can stand calm and unflinching in the path of a charging grizzly, and he can

The great likelihood of bad publicity and public misunderstanding ultimately caused the President to cancel plans for the Yellowstone hunt. Instead, he camped first at Yosemite with his friend John Muir and undertook an extensive tour of Yellowstone with the noted naturalist, John Burroughs.

OPPOSITE: At top, the Sporter bolt-action rifle especially made for President Roosevelt by the Springfield Armory in 1903. Serial #6000, .30-40 caliber, with 24" barrel, matted breech, crescent cheekpiece, and shotgun butt marked: U.S./SPRINGFIELD/ARMORY/MODEL 1903. One of TR's favorite rifles. Below is a near duplicate of the Springfield Sporter #6000, made on special order of the President in 1908. Known to have been used by Kermit and often referred to as his rifle, serial #85806; 23-3/4" barrel; .30-40 caliber; dated 1908 and marked with the Ordnance bomb and U.S. Yet another rifle of similar style, serial #2 Springfield Sporter, was in .30-06 caliber, and was made by R.G. Owen for Kermit (see sidebar on page 137).

SAGAMORE HILL NATIONAL HISTORIC SITE, NATIONAL PARK SERVICE

confront with equal coolness and determination the predaceous corporations and money powers of the country.

He unites the qualities of the man of action with those of the scholar and writer,—another very rare combination. He unites the instincts and accomplishments of the best breeding and culture with the broadest democratic sympathies and affiliations. He is as happy with a frontiersman like Seth Bullock as with a fellow Harvard man, and Seth Bullock is happy, too.

He unites great austerity with great good nature. He unites good sensibility with great force and will power. He loves solitude, and he loves to be in the thick of the fight. His love of nature is equaled only by his love of the ways and marts of men.

He is doubtless the most vital man on the continent, if not on the planet, to-day. He is many-sided, and every side throbs with his tremendous life and energy; the pressure is equal all around. His interests are as keen in natural history as in economics, in literature as in statecraft, in the young poet as in the old soldier, in preserving peace as in preparing for war. And he can turn all his great power into the new channel on the instant. His interest in the whole of life, and in the whole life of the nation, never flags for a moment. His activity is tireless. All the relaxation he needs or craves is a change of work....

It is to such men as [Theodore Roosevelt] that the big game legitimately belongs—men who regard it from the point of view of the naturalist as well as from that of the sportsman, who are interested in its preservation, and who share with the world the delight they experience in the chase.

John Burroughs knew men and he knew nature. Both a respected naturalist and an eminent writer, his tribute to Roosevelt was written with genuine conviction.

The Springfield Sporter #6000

In November 1903, Roosevelt sent a brief letter to the Ordnance Department ordering his second custom made rifle. "I have sent you over my Winchester rifle," he wrote General William Crozier, "so that you may have one of the new Springfield carbines made like it for me. I want the sights reproduced exactly. If necessary they can be obtained from the Winchester Company I want the butt just like my present butt, only one inch shorter."

Roosevelt's new Springfield, a .30-40, had the special serial number 6000. It appears that the Winchester sent to the General as a sample was the Model 1886 takedown, serial #125422, originally shipped to the President in 1902. Its sights are identical to the Springfield's, and the stock is slightly shorter, with the identical butt. Number 6000 was a typically deluxe Roosevelt rifle:

matted breech area up to the buckhorn rear sight; copper or gold bead front sight; varnished deluxe walnut stock, with crescent cheekpiece; 24" barrel; shotgun butt.

TR's first bolt-action rifle, the Springfield Sporter, was a great favorite. With it he took over 300 head of big and small game, from hippopotamus to hyena, from moose to peccary. The rifle was pictured on the cover of *A Book-Lover's Holidays in the Open* (1916) and was referred to in the text as "handy and accurate, has such penetration, and keeps in such good order that it has been my chief hunting rifle for the last dozen years on three continents, and has repeatedly killed heavy game..." Perhaps as a back-up gun, the Armory in 1908 built a matching Model 1903 Sporter on the President's order. It was also a .30-40 caliber had a 23 3/4 barrel, a similarly matted breech, similar sights, the same stock configuration, and bore serial serial 85806.

Although TR was not a "gun expert" from a technical standpoint and had no scientific interest in ballistics or in the miscellaneous technicalities

of small arms, it may safely be said that as a hunter and shooter his practical knowledge of firearms was excellent. He shot with a great variety of rifles, shotguns, and handguns, and owned a battery of nearly 50 weapons of many types and makes.

Winchester was by far his favorite brand. He purchased over a dozen lever action rifles, from the Model 1873 to the Model 1895. He also owned and fired rifles by Sharps, Freund, Ballard, Bullard, the Springfield Armory, Webley, Holland & Holland, Marlin, Mannlicher-Schoenhauer, Flobert, and Stevens; a combination rifle-shotgun and double barrel rifle by Fred Adolph, handguns by Colt, Smith & Wesson, Luger, and Greener; and shotguns by Lefaucheux, Parker, Thomas, Kennedy, Fox, and W. & C. Scott & Son.

He was familiar with practically every kind of basic mechanism: bolt-, lever-, slide-action, and falling-block in rifles, hammer and hammerless double rifles and shotguns, a break-open single shot market gun, double and single action revolvers, automatic pistols, and even varieties of air-guns. The types of ammunition he fired in small arms were numerous: handguns—.32, 9 mm, .38, .41 rimfire, .44-40 and .4....Special; carbines and rifles—.22, .256, .25-35, .32-20, .30-30, .303, .30-40, .38 Long, .40-2 5/8, .40-60, .40-70, .45-2.6, .45-2 7/8, .45-70, .45-75, .45-90, .45-120, .405, .50, .50-115, .50-150, and 500/.450, and in shotguns—4, 10, 12, 16, and 20 gauges.

Quick to adapt to new ideas in firearms, he was always ready to try out the latest cartridge or mechanism if there was a possibility they might be to his advantage in the field. He had abandoned a big-bore Sharps single shot rifle and a British double rifle after his first hunting experiences in the Badlands. With Winchester models he steadily progressed to big game rifles—from the Model 1876 .45-75 to the 1886 .45-90, to the Model 1892 and 1894 in .30-40 and .30-30, to the Model *1895* in .30-40 and .405. And the Model 1903 bolt-action Springfield was the first bolt rifle in his hunting battery. In Roosevelt's longest disquisition on guns and shooting, published in *Hunting in Many Lands* (1895), he showed his practical proficiency in hunting weaponry by forecasting with uncanny accuracy the gradual acceptance

Menu and list of speakers from a May 1903 banquet in San Francisco honoring TR. He had a distinct liking for game food.

**The President negotiating a fence.
Photograph appeared in TR's
*Outdoor Pastimes of an American
Hunter*. The photograph, titled
"Bleistein Jumping," was taken
by Clinedinst.**

THEODORE ROOSEVELT COLLECTION,
HARVARD COLLEGE LIBRARY

of high velocity small-bore ammunition, and the
decline of the large calibers for all but the biggest
of game. Experience in the field and as a hand-
loader of his own cartridges helped TR in making
the small-bore high velocity prediction.

Even in technical matters TR knew what he
wanted, and he was always very strict on sights
and stocks. Writing to gunmaker F.W. Freund of
New Jersey in June 1892, Roosevelt asked the gunmaker if the "line down the rear sight could not
be made of vermilion paint. I have an idea that
a line of vermilion would serve all the purposes
of the white line and yet would not be so apt to
glare or dazzle the eye and would not seem to fade
into the front sight in certain lights..." Roosevelt's
reliance on practical knowledge over theory was
clearly illustrated in the matter of bayonet selection

and rifle accuracy for the armed forces in 1904-
05. Writing to William Howard Taft, then Secretary of War, the President stated his dislike for the
ramrod style of bayonet; and had apprehensions on
the comparative effectiveness of 24" and 30" rifles
at long ranges:

I must say that I think that ramrod bayonet about as poor an invention as I ever saw. As
you observed, it broke short off as soon as hit
with even moderate violence. It would have no
moral effect and mighty little physical effect. I
think the suggestion of a short triangular bayonet a great improvement. After you have gone
over this subject of the bayonet and the sword,
do take it up with me.

I wish our officers could carry rifles. If they
carry any sword they ought to carry a sword
that they can cut or thrust with. Personally I do
not see any point in having the cavalry armed
with a bayonet, even though the modern caval-
ryman is nine times out of ten on foot. He might
have a sword in his belt, only it ought to be a
sword that can do damage.

I am particularly anxious that we should
have a thorough test made of the long and the
short rifle (that is of the 24-inch and 30-inch
rifle) at some place like that in Utah where
several companies of men can be employed at
firing both weapons at long ranges. This ramrod bayonet business does not make me feel
that we can afford to trust too much to theory of the closet variety. I would like to have
the opinion of Captain March, and then the
opinion of the other military attaches who saw
the fighting between the Russians and Japanese, about both the bayonet and the sword. I
would also like to have the opinion of any of
our officers in the Philippines who have seen
the bayonet actually used.

The statement "[we cannot] afford to trust too
much theory of the closet variety" sums up TR's

approach to gun expertise. To judge from his extraordinary hunting and shooting record, this approach was the proper one, at least for him.

The Nature Faker Controversy

During his first Presidential term Roosevelt became personally involved in what came to be called the "nature faker" controversy. Essentially the affair arose over the emergence of a new school of young writers who wrote highly interesting nature books that purported to be based on scientific investigations but in reality were fanciful tales that endowed animals with human characteristics and other preposterous qualities. Ernest T. Seton was the founder of this school and in short time he had many imitators, notably William J. Long and Charles G.D. Roberts. They and others wrote multitudes of pseudo-scientific nature studies that were enormously popular with children. Well-trained naturalists who resented what seemed to them outlandish perversions of natural history took to journals and newspapers to denounce the nature fakers. They felt that these literary concoctions were absurdly unscientific and demonstrably inaccurate.

In 1903 John Burroughs fired the first salvo in an article that appeared in the *Atlantic Monthly*. It was a blistering indictment, charging the "nature fakers" with willfully distorting the facts of natural life and inculcating in the minds of youthful readers untrue information about the characteristics and conduct of various animals. The article rallied many naturalists to Burroughs' side.

Roosevelt read approvingly Burroughs' piece, though he disagreed with a few of his views on animal instincts. The President was positive that the nature fakers were constructing "fairy tales" and were abysmally ignorant of animal life. Over a period of time he slowly and warily involved himself in the controversy. Although he realized that it was undignified for a President to link his office to such an altercation, in 1907 he allowed himself to be interviewed on the subject by Edward B. Clark,

a reporter and naturalist. When the interview was published under the title "Roosevelt on the Nature Fakirs," it caused a nationwide stir because of the President's harsh opinions, especially of William Long whose animal books had deeply rankled him. Roosevelt acted unwisely in singling out Long and lambasting him, not the least because it gave Long the chance to publish a rejoinder in kind.

Long sidestepped the specific criticisms the President had made and instead attacked him personally. He accused Roosevelt of having unfairly and maliciously impugned his veracity while hiding behind the imposing office of the Presidency. Moreover, he went on, Roosevelt was really in no position to talk or write authoritatively on the habits of animals because all he did was shoot them, not study them.

Long's countercharges, though extravagant and baseless, won the support of many people who believed the President had been both rash in getting into the controversy and unfair in concentrating his criticisms on Long. Roosevelt was indeed impolitic for jumping into the breach, but, then again, one could hardly have expected otherwise of him. On the other hand, his stand on the nature faker controversy has been judged by history to be correct and courageous. ☙

The statement "[we cannot] afford to trust too much theory of the closet variety" sums up TR's approach to gun expertise. To judge from his extraordinary hunting and shooting record, this approach was the proper one, at least for him.

CHAPTER 8

The Hunter-President as Conservationist

Roosevelt's performance as President following McKinley's assassination was praised by most of his countrymen. His solicitude for the public interest, his assertiveness against trusts and irresponsible corporate wealth and his fairness to labor unions won him broadly based admiration and respect. Captains of industry and bankers and financiers often resented his progressive posture in matters affecting their vital interests, but the President's overriding desire was to administer the government in the best interests of all groups and classes.

Despite his evident popularity, Roosevelt was worried that certain interests in the Republican Party would seek to deny him the nomination in 1904. Though many Republicans felt this way, there simply was no chance of his being denied the nomination against the will of the people. Indeed, at the Chicago Convention he was unanimously nominated, and in the election he overwhelmingly defeated the Democratic presidential candidate Alton B. Parker by 2-1/2 million votes.

Roosevelt interpreted his stunning reelection as a mandate for more reform. During his second term, the Progressive movement gained impetus. A middle-class upsurge aiming at curbing the evils that flowed from unrestrained *laissez-faire* capitalism, Progressivism was a bipartisan political phenomenon that drew on the dynamic Roosevelt for much of its inspiration, vitality and programs. The President had become the evocative symbol of

On the Oklahoma wolf hunt in the spring of 1906 – TR is center foreground.

THEODORE ROOSEVELT COLLECTION, HARVARD COLLEGE LIBRARY

> "There can be
> no greater issue
> than that of
> conservation in
> this country.
> Just as we must
> conserve our men
> and women and
> children, so we
> must conserve
> the resources of
> the land on which
> they live."

reform as well as the instigator of it. He strenuously supported the Pure Food and Drug Act of 1906, which represented a milestone in the area of consumer protection. To check the often illegal and reckless practices of the railroads, he fought hard for the passage of the Hepburn Act in 1906, which gave the Interstate Commerce Commission greater regulatory powers over railroads. In addition, he directed his Attorney General to institute antitrust suits against some of the largest and most redoubtable financial and industrial trusts in the nation. In all, he infused Progressivism with a new *élan* and sense of direction.

In foreign affairs, he was likewise demonstrative, self-assertive, eminently successful. He was able to bring the Russo-Japanese War to an end in 1905 by serving as the mediator between the two belligerents at Portsmouth, New Hampshire. His adept handling of Russo-Japanese negotiations and later his intervention in the Moroccan crisis won him the Nobel Peace Prize for 1906, an unprecedented honor for an American President.

Probably Roosevelt's most masterful diplomatic stroke was directed against the Japanese government. Relations between the United States and Japan had become strained because Japan was not entirely satisfied with Roosevelt's mediation at Portsmouth and because of the starkly discriminatory treatment of Orientals living on the Pacific coast. When in 1906 the San Francisco Board of Education ruled that Japanese children had to attend separate schools, the government of Japan bitterly remonstrated against the order. Roosevelt strongly disapproved of such discrimination and used all the force of his office to bring about a reversal of the decision. However, not wishing to have Japan interpret his actions as a sign of fear or weakness on the part of the government, Roosevelt arranged for the American fleet to take a majestic cruise around the world, ostensibly to keep the Navy awake and alert but actually to impress Japan (and other countries) with America's vaunted naval might. The maneuver worked brilliantly,

as the Japanese welcomed the American fleet with open arms if not with open hearts. As a diplomatist, Roosevelt habitually acted on the principle that a nation's best defense was a strong offense.

The Conservationist: 1901-1909

Roosevelt's most significant and far-sighted accomplishments as President were undeniably in the field of conservation. Given his tremendous love of wildlife and the outdoors, this is not surprising. He argued that the greatest asset of the United States outside of its people, was its natural resources. Thus, as he stated,

> There can be no greater issue than that of conservation in this country. Just as we must conserve our men and women and children, so we must conserve the resources of the land on which they live.

Prior to his administrations, the United States had pursued desultory and often self-defeating conservation policies. In fact, no such thing as a coherent, consistent, viable policy ever existed. At best, previous Presidents had given the subject low priority, acting only in fits and starts. At worst, previous Presidents had virtually banished the idea from their minds, allowing the natural resources of the country to be ruthlessly exploited and shamelessly squandered. Untrammeled industrialism and urbanism took an appalling toll of natural resources. The indifference and ignorance of federal and state officials—and of businessmen—toward conservation had reached a point early in the twentieth century where a natural disaster lay ahead unless changes were made.

It is difficult to date precisely Roosevelt's interest in conservation. It seems reasonable to suppose that he became aware of the issue at the time he began to study natural history. Unquestionably, his numerous camping and hunting sojourns in the West impressed upon his mind the importance of preserving wildlife and conserving forests. While

ABOVE: A Belgian-made Nagant double-action revolver, presented to TR by Admiral Togo of Japan. On the left side of the frame was engraved: Presented to/President Roosevelt/BY ADMIRAL TOGO/Taken from/Russian battleship after/battle of Sea of Japan. Serial #724. Togo was a visitor to Sagamore Hill in 1911.

LEFT: TR during an election speech in New Castle, Wyoming.

Governor of New York, Roosevelt received a full indoctrination on conservation by fellow Boone and Crockett Club member Gifford Pinchot, one of the nation's most brilliant and dedicated conservationists. Pinchot understood the problem in all of its vast and subtle dimensions. He discerned clearly that conservation involved more than saving a few animal species, a few acres of forest and a certain quantity of various minerals. To him the fullness and quality of life in America was directly dependent on the nation's ability to conserve its natural resources. And this, he believed, required a conscientious, concerted, and comprehensive set of policies on the part of federal and state governments. As Chief Forester, under Roosevelt, Pinchot played a central role in developing conservation programs.

In his first message to Congress Roosevelt underlined the importance of establishing forest reserves throughout the nation. He then moved energetically to support an irrigation and reclamation bill for the arid areas of the West. He jubilantly signed the Newlands Reclamation bill in 1902, which provided for extensive irrigation and land conservation projects at federal expense. Some 28 major irrigation projects were begun. Thousands of culverts, bridges, and dikes were constructed to provide water for 3 million acres embracing 30,000 farms.

Roosevelt's achievements in conservation were striking during his first term, but downright spectacular during the second. His landslide victory in the election of 1904 convinced him that the public staunchly endorsed conservation programs. In 1905, he signed a bill that transferred the federal forests from the Department of the Interior to the Department of Agriculture, where they were put under the aegis of the Bureau of Forestry, rechristened the Forest Service. Gifford Pinchot's responsibilities were thus greatly increased, especially when the President set aside for safekeeping millions of acres of priceless forest reserves.

In addition to the raft of conservation bills he supported, Roosevelt—admirably assisted by Pinchot and other conservationists—instigated a nationwide educational program to enlighten the American public on the importance of the laws he had championed and of those that were forthcoming. Through the press, journals, and other media, he and his fellow conservationists made the subject of conservation seem exciting, patriotic, even absolutely indispensable to national efficiency and welfare. The publicity tended to offset the growing anti-conservation reaction of business moguls and speculators who were alarmed by the fact that Roosevelt, unlike so many of his predecessors, was not giving away the nation's natural resources. The United States Senate, representing powerful economic interests, began in 1907 to object to many of Roosevelt's conservation proposals. Worse still, the timber, oil, and cattle interests also joined in a cacophonous chorus against the President's tight control over natural resources. Even in the face of such opposition Roosevelt plunged straight ahead and accomplished some of his most memorable goals.

In 1907, the Senate approved an amendment by Senator Fulton of Oregon to the Agricultural Appropriations Bill, which expressly forbade the President the authority to set aside additional forest reserves in several northwestern states. The bill passed, and conservatives were confident that they had stolen a march on the President. But

ABOVE: Hunting bear in Mississippi. The rifle is believed to be TR's custom-made Model 1894 Winchester, serial #15659 with a 2/3 magazine, deluxe walnut stocks, and crescent cheekpiece.

THEODORE ROOSEVELT COLLECTION, HARVARD COLLEGE LIBRARY

OPPOSITE: TR sits in the doorway of his West Divide Creek Ranch house and reads a book.

© CORBIS

> "In addition to being a true sportsman, and not a game butcher, in addition to being a humane man as well as keen-eyed, strong-limbed, and stouthearted, the big-game hunter should be a field naturalist. If possible, he should be...adept with the camera..."

Roosevelt and his supporters had other ideas. During the ten-day period he had to sign or veto the bill, they studied the remaining public lands eligible for conversion to National Forests by Presidential proclamation. Roosevelt swiftly issued a series of proclamations that established no less than 21 new forest reserves in the states within the compass of the Fuller amendment; sixteen million acres of land had been saved by the President and his conservationist friends. Having officially proclaimed these national forests, he then proceeded—no doubt with a chuckle or two—to sign the Agricultural Appropriations bill.

Five National Parks were created during Roosevelt's Presidency: Crater Lake in Oregon, Wind Cave in South Dakota, Platt in Oklahoma, Sully Hill in North Dakota, and Mesa Verde in Colorado. Besides this commendable feat, he established four enormous game reserves, one each in Oklahoma, Arizona, Montana, and Washington. Roosevelt was also responsible for setting up 51 bird reservations in 17 states and territories. In 1908, he authorized the creation in Montana of the National Bison Range, embracing 18,000 acres.

Capping off a truly remarkable performance in the field of conservation, Roosevelt, in 1908, invited leading federal and state officials to the White House for the Governors' conference on conservation. Nearing the end of his Presidency, TR wanted to be sure that his manifold programs would be continued and even amplified. Moreover he wanted federal and state agencies to work and plan together in good faith and with high hopes. His address to the luminaries crowded into the East Room was a low-key, earnest appeal for their continued backing of federal and state conservation schemes. He emphasized the noble end they were pursuing and the gratitude that would be lavishly extended to them by future generations. His sincere, often quite moving speech was an appropriate way to climax his own tremendous conservation labors as well as to point the way to a new era. Had Roosevelt done nothing else as President,

his greatness would still have been ensured by what he did in conservation.

The Conservationist as Hunter

For Theodore Roosevelt, as for few other people in the early twentieth century, conservation and hunting were as one. Perhaps in his life and writings can be found some of the answers to the persistent questions asked of hunters-conservationists by their outdoor-loving brothers and (quite often) sisters. TR, typically, did not find himself without blemish. As a Harvard undergraduate, he wrote his friend Henry Minot: "I have not done much collecting this summer, for, as you know, I don't approve of too much slaughter." Later in life, TR admitted that he had taken more than his share of specimens as a teen-age collector: "When I was young I fell into the usual fashion of those days and collected 'specimens' industriously, thereby committing an entirely needless butchery of our ordinary birds. I am happy to say that there has been a great change for the better since then in our ways of looking at these things."

An experienced hunter and naturalist who impressed professionals in ornithology and mammalogy with his knowledge, TR spoke authoritatively on the harvesting of game: "...as Nature is organized, to remove all checks to the multiplication of a species merely means that the very multiplication itself in a few years operates as a most disastrous check by producing an epidemic of disease or starvation." To Sir Harry Johnston he wrote in 1908:

> Your conscience can be reasonably free in the matter of my hunting, altho not entirely so, for tho emphatically against game butchery, or any other kind of butchery of wild things, and emphatically in favor of the preservation of all wild life that can be preserved without detriment to mankind, I still do feel, not only that there is no objection to a reasonable amount of hunting, but that the encouragement of a proper hunting

spirit, a proper love of sport, instead of being incompatible with a love of nature and wild things, offers the best guaranty for the preservation of wild things. Even here on Long Island, which has been settled for three centuries and is no wilder than the least wild districts of England, we can preserve deer, for example, only thru the efforts of sportsmen. If they were never shot at all they would increase so that the farmers would kill them completely out. They have to be kept down somehow, and it is best to have them kept down thru legitimate hunting.

Sport, and particularly hunting, had its proper place in TR's scheme of life:

The chase is the best of all national pastimes, and this none the less because, like every other pastime, it is a mere source of weakness if carried on in an unhealthy manner, or to an excessive degree, or under over-artificial conditions. Every vigorous game, from football to polo, if allowed to become more than a game, and if serious work is sacrificed to its enjoyment, is of course noxious. From the days when Trajan in his letters to Pliny spoke with such hearty contempt of the Greek over-devotion to athletics, every keen thinker has realised that vigorous sports are only good in their proper place. But in their proper place they are very good indeed.

The complete hunter of big game should be many things:

In addition to being a true sportsman, and not a game butcher, in addition to being a humane man as well as keen-eyed, strong-limbed, and stouthearted, the big-game hunter should be a field naturalist. If possible, he should be…adept with the camera.…Wherever possible he should keep a note-book, and should carefully study and record the habits of the wild creatures, especially when in some remote regions

to which trained scientific observers but rarely have access.

Independence, strength, and fortitude were important qualities of manhood:

Laying stress upon the mere quantity of game killed, and the publication of the record of slaughter, are sure signs of unhealthy decadence in sportsmanship. As far as possible the true hunter, the true lover of big game and of life in the wilderness, must be ever ready to show his own power to shift for himself. The greater his dependence upon others for his sport the less he deserves to take high rank in the brotherhood of rifle, horse, and hound. There was a very attractive side to the hunting of the great mediaeval lords, carried on with an elaborate equipment and stately ceremonial, especially as there was an element of danger in coming to close quarters with the quarry at bay; but after all, no form of hunting has ever surpassed in attractiveness the life of the wilderness wanderer of our own time—the man who with simple equipment, and trusting to his own qualities of head, heart, and hand, has penetrated to the uttermost regions of the earth, and single-handed slain alike the wariest and the grimmest of the creatures of the waste.

Theodore Roosevelt's essays on game conservation and on his philosophy of hunting are as timely today as they were when originally published—perhaps more so. The many personal rewards that come from hunting and from observing and studying wildlife are more satisfying when accomplished within a framework of rules and restraints safeguarding the well-being of man and animals alike. Roosevelt's insistence on fair hunting practice, on a responsible attitude toward the outdoor life and on vigorous wilderness adventure offers a well-reasoned point of view for all Americans.

TR... Illustrated

Political cartoons and caricatures of Theodore Roosevelt abound. Many different aspects of TR's political career were documented by pen and ink. These pages show just a few highlighting those that pertained to his hunter persona, his famous trip to Africa, and his policies relating to the outdoors.

Africa
1909–1910

"In every case the result was the same. Good citizens for the moment abandoned their weapons. The bad men continued to carry them. Things grew worse instead of better; and then the good men came to their senses and clothed some representative of the police with power to employ force, potential or existing, against the wrong doers."

Writing the introduction to A.G. Wallihan's *Camera Shots at Big Game*, TR showed his great concern with ineffective game conservation laws and his fear that some species were threatened with extinction. The near destruction of the buffalo herds in the West was all too fresh in his memory:

It will be a real misfortune if our wild animals disappear from mountain, plain and forest, to be found only, if at all, in great game preserves. It is to the interest of all of us to see that there is ample and real protection for our game as for our woodlands. A true democracy, really alive to its opportunities, will insist upon such game preservation, for it is to the interest of our people as a whole. More and more, as it becomes necessary to preserve the game, let us hope that the camera will largely supplant the rifle. It is an excellent thing to have a nation proficient in marksmanship, and it is highly undesirable that the rifle should be wholly laid by. But the shot is, after all, only a small part of the free life of the wilderness. The chief attractions lie in the physical hardihood for which the life calls, the sense of limitless freedom which it brings, and the remoteness and wild charm and beauty of primitive nature. All of this we get exactly as much in hunting with the camera as in hunting with the rifle; and of the two, the former is the kind of sport which calls for the higher degree of skill, patience, resolution, and knowledge of the life history of the animal sought.

His comparison was legitimate at the time, but less so today. With the powerful long distance lenses of modern cameras the hunter with the camera and the hunter with the rifle are on about equal footing.

The size of the bag did not appeal to Roosevelt:

I have never sought to make large bags, for a hunter should not be a game-butcher. It is always lawful to kill dangerous or noxious animals, like the bear, cougar, and wolf; but other game should only be shot when there is need of the meat, or for the sake of an unusually fine trophy. Killing a reasonable number of bulls, bucks, or rams does no harm whatever to the species; to slay half the males of any kind of game would not stop the natural increase; and they yield the best sport, and are the legitimate objects of the chase...

The President and Marksmanship

Roosevelt had much to say and write on marksmanship and its importance in self-defense for the individual and for the nation. The ability of the citizenry to be able to handle weapons was to him indispensable to national preparedness. He insisted that a man should be ready and able to defend himself if necessary. Illogical or unreasonable interference with the individual ownership of firearms by law-abiding individuals was folly. Throughout his life, Roosevelt firmly believed that the proper and legal use of firearms was a fundamental right of all Americans.

Writing a college dissertation on the "Practicability of Equalizing Men and Women Before the Law," Roosevelt's first paragraph emphatically stated his views on self-defense in guarding "against wrong of any kind":

...in an ideally perfect state of society it would... be perfectly needless for any man to learn the use of weapons or to be able to defend himself, as in such a state there would of course be no need to guard against wrong of any kind, yet in the world as it at present exists, I think one of the most important duties, either for an individual or for a nation, is the duty of being able to protect himself (or itself and others against oppression; that is, it is your *duty* to be able to fight effectively....Society [is] still in its semi-barbarous state.)

Much later, Roosevelt apparently considered American society in a less barbarous state, but self-defense was still necessary:

Most Western Americans who are past middle age remember young, rapidly growing, and turbulent communities in which there was at first complete anarchy. During the time when there was no central police power to which to appeal every man worth his salt, in other words every man fit for existence in such a community, had to be prepared to defend himself; and usually, although not always, the fact that he was prepared saved him from all trouble, whereas unpreparedness was absolutely certain to invite disaster.

In such communities before there was a regular and fully organized police force there came an interval during which the preservation of the peace depended upon the action of a single official, a sheriff or marshal, who if the law was defied in arrogant fashion summoned a posse comitatus composed of as many armed, thoroughly efficient, law-abiding citizens as were necessary in order to put a stop to the wrongdoing. Under these conditions each man had to keep himself armed and both able and willing to respond to the call of the peace-officer; and furthermore, if he had a shred of wisdom he kept himself ready in an emergency to act on his own behalf if the peace-officer did not or could not do his duty.

In such towns I have myself more than once seen well-meaning but foolish citizens endeavor to meet the exigencies of the case by simply resolutions of disarmament without any power back of them. That is, they passed self-denying ordinances, saying that nobody was to carry arms; but they failed to provide methods for carrying such ordinances into effect. In every case the result was the same. Good citizens for the moment abandoned their weapons. The bad men continued to carry them. Things grew worse instead of better; and then the good men came to their senses and clothed some representative of the police with power to employ force, potential or existing, against the wrong doers.

President Roosevelt went out of his way to encourage marksmanship. He enthusiastically supported a bill that created the National Board for the Promotion of Rifle Practice, and he instituted the precedent of a congratulatory letter from the White House to the winner of the President's Match of the National Matches competition. In 1905, he endorsed and then signed into law a bill authorizing sales of surplus military ammunition and rifles to dubs affiliated with the National Rifle Association. These sales were under the jurisdiction of the National Board for the Promotion of Rifle Practice.

Roosevelt's opinions on marksmanship were clearly stated in a July 1907, congratulatory letter to a sharp-shooting Brooklyn high school student, Ambrose Scharfenberg:

I heartily congratulate you upon being declared by the Public Schools Athletic League to stand first in rifle shooting among all the boys of the high schools of New York City who have tried during the last year. I am glad to see how well you have done in all the competitions in which you shot during the year; alike in the Whitney Trophy competition; the Individual Match Shoot at Creedmoor, and the Interscholastic Match. Many a grown man who regards himself as a crack rifle shot would be proud of such a score.

Your skill is a credit to you, and also to your principal, your teachers and to all connected with the Manual Training High School which you attend, and I congratulate them all. Practice in rifle shooting is of value in developing not only muscles, but nerves, steadiness and judgment under excitement. It is therefore of value to every man throughout his life.

The Public Schools Athletic League has done fine work for the city, and for the country in introducing and promoting athletics and a love for manly sports in the public schools of New York, especially as the League most wisely

THE WHITE HOUSE
WASHINGTON

February 18, 1907.

My dear General:

I am so heartily interested in the success of the National Rifle Association of America and its work done in cooperation with the National Board for the promotion of Rifle Practise, that I take pleasure in sending you herewith my check for $25 for life membership therein.

Very truly yours,

Theodore Roosevelt

General James A. Drain, President,
    National Rifle Association of America,
    299 Broadway,
    New York.

TR joined the NRA as a lifetime member while in the White House in 1907, as noted by his letter above. TR's advocacy of the NRA and its aims was as sincere as it was effective.

BOONE AND CROCKETT CLUB
PERMANENT COLLECTION

to shoot if he is to be of value as a soldier. In no modern war would it be possible effectively to train men to shoot during the brief period of preparation before the army takes the field. In consequence the training must come in advance and the graduates from our schools and colleges should be thus trained so as to be good shots with the military rifle. When so trained they constitute a great addition to our national strength and great assurance for the peace of the country.

In his 1906 annual message to Congress, Roosevelt urged an expanded program of rifle training throughout the United States. He declared that:

The Congress has most wisely provided for a national board for the promotion of rifle practice. Excellent results have already come from this law, but it does not go far enough. Our regular Army is so small that in any great war we would have to trust mainly to volunteers; and in such event these volunteers should already know how to shoot, for if a soldier has the fighting edge, and ability to care for himself in the open, his efficiency on the line of battle is almost directly proportionate to excellence in marksmanship. We should establish shooting galleries in all the large public and military schools, and should maintain national target ranges in different parts of the country, and should in every way encourage the formation of rifle clubs throughout all parts of the land.

In 1908 he informed Congress that:

There should be legislation to provide a complete plan for organizing the great body of volunteers behind the Regular Army and National Guard when war has come. Congressional assistance should be given those who are endeavoring to promote rifle practice so that our men,

allows no one to compete who is not up to the passing mark both in studies and deportment. I am especially glad of what it has done in establishing instruction in rifle shooting. The United States has a very small standing army In time of war it must depend for defense upon hasty levies of volunteers, and it is of prime necessity that the volunteer should already know how

in the Services and out of them, may know how to use the rifle. While teams representing the United States won the Rifle and Revolver Championships of the World against all comers in England this year, it is unfortunately true that the great body of our citizens shoot less and less as time goes on. To meet this we should encourage rifle practice among schoolboys, and indeed among the classes, as well as in the military services, by every means in our power. Thus, and not otherwise, may we be able to assist in preserving the peace of the world fit to hold our own against the strong nations of the earth, our voice for peace will carry to the ends of the earth. Unprepared, and therefore unfit, we must sit dumb and helpless to defend ourselves, protect others, or preserve peace. The first step—in the direction of preparation to avert war if possible, and to be fit for war if it should come—is to teach our men to shoot.

TR and the National Rifle Association of America

Federal legislation and Roosevelt's encouragement of marksmanship were important factors in the growth of organized competitive shooting during the early twentieth century. At the same time, the National Rifle Association's influence in promoting marksmanship was greatly increased, as its cooperation with the federal government was expanded. Roosevelt joined the NRA in February of 1907. He wrote the president of the Association that he was "so heartily interested in the success of the National Rifle Association of America and its work done in cooperation with the National Board for the promotion of Rifle Practise, that I take pleasure in sending you herewith my check for $25 for life membership therein." Roosevelt's advocacy of the NRA and its aims was as sincere as it was effective. It gave impetus to the Association and to target shooting and marksmanship training and was a major contribution to shooting both as a sport and as a preparation for war.

TR's love of the shooting sports is recognized and celebrated at the National Firearms Museum, Fairfax, Virginia, in exhibits that feature his Browning pistol, Fred Adolph double barrel rifle and a Winchester Model 1895 rifle presented to Colonel Leonard Wood.

Further, the Beretta family and the Beretta company funded a gallery of deluxe firearms, the design of which was influenced by Roosevelt's love of firearms and by the architecture and ambiance of the North Room and the Gun Room at his Sagamore Hill country estate.

Guns and Hunting, 1905-1909

As President, TR embellished the White House with his mounted big game heads, whose silent presence at state dinners must have unnerved some of the less avid hunters among the guests. In *Puck* magazine, cartoonist Albert Levering drew a classic caricature titled, "The Teddyfication of the White House." Levering gave to each animal head the unmistakable look of a Theodore Roosevelt.

During the second administration, TR managed to get in about as much shooting and hunting as he had during the first term. He hunted bobcat, wolf, and bear in April 1906; wild turkey in November 1906; and bear again in October 1907. In 1908 and early 1909, he spent countless hours preparing for the African safari he would make after leaving the White House.

From April 8 through 12, 1905, Roosevelt hunted with a party on the Oklahoma ranch of Cecil Lyon. They coursed wolves (coyotes) on horseback and took three coons and more rattlesnakes than they cared to count. It was a refreshing holiday for the President, reminiscent of riding to the hounds in the 1880s. He wrote to his son, Kermit:

I hope you had as successful a trip in Florida as I have had in Texas and Oklahoma. The first six days were of the usual Presidential tour type, but much more pleasant than ordinarily because I did not have to do quite as much speaking; and there was a certain irresponsibility about

Federal legislation and Roosevelt's encouragement of marksmanship were important factors in the growth of organized competitive shooting during the early twentieth century.

As President, TR embellished the White House with his mounted big game heads, whose silent presence at state dinners must have unnerved some of the less avid hunters among the guests.

it all, due I suppose in part to the fact that I am no longer a candidate and am free from the everlasting suspicion and ill-natured judgment which being a candidate entails. Moreover, both in Kentucky, and especially in Texas, I was received with a warmth and heartiness that surprised me; while the Rough Riders' reunion at San Antonio was delightful in every way.

Then came the five days' wolf hunting in Oklahoma, and this was unalloyed pleasure… General Young, Dr. Lambert and Roly Fortescue were each in his own way just the nicest companions imaginable, and my Texas hosts were too kind and friendly and openhearted for anything. I want to have the whole party up at Washington next winter. The party got seventeen wolves, three coons, and any number of rattlesnakes. I was in at the death of eleven wolves. The other six wolves were killed by members of the party who were off with bunches of dogs in some place where I was not. I never took part in a row which ended in the death of a wolf without getting through the run in time to see the death. It was tremendous galloping over cut banks, prairie dog towns, flats, creek bottoms, everything. One run was nine miles long and I was the only man in at the finish except the professional wolf hunter—Abernathy, who is a really wonderful fellow, catching the wolves alive by thrusting his gloved hands down between their jaws so that they cannot bite. He caught one wolf alive, tied up this wolf, and then held it on the saddle, followed his dogs in a seven-mile run, and helped kill another wolf. He has a pretty wife and five cunning children of whom he is very proud, and introduced them to me; and I liked him much. We were in the saddle eight or nine hours every day and I am rather glad to have thirty-six hours rest on the cars before starting on my Colorado bear hunt.

The bear and bobcat hunt in Colorado lasted three weeks and was thoroughly agreeable to

"The Teddyfication of the White House" by Albert Levering appeared in the February 1909 issue of *Puck* magazine. A bewildered William Howard Taft stands in the doorway at right.

Roosevelt. He recounted the hunt with great detail in *Outdoor Pastimes:*

In mid-April. nineteen hundred and five, our party, consisting of Philip B. Stewart, of Colorado Springs, and Dr. Alexander Lambert, of New York, in addition to myself, left Newcastle, Col., for a bear hunt. As guides and hunters we had John Goff and Jake Borah, than whom there are no better men at their work of hunting bear in the mountains with hounds. Each brought his own dogs; all told, there were twenty-six hounds, and four half-blood terriers to help worry the bear when at bay. We travelled in comfort, with a big pack train, spare horses for each of us, and a cook, packers, and horse wranglers. I carried one of the new model Springfield military rifles [serial #6000], a 30-40, with a soft-nosed bullet—a very accurate and hard-hitting gun.

This Colorado trip was the first on which I hunted bears with hounds. If we had run across a grizzly there would doubtless have been a chance to show some prowess, at least in the way of hard riding. But the black and brown bears cannot, save under exceptional circumstances, escape from such a pack as we had with us; and the real merit of the chase was confined to the hounds and to Jake and Johnny for their skill in handling them.

The first day after reaching camp we rode for eleven hours over a very difficult country, but without getting above the snow-line. Finally the dogs got on the fresh trail of a bobcat, and away they went. A bobcat will often give a good run, much better, on the average, than a cougar, and this one puzzled the dogs not a little at first. It scrambled out of one deep valley, crossing and recrossing the rock ledges where its scent was hard to follow; then plunged into another valley…[The dogs gave chase and finally treed the bobcat]…Shorty and Skip, who always trotted after the horses while the hounds were in

full cry on a trail, recognized the change of note immediately, and tore off in the direction of the bay, while we followed as best we could, hoping to get there in time for Stewart and Lambert to take photographs of the lynx in a tree. But we were too late. Both Shorty and Skip could climb trees, and although Skip was too light to tackle a bobcat by himself, Shorty, a heavy formidable dog, of unflinching courage and great physical strength, was altogether too much for any bobcat. When we reached the place we found the bobcat in the top of a pinyon, and Shorty steadily working his way up through the branches and very near the quarry. Evidently the bobcat felt that the situation needed the taking of desperate chances, and just before Shorty reached it out it jumped, Shorty yelling with excitement as he plunged down through the branches after it. But the cat did not jump far enough. One of the hounds seized it by the hind leg and in another second everything was over.

Next morning we rode off early, taking with us all twenty-six hounds and the four terriers. We wished first to find whether the bear had gone out of the country in which we had seen him, and so rode up a valley and then scrambled laboriously up the mountain-side to the top of the snowcovered divide.

It was hard to follow the scene across such a mountain-side, and the dogs speedily became much scattered. We could hear them plainly, and now and then could see them, looking like ants as they ran up and down hill and along the ledges. Finally we heard some of them barking bayed.…Immediately afterward we saw the bear, half-way up the opposite mountainside. The hounds were all around him, and occasionally bit at his hind quarters; but he had evidently no intention of climbing a tree. When we first saw him he was sitting up on a point of rock surrounded by the pack, his black fur showing to fine advantage. Then he moved off, threatening the dogs, and making what in Mississippi is

called a walking bay. He was a sullen, powerful beast, and his leisurely gait showed how little he feared the pack, and how confident he was in his own burly strength.

Just as we came in sight of him, across a deep gully which ran down the sheer mountain-side, he broke bay and started off, threatening the foremost of the pack as they dared to approach him. They were all around him, and for a minute I could not fire, then as he passed under a pinyon I got a clear view of his great round stern and pulled trigger. The bullet broke both his hips, and he rolled down hill, the hounds yelling with excitement as they closed in on him. He could still play havoc with the pack, and there was need to kill him at once. I leaped and slid down my side of the gully as he rolled down his; at the bottom he stopped and raised himself on his fore quarters; and with another bullet I broke his back between the shoulders.

Immediately all the dogs began to worry the carcass, while their savage baying echoed so loudly in the narrow, steep gully that we could with difficulty hear one another speak It was a wild scene to look upon, as we scrambled down to where the dead hear lay on his back between the rocks. He did not die wholly unavenged, for he had killed one of the terriers and six other dogs were more or less injured. The chase of the bear is grim work for the pack.…The bear was a big male, weighing three hundred and thirty pounds.

ABOVE: A rare photograph of the President in a shooting position, taken while in pursuit of bear in Colorado, c. 1905.

LIBRARY OF CONGRESS COLLECTION

INSET: Dinner on the Colorado bear hunt. Originally published in *Outdoor Pastimes of an American Hunter*. The President is sitting at the far end of the table. Photograph by Philip B. Stewart.

BOONE AND CROCKETT CLUB PERMANENT COLLECTION

The Colorado hunt was Roosevelt's last big game expedition as President. He exclaimed to his friend and fellow Boone and Crockett Club member, Elihu Root, that May:

We had a really good hunt and I think you would have enjoyed it all. The wild gallops after the coyotes in Oklahoma were first-class fun, and in an entirely different way, so was the bear hunting in Colorado. Of the bear only four were good big ones, three of which I got, including a very large old male black bear. In addition we treed six yearlings....It was all horseback work, but on account of the deep snow and the length of time we had to be out each day there was a good deal of exercise in it. The final scramble would be on foot...

Hounds and Hunting

Roosevelt had a special fondness for hunting with hounds. He wrote knowingly and enthusiastically of this form of the chase in *The Wilderness Hunter, Outdoor Pastimes of an American Hunter,* and several of his other outdoor writings. Though he spent far more time in still hunting or stalking game on foot, his experiences with hounds were nevertheless considerable.

He hunted with greyhounds, wire-haired deerhounds, and miscellaneous mongrels. From 1880 through 1901, he followed them afoot or on horseback in England, Colorado, Texas, Oklahoma, Louisiana, New York, and the Badlands; after leaving the Presidency, he followed them in Africa, Brazil, and Arizona. Fox, wolf, rabbit, antelope, deer, bear, javelina, bobcat, jaguar, and mountain lion were all objects of these hunts. Wolf coursing with greyhounds was to Roosevelt the most exciting form of sport imaginable. He greatly admired the raw courage of greyhounds: "Nothing can possibly exceed the gallantry with which good greyhounds, when their blood is up, fling themselves on a wolf or any other foe. There does not exist, and there never has existed, on the wide earth a more perfect type of

dauntless courage than such a hound..." Riding to hounds appealed strongly to Roosevelt's instinctive sense of challenge and adventure:

...of all sports possible in civilized countries, riding to hounds is perhaps the best if followed as it should be, for the sake of the strong excitement, with as much simplicity as possible, and not merely as a fashionable amusement. It tends to develop moral no less than physical qualities; the rider needs nerve and head; he must possess daring and resolution, as well as a good deal of bodily skill and a certain amount of wiry toughness and endurance.

Coursing on the prairie was a favorite form of excitement:

This coursing on the prairie, especially after big game, is an exceedingly manly and attractive sport, the furious galloping, often over rough ground with an occasional deep washout or gully, the sight of the gallant hounds running and tackling, and the exhilaration of the pure air and wild surroundings, all combine to give it a peculiar zest. But there is really less need of bold and skilful horsemanship than in the otherwise less attractive and artificial sport of fox-hunting, or riding to hounds, in a closed and long-settled country

Fox or drag-hunting back East also had its rewards:

A single ride across country, or an afternoon at polo, will yield more exercise, fun, and excitement than can be got out of a week's decorous and dull riding in the park, and many young fellows have waked up to this fact.

At one time I did a good deal of hunting with the Meadowbrook hounds, in the northern part of Long Island. There were plenty of foxes around us, both red and gray, but partly for the reasons given above, and partly because the

> "We had a really good hunt and I think you would have enjoyed it all. The wild gallops after the coyotes in Oklahoma were first-class fun, and in an entirely different way, so was the bear hunting in Colorado."

On his last day in the White House, March 4th, 1909, the President was given this hunting knife. Etched on the blade was the inscription: PRESENTED TO THEODORE ROOSEVELT BY HIS FRIEND JAMES W. GERARD. The blade carried the maker's mark on the left side: J. RUSSELL & CO/GREEN RIVER WORKS. Maker of the silver, gold, and bronze hilt was Dreicer & Company, of New York City. The pommel was cast in the form of an American eagle head, with ruby eyes; one side of the hilt was cast with a Boone and Crockett motif in a forest setting, the other side with a gold and silver TR monogram applied in relief, plus an American eagle, and a wishbone. The crossguard was relief cast with bear-head finials.

PRIVATE COLLECTION

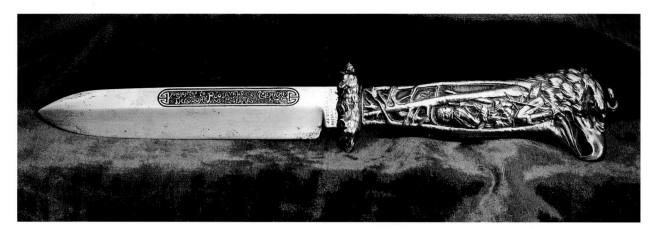

covers were so large and so nearly continuous, they were not often hunted, although an effort was always made to have one run every week or so after a wild fox, in order to give a chance for the hounds to he properly worked and to prevent the runs from becoming a mere succession of steeplechases. The sport was mainly drag-hunting, and was most exciting, as the fences were high and the pace fast...

Whether on foot, as in Louisiana or Colorado, or on horseback, as in New York or England, Roosevelt always retained his interest in hunting with the hounds. The need for stamina, perseverance and coolness, in addition to the rewards of excitement and exhilaration, were what appealed to him. The dangers of a bad fall from horseback or a cuffed face by a mountain lion never cooled his ardor or led him to question the feasibility of such a dangerous form of recreation.

Wild Turkey and Louisiana Bear

In November 1906, the President hunted wild turkey at Pine Knot, his country cottage in Virginia. He hunted for three consecutive days, starting early each morning. He met with indifferent success: "The first two days were failures," he wrote Kermit:

I did not see a turkey and on each occasion when everybody was perfectly certain that I was going to see a turkey, something went wrong and the turkey did not turn up. The last day I was out thirteen hours, and you may imagine how hungry I was when I got back, not to speak of being tired; though fortunately most of the time I was rambling around on horseback, so I was not done out. But in the afternoon at last luck changed, and then for once everything went right. The hunter who was with me marked a turkey in a point of pines stretching down from a forest into an open valley with another forest on its farther side. I ran down to the end of the point and hid behind a bush. He walked down through the pines and the turkey came out and started to fly across the valley offering me a beautiful side shot at about thirty-five yards—just the distance for my ten-bore. I killed it dead, and felt mighty happy as it came tumbling down through the air...

TR's 10-gauge turkey gun was probably his faithful old E. Thomas double barrel from the Badlands days. He preferred the rifle to the shotgun, but he had found so little time for hunting that he was ready to take up any chance that came his way—and the wild turkeys of Pine Knot were good sport.

Roosevelt's final hunt while in office took place from October 6 through 19, 1907, near Stamboul, Louisiana. He hunted bear. A year later he wrote about the trip in an article titled, "In the Louisiana Canebrakes," in *Scribner's* (January, 1908). He also wrote an account of the hunt in various letters to friends. Practically all of his letters describing hunting trips are extremely interesting and illuminating. He generally not only recaptured every important detail of the hunt itself, but usually interspersed his narrative with lively and informed descriptions of the flora and fauna he observed. To John Burroughs he wrote a concise commentary on the various animals he had glimpsed during the Louisiana holiday:

...I am sorry to say I do not think we shall get any bear for so far we have found but one,

which kept in very dense cover and finally fairly outran the dogs before any of us caught a glimpse of it. There are quite a party of us and we have the traditional appetites of hunters, but deer are very plentiful and we have shot four, strictly to keep the camp in meat. I killed one myself—the only shot I have fired; but I caught a glimpse of two wolves this morning, which had come down to the other side of the bayou, in broad daylight, to drink. There are great black squirrels here, the black fox squirrel, and numbers of birds. Most of these birds are simply our northern birds that have come down in the migration, but the commonest woodpeckers around camp are the red-bellied, which are new to me, and in a grove of giant cypress I saw two of the magnificent ivory-billed woodpeckers. I should be sorry to have missed them. The trees are majestic, especially the cypress, red gum, and white oak, which grow to such a stately height that it would be hard to equal them this side of the giant trees of California [P.S.] Since writing the above I killed a good big bear, at bay in a cane brake.

TR's rifle on this trip was the .45-70 Model 1886 Winchester (#125422), ordered from the factory in 1902. "[The] 45-70 which I was using," he wrote in the *Scribner's* article, "is a powerful gun and shoots right through cane or bushes..."

En route back to Washington, TR wrote to his son, Theodore, that "'Bad old father' is coming back after a successful trip... a success in every way including the bear hunt; but in the case of the bear hunt we only just made it successful and no more, for it was not until the twelfth day of steady hunting that I got my bear. Then I shot it in the most approved hunter's style, going up on it in a canebreak as it made a walking bay before the dogs..." Appropriately enough, his last hunt as President had been "a success in every way." ✦

CHAPTER 9

The Great African Adventure

Theodore Roosevelt's last full year as President was 1908. But by March of that year, he already had an idea of what he would do after he left the White House. "A year hence I shall leave the Presidency," he wrote to Colonel John Henry Patterson, a noted British big game hunter, explorer, and author:

...while I cannot now decide what I shall do, it is possible that I might be able to make a trip to Africa. Would you be willing to give me some advice about it? I shall be fifty years old, and for ten years I have led a busy, sedentary life, and so it is unnecessary to say that I shall be in no trim for the hardest kind of explorers' work. But I am fairly healthy, and willing to work in order to get into a game country where I could do some shooting. I should suppose I could be absent a year on the trip. Now, is it imposing too much on your good nature to tell me when and where I ought to go to get some really good shooting....Would it be possible for me to go in *from* Mozambique or some such place and come out down the Nile? How much time should I allow in order to give ample opportunity for hunting? Would it be possible for you to give me any idea of the expense, and to tell me how I should make my preparations; whom to write to in advance, etc.? Is there anyone who outfits for a trip like that to whom I could turn to know what I was to take?

I trust you will excuse me if I am trespassing too much on your good nature. It may be

Armed with a .405 Winchester, TR cautiously approached a rhinoceros. One gun bearer was carrying the backup .405 and the other held the Holland & Holland.

THEODORE ROOSEVELT COLLECTION, HARVARD COLLEGE LIBRARY

"In other words I shall be able to make it a scientific instead of merely a hunting trip, and all my trophies will go to the National Museum—a great relief to Edith, who, I think, felt she would have to move out of the house if I began to fill it full of queer antelopes, stuffed elephants, and the like."

that I shall not be able to go at all; but I should like mightily to see the great African fauna, and to kill one or two rhino or buffalo and some of the big antelopes, with the chance of a shot at a lion. [P.S.] I suppose that in a year's trip I could get into a really good game country; I am no butcher, but I would like to *see* plenty of game, and kill a few head.

After eight taxing years guiding the destiny of the nation, Roosevelt rewarded himself with the ultimate treat of all big game hunters—the African safari. "I am no butcher," he was sure to point out, "but I would like to *see* plenty of game, and kill a *few* head. TR's query to Patterson was but one of several letters to experienced and knowledgeable African hunters and naturalists, many of whom were fellow Boone and Crockett Club members. Patterson, Frederick C. Selous, R. J. Cuninghame, Carl Akeley, and Edward North Buxton formed the nucleus of a select coterie of Presidential advisers for the expedition.

On the 11th of April, Roosevelt wrote to Kermit, whom he was considering taking along:

...I have begun my correspondence about the African trip, altho it is not possible yet to say whether or not I can make it. Mr. Selous thinks we ought to go in by Mombasa, because the Uganda-Nile regions are not healthy, and we will get acclimated in the healthy regions; moreover, we would then have some hunting to the good anyway, even if we did not get out well from the Nile trip....

By late in June Roosevelt was already well along in plans for the African safari. He wrote on the 19th to Sir George Otto Trevelyan:

...When I get thru the Presidency next year, I *am* going for ten months or a year to Africa, and I am already in consultation with Edward North Buxton and Selous about the details of my trip.

As I wrote to Selous, my aim is to visit the Pleistocene and the world "as it lay in sunshine unworn of the plow;" to see the great beasts whose like our forefathers saw when they lived in caves and smote one another with stone-headed axes. I do not want to do any butchering, but I would like to get a few trophies. Probably all to be put in the National Museum here at Washington. My second son will go with me; and if I come out by the Nile the following spring I shall hope to meet Mrs. Roosevelt and my younger daughter there. I should then greatly like to spend a few weeks in North Italy, France and England; but I shall not try to if I find I have to be presented at the various courts, & meet the sovereigns, prime ministers, and others. When I am thru with the Presidency I am thru with it, definitely and once and for all. The second my successor takes the oath of office I become a private citizen, and then I wish to go downstream among the earthen pots and not among the brazen pots....

The next day TR sent a long letter to Boone and Crockett Club member, Dr. Charles Doolittle Walcott, Secretary of the Smithsonian Institution, offering to collect specimens of animal and bird life in Africa for the U.S. National Museum collection. Walcott was delighted by the President's proposal. The safari-vacation became a scientific expedition as well, one of great consequence. No trip before or since would make a more substantial contribution to the National Museum's collections of African natural history.

By early August, Roosevelt revealed his completed plans for the expedition in a letter to his old friend Henry Cabot Lodge:

...My African trip is all decided, and I am more and more convinced, as you always have been convinced, that it is the wisest thing I could possibly do. On March 23d I leave New York, and, going by Naples, reach Mombasa about a

"Only a few more days." The President could hardly wait for his successor to take over and for the safari to begin.

FROM THE CLEVELAND *PLAIN DEALER*

''Only a few more days.''

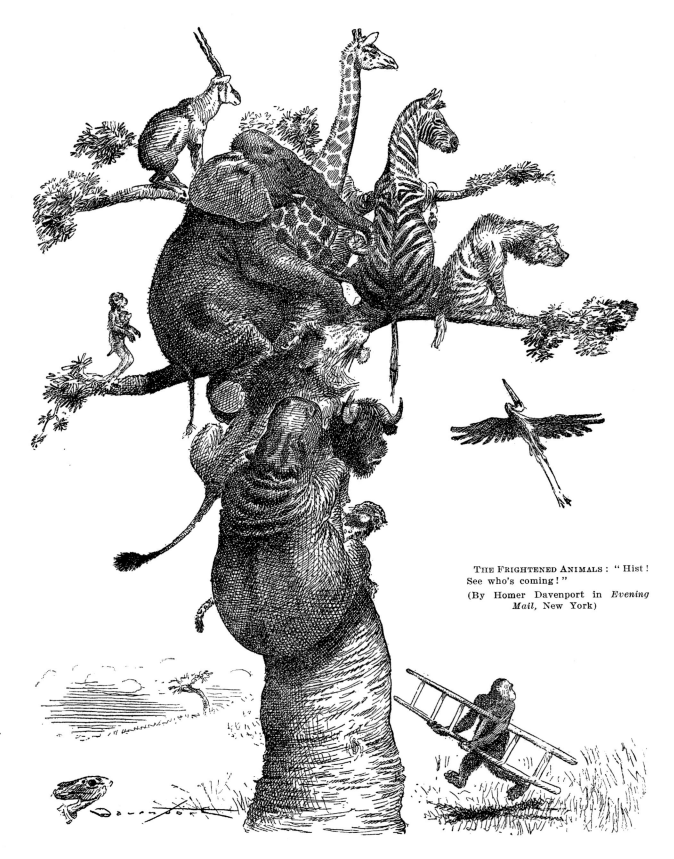

THE FRIGHTENED ANIMALS: "Hist! See who's coming!"
(By Homer Davenport in *Evening Mail*, New York)

"Hist! See Who's Coming!" by Homer Davenport. Africa's wildlife watched for the arrival of the big game hunter and ex-President.

FROM THE NEW YORK *EVENING MAIL*

month later. Probably about December I shall reach the headwaters of the Nile, via the Nyanza lakes, and will leave Cairo somewhere about the last of March. I shall travel for the National Museum at Washington, they giving me two taxidermists and paying for the expense of these taxidermists and for the transport of the specimens home. In other words I shall be able to make it a scientific instead of merely a hunting trip, and all my trophies will go to the National Museum—a great relief to Edith, who, I think, felt she would have to move out of the house if I began to fill it full of queer antelopes, stuffed elephants, and the like. As a matter of fact I don't want any more trophies....

His expressed intentions notwithstanding, selected trophies from the African bush would be prized souvenirs to add to the splendor of Sagamore Hill. Mrs. Roosevelt knew full well that her husband was much too enraptured over the African safari to come home without "queer antelopes, stuffed elephants, and the like" for their home. In fact, had he not done so it would have been a thorough surprise—and disappointment—to the entire Roosevelt household.

Fall and winter could not go by quickly enough for Theodore Roosevelt. "...I am looking forward to my African trip," he wrote Western artist Frederic Remington in October, "with just as much eagerness as if I were a boy." Preparation for each and every detail of the expedition brought many advisers on hunting and big game to the White House and to Sagamore Hill. TR listened intently to these experts. He wrote Kermit late in November:

...Col. Patterson, the man who killed the man-eating lions of Tsavo, spent Friday night with us, and was most interesting. Next day I had Carl Akeley, the Chicago man who has also hunted elephant & rhino in Africa, at lunch, and it was interesting to hear the two. I think I got some valuable advice from both. There is no question

that you and I must be extremely careful in dealing with lion, elephant, buffalo, and rhino; they are dangerous game. Both of us must be extremely cautious, and of course I shall want some first-class man with you until you grow accustomed to what is being done. All our arrangements are made; the stores have been sent to Africa, etc. etc. Both Patterson and Akeley were very much pleased at my having engaged Cuninghame [as a white hunter], and said that with a caravan the size of ours I would have been unable to have done much hunting if I had been obliged to manage the caravan myself.

It is not in the least like Buxton's trips, which are merely for a few days at a time away from the railroad. You and I want to go up into the really wild country....

The press was also preparing itself for Africa, much to the President's chagrin. TR was determined to avoid further press intrusions into his private life, as he made clear to newsman Melville E. Stone early in December:

...The other day I was concerned to find from one of the steamship lines, on which it was erroneously announced that I had taken my passage for Africa, that certain newspapermen, representatives of the press associations and individual newspapers, had also taken passage. Now, my trip is to be an entirely private trip, and I very earnestly hope, and shall very earnestly request, that the press associations and the newspapers of this country will under no circumstances send any representative with me, or try to see me or to have interviews with me or report my doings while I am on the trip. As you know, while I have been President I have done my best to give every proper and reasonable facility to every reputable newspaperman to know about all my public acts....

But when I start on this African trip I shall have ceased to be President, and shall be simply

"There is no question that you and I must be extremely careful in dealing with lion, elephant, buffalo, and rhino; they are dangerous game. Both of us must be extremely cautious..."

RIGHT: The Roosevelt Expedition, April 9, 1909 to March 30, 1910. Map by C.S. Hammond & Company.

BELOW: One can only imagine the delight TR felt when opening the package containing this elegant silver-mounted Tiffany & Co. compass, its case, and accessories. New York businessman and politician Alfred Hodges, of Brooklyn, made the presentation, accompanied by a brief letter:

> *469 Bedford Avenue*
> *February 22, 1909*
>
> *My dear Roosevelt:*
> *Herewith I send to you a compass, an aneroid barometer and a thermometer all contained in a gun metal case and a leather case for convenience in carrying.*
> *It seems to me that this will be useful to you in Africa and I ask you to accept it for "old times sake."*
> *Hoping you will have a successful expedition and return home safely and in good health, I am,*
> *Very cordially yours,*
> *Alfred Hodges*

On the 27th, TR responded:

> *My dear Hodges:*
> *That is a very beautiful and useful gift you have sent me. I prize it and I prize the inscription on it.*
> *With hearty thanks and regards, believe me...*

Note inscription encircling the gun metal case: President Theodore Roosevelt from an Old Time Friend Alfred Hodges February 22, 1909.

<small>PRIVATE COLLECTION;
PHOTOGRAPH COURTESY OF JOHN KILPATRICK</small>

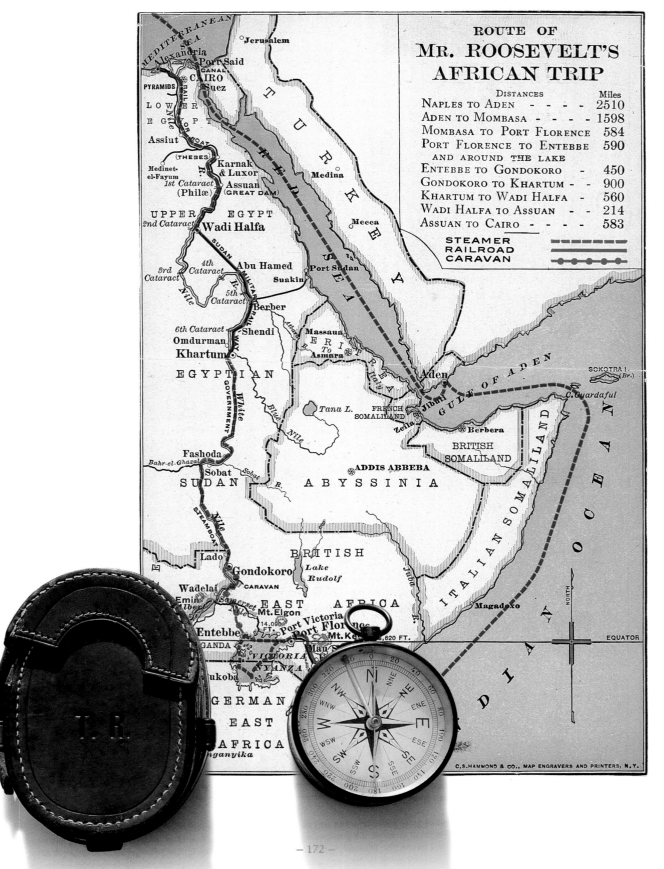

ROUTE OF MR. ROOSEVELT'S AFRICAN TRIP

DISTANCES	Miles
NAPLES TO ADEN	2510
ADEN TO MOMBASA	1598
MOMBASA TO PORT FLORENCE	584
PORT FLORENCE TO ENTEBBE	590
AND AROUND THE LAKE	
ENTEBBE TO GONDOKORO	450
GONDOKORO TO KHARTUM	900
KHARTUM TO WADI HALFA	560
WADI HALFA TO ASSUAN	214
ASSUAN TO CAIRO	583

STEAMER
RAILROAD
CARAVAN

C.S. HAMMOND & CO., MAP ENGRAVERS AND PRINTERS, N.Y.

a private citizen, like any other private citizen....It will be an indefensible wrong, a gross impropriety from every standpoint, for any newspaper to endeavor to have its representatives accompany me on this trip, or to fail to give me the complete privacy to which every citizen who acts decently and behaves himself is entitled. To send any reporters with me would really be a wanton outrage....Now don't you think that we can get the newspaper press of this country to acquiesce in this view and leave me alone when I am out of office and have left the country? Can't you make the request of the newspapers generally, by circular or otherwise?

Notwithstanding these efforts at protecting his privacy, Roosevelt was always a newsworthy public figure. Wherever he was the press was usually not far behind. Since no newsman went into the bush with Roosevelt, however, the only authoritative account of the safari is his own book, *African Game Trails*.

In the late fall and winter of 1908, newspapers ran copious stories about Roosevelt's impending African hunt. Not all of the stories were friendly and a few made jest of the proposed venture. In October, Sir Harry Johnston, a British diplomat serving in South Africa and then visiting the United States, uttered some caustic comments about the projected hunt. "If I had my say," he publicly stated, "I should present a telephoto camera instead of a rifle to the President and entreat him to take shots at long range with that. Everywhere we witness the destruction of animals and birds indigenous to their native soils, and I am for preserving them rather than destroying them. Africa is no exception and big game there is slowly being exterminated."

Antagonistic publicity about Roosevelt's well-advertised hunting plans began to spread and did not subside until the Smithsonian Institution released a news story indicating the scientific significance of the exploration and the benefits to be derived from the specimens that would be acquired.

Roosevelt had worked out an agreement with the Smithsonian to collect specimens for them; he would pay the expenses of himself and Kermit, while the museum would supply the technicians and preserve the specimens. In his initial letter to the Smithsonian, Roosevelt had said: "As you know, I am not in the least a game butcher. I like to do a certain amount of hunting; but my real and main interest is the interest of a faunal naturalist... the specimens will all go to the National Museum, save a very few personal trophies of little scientific value, which for some reason I might like to keep." Thus the Smithsonian Institution informed the world that President Roosevelt's trip to Africa was primarily for the advancement of knowledge and the enrichment of their scientific collections.

To accompany Roosevelt in the "great adventure" the Smithsonian chose a U.S. Army naturalist, Dr. Edgar Mearns. Edmund Heller, a 26-year-old professor at the University of California, who later became a professional member of the Boone and Crockett Club, was personally chosen by TR to assist on the expedition. Heller had already traveled extensively in Mexico, Central and South America and Alaska. In 1914, he and Roosevelt would author a two-volume work, *Life-Histories of African Game Animals*, still considered a basic reference on the subject. Alden Loring, of Owego, New York, was another naturalist who went along.

The arrangements for the hunt itself had been made by big game hunters Frederick C. Selous and Edward North Buxton. They, in turn, would be assisted on the safari by R.J. Cuninghame and Leslie Tarlton, both renowned hunters who were familiar with Africa and its game. Two hundred natives were needed to carry the expedition across Africa. The cost of the entire adventure, subsidized in part by Andrew Carnegie, was estimated at $75,000. Roosevelt had arranged to pay for his share by writing articles for *Scribner's* magazine with the eventual idea of collecting them into a book. *Scribner's* agreed to give him an honorarium of $50,000, plus royalties from the book.

Antagonistic publicity about Roosevelt's well-advertised hunting plans began to spread and did not subside until the Smithsonian Institution released a news story indicating the scientific significance of the exploration and the benefits to be derived from the specimens that would be acquired.

Early in 1909 Roosevelt sent a note to Winston Churchill of England in which he praised the latter's book, *My African Journey*:

I have just received the beautiful copy of your book, and I wish to thank you for it. I had read all the chapters as they came out, with a great deal of interest; not only the chapters upon the very important and difficult problems of the Government itself, but also the hunting chapters and especially the one describing how you got that rare and valuable trophy, a white rhinoceros head. Everyone has been most kind to me about my proposed trip to Africa. I trust I shall have as good luck as you had.

Arming the Roosevelt Expedition

The acquisition of firearms for the safari is a story in itself. Since taking along the proper arms was crucially important, Roosevelt gave the matter extended consideration. In a letter to Kermit he outlined the kinds of weapons he thought suitable for the trip:

...I enclose you letters from Buxton and Selous, and maps, together with an envelope in which please place them, after you have looked at them, and send them back to me. I shall not answer them until I have consulted with you. The time is near enough now for us to make our plans pretty definitely. I think I shall get a double-barrelled 450 cordite, but shall expect to use almost all the time my Springfield and my 45-70 Winchester. I shall want you to have a first-class rifle, perhaps one of the powerful new model 40 or 45 caliber Winchesters. Then it may be that it would be a good thing to have a 12-bore shotgun that could be used with solid ball. Perhaps you should also have a spare rifle. I am afraid the 30-30 is too light for African game. In any event we would thus have four rifles and the shotgun between us so as to allow for accidents. It is no child's play going after lion, elephant,

rhino and buffalo. We must be very cautious; we must be always ready to back one another up, and probably we ought each to have a spare rifle when we move in to the attack...

The battery of Roosevelt and his son is described in *African Game Trails:*

My rifles were an army Springfield, 30-calibre, stocked and sighted to suit myself; a Winchester 405; and a double-barrelled 500-450 Holland, a beautiful weapon presented to me by some English friends....Kermit's battery was of the same type, except that instead of a Springfield he had another Winchester shooting the army ammunition, and his double-barrel was a Rigby. In addition I had a Fox No. 12 shot-gun; no better gun was ever made.

The "army Springfield, 30-calibre" was his old standby custom-made Sporter, serial #6000. The Rigby double rifle was lent by African hunter John Jay White, and the Holland & Holland 500-450 was given to Roosevelt early in 1909. The Fox shotgun was also delivered at the White House, and like the Springfield, the Holland, and the Winchesters, was fully custom-made. The two Winchesters, .405 caliber Model 1895 lever actions, were the regular rifles for big game, and they were augmented by a back-up .405 and a .30-40, both also Model 1895s. TR on safari would affectionately refer to his regular .405 Winchester as his "medicine gun" for lion.

Winchester had the honor of supplying the President with the most important guns for the safari. He had always had a high regard for the company's products, and they in turn took special pains to satisfy the President's wishes, even when a few of these were—or so they must have seemed at times to Winchester—whimsical. Excerpts from the Winchester-Roosevelt correspondence tell a story in themselves, and are included in the Appendix.

OPPOSITE: Cased Holland & Holland, its interior cover with elegant gold-imprinted trade label in leather, and the list of presenters imprinted on paper within the lid. Wear on metal and wood indicative of extensive and hard use on the 1909-1910 safari.

FRAZIER HISTORICAL ARMS MUSEUM

A few months before the expedition embarked Roosevelt sent a detailed letter to Kermit, devoting a full paragraph to their battery of hunting guns:

...John Jay White, that African hunter who struck us as being a little nervous, to judge by his letters, was on here to lunch. He was very interesting and gave me one or two points. He was also very kind; he has left his double-barreled 450 cordite [a Rigby] in Nairobi. He says it is in fine trim and that he will give it to us. Accordingly I wrote to Newland, Tarlton & Company; our agents in Nairobi, who have the gun, to get it all ready and get cartridges for it. If necessary either you or I can take this gun and the other take the double-barreled Holland, and therefore we now have each a type of the hard-hitting double-barreled English gun which they say is necessary. Personally I cannot help feeling that the Winchester will be our ordinary weapon, but of course I may be utterly mistaken. Moreover, nice George Meyer has given me his little Manlicher rifle, which has a telescopic sight. The weapon is a perfect beauty; and with the telescopic sight one certainly does see marvelously up to say 300 yards. I have made up my mind not to take out my 45.70 rifle, and shall take this little Manlicher in place of it. The more I have thought over the matter the more convinced I have become that I would prefer the 405 Winchester for any purpose for which I desired to take the 45.70 and as long as I now have an extra 405 it is not worth while taking the 45.70 at all. My Holland double barrel is on the way here for me to try....

I enclose the list of the English donors of my rifle.

Some mystery surrounds the Rigby double barrel rifle which was used by Kermit on the safari. No details have been located as to its serial number, though the caliber is known as .450 nitro or cordite. Since it was left by sportsman John Jay White in Nairobi for the Roosevelts to collect, no doubt the rifle was left there (with Newland, Tarlton & Co.) at the safari's completion.

It has been suggested that the rifle was serial number 17311, which had been built by Rigby for Captain The Honorable Guy Wilson, in 1906, for safari abroad. The rifle has an unusually long forend, in which the wood extended beyond the forend latch release, a few inches. Further, there is the possibility that White obtained the rifle from Wilson.

An examination of a photograph showing Kermit with his Rigby, and his father with his Holland & Holland, suggests that the former rifle did indeed have a longer than standard forend.

Roosevelt's Holland & Holland double rifle, #19109, a .500/.450, was the London firm's finest grade. TR considered it a "beautiful weapon" and told in *African Game Trails* how his friend E.N. Buxton had conscripted the support of many English friends and admirers of TR to order the custom gun.

The original Holland & Holland company records show that work began in the fall of 1908, that the rifle was a "best quality 450 bore Royal [grade]," and it was "not to be sent to U.S. for trial Finish outright." Planning well in advance, Buxton had first discussed the rifle with TR by letter in the summer of 1908. Writing from the White House on August 8, the President had told Buxton:

I have never used a peep sight. I do not know whether it is just a prejudice of mine, or whether it is really that my eyes are not suited to one. I have always used open sights. At long range, I am sorry to say, I never was really good for anything. I enclose you the type of front sight I like most. The rear sight I like very open, but with a little U that takes the bead of the front sight.

A delighted Theodore Roosevelt finally received his Holland & Holland double rifle early in

1909, in plenty of time for the safari. It had been made to his tastes in every respect, with the added and elegant touch of a gold circular inlay on the buttstock, engraved with the Presidential eagle and the inscription: TR/1909. The crescent cheekpiece, the pistol grip stock, the rubber recoil pad, the sling swivels, the flat-topped leaf rear sights (graduated for 100, 200, and 300 yards), the gold-beaded steel blade front sight, the rich blue and case-hardened finish and the first-class workmanship were all in keeping with Roosevelt's taste for fine guns.

Worthy of the title "History's Most Important and Valuable Sporting Rifle," the presentation Holland & Holland express double rifle has no rivals. Presently, the center of an elaborate and costly display at the Frazier Historical Arms Museum, Louisville, Kentucky, TR's Holland & Holland weathered eleven months of intense use by the 26th President of the United States, and was featured in his articles in *Scribner's*, as well as in *African Game Trails*. Upon return to the U.S., by way of Europe, a gala dinner was held in England, saluting TR, who was guest of the donors who had funded the presentation.

The Ansley H. Fox Deluxe Presentation Shotgun

While the Holland & Holland was in manufacture, still another fine grade gun was in the works. This was an Ansley H. Fox double-barrel shotgun, 12 gauge, constructed in the company's finest style. Very little is known of this piece from the President's battery, though two letters tell much of the story. The first of these was sent to the President by Fox himself, on August 13, 1908:

> The Directors of this Company, having read of your proposed hunting trip, have instructed me to offer to make to order for you the finest gun this company can produce.
>
> I am mailing to you one of our art catalogues under separate cover and call your

particular attention to the great simplicity and strength of our gun which should commend it for the hard use we hope you will give it.

> We are prompted in this purely by our high regard and esteem for you as well as our desire that you should do your shooting with an American product, made by Americans specially for you.
>
> In granting us this privilege of thus serving you, I desire it to be thoroughly understood that the offer is not made with an idea or thought of using it as an advertising scheme in any sense of the word, but, on the contrary, I pledge my word, that of each Director separately on the honor gentlemen that your acceptance will not be so construed, and solicit the pleasure of an early reply.
>
> Yours respectfully,
> A.H. Fox
> Pres't
> P.S.—I herewith enclose a lists of our Directors and their business connections.

An exchange of letters between TR and Fox is missing, since TR wrote to Fox, September 10, 1908:

> When I wrote you I did not intend to take a shotgun to Africa. I find, however, that I would like to take such a gun, provided that at close quarters I could use it with ball also. In other words, I should like in case of an emergency to have it loaded with ball and use it as a spare gun for a lion. Now I have rather a pride in taking American rifles on this trip, and in the same way I should like to take an American gun; but of course you may have by this time decided that you do not care to repeat your very kind offer; in that event will you tell me what the cost of such a gun as I have described, twelve-bore and plain finish, would be?
>
> [P.S.] Of course the use with ball would be wholly exceptional; normally I should use it for geese, ducks, guinea fowl & etc.

"We are prompted in this purely by our high regard and esteem for you as well as our desire that you should do your shooting with an American product, made by Americans specially for you."

Fox did agree to build a gun for Roosevelt, but it was hardly of "plain finish," though indeed of 12 gauge.

These advertisements by the A.H. Fox Gun Company, after the safari, were surely agreed to by TR, rather than Fox going against his stated word.

The original Fox factory record (dated September 18, 1908), identifies the TR shotgun as serial #13292, an F grade, with 30" barrels, the right with modified choke, the left full, the stock of 14" length, with drop at comb of 1-5/8", drop at heel of 2-1/2"; the overall weight of 7 pounds 8 ounces; trigger pull of 5 pounds for the right trigger, and 6 pounds for the left; automatic safety. Remarks in the record note: "This gun is for exhibition purposes and must be as perfect as skill can make it...thin comb....Shop records simply say Exhibition gun [.] Mr. Fox will select stock frame and barrels." The reverse side of the original record is marked: "Pres. Roosevelt."

The top of the right barrel is inscribed:
MADE EXPRESSLY FOR HON.
THEODORE ROOSEVELT

The top of the left barrel is inscribed:
BY A.H. FOX GUN COMPANY
PHILADELPHIA U.S.A.

Early in 1909, TR sent Fox a glowing letter about the deluxe shotgun made subsequent to his note of September: "The double-barreled shotgun has come, and I really think it is the most beautiful gun I have ever seen. I am exceedingly proud of it. I am almost ashamed to take it to Africa and expose it to the rough usage it will receive. But now that I have it, I could not possibly make up my mind to leave it behind. I am extremely proud that I am to have such a beautiful bit of American workmanship with me." TR. would repeat himself in *African Game Trails* when he proudly said: "I had a Fox No. 12 shotgun; no better gun was ever made."

This historic American shotgun is accompanied by its original oak and leather casing.

"Made Ready in Every Way"

In his book, *The Happy Hunting Grounds*, Kermit remembered how his father had thoroughly dedicated himself to preparing for Africa:

For the African expedition [Father] made ready in every way. I was at the time at Harvard, and almost every letter brought some reference to preparations... "You and I will be so rusty when we reach Sir Alfred Pease's ranch [first hunting grounds of the party in Africa] that our first efforts at shooting are certain to be very bad. In March we will practise at Oyster Bay with the 30-30 until we get what I would call the 'rifle sense' back again, and this will make it easier for us when, after a month's sea trip, we take up the business of hunting....At last I have tried the double-barrelled Holland Elephant rifle. It is a perfect beauty and it shoots very accurately, but of course the recoil is tremendous, and I fired very few shots. I shall get you to fire it two or three times at a target after we reach Africa, just so that you shall be thoroughly familiar with it, if; or when, you use it after big game."...The recoil of the big gun was so severe that it became a standing joke as to whether we did not fear it more than a charging elephant!

As the Presidency had been the great adventure of Theodore Roosevelt's political life, so the safari would be the great moment of his private life. Within a month after William Howard Taft's inauguration, TR and Kermit, accompanied by a large retinue of fellow hunters, aides, and naturalists, sailed aboard the *S.S. Hamburg* for Africa. On April 21, the party glided into the picturesque harbor of Mombasa. Those in the party who had come to Africa for the first time experienced a vivid sense of expectation

OPPOSITE: Three views of TR's Fox side-by-side, double-barrel shotgun, serial #13292, F grade, with 30" barrels – right with modified choke and left with full choke; 14" length of pull. Made for the Honorable Theodore Roosevelt and so inscribed.

PRIVATE COLLECTION;
PHOTOGRAPHS COURTESY OF THOMAS C. KIDD

BACKGROUND: "In addition I had a Fox No. 12 shotgun; no better gun was ever made." Quoting TR writing in *Scribner's* magazine, on his African safari, and as used by the A.H. Fox Gun Company in its advertising brochure, "What Theodore Roosevelt Said About the Fox Gun." The latter included letters of February 11 and 16, 1909, from the White House. TR's endorsements were powerful marketing tools for the company.

The vast continent teemed "with beast of the chase," Roosevelt wrote, "infinite in number and incredible in variety." Africa was a naturalist's and hunter's paradise. "It holds the fiercest beasts of raven... It holds the mightiest creatures that trek the earth or swim in its rivers."

as they took their first steps on African soil. None could even faintly anticipate what the safari would actually be like, not even the usually prescient ex-President; all knew, however, that in one way or another it was bound to be fulfilling and satisfying.

The Long-Awaited Hunt

From Mombasa, Roosevelt and several members of his party headed by train for the Kapiti Plains, the starting point of the long-awaited hunt. For the next eleven months the safari traversed a good part of East Africa, slowly following a route northwest and then north, from Nairobi to Kijabi, then on to Mt. Kenya and Mt. Elgon, after which the party moved methodically across Lake Victoria to Uganda. Ultimately, the expedition traveled across the White Nile and finally reached Khartoum. The journey itself, highlighting as it did the sometimes stark, sometimes sublime grandeur of the Dark Continent, seemed reward enough for the painstaking labors the safari had required.

Africa was a land of marked contrasts and mystery. Roosevelt wrote in *African Game Trails* that he saw:

> ...mountain peaks whose snows are dazzling under the equatorial sun; swamps where the slime oozes and bubbles and festers in the steaming heat; lakes like seas; skies that burn above deserts where the iron desolation is shrouded from view by the wavering mockery of the mirage; vast grassy plains where palms and thorn-trees fringe the dwindling streams; mighty rivers rushing out of the heart of the continent through the sadness of endless marshes; forests of gorgeous beauty, where death broods in the dark and silent depths.

The vast continent teemed "with beast of the chase," Roosevelt wrote, "infinite in number and incredible in variety." Africa was a naturalist's and hunter's paradise. "It holds the fiercest beasts of raven... It holds the mightiest creatures that trek the earth or swim in its rivers." Those

hunters and naturalists who had the good fortune to travel through Africa see "sights which ever after remain fixed in the mind. In after years there shall come to him memories of the lion's charge; of the gray bulk of the elephant...of the buffalo...of the rhinoceros."

African Game Trails, Roosevelt's *magnum opus* on the safari, is a splendid narrative depicting the natural beauty and awesomeness of the African landscape. Its description of the endless variety of animals, their habits and characteristics, is always compelling and usually very moving. Roosevelt felt genuine respect for the great beasts. He admired their instinctive courage and massive strength and marveled at their self-sufficiency. In the wild jungles the animals lived each day in a constant struggle against both the elements and, often, each other. It was a tooth-and-claw existence, and only the fittest survived. His observation of animal life in Africa reinforced his avid belief in Darwinian evolution. It also reaffirmed a longstanding conviction of his: life itself was a continual struggle and only those able to adapt to changing conditions were capable of survival. Roosevelt reveled in Africa because he believed it was as close as one could get to the natural world as it existed at the dawn of creation. The ruling principle of that world was violence:

> Death by violence, death by cold, death by starvation—these are the normal endings of the stately and beautiful creatures of the wilderness. The sentimentalists who prattle about the peaceful life of nature do not realize its utter mercilessness; although all they would have to do would be to look at the birds in the winter woods, or even at the insects on a cold morning or cold evening. Life is hard and cruel for all the lower creatures, and for man also in what the sentimentalists call a "state of nature." The savage of to-day shows us what the fancied age of gold of our ancestors was really like; it was an age when hunger, cold, violence, and iron cruelty were the ordinary accompaniments of life...

Roosevelt did not countenance the promiscuous slaughter of wildlife. Few have been as deeply concerned over the preservation of animal species as he was. But he was no sentimentalist. He understood perfectly well that wild animals could not multiply geometrically. Nature had to have a way of striking a balance between the populations of various species. Shooting wild animals, therefore, was not *ipso facto* morally wrong or cruel. Roosevelt maintained that:

…game laws should be drawn primarily in the interest of the whole people, keeping steadily in mind certain facts that ought to be self-evident to every one above the intellectual level of those well-meaning persons who apparently think that all shooting is wrong and that man could continue to exist if all wild animals were allowed to increase unchecked. There must be recognition of the fact that almost any wild animal of the defenceless type, if its multiplication were unchecked while its natural enemies, the dangerous carnivores, were killed, would by its simple increase crowd man off the planet, and of the further fact that, far short of such increase, a time speedily comes when the existence of too much game is incompatible with the interests, or indeed the existence, of the cultivator. As in most other matters, it is only the happy mean which is healthy and rational. There should be certain sanctuaries and nurseries where game can live and breed absolutely unmolested; and else where the laws should so far as possible provide for the continued existence of the game in sufficient numbers to allow a reasonable amount of hunting on fair terms to any hardy and vigorous man fond of the sport, and

TR with one of his big lions—a photogravure from a photograph by Kermit Roosevelt. Appeared as the frontispiece in *Africa Game Trails.*

6 61. From left to right; Cuninghame, self, Father, Heller, and Heatley at Buffalo Camp.

AFRICAN SAFARI

CLOCKWISE FROM LEFT: "Our three bulls were fine trophies." The party with skulls from the buffalo shot on the second day at Hugh H. Heatley's farm. From left to right: R.J. Cunninghame, Kermit, TR, Edmund Heller, and Heatley. Note the American flag, which accompanied the expedition throughout Africa. ❧ The party's first big lion – Kermit at left, Sir Alfred Pease at center. TR and Kermit are both armed with Model 1895 Winchester, in .405 caliber. ❧ The President with Kermit and a Cape buffalo taken with the Holland & Holland in Kenya 1909. ❧ TR and Captain Arthur Slatter, with a black rhinoceros taken by TR at Kilimakiu with the Holland & Holland double rifle. The rhino's charge was stopped at "just thirteen paces from where we stood." ❧ At Juja Farm with H. Judd and one of TR's seven hippopotamus. TR was holding the Holland & Holland, but all of his hippos were taken with the Springfield Sporter and the Model 1895 Winchester rifle. ❧ Kermit holding his Winchester 1895 with a cheetah – one of seven – shot by him.

Excerpts from TR's African diary. Drawings show position of game and where each was hit. His notes usually record the site of the hunt, the species of game and the distance of each shot.

THEODORE ROOSEVELT
BIRTHPLACE COLLECTION

A wildebeest taken by TR with his .30-06 Springfield Sporter. R.J. Cunninghame at left.

THEODORE ROOSEVELT COLLECTION,
HARVARD COLLEGE LIBRARY

yet not in sufficient numbers to jeopard[ize] the interests of the actual settler, the tiller of the soil, the man whose well-being should be the prime object to be kept in mind by every statesman. Game butchery is as objectionable as any other form of wanton cruelty or barbarity; but to protest against all hunting of game is a sign of softness of head, not of soundness of heart.

Game Bags, Guns, and Shooting

The hunt itself was an unqualified success. Roosevelt and Kermit took 512 head of game, Roosevelt accounting for 296 and Kermit 216. Of the most dangerous beasts included in this number were: 11 elephant, 17 lion, 3 leopard, 7 cheetah, 20 rhinoceros, 8 hippopotamus, and 10 buffalo. Most of these were brought down by the .405 Model 1895 Win-

chesters; many were shot with the Holland & Holland and the Rigby double rifles, and the Springfield Sporter. Over 75 species of smaller or less dangerous game were shot by the ex-President and his son. Most of them taken with TR's .30-40 caliber Springfield Sporter or with Kermit's .30-40 Model 1895 Winchester. Of these species, the bag numbered 9 hyena, 7 wildebeest, 12 warthog, 29 zebra, 9 giraffe, 10 eland, 2 kudu, 15 bushbuck, 53 hartebeest, 24 kob, 12 impala, 47 gazelle, *3* baboon, 4 crocodile, 4 python and many more.

Using the Fox shotgun, the Roosevelts took "Egyptian geese, yellow-billed mallards, francolins, spurfowl and sand grouse for the pot, and certain other birds for specimens." The great bulk of animals shot were turned over to the Smithsonian. Roosevelt proudly reported that:

> Kermit and I kept about a dozen trophies for ourselves; otherwise we shot nothing that was not used either as a museum specimen or for meat—usually for both purposes. We were in hunting grounds practically as good as any that have ever existed; but we did not kill a tenth, nor a hundredth part of what we might have killed had we been willing. The mere size of the bag indicates little as to a man's prowess as a hunter, and almost nothing as to the interest or value of his achievement.

References to the .30-40 Springfield, the Winchester, and the Holland & Holland abound in *African Game Trails*. TR even "made a point of keeping as many as possible of the bullets with which the different animals were slain so as to see just what was done by the different types of rifles we had with us." He assessed the effectiveness of the Winchester .405 and the Holland & Holland .500/.450 on rhinoceros:

> As we brought home the whole body of this rhinoceros, and as I had put into it eight bullets, five from the Winchester and three from

the Holland, I was able to make a tolerably fair comparison between the two. With the full-jacketed bullets of the Winchester I had mortally wounded the animal; it would have died in a short time, and it was groggy when it came out of the brush in its final charge; but they inflicted no such smashing blow as the heavy bullets of the Holland. Moreover, when they struck the heavy bones they tended to break into fragments, while the big Holland bullets ploughed through.

About the Springfield .30-40 Sporter he remarked:

The Winchester and the Springfield were the weapons one of which I always carried in my own hand, and for any ordinary game I much preferred them to any other rifles. The Winchester did admirably with lions, giraffes, elands, and smaller game, and, as will be seen, with hippos. For heavy game like rhinoceros and buffaloes, I found that for me personally the heavy Holland was unquestionably the proper weapon. But in writing this I wish most distinctly to assert my full knowledge of the fact that the choice of a rifle is almost as much a matter of personal idiosyncrasy as the choice of a friend. The above must be taken as merely the expression of my personal preferences. It will doubtless arouse as much objection among the ultra-champions of one type of gun as among the ultra-champions of another. The truth is that any good modern rifle is good enough. The determining factor is the man behind the gun.

Roosevelt's marksmanship on the safari was in the main good, but he had his erratic moments. Vision in his left eye was very poor as a result of a boxing accident in the White House in 1906. He did not tell anyone of his impaired vision until after the African expedition. In the light of Roosevelt's imperfect depth perception, his hits in Africa, many at long distances, were no mean accomplishment.

A superior knowledge of game, especially of their relative sizes, plus stubbornness and courage, accounted for his success under trying circumstances.

A few statements in *African Game Trails* suggest that TR had difficulty seeing clearly:

In the afternoon I came on giraffes and got up near enough to shoot at them. But they are such enormous beasts that I thought them far nearer than they were. My bullet fell short....

Distances are deceptive on the bare plains under the African sunlight. I saw a fine Grant [gazelle], and stalked him in a rain squall; but the bullets from the little Springfield fell short as he raced away to safety; I had underestimated the range.

Again I knelt and fired; but the mass of hair on the lion made me think he was nearer than he was, and I undershot, inflicting a flesh wound…[approximately 200 yards]

TOP: "Charged straight for the boat, with open jaws, bent on mischief." A photogravure from a drawing by Philip R. Goodwin featured in a special two-volume edition of *African Game Trails*.

BOONE AND CROCKETT CLUB
PERMANENT COLLECTION

Excerpts from TR's African diary. A few pages in the diary are marked "writing," and were days devoted to the *Scribner's* series and to correspondence.

THEODORE ROOSEVELT
BIRTHPLACE COLLECTION

TR pictured with a mammoth black rhinoceros bull proudly displaying his Winchester .405.

THEODORE ROOSEVELT COLLECTION
HARVARD COLLEGE LIBRARY

INSET: Celebrated Winchester advertisement, "Coming Events Cast Their Shadows."

JIM WALTER COLLECTION

IN BACKGROUND: "Truth Will Out," a Winchester advertisement in *Scribner's* magazine, published soon after TR's series on the expedition began.

Roosevelt never tried to extenuate his shooting lapses. He always gave a balanced version of his performance:

I rarely had to take the trouble to stalk anything; the shooting was necessarily at rather long range, but by maneuvring a little, and never walking straight toward a beast, I was usually able to get whatever the naturalists wished. Sometimes I shot fairly well, and sometimes badly. On one day, for instance, the entry in my diary ran: "Missed steinbuck, pig, impala and Grant; awful." on another day it ran in part as follows: "Out with Heller. Hartebeest, 250 yards facing me; shot through face, broke neck. Zebra, very large, quartering, 160 yards, between neck and shoulder. Buck Grant, 220 yards, walking, behind shoulder. Steinbuck, 180 yards, standing, behind shoulder." Generally each head of game bagged cost me a goodly number of bullets; but only twice did I wound animals which I failed to get [this statement remained true until later in the safari]; in other cases the extra cartridges represented either misses at animals which got clean away untouched, or else a running fusillade at wounded animals which I eventually got. I am a very strong believer in making sure, and, therefore, in shooting at a wounded animal as long as there is the least chance of its getting off. The expenditure of a few cartridges is of no consequence whatever compared to the escape of a single head of game which should have been bagged. Shooting at long range necessitates much running. Some of my successful shots at Grant's gazelle and kongoni were made at 300, 350, and 400 yards; but at such distances my proportion of misses was very large indeed—and there were altogether too many even at shorter ranges.

The so-called grass antelopes, the steinbuck and duiker, were the ones at which I shot worst; they were quite plentiful, and they got up close, seeking to escape observation by hiding until the last moment; but they were small, and when they did go they rushed half hidden through the grass and in and out among the bushes at such a speed, and with such jumps and twists and turns, that I found it wellnigh impossible to hit them with the rifle. The few I got were generally shot when they happened to stand still.

On the steep, rocky, bush-dad hills there were little klipspringers and the mountain reedbuck or Chanler's reedbuck, a very pretty little creature… I shot two [reedbuck] does with three bullets, all of which hit. Then I tried hard for a buck at last, late one evening, I got up to one feeding on a steep hill-side, and actually took ten shots to kill him, hitting him no less than seven times.

African Game Trails is replete with kills from short range to beyond 400 yards; most of these were with one or two shots, and all of them with open sights. TR kept an interesting and candid record of the distances at which he shot wild beasts, the number of shots needed, and, of course, the number of misses.

Within 25 yards. Roosevelt dropped a hippo (one shot), a lioness (two hits out of three shots), a rhinoceros (two shots), and an elephant (several shots). At 30 yards he felled a charging rhinoceros with one shot, at 40 yards an elephant with seven shots, and at 50 yards two rhinos (two shots on one and one on the other).

At 60 yards TR dropped a rhino with four shots and an ostrich with one. At 80 yards he brought down an elephant with two shots and a buffalo with three. And at 85 yards he killed an ostrich.

Most of his recorded kills were made at distances from 100 to 400 yards. Of these, approximately one half were from 100 to 200 yards: Among those at 100 were an elephant (several shots), a charging lion (four shots), a bushbuck, a water buck, and a bustard. Hit but not killed at that distance were a hippopotamus, which escaped, and a giraffe, which was brought down in a subsequent chase.

"Rhino when hunted, though at times ugly customers, seem to me certainly less dangerous than the other three; but from sheer stupid truculence they are themselves apt to take the offensive in unexpected fashion, being far more prone to such aggression than are any of the others - man-eating lions always excepted."

Of the recorded 150 yard kills there were: one buffalo, a hartebeest, and a klipspringer running, and a Kavirondo crane flying (hit after several misses).

Most of TR's shooting at beyond 150 yards was done at species of antelope, gazelle, zebra, and the like. At 180 yards he brought down an eland on the run, and at 200 killed a lechwe running (one shot), a gazelle, and a kob. Two more gazelle fell at 210 and 225 yards, respectively. From 250 to 260 yards, there were impala, boar, gazelle, topi, and a giraffe.

An eland partially facing TR was a one shot kill at 280 yards, another was down in a fusillade at 300+ yards, a wildebeest was brought down in one shot at 300 yards running and four hartebeests and a zebra were killed at the same distance, with several shots at standing and some at running heads.

At 350 yards and beyond, there were usually expended a quantity of cartridges before TR had his range zeroed in. He hit an oryx at 350 yards, then missed it twice and finally killed it at 300 yards. A topi was killed at 350, and a wildebeest was shot at approximately twelve times from 300 to 500 yards and was finally brought down. At 400 yards, a kongoni was killed and another wounded and successfully chased by horseback. At the same distance, TR killed an eland after several misses, and at 450 yards, he brought down an oryx— again after several shots. One of the longest kills was of a topi at 520 yards—after several shots.

Naturally, Roosevelt did not enjoy missing, but he had been a hunter too long ever to become distracted over a miss. He hunted, as he good-naturedly put it, "on the Ciceronian theory, that he who throws the javelin all day must hit the mark some time." Occasionally, some of his shots hit the mark, but not always the right one. He hit a lion in the paw at 200 yards, and a few game, both big and small, he shot in the rump!

Though his marksmanship faltered from time to time, his courage and resoluteness remained unspotted. TR faced more than his share of close calls from charging wild beasts, but he never wavered. He never hunted big game unfairly and he never killed for the sake of killing. Roosevelt was a hunter's hunter and a sportsman's sportsman.

The Big Five and Other Game

The most prized and dangerous big game of Africa—lion, leopard, elephant, rhinoceros, and buffalo — understandably offered Roosevelt his greatest challenge. He was fully alive to the dangers attendant on such hunts:

The hunter who follows any of these animals always does so at a certain risk to life or limb; a risk which it is his business to minimize by coolness, caution, good judgment, and straight shooting. The leopard is in point of pluck and ferocity more than the equal of the other four; but his small size always renders it likely that he will merely maul, and not kill, a man....

During the last few decades, in Africa, hundreds of white hunters, and thousands of native hunters, have been killed or wounded by lions, buffaloes, elephants, and rhinos. All are dangerous game; each species has to its gruesome credit a long list of mighty hunters slain or disabled. Among those competent to express judgment there is the widest difference of opinion as to the comparative danger in hunting the several kinds of animals....The experts of greatest experience...absolutely disagree among themselves; and there is the same wide divergence of view among good hunters and trained observers whose opportunities have been less....

Personally, I believe the actual conflict with a lion, where the conditions are the same, to be normally the more dangerous sport, though far greater demands are made by elephant hunting on the qualities of personal endurance and hardihood and resolute perseverance in the face of disappointment and difficulty. Buffalo, seemingly, do not charge as freely as elephant, but

OPPOSITE: "The chase of the elephant, if persistently followed, entails more fatigue and hardship than any other kind of African hunting." TR's first bull elephant was brought down with two shots from the Holland & Holland. The pair of tusks weighed 130 pounds, each side.

219.   Giant eland.   Eland trip.

are more dangerous when they do charge. Rhino when hunted, though at times ugly customers, seem to me certainly less dangerous than the other three; but from sheer stupid truculence they are themselves apt to take the offensive in unexpected fashion, being far more prone to such aggression than are any of the others - man-eating lions always excepted.

In hunting the lion, TR put his trust in the Winchester Model 1895 .405, his "medicine gun for lions." His first big cat was shot on the Kapiti Plains, late in April 1909:

...Almost as soon as we reached [the creek] our leader found the spoor of two big lions; and with every sense acock, we dismounted and approached the first patch of tall bushes. We shouted and threw stones, but nothing came out, and another small patch showed the same result. Then we mounted our horses again, and rode toward another patch a quarter of a mile off. I was mounted on Tranquility, the stout and quiet sorrel.

This patch of tall, thick brush stood on the hither bank - that is, on our side of the watercourse. We rode up to it and shouted loudly. The response was immediate, in the shape of loud gruntings, and crashings through the thick brush. We were off our horses in an instant, I throwing the reins over the head of mine; and without delay the good old fellow began placidly grazing, quite unmoved by the ominous sounds immediately in front.

I sprang to one side; and for a second or two we waited, uncertain whether we should see the lions charging out ten yards distant or running away. Fortunately they adopted the latter course. Right in front of me, thirty yards off, there appeared, from behind the bushes which had first screened him from my eyes, the tawny galloping form of a big maneless lion. Crack! the Winchester spoke; and as the

soft-nosed bullet ploughed forward through his flank the lion swerved so that I missed him with the second shot, but my third bullet went through the spine and forward into his chest. Down he came, sixty yards off, his hindquarters dragging, his head up, his ears back, his jaws open and lips drawn up in a prodigious snarl, as he endeavored to turn to face us. His back was broken; but of this we could not at the moment be sure, and if it had merely been grazed, he might have recovered, and then, even though dying, his charge might have done mischief. So Kermit, Sir Alfred [Pease], and I fired, almost together, into his chest. His head sank, and he died.

Some nine miles from camp by Kilimakiu mountain, early in May, TR shot his first rhinoceros:

...The huge beast was standing in entirely open country, although there were a few scattered trees of no great size at some little distance from him. We left our horses in a dip of the ground and began the approach... The big beast stood like an uncouth statue, his hide black in the sunlight, he seemed what he was, a monster surviving over from the world's past, from the days when the beasts of the prime ran riot in their strength, before man grew so cunning of brain and hand as to master them. So little did he dream of our presence that when we were a hundred yards off he actually lay down.

Walking lightly and with every sense keyed up, we at last reached the bush, and I pushed forward the safety of the double-barrelled Holland rifle which I was now to use for the first time on big game. As I stepped to one side of the bush so as to get a clear aim, with Slatter [a local ostrich-rancher] following, the rhino saw me and jumped to his feet with the agility of a polo pony. As he rose I put in the right barrel, the bullet going through both lungs. At the same moment

OPPOSITE: TR's giant eland, shown here with the skinner and gun bearers.

INSET: En route to Redjaf to hunt giant eland. Standing behind TR were two gun-bearers and one of seven Belgian askari guards who accompanied the Roosevelt party on this side trip.

THEODORE ROOSEVELT COLLECTION, HARVARD COLLEGE LIBRARY

Mannlicher-Schoenauer bolt-action rifles were of considerable popularity with sophisticated sportsman very soon after their introduction early in the 20th century. Among enthusiastic users were the American ex-patriot, sportsman and champion shot, Walter Winans, the artist Alexander Phimister Proctor, Delia (Mrs. Carl) Akeley, and – in later years – George Eastman. The rifle presented to TR in Austria after the African trip, a Model 1905, bears. serial #5220; and has a 22 1/2" barrel. Inlaid on the right side of the buttstock is an inscribed silver plaque:

This Mannlicher-Schoenauer
.256 Sporting Rifle md 1903
with the Baillie Grohman peep
sight & his mechanism to take the rifle
apart is presented to
Mr. Theodore Roosevelt
by the Oest. W.F.G. of Steyr
as a souvenir of his recent visit
to Austria

Although the Mannlicher-Schoenauer rifle taken by TR on the African expedition, likely a Model 1905, in 9x56 M/S caliber, has yet to be located, several references are made to it, not only in *African Game Trails*, but in TR's lengthy correspondence with Winchester, preparing for the safari. Yet to be seen by the writer are any photographs of TR or Kermit with the safari Mannlicher.

THEODORE ROOSEVELT
BIRTHPLACE COLLECTION

he wheeled, the blood spouting from his nostrils, and galloped full on us.

Before he could get quite all the way round in his headlong rush to reach us, I struck him with my left-hand barrel, the bullet entering between the neck and shoulder and piercing his heart. At the same instant Captain Slatter fired, his bullet entering the neck vertebrae. Ploughing up the ground with horn and feet, the great bull rhino, still head toward us, dropped just thirteen paces from where we stood.

This was a wicked charge, for the rhino meant mischief and came on with the utmost determination...

Stalking the elephant provided the acid test for big-game hunters. "No other animal, not the lion himself," Roosevelt observed, "is so constant a theme of talk round the camp-fires of African hunters and in the native villages of the African wilderness.. . ." Pursuit of the elephant "entails more fatigue and hardship than any other kind of African hunting." Roosevelt shot his first elephant in Mount Kenya, in August 1909. In so doing, he narrowly escaped being killed himself:

At last we came in sight of the mighty game. The trail took a twist to one side, and there, thirty yards in front of us, we made out part of the gray and massive head of an elephant resting his tusks on the branches of a young tree. A couple of minutes passed before, by cautious scrutiny, we were able to tell whether the animal was a cow or a bull, and whether, if a bull, it carried heavy enough tusks. Then we saw that it was a big bull with good ivory. It turned its head in my direction and I saw its eye; and I fired a little to one side of the eye at a spot which I thought would lead to the brain. I struck exactly where

I aimed, but the head of an elephant is enormous and the brain small, and the bullet missed it. However, the shock momentarily stunned the beast. He stumbled forward, half falling, and as he recovered I fired with the second barrel, again aiming for the brain. This time the bullet sped true, and as I lowered the rifle from my shoulder, I saw the great lord of the forest come crashing to the ground.

But at that very instant, before there was a moment's time in which to reload, the thick bushes parted immediately on my left front, and through them surged the vast bulk of a charging bull elephant, the matted mass of tough creepers snapping like packthread before his rush. He was so close that he could have touched me with his trunk. I leaped to one side and dodged behind a tree trunk, opening the rifle, throwing out the empty shells, and slipping in two cartridges. Meanwhile Cuninghame fired right and left, at the same time throwing himself into the bushes on the other side. Both his bullets went home, and the bull stopped short in his charge, wheeled, and immediately disappeared in thick cover.... [This bull escaped.]

If we had been only after ivory we should have followed him at once but there was no telling how long a chase he might lead us; and as we desired to save the skin of the dead elephant entire, there was no time to spare....

Some Publicity for Winchester

TR had no quarrel with the performance of the Winchesters and the .30-40 Springfield Sporter. Within a month after the safari began, he had written Henry Cabot Lodge that he was "pleased to find that my American rifles, which everyone warned me against taking, have done well." In *Af-*

rican Game Trails his esteem for Winchester rifles is dearly evidenced by such affectionate allusions as "my medicine gun for lion," "the beloved Winchester" and "the faithful Winchester." The company could not have asked for a more commanding endorsement of its products.

Before embarking on his African safari, Roosevelt had been assured by Winchester that it would "take all pains to see that the privilege [of supplying firearms for the safari] is not abused or made use of by us for advertising purposes" But the temptation to capitalize was too strong for the advertising manager, William Clark. Harold Williamson, in *Winchester - The Gun That Won the West* reports that Clark ran advertisements prior to the safari's departure "showing a picture of the map of South Africa with a hand thrust thru the map from the rear holding a Winchester rifle, the shadow of which fell directly across the central part of Africa—beneath the picture was a caption in large letters, 'COMING EVENTS CAST THEIR SHADOWS'....Williamson was quoting a former company official, Henry Brewer, who had first-hand knowledge of that era of Winchester history. Clark's ads, according to Brewer, were run without the knowledge of company President, T.G. Bennett, who became quite upset. Roosevelt's reaction, however, was said to have been not at all what Bennett expected. Williamson states that the "President did not seem to be a bit annoyed—in fact, loving publicity as he did, he seemed to be rather amused and rather tickled with the situation..."

The advertisement has the headline in the Winchester lightning style logo, beneath which is a map of Africa, with a gauntleted hand thrust through, holding a Winchester Model 1895 rifle. The rifle's shadow is silhouetted WINCHESTER. At the bottom of the advertisement is the boldface statement "Coming Events Cast Their Shadows"—accompanied by the text:

Winchester
Winchester rifles and

Winchester Ammunition—the invariable choice of experienced and discriminating big game hunters.
[decorative mark]
Sold everywhere. Ask for
THE RED W BRAND

Yet another advertisement appeared in *Scribner's* late in 1909. Headlined "Truth Will Out," this ad also depicted a map of Africa, also thrust through with a gauntleted hand, this time clutching a large scroll. On the scroll were Roosevelt's remarks on his rifles that had been published in the October, 1909, issue of *Scribner's*:

My rifles were an Army Springfield, 30-calibre, stocked and sighted to suit myself; a Winchester 405 [the underscoring was by Winchester's advertising department]; and a double-barrelled 500-450 Holland ....

To the left of the map was the underscored word Winchester, and the statement "Winchester Rifles and Winchester Ammunition are the invariable choice of experience-taught and discriminating big game hunters." How TR reacted to this unauthorized publicity is unknown, but having a high regard for the company, and no longer holding public office, he probably did not mind. Still, there must have been some anxious moments in the Winchester front office.

Back to America

Steaming up the Nile on the last leg of the trip to Khartoum, Roosevelt got his last full view of Africa's dark and strange beauty:

At night we sat on deck and watched the stars and the dark, lonely river. The swimming crocodiles and plunging hippos made whirls and wakes of feeble light that glimmered for a moment against the black water. The unseen birds of the marsh and the night called to one another

"The big beast stood like an uncouth statue, his hide black in the sunlight, he seemed what he was, a monster surviving over from the world's past, from the days when the beasts of the prime ran riot in their strength, before man grew so cunning of brain and hand as to master them."

"He came on steadily, ears laid back and uttering terrific coughing grunts." A photogravure from a drawing by Philip R. Goodwin featured in a special two-volume edition of *African Game Trails*.

in strange voices. Often there were grass fires, burning leaping lines of red, the lurid glare in the sky above them making even more sombre the surrounding gloom.

The expedition reached Khartoum on March 14, 1910, where the party separated. "Kermit and I parted from our comrades of the trip with real regret," Roosevelt wrote, adding, "it was a sad parting from our faithful black followers, whom we knew we should never see again."

The trip had been a tremendous success. There were no major accidents, and the health of Roosevelt and his son was excellent. Kermit had been sick from tick fever for a total of three days, while his father was sick for but five days. "I think my fever had nothing to do with Africa at all," TR noted,

...and was simply a recurrence of the fever I caught in the Santiago campaign and which ever since has come on at long and regular intervals....The couple of attacks I had

in Africa were very slight; by no means as severe as one I had while bear hunting early one spring in the Rocky Mountains.

Over 11,000 specimens had been captured and preserved. The 4,897 mammals, 4,000 birds, 500 fishes, 2,000 reptiles and many invertebrates collected are still available for study in the Smithsonian Institution and in other museums. It is one of the most prized collections of its kind in the world.

Some measure of the general high regard in which the expedition was held may be seen from two reviews of books TR wrote about his adventures. The *National Geographic Magazine* devoted six pages to reviewing *African Game Trails*:

The sights which [Roosevelt] saw are described so vividly and accurately that even the most quiet and unimaginative citizen thousands of miles from the scene of Africa's grandeur can easily picture the extraordinary contract which remain so fixed in Mr. Roosevelt's mind... The book is an unusual contribution to science, geography, literature, and adventure... the strongest and best work of literature Mr. Roosevelt has yet written...

Reviewing *Life-Histories of African Big Game Animals*, the *Bulletin of the American Geographical Society* stated: "...the work is a very valuable contribution to geography and zoology and no other book covers the same field...the authors have given us a work which will long be standard in its field."

Mrs. Roosevelt and her daughter Ethel met the expedition in Khartoum. It was a happy reunion for the big-game hunter. He guided his wife and daughter on a tour of the desert from the back of a camel. From Khartoum, where they were lavishly entertained by Saltin Pasha, the Roosevelts went to Cairo, where the President infuriated Egyptian nationalists by predicting ruin to the Sudan and Egypt if British rule came to an end.

Roosevelt's original plan to return directly

home from Egypt was abandoned because of the many requests for lectures and personal appearances. He had been planning for some time to deliver his Nobel Peace Prize address in Norway, the Sorbonne had requested a lecture and Oxford had invited him to give the Romanes Lecture. Even Kaiser Wilhelm wanted him to speak to German university students in Berlin. He soon found, however, "that while the different rulers did not really care a rap about seeing me they did not like me to see other rulers and pass them by." From Egypt he traveled to Italy and from there to Austria-Hungary, France, Belgium, Holland, Norway, and England. On his tight schedule in England was a dinner held by the donors of his Holland & Holland rifle. TR was received by cheering crowds everywhere but Germany, where "the Germans did not like me and did not like my country; and under the circumstances...showing me every civility and making no pretense of an enthusiasm that was not present."

In early June 1910, an anxious nation waited for the ex-President's return. Twenty-five hundred people gathered in New York harbor to greet him, and he was given an escort up Broadway and Fifth Avenue in the midst of a huge parade. A splendid "welcome home" dinner was planned for June 22 at Sherry's in New York, with a highly select guest list and a profusion of delicacies. After the fancy dinner and cheering crowds, Americans sat back and wondered what the big-game hunter planned to do next. ❦

Front cover of six-page brochure prepared by London gunmakers Holland & Holland, Ltd., for the "African Hunter Series," in 2009. The .500/.450–3 1/4" caliber double "Royal" grade rifle was built as a centennial salute to TR's African safari, and to the original presentation cased rifle, as depicted on pages viii-ix and 175. As stated in the brochure, the 2009 rifle, serial #35555, "is the direct descendant of the rifle #19109." Others in the "African Hunter Series of Rifles" are The Sir Samuel Baker, The Captain Frederick Courtney Selous, The W.D.M. Bell, The John Taylor, and The James Sutherland. The firm's gunrooms are noted on the brochure, in London, New York and Moscow.

CHAPTER 10

Farewell to a Bull Moose

Roosevelt was 51 years old when he returned to the United States from his African safari. He could have slipped into a comfortable and well-earned retirement and spent the remainder of his life writing, traveling, lecturing, and hunting. He, himself, would not have been opposed to pursuing such activities because they had always been favorite pastimes. Roosevelt's interests were so broad and his hobbies so varied that the "idle" years ahead of him would have scarcely been dull or lackluster.

There seems little doubt that Roosevelt would never again have become engaged in politics had not the Republican Party become a house badly divided against itself while he was in Africa. President William Howard Taft was a good and sincere man who tried to continue the progressive programs of his predecessor. But he was a weak executive who shrank from making decisions. In addition, he was susceptible to strong political pressures and in a crisis tended to follow the line of least resistance. It was difficult for any man to succeed Roosevelt, but Taft compounded his problems by a propensity for vacillation. He was certainly no willful tool of corporate wealth, but he was awed by the political influence that big business wielded. Rather than exercise the vast powers and resources of his office to keep a rein on various capitalist interests, Taft drifted into indecision and timidity. The more he temporized and equivocated, the stronger conservative groups in the Republican Party became.

Republican Progressives in Congress were profoundly dismayed by Taft's unintended alliance

January 7, 1919—Pallbearers carrying the flag draped casket containing the body of Colonel Roosevelt to its final resting place in the Young Memorial Cemetery at Oyster Bay.

© BETTMAN/CORBIS

"Friends, I shall ask you to be as quiet as possible. I don't know whether you fully understand that I have just been shot; but it takes more than that to kill a Bull Moose....The bullet is in me now...Friends, I am thinking of the movement....I do not care a rap about being shot; not a rap....Now friends, what we Progressives are trying to do is to enroll rich or poor...to stand together for the most elementary rights of good citizenship."

with congressional spokesmen for corporate interests. Though personally not in favor of excessively high protective tariffs, Taft found himself in the unenviable position of having to defend the Payne-Aldrich tariff of 1900. Though a true believer in conservation, Taft dismissed Gifford Pinchot as Chief Forester because of the allegations the latter had made concerning gross improprieties in the sale of valuable coal lands in Alaska. Almost without meaning to, Taft had alienated himself from the Progressive wing of his Party

News of Taft's difficulties reached Roosevelt while he was in Africa. He was appalled to learn that Taft had dismissed Pinchot, but when he returned to the United States in 1910, he refrained at first from openly criticizing the Taft administration. As TR watched insurgent Republicans repudiate the President's leadership, he became convinced that Taft had shattered party unity. Slowly Roosevelt came round to the conviction that, in the interests of the public and the Republican Party, Taft ought not to be renominated for the Presidency in 1912. The ex-President had not as yet made up his mind to seek the nomination for himself, but he no longer had any faith in Taft.

Roosevelt's open break with the Taft administration was occasioned by the famous "New Nationalism" speech, which he delivered in Kansas in August 1910. It was a bold and brilliant espousal for increased federal intervention in economic matters, a graduated income tax, anti-child-labor laws, and a host of comparable measures to ensure social justice for all classes. Conservatives throughout the nation were shocked by Roosevelt's radicalism, and President Taft at last realized the complete estrangement of himself from his former political mentor.

Progressives in the Republican Party rallied round TR and began endorsing him for the Presidential nomination in 1912. He, himself, did not believe that the Republican Party would fare well in 1912 and thus would have preferred to run four

years later. The Party was in such a state of disarray, however, and the pleas of Progressives were so importunate, that Roosevelt determined to seek the nomination. In February 1912, he announced, "My hat is in the ring."

A bitter political struggle between Roosevelt and Taft supporters ensued. Roosevelt undertook a strenuous campaign to win the endorsement of delegates to the Republican nominating convention in Chicago. Everywhere he went he was received enthusiastically. The people responded to his charisma as much as they had in the past. But it was a losing battle. Taft supporters had taken the necessary steps to make sure that delegates sympathetic to their cause would be in the majority at Chicago. At the convention a fight immediately broke out over which delegate ought to be officially seated. When practically all of the contested seats went to Taft men, Roosevelt delegates bolted the convention and proceeded to organize the Progressive Party and to nominate Roosevelt as its presidential candidate. Declaring himself to be as "fit as a Bull Moose," Roosevelt entered the campaign with his usual buoyancy, but he was not at all optimistic about his chances. The Democrats had nominated a popular liberal candidate in Governor Woodrow Wilson of New Jersey and adopted an enlightened and progressive platform of their own. With the Republican Party split into Roosevelt and Taft forces, Democrats felt assured of a Wilson triumph.

Fighting uphill, Roosevelt waged a relentless assault on trusts and on special interest groups that manipulated the federal government for their own selfish end. He attacked the complacency of the Taft administration and the tepid Progressivism advocated by Wilson. Only a strong federal government, he argued, could keep big business in line and make it amenable to the public welfare. His New Nationalism was predicated on a vigorous employment of governmental powers to bring equal rights and fair opportunities to all classes of Americans.

A sour and near fatal event obtruded itself on the campaign scene when on October 14, a fanatic shot Roosevelt as he was about to get into his car in Milwaukee. The bullet, fired from a revolver point-blank, tore through Roosevelt's coat, steel spectacle case, and folded speech before lodging near his right lung. Dazed by the projectile, Roosevelt managed to stand up and shout to the onrushing crowd, "Don't hurt the man." Refusing to be driven to a hospital, he insisted on being taken to the auditorium where he was scheduled to deliver a speech. Before a stunned audience and with complete presence of mind, he declared:

> Friends, I shall ask you to be as quiet as possible. I don't know whether you fully understand that I have just been shot; but it takes more than that to kill a Bull Moose....The bullet is in me now.... Friends, I am thinking of the movement....I do not care a rap about being shot; not a rap.... Now friends, what we Progressives are trying to do is to enroll rich or poor...to stand together for the most elementary rights of good citizenship.

Roosevelt spoke for nearly an hour and the audience was absolutely mesmerized by the incredible display of courage and stamina they were witnessing.

Convalescing at Sagamore Hill, Roosevelt made one final pre-election speech at Madison Square Garden on October 30. Twelve thousand people wildly cheered his ringing address reaffirming his faith in the New Nationalism. As the dramatic election campaign came to a close, however, Roosevelt was aware that he had only an outside chance of winning. Outwardly, he appeared sanguine and confident, inwardly, he knew that the outlook was not bright. He was right. Wilson won the election, but Roosevelt far outdistanced Taft, both in the electoral count and in the popular vote. Considering the serious handicap of a split party, Roosevelt had nothing to be ashamed of. Although he did not remove himself from the political life of the nation, this was his last election campaign. He was now able to bring his public life and his private life into balance. A deep personal

sense of responsibility and urgency had taken him away from private pleasures in 1912. He now returned to his writing, his family, his hunting, his "bully" life, with gusto.

From Kaiser Wilhelm II to President Roosevelt— The Deluxe Luger Carbine

Among the most exotic of modern firearms is the carbine version of the Luger semi-automatic pistol. The Luger was a totally new handgun early in the 20th century, and one of its dedicated advocates was Kaiser Wilhelm II. Due to his crippled left arm, the Kaiser found the Luger Carbine ideal for shooting roe deer. Knowing of Roosevelt's hunting interests, it was long thought that the Kaiser invited TR to hunt when traveling through Germany enroute back from the African expedition. It was also believed that Kaiser Wilhelm had then presented a deluxe, cased Luger Carbine to the President. Initially it appeared that the case and the attachable shoulder stock for the presentation were in the Theodore Roosevelt Birthplace Collection.

Kermit's affection for what appeared to be this carbine was demonstrated by his use of a Luger with stock while on the River of Doubt Expedition.

Considerable research has been done in the set's documentation in the 1990s and early 21st century. The results suggest that TR was presented with only one cased Luger Carbine, and the likely date was early in 1902.

Bearing serial number 10012C, a TR Model 1902 Luger Carbine is known embellished on the top of the breech with an American eagle motif, and the GL initials of the inventor, George Luger (on the third toggle piece). In his column, "Lugers at Random," Charles Kenyon, Jr., Sr. Staff Editor of *The Gun Report* magazine, noted that there were *two* Luger Carbines belonging to the President, the first of them the Model of 1902, and received as a presentation while Roosevelt was in the White House. The second of these was a presentation believed made during TR's visit to Austria and Germany, in 1910.

A July 3, 1902 letter directed the Commanding Officer at the Springfield Armory to:

forward the Luger Automatic Pistol sent you June 6, 1902, for correction of sights and general overhauling, to The President at Oyster Bay, New York, immediately upon completion of repairs, reporting your action by endorsement here-on with the return of this paper to this Office.

The brief directive was signed by William Adzier, Brigadier General, Chief of Ordnance, Washington, D.C.

Revealing of a considerable amount of energy and effort devoted to making the Luger work properly and accurately, a lengthy letter dated July 18, 1902, was addressed to the President, from Lt. Colonel Phipps, advising that on:

the 9th of June last I received from the Chief of Ordnance, U.S.A., a Luger automatic carbine belonging to you, with instructions to correct the following faults, viz:

"The carbine shoots 6 or 8 inches too high at 100 yards. Have the rear sight cut down and opened so as to be a 'U' instead of a 'V' and then the bead of the front sight will be more distinct."

In addition to this the pistol was to be generally overhauled and put in perfect working condition.

As this arm has been kept here so long, it is but fair that an explanation should be made of the cause of the delay: The carbine was received here without any ammunition for it. It was therefore tested with the pistol ammunition which we had on hand. This ammunition, it was found, did not give sufficient recoil to work the pistol automatically, and it became evident that a cartridge with a heavier powder charge was required to move a barrel 7-1/2 inches longer than that of the pistol.

ABOVE: Deluxe case and buttstock of TR's Model 1902 Luger Pistol Carbine, possibly presented by Kaiser Wilhelm II, early in 1902. Pistol and stock carried by Kermit on the Brazilian expedition of 1913-14.

THEODORE ROOSEVELT
BIRTHPLACE COLLECTION

OPPOSITE: Kaiser Wilhelm, German Emperor during World War I, and President Theodore Roosevelt riding horses together.

© BETTMAN/CORBIS

Kenyon's research had determined that in 1902, a Luger Carbine had been sent from the White House to the Springfield Armory, for alterations to the sight, and also to investigate why there were problems with the mechanism while firing. A letter dated July 2, 1902, from Lt. Colonel, Ordnance Department, U.S. Army, Commanding the Armory, Frank H. Phipps, was addressed to the Chief of Ordnance, U.S. Army, and dealt with those problems. Phipps noted that the agent for the maker, a Mr. [Hans] Tauscher, was "traveling about so much that it is difficult to reach him." Correspondence had also been undertaken with the Union Metallic Cartridge Co., in an attempt to purchase ammunition which would work in the pistol. The cartridges at hand did not produce enough recoil to allow the action to reload automatically on firing.

If you had any difficulty with the automatic working of the carbine, it was due probably to the fact that you were using pistol ammunition.

A letter was written to Mr. Tauscher, agent of the manufacturers of the Luger arms, explaining our difficulty and requesting that he send ammunition intended for the carbine. It was not until June 30th that 50 cartridges were received from him. Mr. Tauscher has sailed in the meantime for Europe. The 50 cartridges were exhausted before the necessary firing to properly graduate the sights for the carbine could be made. An effort was made to secure more cartridges like those sent by Mr. Tauscher, in which the charge should be 1.45 grains heavier than that in the pistol ammunition. None of these being procurable, in this country at least, it was necessary to have some made. This manufacture the Winchester Repeating Arms Company undertook, from that data I furnished it.

In graduating the sights, it was found necessary to cut the rear sight down as low as possible and to make a new front sight—higher.

Lt. Colonel Phipps then noted test firings at 100, 200, 300, 400, and 500 yards, with the elevation to the sights set accordingly. The ammunition used was noted, as well as the "Elevation of Shots on Target," and remarks, such as "Strong wind at 400 & 500 yds." And "Weather and light—good." Phipps concluded his letter by stating:

Up to and including 300 yards the showing was excellent, but at 400 and 500 yards the shots were too low. By bringing the rear sight slide catch to the edge of the 500-yard notch, the shots truck about 8-1/2 inches above the center of the target at 400 yards. From the construction of this sight it is impracticable to make any alteration. A new sight will be necessary. This can be done, of course, if desired, but as it is probable this carbine will not be used at these longer ranges, it is thought best to send the carbine as it is and await further instructions.

I am sending with the carbine, by direction of the Chief of Ordnance, U.S.A., 500 cartridges similar to those used in the test. They go forward to you at Oyster Bay by express to-day.

One can only imagine the delight the President took in having such expert assistance as the Springfield Armory *and* the Winchester Repeating Arms Company, looking after his wishes with his new pistol.

In addition to discovering the 1902 correspondence about TR's Luger, Kenyon corresponded with the German authority, Reinhard Kornmayer, who investigated records pertaining to TR's visit in Berlin, from May 12 to 15, 1910. Kornmayer determined that TR visited with the Kaiser on May 13, and found a telegram sent by the President to Wilhelm (May 15), in which TR noted gifts he had received: "I prize the books, I prize the beautiful vase, which will ever stand in my house. I prize the photos with your characteristic comments on the backs of them." But TR makes no mention whatever of a German Luger Carbine. The conclusion of Kornmayer was that the President was not presented with the cased Luger Carbine on that visit. It therefore appears that the cased set had been a gift sent during the early period of TR's presidency.

Presentations from Master Gunmaker Fred Adolph

Ferlach immigrant gunsmith Fred Adolph settled in Genoa, New York, and was an ardent admirer of Theodore Roosevelt. Unlike most of his contemporary custom gunmakers, Adolph printed a handsomely illustrated catalogue with detailed text. Titled, "Modern Guns," the catalogue describes a visit Adolph made with President Roosevelt, at his Sagamore Hill estate, for presentation of an over-and-under combination gun. Two exquisite firearms were built by Adolph for the President.

OPPOSITE: The Browning semi-automatic pistol serial #8664, with the Fred Adolph big game double rifle, serial #4108 in .500/.450 caliber. Note the presidential eagle engraved on each barrel. R.J. Kornbrath was the engraver of this rifle, as well as the Adolph over-and-under.

NATIONAL FIREARMS MUSEUM

"Teddy's" New Gun

Fred Adolph of Genoa, the maker of the finest guns in America, if not the world, returned Wednesday morning from Oyster Bay, Long Island, where he went to deliver the gun which he has been making during the last year for Colonel Theodore Roosevelt. Mr. Adolph visited Sagamore Hill, the home of Mr. Roosevelt, Tuesday.

The ex-President, in a khaki suit, waving a big Alpine stick, was just ready to start on a trip across the fields, accompanied by his son Archie, when Adolph drove up in an auto, and handed the gun to him. Roosevelt expressed his delight about the gun in very flattering terms, opened and closed the action several times, praised the workmanship, engraving and . . .

. . . in gold on the left side Hiawatha and Minnehaha, after a painting by Taylor; on the right side, Hiawatha with bow and arrow and a swan on his shoulder, and on the top the insignia of the Camp Fire Club of America in gold, surrounded by heavy relief engraving. Stock and fore end are fully carved with deer, fox and phea . . . gun is without the slightest d . . . ful gun ever built in A . . . highest sense.—*Tribu*

Lieut. Whelen, w . . . in "*Field and S . . .*"

Both were richly engraved and of quality equal to the Holland & Holland double barrel rifle. With a 20-gauge upper barrel and .25-35 rifled lower barrel, the Fred Adolph over-and-under was one of the few combination guns in the Roosevelt collection. A particularly personal embellishment was the low relief gold inlaid logo of The Camp Fire Club of America, on the top of the breech. This appears to be the only instance in which that motif appeared on any of Roosevelt's firearms. Tragically, the over-and-under Adolph special was severely burned in a fire on the 1986 "In the Blood" film safari, in Tanzania. The badly damaged remains were then stolen from the shipment of film material sent on KLM Airlines from Tanzania to Amsterdam to New York City, along with a handful of other arms which had also survived the fire. Ironically, the much more valuable Holland & Holland double rifle cased set arrived safely in New York, while the fire-damaged guns did not.

The Final Hunts

By the end of spring 1913, Roosevelt had finished writing his autobiography, a candid and absorbing recollection of an extremely busy and varied life. He continued writing a flock of informed articles for major journals and periodicals on almost every imaginable subject. With friends scattered throughout the world, he carried on an indefatigable correspondence. He took long walks in the country and exercised rigorously and religiously. His body was still sound, and his mind was as acute and receptive as ever.

For two weeks in July, TR, sons Archibald and Quentin, and nephew Nicholas hunted mountain lion in the Grand Canyon. Accompanied by guides and a pack of hounds, the party shot three mountain lion and several rattlesnakes. The Roosevelts finished up their holiday by crossing the Navajo Desert, visiting with the Hopi Indians and camping in the Colorado wilderness. This was Roosevelt's last hunt for big game in the United States. Details of the adventure were later published in *A Book-Lover's Holidays in the Open*, written with verve and vividness.

By the early fall of 1915, Roosevelt had lost the sight of his left eye, which had been injured in the White House boxing accident. But in no way did this loss interfere with either the pace or nature of his activities. His most perilous adventure—the exploration of Brazil's mysterious "River of Doubt"—was yet to take place. It was, as he coyly stated, his "last chance to be a boy," and he resolved not to let a sightless left eye stand in the way of an expedition that promised so much adventure.

The South American Expedition

In June 1913, Roosevelt had been invited by Romulo Naón, the Argentine Minister to the United States, to speak in his country on the principles of democratic government. TR accepted the invitation and within a short time other requests for speaking engagements came from officials in Brazil and Chile.

When Roosevelt had been in the White House, his friend Father John Zahm had suggested a trip to the South American wilderness, but TR had chosen Africa instead. The speaking invitations, however, presented a new opportunity for South American adventure. Accordingly, he hired the famed Arctic explorer, Anthony Fiala, who was helpful to Zahm in making most of the arrangements for the Amazon expedition (Zahm was also present on the early part of the trip). TR also enlisted the aid of Henry Fairfield Osborn, Director of the American Museum of Natural History in New York City, and Frank M. Chapman, a curator of ornithology at the same museum – both fellow Boone and Crockett Club members. Osborn tried to dissuade Roosevelt from undertaking the dangerous trip. But the ex-President would not be diverted from his plans: "Tell Osborn I have already lived and enjoyed as much of life as any nine other men I know; I have had my full share, and if it is necessary for me to leave my bones in South America, I am quite ready to do so."

Tragically, Roosevelt's remark nearly become prophetic. The expedition was partly inspired by

OPPOSITE BACKGROUND: "Teddy's New Gun" from a Fred Adolph "Modern Guns" catalogue – circa 1914.

JOHN HOVANESS HINTLIAN COLLECTION

OPPOSITE: Details showing Fred Adolph over-and-under combination rifle/shotgun. Note the gold inlaid crest of The Camp Fire Club of America on top of the breech.

a need for TR to deal with the intense disappointment of his failed bid for yet another term as President. His years in the West following the sudden deaths of his mother and first wife had provided an outlet for that early trauma. His always intense and vigorous hunting trips had long provided a means of dealing with the rough and tumble of politics, and as a form of release and relaxation from the intrepid and unyielding pace of his everyday life. "Black care," he had said, "rarely sits behind a rider whose pace is fast enough."

Chapman assigned George Cherrie, an ornithologist, and Leo Miller, a mammalogist, both experts in South American zoology, to go along on the expedition. Colonel Candido Rondon, a Brazilian army officer, took charge of the arrangements in South America. Frank Harper, Roosevelt's personal secretary, also went on the trip as did Jacob Sigg, an army hospital nurse. Kermit Roosevelt was already working in Brazil, and it was only natural that he should join his father.

Fiala was put in charge of all the equipment for the trip because Roosevelt had great confidence in his good judgment. Of particular interest to TR were the firearms to be selected:

For arms the naturalists took 16-bore shotguns, one of Cherrie's having a rifle barrel underneath. The firearms for the rest of the party were supplied by Kermit and myself, including my Springfield rifle [#6000], Kermit's two Winchesters, a 405 and 30-40 [from the African safari], the Fox 12 gauge shotgun [also from the African trip], and another 16 gauge gun, and a couple of revolvers, a Colt, and a Smith and Wesson.

Years of camping and hunting in America and Africa made him pay close attention to other equipment needs, too:

We took from New York a couple of canvas canoes, tents, mosquito bars, plenty of cheese cloth, including nets for the hats, and both light cots and hammocks. We took ropes and pulleys, which proved invaluable on our canoe trip. Each equipped himself with the clothing he fancied. Mine consisted of khaki, such as I wore in Africa and a couple of silk shirts, one pair of hobnailed shoes with leggings, and one pair of laced leather boots coming nearly to the knee.…I also had gauntlets because of the mosquitoes and sand flies. We intended where possible to live on what we could get from time to time in the country, but we took some United States Army emergency rations, and also ninety cans, each containing a day's provision for five men.…

Roosevelt and his party left New York on the *Vandyct* in October 1913. The primary aim of the expedition was to collect animal and botanical specimens for the American Museum of Natural History, and to map the River of Doubt, an unexplored tributary of the Amazon. The undertaking proved to be more dangerous and strenuous than the African safari.

The "trip [was] a thorough success," Roosevelt later wrote in *Through the Brazilian Wilderness:*

Cherrie and Miller…collected over twenty-five hundred birds, about five hundred mammals, and a few reptiles, batrachians, and fish. Many of them were new to science… of course, the most important work we did was the geographic work, the exploration of the unknown river…we put upon the map a river some fifteen

ABOVE: Kermit in the Brazilian wilderness, armed with the Luger 9mm Parabellum Pistol Carbine.

THEODORE ROOSEVELT COLLECTION HARVARD COLLEGE LIBRARY

OPPOSITE: The "River of Doubt" pointed out by TR. In contrast to the African trip, the Brazilian adventure was primarily exploratory. Hunting was secondary.

THEODORE ROOSEVELT COLLECTION HARVARD COLLEGE LIBRARY

INSET: Clothing buttons issued for the Congressional election of 1910, commemorating TR's expedition to Africa. Now considered among the rarest of TR's political tokens.

THEODORE ROOSEVELT COLLECTION HARVARD COLLEGE LIBRARY

Colonel Roosevelt and the first jaguar
From a photograph by Kermit Roosevelt

A jaguar taken in Brazil by TR with his .30-40 Springfield.

THEODORE ROOSEVELT COLLECTION, HARVARD COLLEGE LIBRARY

The hunting was good, but by no means comparable to that on the African safari. Roosevelt's accounts of hunting adventures were limited to jaguar and peccary, with random notes on other game: agouti, armadillo, bush-deer, coati, giant anteater, capybara, curassow, monkey, pampas deer, jabiru storks, muscovy duck, tapir, and wood-ibis. "We see all kinds of queer birds," he wrote to Quentin in January:

> …and we now and then collect very queer beasts. The queerest of all was the giant anteater. It was the size of a bear, with a tail like an enormous skunk, and a head that looked more like that of a long-billed bird than of any normal quadruped. The most dangerous things I hunted were the white-lipped peccaries, because they are such savage little beasts which make a kind of moaning noise of defiance and clatter their teeth like castanets. It

was also very interesting to hunt the jaguar. Kermit is, however, by this time a far better hunter than I am.

Roosevelt still found hunting stimulating, but his hunts in South America seemed anti-climatic when compared to his experiences in Africa. He enjoyed hunting jaguar, but found it unusually fatiguing because of the scorching heat:

> The jaguar is the king of South American game, ranking on an equality with the noblest beasts of the chase of North America, and behind only the huge and fierce creatures which stand at the head of the big game of Africa and Asia.…
>
> [In the morning near the Taquary River] we rose at two, and had started on our jaguar-hunt at three. Colonel Rondon, Kermit, and I, with the two trailers or jaguar-hunters, made up the party, each on a weedy, undersized marsh pony, accustomed to traversing the vast stretches of morass; and we were accompanied by a brown boy, with saddle-bags holding our lunch, who rode a long-horned trotting steer which he managed by a string through its nostril and lip. The two trailers carried each a long, clumsy spear. We had a rather poor pack. Besides our own two dogs, neither of which was used to jaguar-hunting, there were the ranch dogs, which were well-nigh worthless, and then two jaguar hounds borrowed for the occasion from a ranch six or eight leagues distant.…
>
> As our shabby little horses shuffled away from the ranch-house the stars were brilliant and the Southern Cross hung well up in the heavens, tilted to the right. The landscape was spectral in the light of the waning moon. At the first shallow ford, as horses and dogs splashed across, an alligator, the jacaré-tinga, some five feet long, floated unconcernedly among the splashing hoofs and paws; evidently at night it did not fear us. Hour after hour we shogged along. Then the night grew ghostly

The hunting was good... hundred kilometres in length, of which the upper course was not merely utterly unknown to, but unguessed at by anybody…

ture in law, Sheldon was keen on natural history. An accomplished hunter, he shared a dedication to big game hunting and wildlife conservation with the likes of Theodore Roosevelt.

Sheldon became a member of the Boone and Crockett Club and was particularly interested in North American wild sheep and the Alaskan wilderness. The respect held by TR for Sheldon is evident in the President's review of Sheldon's *The Wilderness of the Upper Yukon*, published in 1911:

Mr. Sheldon is not only a first-class hunter and naturalist but passionately devoted to all that is beautiful in nature, and he has the literary taste and ability to etch his landscapes into his narratives, so they give to the reader something of the feeling that he must have had when he saw them—and that this is no mean feat is evident to everyone who realizes how uncommonly dreary most writing about land-scape is, for the average writer either treats the matter with utter bareness, or, what is worse, indulges at much length in "fine writing" of the abhorrently florid and prolix type.

Mr. Sheldon hunted in the tremendous Northern wilderness of snow-field and torrent, of scalped mountain and frowning pine forest; and in all the world there is no scenery grander in its lonely desola-tion than that which he portrays. He is no holiday hunter. Like Stewart Edward White, he is as skillful and self-reliant a woodsman and a mountaineer as an old-time trapper, and he always hunts alone. The chase of the Northern mountain sheep, followed in such manner, means a test of every real hunter's quality—marksmanship, hardihood and endurance, nerve and skill as a cragsman, keen eyesight, and high ability as still hunter and stalker. Mr. Sheldon possesses them all. Leaving camp by himself, with a couple of crackers and a piece of chocolate and perhaps a little tea in his pocket, he would climb the mountains until at last he saw his game, and then might have to spend twenty-four hours in the approach, sleeping out over-night and not returning to camp until late the following evening, when he would stagger downhill through the long sub-arctic dusk with the head, hide, and some of the meat of his game on his back…

But the most important part of Mr. Sheldon's book is that which relates not to hunting but to natural history. No professional biologist has worked out the problems connected with these Northern mountain sheep as he has done. He shows that they are of one species; a showing that would have been most unexpected a few years ago, for at one extreme this species becomes the black so-called Stone's sheep, and at the other the pure white, so-called Dall's sheep. Yet as Mr. Sheldon shows in his maps, his description, and his figures, the two kinds grade into one another without a break, the form midway between having already been described as Fannin's sheep. The working out of this fact is a matter of note. But still more notable is his description of the life history of the sheep from the standpoint of its relations with its foes—the wolf, lynx, wolverine, and war eagle.

Sheldon early encouraged the establishing of parkland and game refuges in Alaska and fostered support for granting that status to Mount McKinley. A year Sheldon had spent in the Denali wilderness heavily influenced his activism. Sheldon also served for many years as the Club's chairman of the Game Conservation Committee, in which capacity he helped to "lead the club's evolution from the original idea of a comradeship of rifleman and hunters toward a far-reaching ethic of conservation."

CHARLES SHELDON

Boone and Crockett Club

Report
of the
Game Preservation Committee
1912

The preservation of some of the species of North American large Mammals is no longer a question of providing for the next generation of sportsmen.

The inevitable spread of civilization will render that impossible.

We shall do well if we can locate the existing rem-nants in safe places and avert their impending exterm-ination.

To the Members of the Boone and Crockett Club:

The Game Preservation Committee respect[...] offers herewith its report, which includes the wo[...] the year, the game situation, legislation, and g[...] remarks on game protection.

Owing to the rapidly increasing interest in g[...] preservation, the Committee offers for consideration some constructive criticism on the existing tendencies of game protection in this country.

CHARLES SHELDON, *Chairman*,
CHAS. H. TOWNSEND, *Secretary*,
J. WALTER WOOD,
W. REDMOND CROSS,
EDWARD HUBERT LITCHFIELD,
E. W. NELSON,
ALEXANDER LAMBERT, M.D.
GEORGE BIRD GRINNELL } *Advisory*
DR. LEWIS RUTHERFURD MORRIS } *Members*

"there befell me one of the most curious and interesting adventures with big game that have ever befallen me during the forty years since I first began to know the life of the wilderness."

with the first dim gray of the dawn. The sky had become overcast. The sun rose red and angry through broken clouds; his disk flamed behind the tall, slender columns of the palms, and lit the waste fields of papyrul. The black monkeys howled mournfully. The birds awoke. Macaws, parrots, parakeets screamed at us and chattered at us as we rode by. Ibis called with wailing voices, and the plovers shrieked as they wheeled in the air. We waded across bayous and ponds, where white lilies floated on the water and thronging lilac-flowers splashed the green marsh with color.

At last, on the edge of a patch of jungle, in wet ground, we came on fresh jaguar tracks. Both the jaguar hounds challenged the sign. They were unleashed and galloped along the trail, while the other dogs noisily accompanied them. The hunt led right through the marsh. Evidently the jaguar had not the least distaste for water. Probably it had been hunting for capybaras or tapirs, and it had gone straight through ponds and long, winding narrow ditches or bayous, where it must now and then have had to swim for a stroke or two. It had also wandered through the island-like stretches of tree-covered land, the trees at this point being mostly palms and tarumans; the taruman is almost as big as a live-oak, with glossy foliage and a fruit like an olive. The pace quickened, the motley pack burst into yelling and howling; and then a sudden quickening of the note showed that the game had either climbed a tree or turned to bay in a thicket. The former proved to be the case. The dogs had entered a patch of tall tree jungle, and as we cantered up through the marsh we saw the jaguar high among the forked limbs of a taruman-tree. It was a beautiful picture - the spotted coat of the big, lithe formidable cat fairly shone as it snarled defiance at the pack below. I did not trust the pack, the dogs were not stanch, and if the jaguar came down and started I feared we might lose it. So I fired at

once, from a distance of seventy yards. I was using my favorite rifle, the little Springfield with which I have killed most kinds of African game, from the lion and elephant down; the bullets were the sharp, pointed kind, with the end of naked lead. At the shot the jaguar fell like a sack of sand through the branches, and although it staggered to its feet it went but a score of yards before it sank down, and when I came up was dead under the palms, with three or four of the bolder dogs riving at it....

The expedition encountered many major problems while exploring the River of Doubt. Several canoes were lost in the rapids, and one of the native assistants drowned. Another native porter, deranged by the strain of struggling through the almost impenetrable Amazon wilderness, killed his supervisor. In a near fatal canoe accident, Kermit lost his .30-40 Winchester rifle, one of the custom-made battery of arms from the African safari. The party ran out of food and had to live off the land. Both Zahm and Fiala proved inept and were dismissed. When a canoe got jammed in the river, Roosevelt's attempts to pry it loose resulted in a damaged knee that made it impossible for him to walk. He had to be carried through tropical downpours and temperatures that frequently went well over 100 degrees fahrenheit. Exposed to such extreme vicissitudes of weather, he contracted jungle fever, which was further complicated by an abscess that had developed on his injured leg. When the fever grew worse, TR asked to be left in the jungle, not wanting to slow down the others and thereby jeopardize their chances of getting out alive. He was prepared to fend for himself, even to die alone. Of course, for one of the few times in his life, he was overruled.

The party plodded on and after nearly three months of incredible hardship at last emerged from the jungle; lucky to have survived. Exhausted, crippled, and thirty-five pounds underweight, Roosevelt left for New York in May 1914.

Still tired and frail, he sailed for Spain ten days later to attend Kermit's wedding.

Despite the tortured hardship and long-term damage to TR from the Brazilian Expedition, he arranged for presentation firearms to be sent in appreciation to certain of those who had played vital roles. Colt factory records reveal that TR presented several automatic pistols, all in 1914. These were a Model 1911 Automatic Pistol, with a gold plate in the left grip, inscribed for Colonel Candido Rondon (serial #C7847, shipped August 17); another Model 1911 engraved on the left side of the slide to Colonel Carepe from Theodore Roosevelt (#C7542, shipped August 10); still another Model 1911 was engraved to Pedrinho Craveiro from Roosevelt (#C8037, shipped August 29). At this writing the location of none of these pistols is known to the author. Each stands as testimony to the generosity and thoughtfulness of their donor.

Charged by a Bull Moose

In September 1915, Theodore Roosevelt hunted big game for the last time. As guest of his old friend Dr. Alexander Lambert, TR journeyed to the Tourilli Club in Quebec to "enjoy the great northern woods, and the sight of beaver, moose; and caribou..." He "had not expected any hunting experience worth mentioning." But to his complete surprise "there befell me one of the most curious and interesting adventures with big game that have ever befallen me during the forty years since I first began to know the life of the wilderness." In a deposition made before a Canadian government official, Roosevelt told the story of this strange experience:

I, Theodore Roosevelt, residing at Oyster-Bay in the United States of America, do solemnly declare as follows:

Guide Arthur Lirette and TR, with antlers from the moose that charged Roosevelt and his hunting party on September 19, 1915.

<small>Charles Scribner's Sons</small>

INSET: In this illustration from *A Book Lover's Holiday in the Open*, TR paid tribute to his .30-40 Springfield. "With it I have shot some three hundred head of all kinds..."

<small>Boone and Crockett Club Permanent Collection</small>

That I have just returned from a trip in the Tourilli Club limits as a Guest of Dr. Alexander Lambert, I had the ordinary game license No.25 issued to me on the 6th day of September instant. On September the nineteenth, on Lake Croche, having with me as guides, Arthur Lirette and Odilon Genest, I killed an old bull moose as authorized by the license, which only permitted to me to kill one moose. That afternoon, shortly after three o'clock, we were returning in our canoe to the West end of the Lake; where a portage trail led to our camp; a small stream runs beside the portage trail; when half a mile from our proposed landing place; we saw an old bull moose on the shore. We paddled to within a hundred yards of it. We supposed that when it saw us, it would take to the woods. It however walked along the edge of the water parallel to our canoe, looking at us. We passed it, and gave it our wind, thinking this would surely cause it to run. But it merely raised its hair on its withers and shook its horns and followed after the canoe. We shouted, but it paid no heed to us; we then reversed our canoe and paddled in the opposite direction; but following us and threatening us, the bull moose turned and walked the same way we did, we renewed our former course, and thereupon so did the moose, where the water was shallow, we did not venture near it, but where the water was deep, we went within fifty yards; and it then thrashed the branches of a young tree with its antlers, and pawed the earth and advanced a little way into the water towards us, walking parallel to our canoe, it reached the portage trail, it turned and walked up this trail and sniffed at our morning's tracks, and we supposed it had fled; but on nearing the landing place; we saw it standing in the trail, and it rushed down towards us and we had to back quickly into deep water; we paddled on round the shore, hoping it would get tired and go; we shouted and tried to frighten it, but it merely shook its head and stamped on the ground and

bounded in a circle; then it swaggered along grunting, it kept its mouth open, and lolled out its tongue and when it turned towards us, it ran its tongue over its muzzle thus it accompanied us to and fro for an hour, cutting us off whenever we tried to land; then it turned, and went up the little stream, shaking its head, and galloping or bounding not trotting, for fifty yards, it disappeared around a bend of a stream, we waited a few minutes, and landed, and started along the portage trail for camp, after about ten minutes, the trail approached the little stream then the moose suddenly appeared rushing towards us at a slashing trot, its hair ruffled and tossing its head.

Arthur Lirette; who is one of the game wardens of the Tourilli Club, called out to me to shoot, or the moose would do us mischief, in a last effort to frighten it, I fired over its head, but it paid no heed to this and rushed over the stream at us; Arthur again called: "Tirez, monsieur, tirez, vite, vite, vite," and I fired into the moose's chest, when he was less than twenty feet away, coming full tilt at us, grunting, shaking his head, his ears back and his hair brindled; the shot stopped him, I fired into him again; both shots were fatal; he recrossed the little stream and fell to a third shot, but when we approached, he rose; grunting, and started towards us. I killed him. If I had not stopped him, he would have certainly killed one or more of our party; and at twenty feet I had to shoot as straight as I knew how, or he would have reached us. I had done everything possible in my power to scare him away for an hour and a quarter, and I solemnly declare that I killed him only when it was imperatively necessary, in order to prevent the loss of one or more of our own lives, and I make this solemn declaration conscientiously, believing it to be true; and knowing that it is of the same force and effect as if made under oath, and by virtue of the Canada EVIDENCE ACT, 1893. *(Signed)* THEODORE ROOSEVELT

Standing off a charging bull moose was a fitting finale to a hunting life packed with adventure and peril. But Roosevelt was now beginning to show signs that even he was not impervious to the toll that advancing age necessarily takes on any man. Anna Roosevelt Cowles "saw evidence for the first time that this mighty human dynamo is working with a somewhat diminished energy. He has just returned from a hunting trip to Canada where, as the newspapers said, he killed a second moose because the animal charged upon him. He told me that it was his last hunting trip, that he didn't want to be 'taken care of...' He said that he had sent in the manuscript of what was probably his last book on hunting [*A Book-Lover's Holidays in the Open*] to the publisher, and that his work was largely done....I do not mean that he was in any way despondent, but that he recognized that there are some limitations to his capacity for work—something new for him." He was the first to recognize and to admit that his physical powers were not what they had been, and that he would have to conserve his energy by slowing down his work pace.

Souvenirs of a Bully Life

Perhaps in the relatively placid days that came more and more frequently to the ex-President after 1915 he had time to examine and reflect upon the memorabilia that filled the mansion at Sagamore Hill. In the best tradition of hunters of big game, Roosevelt had amassed a substantial collection of mounted heads and skins, of pictures, sculpture and other reminders of the chase. He first began seriously collecting these items during his stay in the Badlands in the mid-1880s. He added new mounts almost annually until shortly before World War I. The largest single addition came in 1909-10, from the African safari. His big-game trophies formed one of the finest and most complete private collections in America. Representing over 40 years of hunting on three continents, skins, heads, horns, antlers, feet and tusks were displayed in most of the rooms at Sagamore Hill. There were skins from

grizzly, brown, and black bear, mountain lion, African lion, leopard, zebra, bobcat, and antelope; mounted heads of buffalo, blacktail and whitetail deer, antelope, mountain goat, bighorn sheep, moose, caribou, elk, wolf, javelina, Cape buffalo, eland, gnu, oryx, and bear, antlers of deer, elk, and moose; rhinoceros horns and elephant tusks; an elephant foot umbrella stand, a rhinoceros foot inkstand, a rhino feet gong and a wolfskin robe.

When Sagamore Hill was first built, elk antlers had been fitted on some roof peaks. With the addition of the North Room, in 1905, the stately home took on the aura of a big game hunter's paradise. But far more trophies were given to friends and relatives or became museum displays than were kept by TR. Most of these went to the Smithsonian Institution, though several of the rare early mounts of small game and birds—done by Roosevelt as a boy—were presented to the American Museum of Natural History.

A competent amateur taxidermist, Roosevelt in his youth had skinned and mounted a great many birds, and some small animals. But for big game trophies, he turned to such professionals as John G. Bell, Boone and Crockett Club member James L. Clark, and the New York furriers C. G. Gunther's Sons. On the African hunt the specimens were prepared for shipment under the supervision of Edgar A. Means, Edmund Heller, and J. Alden Loring. The taxidermy for nearly all the African game intended for mounting was done by scientists of the Smithsonian Institution and by private firms contracted by the museum. Preserving these specimens was a mammoth undertaking, the largest of its kind in museum history. Taxidermists estimated that the project would require from two to three years, and perhaps longer. When the Smithsonian decided they would be able to mount only a fraction of these trophies, TR was understandably disappointed. Roosevelt also brought together at Sagamore Hill a tasteful selection of hunting and outdoors bronzes, paintings, drawings, and prints. Most of the artists of these works were friends or contemporaries of

"I love flower gardens; but this is the time to use the space for vegetables. In short, let every form of expenditure and labor be for productive purposes; so as to meet the vital needs created by this great war...."

Winchester takedown Model 1894 rifle, .30-30 caliber, fitted with a Maxim silencer, c. 1909-1910, serial #410495, 25-1/2 inch barrel. Son Archibald told the author that this rifle was used to shoot rodents and other pests on the Sagamore Hill property, without disturbing the neighbors.

SAGAMORE HILL NATIONAL HISTORIC SITE, NATIONAL PARK SERVICE

OPPOSITE: The North Room of Sagamore Hill, designed by Boone and Crockett Club member, C. Grand LaFarge, and built in 1905, was a magnificent trophy room with 1,200 square feet of floor space. Here TR could greet special guests in near-regal splendor.

THEODORE ROOSEVELT COLLECTION, HARVARD COLLEGE LIBRARY

Roosevelt, including Albert Bierstadt, A.B. Frost, Henry Sandham, R. Swain Gifford, Carl Rungius, Frederic Remington. Alexander Phimister Proctor, Antoine Louis Barye, Frederick MacMonies, and James L. Clark. Two of TR's favorite pieces were Remington's bronze "The Bronco Buster," a gift from the Rough Riders, and a bronze cougar by Proctor, presented by the "Tennis Cabinet" in 1909.

The ex-President had also built up over the years a substantial library of books on the outdoors. As he wrote in the *Autobiography:*

Of course each individual is apt to have some special tastes in which he cannot expect that any but a few friends will share. Now, I am very proud of my big-game library. I suppose there must be many big-game libraries in Continental Europe; and possibly in England, more extensive than mine, but I have not happened to come across any such library in this country. Some of the originals go back to the sixteenth century, and there are copies or reproductions of the two or three most famous hunting books of the Middle Ages, such as the Duke of York's translation of Gaston Phoebus, and the queer book of the Emperor Maximilian....

TR read voraciously, and his knowledge and expertise are convincingly demonstrated in his essays, "Literature on American Big-Game Hunting" (in *American Big-Game Hunting,* 1893). Books on Big Game" (*Trail and Campfire,* 1897), and "Books on Big Game" (*Outdoor Pastimes of an American Hunter,* 1905). He drew on his own huge library in preparing these works, each of which was a masterly study.

Most of TR's hunting library was kept in the gun room at Sagamore Hill: "the gun-room at the top of the house; which incidentally has the loveliest view of all, contains more books than any of the other rooms....Among his favorite works on hunting and the outdoors were Williamson's *Oriental Field Sports,* Harris' *Wild Sports of South Africa,* Gordon Cumming's *Hunter's Life in South Africa,* Selous' *A Hunter's Wanderings in South Africa* and *Travel and Adventure in Southeast Africa,* Baldwin's *African Hunting,* Drummond's *Large Game and Natural History of South Africa,* Millais' *A Breath from the Veldt,* Buxton's *Short Stalks,* Astor Chanler's *Through Jungle and Desert,* Forsyth's *Highlands of Central India,* Shakespeare's *Wild Sports of India,* Kinloch's *Large Game Shooting;* Sanderson's *Thirteen Years Among the Wild Beasts of India,* Elliott's *Carolina Field Sports,* Palliser's *Solitary Hunter,* Dodge's *Hunting Grounds of the Great West,* Van Dyke's *Still Hunter,* Caton's *Deer and Antelope of America,* the Century's *Sport with Gun and Rod,* Davenport's *Sport,* Scrope's *Art of Deerstalking,* Greener's *The Gun,* Grobman's *Sport in the Alps,* Lamont's *Seasons with the Sea Horses,* and the *Big Game Shooting* series of the Badminton Library.

Sir Samuel W. Baker, a prolific writer on big game hunting, was a Roosevelt favorite:

If we were limited to the choice of one big game writer, who was merely such, and not in addition a scientific observer, we should have to choose Sir Samuel Baker, for his experiences are very wide; and we can accept without question all that he says in his books. He hunted in India, in Africa, and in North America; he killed all the chief kinds of heavy and dangerous game; and he followed them on foot and on horseback, with the rifle and the knife; and with hounds.

Massive, 18-pound Hawken Target Rifle, dispersed from the Boone and Crockett Club Collection in 1972. Listed as item no. 10, the rifle was one of 30 pieces which were sold, while 13 were retained – the latter all with TR significance. The intent had been to retain the 13 for exhibit at the Gun Room at Sagamore Hill. For security reasons, the firearms are no longer on display. The Hawken Target Rifle was described in the catalogue for the *Colt/Christie's Rare and Historic Firearms* catalogue of October 7, 1981 (lot 31), as:

An Historic American Percussion Heavyweight Target or Hunting Rifle with browned octagonal barrel of .70 caliber cut with seven deep grooves and stamped to the rear of the buckhorn style rear sight. 'S. Hawken St. Louis', long tang fitted with folding peep sight, case hardened lock, varnished American walnut half-stock checkered at the wrist, iron mounts, pewter forend cap, double set triggers, brass-mounted heavy hickory ramrod, and much of its original finish. Circa 1850, 36-1/2 inch barrel. Weight 18 pounds. Provenance The Theodore Roosevelt gun room, Sagamore Hill, Oyster Bay, Long Island. According to Roosevelt family tradition the rifle belonged to Kit Carson.

Roosevelt believed that "Hunting should go hand in hand with the love of natural history, as well as with descriptive and narrative power." Writing the foreword to *Animal Life in Africa* (1912), he described the ideal big game book: "A book about big game nowadays should be much more than a mere book about the slaughter of big game. The writer should be not only a mighty hunter, but a trained field naturalist, and therefore a skilled observer; and finally he should he a good writer, able to bring in vivid fashion before the eyes of others what he himself has seen."

Roosevelt's own writings on hunting were substantial: over 100 essays in *Scribner's* and other periodicals, *Hunting Trips of a Ranchman* (1885), *Ranch Life and the Hunting Trail* (1888), *American Big-Game Hunting* (co-edited with George Bird Grinnell, 1893), *The Wilderness Hunter* (1893), *Hunting in Many Lands* (co-edited with Grinnell, 1895), *Trail and Campfire* (also with Grinnell as co-editor, 1897), *Outdoor Pastimes of an American Hunter* (1905), *African Game Trails* (1910), and *A Book-Lovers Holidays in Me Open* (1916). All were notable contributions to the literature on big game. *Through the Brazilian Wilderness* (1914) and *Life-Histories of African Game Animals* (with Edmund Heller, 1914) were technical studies more than studies of hunting. *Life-Histories* is an especially valuable source of reference for anyone with an interest in the big game of the African continent. His contributions to *The Encyclopaedia of Sport*, published in 1897 (v. 1) and 1898 (v. 2), were the observations of a hunter-naturalist on the pursuit of bison, caribou, Rocky Mountain goat, opossum and raccoon, peccary, prairie chicken, pronghorn (antelope), puma, wild turkey, wapiti, and wolf. Among the contributing authors were old friends F.C. Selous, Caspar Whitney, and E.N. Buxton. *The Rough Riders* (1899)

and *An Autobiography* (1913) are two lively and interesting books that include much information on Roosevelt's use of firearms.

The Roosevelt home was a kind of private museum, with its several animal heads, vast library, innumerable objects of all kinds. TR's passion for hunting and the outdoors life was overpoweringly obvious to any visitor to Sagamore Hill. These souvenirs, representing over forty years of hunting, added a great deal to the character of Sagamore Hill, and were a constant reminder to Roosevelt of all that he had achieved and enjoyed as a hunter, as a naturalist—and most significantly—as a conservationist.

World War I

In the summer of 1914, war broke out in Europe. Germany and Austria-Hungary were the principal belligerents against France, Great Britain, and Russia. At first Roosevelt was of the opinion that America should remain neutral, but as ominous reports of a German victory were received, he began to change his mind. In May 1915, a German submarine torpedoed the *Lusitania*, causing over a thousand deaths including many Americans, and setting off a wave of indignation in the United States. President Wilson sent a stern message of protest to the German government. Roosevelt was ready for strong action and was openly critical of Wilson's desire to seek a peaceful settlement of the crisis: "I feel that Wilson is not carrying out genuine American policy," he wrote in June 1915. "I feel he is not carrying out any policy at all save one of words merely, which he tries to make strong enough satisfy our people that something is being done and at the same time to enable him to dodge out of doing anything to Germany…" As the country's hostility toward German U-boat attacks grew more intense, Roosevelt's strictures on Wilson sharpened. TR assumed leadership of the national movement for military preparedness. Across the nation Americans debated the merits of war against Germany.

In encouraging American involvement in World War I, TR wrote and spoke profusely on marksmanship and on matters of preparedness. He wrote in *America and the World War* (1915):

There should be at least ten times the number of rifles and the quantity of ammunition in the country that there are now. In our high schools and colleges a system of military training like that which obtains in Switzerland and Australia should be given. Furthermore; all our young men should be trained in actual field-service under war conditions; preferably on the Swiss, but if not on the Swiss then on the Argentinian or Chilean model.

The Swiss model would probably be better for our people. It would necessitate only four to six months' service shortly after graduation from high school or college; and thereafter only about eight days a year. No man could buy a substitute; no man would be excepted because of his wealth; all would serve in the ranks on precisely the same terms side by side.

Under this system the young men would be trained to shoot, to march, to take care of themselves in the open, and to learn those habits of self-reliance and law-abiding obedience which are not only essential to the efficiency of a citizen soldiery, but are no less essential to the efficient performance of civic duties in a free democracy. My own firm belief is that this system would help us in civil quite as much as in military matters. It would increase our social and industrial efficiency. It would help us to habits of order and respect for law.

By January 1917, Germany decided to unleash submarine warfare against American shipping to the Allied powers. Congress responded by a declaration of war on April 2, 1917.

Three days later, Roosevelt hurried to Washington to ask President Wilson for permission to recruit and train a division of volunteers. The request was denied and Roosevelt accepted the decision with unconcealed bitterness. In support of America's cause, TR reconciled himself to a welter of writings and speeches:

I love flower gardens; but this is the time to use the space for vegetables. In short, let every form of expenditure and labor be for productive purposes; so as to meet the vital needs created by this great war....

In June, the American Expeditionary Force that left New York under the command of General John J. Pershing included four Roosevelts: Quentin, Theodore Jr., Archibald, and Kermit. The old Rough Rider reluctantly remained at Sagamore Hill.

Roosevelt's frustration and fury over America's lack of preparedness was vented at every opportunity. In a letter to the editorial department of the *New York Sun*, he expressed dissatisfaction with that paper's failure to perceive who was responsible for the nation's military unpreparedness:

...please pass this letter on to the man [who wrote the editorial "Arms and Our Men"].

The *Sun* is so very straight and so very sane in war matters that I really regret it has written this editorial. This speech of mine to which it refers was an indictment of our whole people for having failed to prepare in advance; just such an indictment as in the last paragraph in the article is wrongfully made against Congress alone. To show the damage done by

failing to prepare in advance; I instanced the shortage of rifles. General Crozier [Chief of Ordnance] in his articles expressly admits that what I said was true. His excuse is utterly unworthy. I have trained raw troops. I know how regulars are trained. I know that really efficient officers after training a recruit a week without arms, always like to give him his rifle; train him with that rifle; and train him to take care of it. General Crozier was at one period a very good bureau man for bureau work. He never was a field man, and for the last few years his work has not been done in a way that should make him the head of his bureau at this time.

Two of the Major Generals in charge of the cantonments have told me that they were gravely handicapped in their work by the shortage of rifles and by the complete absence of guns for the artillery. Of course, they can't say this publicly or attack the Administration.

General Crozier's statement as to the "perfectly endurable delay" is entirely wrong. If we were to make new rifles, it was in my judgment, and is I believe in the judgment of the best military men, such as General Leonard Wood, a capital mistake not to have taken either the French or English rifle and its ammunition. Crozier is directly responsible for our not having many hundred thousands of the new rifles now.

You say in your article that "naturally we have no million new rifles stored in arsenals." There is nothing natural about this, and was the gross fault of President Wilson and his officers of the War Department including General Crozier. All that was necessary was to run the Springfield Arsenal full time day and night, just as big private businesses are habitually run; then between the time of our first ultimatum to Germany and the declaration of war we would have had over a million more rifles than we actually did have.

In the last paragraph you say that the real responsibility rests on Congress. It does not. It rests on the Administration, that is President Wilson. It is he who is primarily responsible for our unpreparedness; it was he who remained deaf to appeals and who misled Congress and the people by his attitude. For a year and a half he did everything in his power to prevent all preparedness. Then for a year and a half he went every which way, speaking for preparedness sometimes, sometimes speaking and always acting against it....

Our real difficulty in securing preparedness at present comes from the fact that Mr. Wilson's great adroitness and cleverness (and entire absence of conviction) were during two and a half vital years used to persuade the people *not* to prepare.

In July 1918, Quentin, the youngest son, was killed in an aerial duel. Although profoundly aggrieved by Quentin's death, Roosevelt could bravely write: "Only those are fit to live who do not fear to die; and none are fit to die who have shrunk from the joy of life....Both life and death are parts of the same Great Adventure." To King George V of England, who had sent Roosevelt a touching message of sympathy, Roosevelt wrote proudly:

It was very kind and thoughtful of Her Majesty the Queen, and you Sir, to cable us about the death of our son Quentin, and Mrs. Roosevelt and I thank you both, with all our hearts. Of his three brothers Ted, who is a Major of Infantry, has been gassed once and is now in hospital with a bullet through the leg; Archie, a Captain of Infantry, has been badly wounded by a shell; both were cited for gallantry, in orders; Kermit has been Captain of an armored machine gun motor battery with your army in Mesopotamia, has been given the Military Cross, and is now with our army under Pershing. Unlike most of their fellow-countrymen they had prepared in advance! They sailed from our shores over a year ago;

their mother and I knew their temper and quality; and we did not expect to see all of them come back....

Early in 1918, Roosevelt suffered a recurrence of jungle fever. Operations were necessary to remove abscesses on his thigh and in his ear, and afterward he walked with difficulty and was partially deaf. Doctors told him he might be confined to a wheelchair for the rest of his life: "All right!" he replied, "I can work that way too." Through the spring and summer of 1918, he retained an active interest in national and international affairs. He was forced to spend much of his time in bed but still managed to write articles for newspapers and to call for increased support of American troops in Europe. In October, Roosevelt was back in the hospital because of an attack of inflammatory rheumatism. He returned to Oyster Bay two months later, but was confined to bed. His health was rapidly failing. He could do no work. The end seemed near.

While President Wilson was in Europe negotiating peace terms and trying to enlist support for his Fourteen Points, Roosevelt's condition worsened. James Amos, his personal valet, wrote that the ex-President, "suffered cruelly....I am convinced that Mr. Roosevelt sensed the approach of his end. He was not the man to talk of death. His mind had always been busy with plans for his adventures in politics and life. But in the last year he talked much of death."

Roosevelt realized that death was not far off. "...you and I are in the range of the rifle pits," he wrote to a friend. "From now on until we ourselves fall—and that date can not be so many years distant—we shall see others whom we love fall. It is idle to complain or to rail at the inevitable; serene and high of heart we must face our fate and go down into the darkness."

On January 5, 1919, at 11 p.m., Roosevelt turned to his valet and quietly said, "James, will you please put out the light?" That night the "Old Lion," as his sons called him, died in his sleep. 🖉

OPPOSITE: Monumental memorial sculpture to Theodore Roosevelt, on the front steps of the Roosevelt Memorial Building, American Museum of Natural History, New York.

TE HOUSE,
WASHINGTON.

October 21, 1902.

Dear John:

If I am in luck about the 13th of next month, I shall try a bear hunt in Mississippi or Arkansas. It has been arranged for me by Stuyvesant Fish, of the Illinois Central Road. I am trying to keep everything about it very secret. Do you think you could come along? I should so like to see you.

Always yours,

Theodore Roosevelt

Mr. John A. McIlhenny,
Averys Island, Louisiana.

ABOVE: Letter from TR to Mr. John A. McIlhenny of Avery Island, Louisiana.

TOP RIGHT: Clifford K. Berryman first version of the famous cartoon, "Drawing the Line in Mississippi" as it appeared in the *Washington Post* on November 16, 1902.

NEAR RIGHT: Berryman also drew this more publicized second version of the famous "Mississippi" cartoon.

BACKGROUND: TR returned to the South with Holt Collier as his expert bear guide once again. TR (3) is pictured here with Harley Metcalfe (2) and Clive Metcalfe (4). Collier is pictured behind Harley and TR.

Appendix

Theodore Roosevelt and the Winchester Repeating Arms Co.

No episode in Theodore Roosevelt's life more clearly and definitively documents his dedication to and depth of knowledge of firearms, accessories and their use in hunting than the exhaustively detailed preparation for the African expedition of 1909-10. Unique in numerous ways, the Roosevelt safari demanded complete preparation, and TR oversaw the most minute of details. The bulk of the papers here quoted are housed in the permanent collection of the Cody Firearms Museum, Buffalo Bill Historical Center, which also exhibits some of Roosevelt's firearms.

The President's first letter to Winchester about his projected safari was written by his personal secretary, William Loeb, Jr., on July 16, 1908. It implied that only guns for his son Kermit would be purchased:

> The President is going to Africa with his son a year hence. He probably has all the rifles he needs, but his son has not. Before deciding what he will buy, the President would like to see your catalog, his idea being to give his son two— one a high-power *small* caliber rifle of the 30-40 type, or one approaching it; and the other a very much more powerful rifle, such as he could use for buffalo, rhinoceros and even elephant. Will

Loading the *S.S. Hamburg* with equipment and supplies for the Roosevelt expedition. These crates were from the Abercrombie & Fitch Company, New York.

THEODORE ROOSEVELT COLLECTION, HARVARD COLLEGE LIBRARY

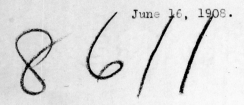

THE WHITE HOUSE
WASHINGTON

June 16, 1908.

Gentlemen:

The President is going to Africa with his son a year hence. He probably has all the rifles he needs, but his son has not. Before deciding what he will buy, the President would like to see your catalog, his idea being to give his son two - one a high-power small caliber rifle of the 30-40 type, or one approaching it; and the other a very much more powerful rifle, such as he could use for buffalo, rhinoceros and even elephant. Will you send your catalog to the President at Oyster Bay, where he will arrive Saturday next?

Very truly yours,

W. Loeb

Secretary to the President.

The Winchester Repeating Arms Company,
New Haven, Connecticut.

---

you send your catalog to the President at Oyster Bay, where he will arrive Saturday next?

The Winchester company's reply, written by Winchester Bennett, 2nd Vice President, was immediate and courteous. The company, Bennett wrote, would be delighted to render any service.

What the President studied before replying to Winchester is shown by the extracts from the 1908 catalog, reproduced on the following page. What must have particularly caught the President's eye was the statement: This gun offers many advantages in rapidity of action, high velocity, and excellence of material and workmanship. Roosevelt's reply, on June 29, made it clear that he was as interested in rifles for himself as he was for Kermit. It was also obvious that the President wanted everything to be perfect:

Your letter of the 17th instant to Mr. Loeb has been received. I would like my son Kermit to go to New York and inspect the guns I wish, taking them out here for me to look at, as I want to be sure there is no slip—up. What I think I would like would be a 30-40 shooting the same ammunition I use in my Springfield, and two 405 caliber rifles. Does your Winchester shoot the Springfield Army rifle ammunition with as much power as the Springfield gun? Or is it the Krag ammunition which it shoots? Of course it would be a great convenience to me to have both my son's gun, the 30-40, and my Government Springfield shooting the same ammunition, and then in addition each of us would sometimes use the 405 caliber. We would have full jacket cartridges, and also cartridges with the lead point exposed, for both, of course. My son will bring in his 30-30 Winchester to have the sights and stock duplicated, unless we decide to have the front sight with a gold bead. In addition I shall take my 45-70 take-down Winchester [1886, #125422], which certainly ought to be good for lion, zebra, and the smaller antelopes in the bush and probably a double-barreled 450 cordite English rifle. Your rifles will be shooting in competition with the latter, so I want to be sure that they are good ones.

Where is your New York house, and when will you be able to have those rifles in for my son to look at?...

[Handwritten P.S.] Can I get two telescope sights for two of the rifles?

TR was already interested in two 405 Model 1895 rifles, knew what type of cartridges he wanted and was reasonably certain of his wants for sights. Because the Winchesters would be competing with a 450 English double rifle, he wanted to be sure that they were good ones.

On July 1, Winchester sent a detailed and rather technical reply, with not a little carefully considered and tactfully worded advice:

In response to your inquiry of the 29th ultimo, acknowledging our letter of the 17th, we are pleased to advise that we shall be glad to forward to you at Oyster Bay Model *1895* rifle adapted to use the 30 U.S. Govt M'06 Cal. cartridge such as you would use in your Springfield, and a Model *1895 405* Cal. rifle, for trial purposes—together with ammunition fur the same. We are prepared to furnish our Model 1895 rifle to handle either the old 30-40 cartridge similar to that used in the M'98 Krag the U.S. Govt M'03 cartridge, or the US. Govt M'06 cartridge. The M'06 cartridge with pointed bullet is of course hardly the cartridge which we could advise for use on game, as proper upset or mushrooming effect is not satisfactorily obtained with the pointed bullet; but we can equip the M'06 shell with a soft nose bullet similar to that used in the M'03 cartridge—that is, with rounded nose in soft point, which will give very nice mushrooming effect. This bullet; being a 220 grain bullet, would not develop quite the velocity obtained in the M'06 Springfield cartridge—which has 2,300 to 2,400 FPS.

velocity—but will develop a velocity of somewhat over 2,100 FPS. For purposes of comparison we might add that the velocity of the 30-40 with 280 grain ball is but 1,960 FPS.

The arms which we will ship you will be the plain stock article, simply fur trial, after which you can select such specialties as special length and drop of stock, form of sight, etc., as you might desire.

In reference to the 30-30 Winchester rifle which you are planning to forward to us to have the sights and stock duplicated, would say we will have no difficulty in doing this unless this arm has a pistol grip stock—which form of stock we cannot furnish on the Model 1895 rifle.

As per the above we are shipping tonight to our New York Department, No.812 Broadway to be delivered to you at Oyster Bay (unless they are otherwise advised by you):

1 Model 1895 rifle 30 U.S. Govt. M'06 Caliber;
1 Model 1895 rifle 405 Caliber;
together with an assortment of ammunition fur trial.

With regard to the matter of telescope sights, would advise that we can equip these arms with such telescope sights as you might select but we ourselves rather hesitate to make a selection for you as there is so much opportunity for personal choice in a device of this character. Sights of this kind are manufactured by

Malcolm Rifle Telescope Mfg. Co., Auburn, N.Y
Julius King Optical Co., No. *10* Maiden Lane, N.Y City
Bausch & Lomb Optical Co., Rochester, N.Y

So far as their use is concerned, aside from being somewhat cumbersome on the gun and

OPPOSITE: William Loeb, Jr.'s letter to Winchester, which began the long and detailed correspondence on the President's African hunting rifles.

necessitating rather careful handling, they have the drawback that on guns of great power and consequent heavy recoil similar to the *405* Caliber, there is some difficulty in so placing the mountings on the barrel as to insure their staying in place.

No further mention was made of telescopic sights, a feature wisely omitted for the reasons given by Bennett.

On July 9, the President sent his reply. As always, the letter was simply addressed to the company, for the attention of "Gentlemen." Not once was a communication received with any personal heading:

I am returning to you herewith the two guns you sent out to me, together with 30-30 Winchester rifle and my Springfield rifle [#6000]. The latter (the Springfield) merely desire that you have cleaned and returned to me; and I wish to know also whether your cartridges, such as you sent out to me, are the same as the Government cartridges so that I can use them in my Springfield. It would be very bothersome to have different cartridges looking so much alike as my Government cartridges and yours for your corresponding rifle.

I return you the reloading tools, as I do not wish to do any reloading [Roosevelt was known to have done his own hand-loading, but for the African safari he was not interested].

I send you the 30-30 as a model for the two 405's which I desire to have from you Please have the top of the barrel roughened, as in the case of the 30-30 Have the sight like those of the 30-30, and the stocks, excepting of course the pistol grip. For the last inch and a half of the stock have put on each gun (I think it is called) Silver's gun pad.

About the 30-40 I shall write you later, because my son has been informed that he will be presented with a 30-40.

How soon can you have the two 405's sent

OPPOSITE: Pages from Winchester's Catalogue No. 74 March 1908, studied by Roosevelt in selecting his battery of rifles and ammunition for Africa.

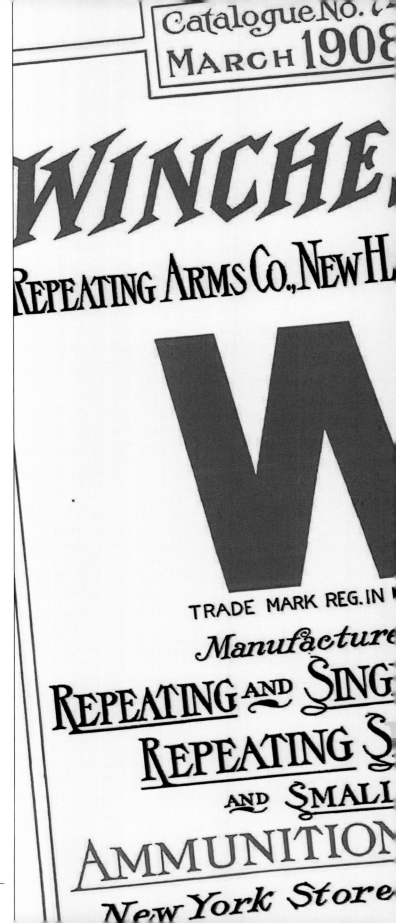

Sporting Rifle, Model 1895, .30 Army And .303 British. $30.00

Twenty-eight Inch Round Nickel Steel Barrel, Weight about 8¼ pounds, Number of Shots 6, ...

Sporting Rifle, Model 1895, .38-72 And .40-72 Winchester. $23.50

Twenty-six Inch Round Barrel, Weight about 7½ pounds, Number of Shots 6, ... 25.00

Twenty-six Inch Octagon Barrel, Weight about 8¼ pounds, Number of Shots 6, ...

Fancy Sporting Rifle, Model 1895, .30 Army And .303 British.

Twenty-eight Inch Round Nickel Steel Barrel, Fancy Walnut Checked Stock and Forearm,
Weight about 8½ pounds, ...

Fancy Sporting Rifle, Model 1895, .38-72 And .40-72 W

Twenty-six Inch Round Barrel, Fancy Walnut Checked Stock and Forearm, Shotgun
7¾ pounds, ...

Twenty-six Inch Octagon Barrel, Fancy Walnut Checked Stock and Forearm, Shotgu
8½ pounds, ...

When ordering, specify whether rifle should be sighted for Black or Smokeless
specify whether rifle should be sighted for Black or Smokeless
Shotgun Butt Stock, with either metal or rubber Butt Plate, same p

The first opening motion
sear, before the gun is unl
fully locked. The continu
and withdraws the breech-
The breech-bolt, passing o
and makes fast the firing p
hammer is made to hold it
When in this position, the
the breech-bolt.

The closing action of
out of the magazine into t
osition, the locking bolt i
g the firing pin. The fir
e sear, leaving the gun i

The magazine is of the
ays be known by openi
azine follower present
tion to be forced into
idge following before

.303 BRITISH SOFT POINT

Smokeless Powder, Metal Patched, Soft Point

Cartridges.	Per 1,000	
Primed Shells.	$50.00	Smokeless Powder, Me
Bullets.	20.00	Soft Point or Full Me
	15.00	Bullet
		Cartridges packe

.35 WINCHESTER MODEL 1895 SOFT POINT

Smokeless Powder, Metal Patched, Soft Point Bul

Cartridges.	Per 1,000	
Cartridges packed 1,000 in a case.	$55.00	Smokeless Powder.
		Soft Point or Full Metal
		Bullet

.405 WINCHESTER MODEL 1895 SOFT POINT

Smokeless Powder, Metal Patched, Soft Point Bullet.

Cartridges.	Per 1,000	
Cartridges packed 1,000 in a case.	$60.00	Smokeless Powder.
		Soft Point or Full Metal Pa
		Bullet

.38-72-275 WINCHESTER MODEL 1895

Cartridges, Black Powder, Lead Bullet.	Per 1,000	
Full Metal Patched or Soft	$34.00	Bullets, Soft Point or Full Metal Pa
Point Bullet		Powder.
Primed Shells.	35.00	
Bullets, Lead (275 grains)	24.00	Cartridges packed 1,000 in a
	10.00	

SMOKELESS CARTRIDGES,
Metal Patched or Soft Point Bullet, per 1,000, .38-72 Winchester, Smokeless Powder, 275 ...

.40-72-330 WINCHEST

ating
s '03 an
r Center
ver put u
rts are fe
xperienc

Model 1895 .405 rifle, one of the three Winchesters shipped by the factory to Roosevelt on September 10, 1908. The shotgun buttplate, crescent cheekpiece, select walnut, oiled and checkered stocks, the big caliber, and the flat topped open sights were typical of TR's choices in most of his previous Winchesters. Serial #63736. 24" barrel with matted top. Made with a pink bead on the front sight.

BUFFALO BILL HISTORICAL CENTER, CODY, WYOMING; LOAN FROM SAGAMORE HILL NATIONAL HISTORIC SITE AND THE BOONE AND CROCKETT CLUB

to me? Will you send me at the same time some targets, pasters, and three or four sets of cleaning rods such as would be suitable for an African trip. Also two woven cartridge belts to carry the 405 cartridges, and two to carry the 30-40 cartridges; one of each for a 42 waist—& one for a 28.

Also please send me for my *45-70* Winchester 100 full-jacketed smokeless powder cartridges, with the bullet weighing four hundred and five grains. This is the rifle I used in Louisiana last year, and which both my son Ted and Dr. Lambert used in killing moose in Canada. We all of us used soft-nosed bullets, and certainly for moose and black bear it is as efficient a weapon as could be desired. It is so efficient that I am going to take it to Africa to use, altho I have been warned that the gun is not right for African game. I am rather inclined to doubt this. How will the penetration of the full metal covered bullet for this 45-70 rifle compare with the penetration of the similar full-jacketed bullet for the *405?* Have you any data which would show how this *45-70* would do on African buffalo and rhino, for instance? I should use the soft-nosed bullet for lion, for I do not believe that a lion is a tougher animal than a moose or a bear. As I have said to you, I do not want to use any one of our American guns for any game

for which it is unsuited, because there will be a good deal of attention attracted to my trip and I want to be sure that it comes out all right.

When I have tried your guns could you arrange to ship them & the cartridges to Mombasa, care of Smith and Mackenzie? I can not afford to take any chances, and I should have to be sure that you would ship them in such time that you would get a cable stating they were there before I myself start. Have you facilities for doing this? Can you put your cartridges up in cases suitable for transportation on the backs of porters? I will later give you in detail the number and kind of cartridges I wish.

In your catalog you speak of a 45-70 cartridge with a heavier bullet than the 45-70 cartridge I have been using, that is, with a 500-grain bullet. Could I use this in the same 45-70 rifle? If so, what advantage would it give me in shooting big game? It seems to me that the additional weight of the bullet might count a good deal with heavy game.

In this letter, as in many others signed by Roosevelt, there were annotations and corrections in his own hand-apparently each note was reread by him carefully. It seems presumptuous of Roosevelt to send his Springfield to *Winchester* for cleaning! But after all, he was President of the

United States-and a long-time Winchester fancier. The three features of greatest importance to TR on the pair of 405's were the sights, the stocks and the roughened or matted barrels. There is also a certain chattiness about the letter, which indicates the President was enjoying the technical aspects of selecting these big-game rifles. The question of bullet performance, particularly penetration, did not escape his attention.

On July 11, Bennett addressed an interoffice memorandum to I.L. Lippencott of the shipping department; asking, "What can we do in the way of time in furnishing [TR] the two 405 rifles which he wants? Possibly it would be advisable to wait until we see the 30-30, and are able to determine what special work we will have to do...."

Lippencott replied promptly:

In reply to yours..., in reference to guns for Pres. Roosevelt's African trip, we have received the 30-30 which he desires copied in the Model '95 405 and find it is fitted with a matted barrel carrying flat top sporting rear and Lyman Gold Bead front sights. It has an oil-finished short butt stock with cheek piece and is fitted with screw-eyes for our sling strap. We can furnish the Model '95 405 with all of these extras and can give him a Silvers Recoil Pad. This latter he asks to have about 1 1/2 inches thick. Our regular pads are 3/4 inches thick, but I find we can get the thicker pads from the other side in four to six weeks' time. We have no matted barrels in stock for the *405*, and special stocks with cheek piece would, of course, have to be made. We can furnish him the cartridge belts which he asks for, and they will cost us about $1.00 each.

In regard to shipping to Mombasa, British East Africa, we have had New York make enquiries, and under ordinary conditions it would

take from six to eight weeks to reach destination. They would probably have to be shipped to Aden as shipments to Mombasa are very infrequent. The rates are about $3.00 to $8.50 a 100 lbs. on cartridges; from $2.00 to $2.50 a 100 lbs. on guns with a minimum bill-of-lading from $20.00 to *$25.00*. We understand there is a duty on guns of £2 per weapon, and an ad valorem duty on ammunition of 10%.

Bennett reminded Lippencott to note TR's request for target materials, cleaning rods, cartridge belts, and "other small details," and added, "I have advised the President that we will retain his 30-30, unless he otherwise advises, until the work on the 405 caliber stocks is completed."

On July 16 Bennett wrote a six-page letter to the President, then at the "summer White House," at Sagamore Hill, answering in great detail the questions TR had posed in his lengthy letter of the 9th:

In regard to your enquiry as to ammunition, would say that we find on investigation that your Springfield rife is chambered for the 50 Government Model 1908 cartridge [30-40]. Our ammunition of this class is made according to government standards and will give good service in your Springfield rifle. Our Model 1895 arm we can furnish for this ammunition. We sent you Model 1906 ammunition with 190-grain pointed bullet also 1906 ammunition with 220-grain soft point bullet, together with some Model 1908 ammunition with soft point bullet.

We note your specifications as to the 405 caliber rifles which we can readily comply with, furnishing them with special stocks, and finish, with cheek piece, matted barrels, Flat Top Sporting Rear and Lyman Gold Bead Front sights, sling straps and swivels....

As you are probably aware, the 30-40 Model 1895 rifle which you mention in your letter, is not adapted to use ammunition similar to that

"The rifles have come. They are beautiful weapons and I am confident will do well..."

which you would use in your Springfield rifle. If an aim to use similar ammunition is desired, the same can be obtained by ordering our Model 1895 rifle for the 30 Government Model 1908 Rimless cartridge.

As before stated, the 405's can be forwarded to you in about six weeks.

We note your request as to targets, pasters, cleaning rods, etc., and will see that these are included....

As to the use of this arm in Africa, we are inclined to believe that it is amply powerful if the bullet is placed in the right spot, but it is not as powerful as arms generally used in that country. It does not; in fact, even compare favorably in power with the 30-40, developing but 1,486 foot-pounds muzzle energy, against 1,880 foot-pounds developed by the 30-40. Nevertheless, quite a few have been used, and quite successfully with soft point bullet, for lion. For larger animals, such as rhinoceros, where the full metal patched ball would be desired, we certainly would not recommend it while we have the *405* to offer, for this arm (the *405)* develops muzzle energy of 3,077 foot-pounds, almost twice that of the 45-70-405.

Besides the regular 45-70 cartridge in either black or smokeless powder, using the 405-grain ball and developing velocity of 1,286 foot-seconds, we have to offer the 45-70 Winchester High Velocity cartridge, which would work in the same gun, but would require different elevation of sights. With the 300-grain ball, developing 1,825 foot-seconds velocity, it gives a muzzle energy of 2,214 foot-pounds, but this cartridge we cannot recommend for anything but very moderate ranges as its accuracy beyond 150 yards is by no means satisfactory. This is a makeshift development of the black powder 45-70 cartridge in order to obtain greater power, and, like almost all compromises, while there is a gain in one detail,

there is a distinct loss in another. The 45-70-405 cartridge was always considered a very accurate cartridge until smokeless powder came into use, when it was at once eclipsed by other cartridges, such [as] the 30-40 Government, the 30 Government Model 1908, 1906, etc.

As to the matter of comparative penetration. The penetration of the 405 (on the basis of 7/8 in. pine boards at 15 inches from the muzzle) is 48 boards; that of the 45-70-405 full metal patched, 18 boards; that of the 45-70-300 W.H.V. 25 boards. Muzzle energy in foot-pounds we have given above, and this muzzle energy is the best measure that we know of of the actual shocking or knockdown blow delivered by the bullet.

In short, while we have the 405 to offer, we would not recommend the 45-70 for use on dangerous big game. Successful use has been made of it; but there is not the same factor of safety for the deer that there is with the 405.

In regard to the matter of forwarding your guns, we should be glad to do this as it will give us a last opportunity to look them over, clean them thoroughly and pack them in tin-lined cases. Under ordinary conditions, it would take from six to eight weeks, after the arms leave New York, for them to reach destination. They would in all probability have to be shipped to Aden as shipments from New York to Mombasa are very infrequent. We have made inquiries of our London correspondents as to shipping to them for reshipment out of London for Mombasa but have not as yet heard from them When we do we shall be pleased to advise you....

In regard to your inquiry as to the 45-70 with 500-grain bullet, we are pleased to advise that you could use this in your 45-70 rifle, of course making somewhat different [elevation] of the sights. The particular advantage of the 500-grain bullet is that it has somewhat steadier flight at ranges above 800 yards (an almost impossible range for sporting work, particularly

in thick country). Other than this there is no particular advantage, for the cartridge with 500-grain ball develops but 1,179 foot-pounds velocity against 1,286 for the same cartridge with the 405-grain ball, and the advantage in shocking blow is comparatively small as the muzzle energy of the 500-grain cartridge is but *1,542* foot-pounds against 1,486 for the cartridge with 405-grain ball. The penetration of the 500-grain ball is naturally somewhat better, as, with that cartridge in full metal patched bullets the penetration of 20 boards is obtainable. On the whole, for sporting ranges, there is very little to choose between the two....

On the 17th of July, the President despatched a letter which crossed in the mails with Bennett's. TR's note dealt with technicalities of ammunition and the problems of shipment:

I enclose you the cartridges I have been using for the Springfield and for the 45-70. Is the Winchester I sent you, that has been given to my son Kermit, able to chamber this same ammunition as the Springfield? If not, I want a Winchester gun for him that will chamber the same ammunition. I do not like the model 1906 ammunition with the 190-grain pointed bullet;

and I want the bullets that are soft-nosed and those that are of full metal jacket to be of equal weight. What I want is a Winchester that will shoot exactly the ammunition that my Springfield shoots; in addition to the two 405 Winchesters. I understand you can furnish both the full-jacketed and soft-nosed bullet as good as the Government ammunition for both the rifles? Please send out the targets and pasters, together with my Springfield rifle, and the ammunition for it, and the ammunition for the 45-70; for the last, the ordinary ammunition such as I used last year in Louisiana. Send me for both rifles both full-jacketed and soft-nosed ammunition. I shall take out this 45-70 as it is such a convenient saddle gun; and I shall carry both the hard- and the soft-nosed bullets; but from what you say I shall expect to use almost always either the Springfield, the Winchester shooting the same ammunition, or one of the two 405's.

Now about forwarding the guns. You certainly must not send them to Aden to be reshipped. You must send them to London, to be shipped straight to the firm of Mackenzie and Smith, Mombasa. But unless you know all about the matter and can guarantee having them reshipped, all right, I would not think of having you do it, but should send them to London

Winchester Model 1895 .405, serial #63727 shipped to the President for trial on September 10, and shipped again on November 25. On both occasions the .405 serial #63736 and a .30-40 Model 1895 were also shipped. When these rifles reached TR in November, all work had been completed, and he expressed great delight.

THEODORE ROOSEVELT
BIRTHPLACE COLLECTION

myself to be shipped. Surely, however, your agent in London ought to be able to attend to this. I shall carry one rifle with me and my son will carry another, but the balance may want shipped together with almost all of the ammunition. I would simply take for each of us a couple of belts of ammunition, so that we would not be absolutely stranded for a few days in case there was a hitch about the matter. I would want you, however, to forward the guns and ammunition so far in advance that you would have time to receive cable information that they were there before I started. I can not afford to have any slip-up in this. Make your inquiries, and meanwhile I will make my own, and when you report to me I shall be able to give directions as to what should be done. I may decide to take the rifles with me, after all.

The company responded promptly:

We have yours of the 17th instant, and the sample cartridges are also at hand. The Model '94 gun, belonging to your son Kermit, is also here, and we find this is not chambered for the Rimless ammunition, but is an old gun which left the factory ten or eleven years ago and takes the old Krag ammunition; viz., the cartridge with the rim. We can get you up a '95 gun taking the same ammunition as your Springfield, and will be glad to make it up with the other guns we are now putting through the works, Please advise us if it is your desire that we make these up in style similar to the 405's now in process; viz., with stocks with cheek pieces similar to the Model '94-30 which we are using as a model for the stocks on the new guns; the Silver's recoil pad, etc.

Your Springfield rifle has already been returned to you, having been shipped on the 16th, and today we are sending you a quantity of targets with some black and white pasters, also the ammunition which you ask for, this latter

for your 45-70, and for your Springfield rifle no quantities are mentioned, but in a previous letter you asked us to send you 10045-70 full patched. We will therefore send you the same quantity of soft point; and also 100 each of the same style for your Model 1908 Springfield. We trust this ammunition will be found entirely satisfactory

In regard to shipment of your guns to Africa, we certainly will not ship via Aden as we have no agents at that point whom we would care to trust to look after the reshipment of the goods. We have, however, as promised, made enquiries of our London agents, and we have no doubt that they will advise us very shortly. There are undoubtedly several lines running direct from London to Mombasa which will handle these goods, and our London agents will look after trans-shipment at that point. They are thoroughly reliable and have many years experience, and if the goods are sent in their cars the matter will be most carefully attended to.

We await your reply in regard to the Model '95 rifle....

On July 23, William Loeb, Jr., sent TR's reply; the President had decided that Kermit should have a Model 1895 rifle, "taking the same ammunition as the Springfield [30-40 caliber] and exactly similar in style to the 405 now in process of making." Loeb, ignorant on the matter of firearms, mistakenly referred to the rifle as a Model 1905. 'The lack of gun know-how among TR's staff—especially Loeb—was partly to blame for some errors that were greatly to annoy the President later that summer.

Lippencott promptly acknowledged Loeb's order for the 30 caliber Model 1895 rifle for Kermit; with assurances that the 'matter shall have our careful attention.' On the 29th, Loeb wrote Winchester from Oyster Bay to order for the President "some targets with regular rings marked, and also some pasters to cover the shots on the target. What the President desires is regular rifle targets."

He also asked: "Do you understand that the 30-40 rifle for Kermit is to carry the same ammunition as the President's Springfield rifle?"

On the 1st, Bennett wrote that the shipment of a selection of standard military targets for 200, 100 and 50 yards had been made, with the exception of 50-yard targets, which would "be forwarded at the earliest possible moment." The previous day he had advised Loeb that these would be supplied through Winchester's New York office, and also had explained that the chambering for Kermit's Model 1895 rifle in 30 caliber would be "for the use of the 1903 rimless cartridge, identical with that intended for use in the Sporting Springfield rifle which the President forwarded us for inspection and repairs some little tune ago."

On the 1st of August, Roosevelt sent to Winchester a glowing letter on his Model 1886 takedown rifle and on a stream of other matters:

I herewith send you my 45-70 rifle. Really I can not make my mind act to take this rifle with me on my African trip. It is as handy as a knife and fork, and it shoots just where I want it to. I have never had a rifle I was as fond of, or felt as confident of, since twenty years ago when I broke my old *45-75* Winchester in falling over a cliff while after white goat. I suppose the 405 Winchester will be the one I shall work often…but surely this 45-70 ought to be good for lion, zebra, and the smaller antelopes. In any event; as it has exactly the right pull of trigger, I send it to you so that on the three rifles you are making for me you may get a trigger-pull precisely like this. The stock of this rifle is a little too short for me, and therefore in the stock you will follow the model of the 30-30 which you already have. Would it not be well to have the front sight of gold, and if possible, roughened or dull gold, in each case? White metal is apt to be a little too bright.

Please send this 45-70 back at once, and also the 30-30 as soon as possible. I suppose you can fix the trigger without keeping the 45-70

very long as a model. I should like to get it back within a fortnight.

In reply, Bennett discussed the shipping situation to Africa, the 405 Model 1895 rifle the 45-70 Model 1886 pattern gun, and the subject of sights. Bennett acknowledged with pleasure Roosevelt's "attachment to the 1886 45-70 rifle, and the confidence which you feel therein. Certainly for zebra, the smaller antelope, and much other African game, this arm ought to be sufficient."

On August 10, the President wrote again:

Will you have the 30-30 [M 1894, #15659], which was sent you as a model, cleaned before returning it?

Have you made inquiries yet about shipping the ammunition to Mombasa? I expect to be in Africa about eleven months, and I shall be hunting certainly half the time perhaps almost all the time. In addition to taking 300 or 400 cartridges with us in our trunks, I will want to ship 6,000 rounds to Mombasa or Nairobi, care Smith, Mackenzie & Co., this including 2,500 of the Government rifle ammunition, 2,500 of the 405, an 1,000 of the 45-90 [45-70; typist's error at the White House]. I think that this will be double the amount of ammunition that we shall use; but I would a great deal rather hay 8,000 cartridges more than I want than 100 cartridges less than I want. For each make of cartridge I shall want about twice as many of the soft-nosed as of the full metal patched, that is, of the 1,000 for the 45-90 [45-70], I will wish 850 full metal patched and 650 soft-nosed. Of the 2,500 for the Government caliber, and the 2,500 for the 405 caliber, I shall want in each case 800 full metal patched and 1,700 soft-nosed. I shall want you to get these out so far in advance that you can receive a telegram saying they have come there not later than the 1st of March (and preferably by the 1st of February),

"I herewith send you my 45-70 rifle. Really I can not make my mind act to take this rifle with me on my African trip. It is as handy as a knife and fork, and it shoots just where I want it to. I have never had a rifle I was as fond of, or felt as confident of, since twenty years ago when I broke my old 45-75 Winchester in falling over a cliff while after white goat."

without fail, so that if there should be any hitch we can then arrange to have another shipment made. I am not going to run any chances, nor must you run any chances.

As you know, I have always used your rifles and I am using them now instead of the English rifles which my English friends are giving to me, because it is a matter of pride with me to use an American rifle. Now I won't want to have any slip-up. A friend of mine, young Forbes of Boston, was in to see me the other day. He has been using your 405 in Africa for elephant, rhinoceros, buffalo and lion. He found it worked well except that twice the cartridges jammed (once with a lion). Now do try these guns you are to send me for my son and myself so as to be sure that they will not jam. Ought we not to carry spare sights, and perhaps spare pieces? As we will have five rifles, of course we could get along even if one or two of the rifles went wrong, but, again, I don't want to run any chances.

When will you send out the four woven cartridge belts, the two for the 405 rifles and the two for the Government ammunition?

TR was taking no chances—"nor must you run any chances." He was preparing for his cartridge shipments with typical brisk thoroughness, preparing nearly eight months in advance of leaving for Africa. And again he underscored the use of "an American rifle" and admonished "I won't want to have any slip-up." The possibility of a jammed action was another matter he pondered, as was the possibility of broken parts.

Bennett's detailed and reassuring response, sent August 11, was five pages in length. It appraised the President of the status of Kermit's old Model 1894 (it would he thoroughly repaired and put in first class order" before being returned), confirmed the President's order for ammunition, and reviewed the status for the shipment of guns and cartridges. Bennett also stated Winchester's "appreciation of the fact that you are using our rifles,"

and promised "that we will take every precaution to see that your arms are turned out in such shape that no criticism can he found with them." The matter of jammed cartridges was dealt with in the flat statement that the "Model 1895 rifle is generally in use throughout this country and complaint is almost unheard of." Bennett did add, however, that some spare parts should he taken along as a contingency of equipping "parties going for as long and serious a hunt as you are planning...." In the final half of the letter Bennett told of an African hunt in which the rifles used were the 82 Special Model 1894 and the 405 Model 1895. From the detailed kills of big game cited (among them an elephant with one abut from the 82 Special!) he noted that Winchester was "inclined to believe you will find the 30-30 a very bandy gun." Bennett concluded his letter by advising that "two of the four [butt pads] have had to be made and they are still in the hands of the manufacturer, so we are unable at this writing to name a definite shipping date..."

Still another letter from Winchester was sent to Oyster Bay on August 18, as a correction of TR's last letter on the subject of 45-90 (as opposed to 45-70) ammunition. Mention was also made of the shipping time between London and Mombasa—three weeks. Not an i would be left undotted in this detailed correspondence until the arms, ammunition, and accessories were finally despatched in their entirety.

The next Presidential letter straightened out much of the shipping situation. It read simply:

August 14, 1908.

Gentlemen:

The President desires me to advise you that he is expecting to take all his rifles with him, and it will not be necessary therefore for you to ship anything but the ammunition.

Bennett's response was immediate: "This decision very much simplifies matters of making shipments, as if they related to ammunition there will he no difficulty about passing them through England without delay...." On the same day TR's acting secretary Forster corrected the 45/90-45/70 cartridge error with a brief note acknowledging that the "President meant to order 45-70 cartridges, not *45-90*."

On August 21, Lippencott of Winchester let the President know they were prepared to ship his 6,000 rounds of sundry cartridges through their London agent, and would attempt to time the consignment so "there will be little or no delay in trans-shipment at London...shipment can probably be made in a couple of weeks...."

The President replied the next day:

To my great pleasure I find that I shall be allowed to take cartridges with me on the steamer. Such being the case, I shall take 8,000 cartridges with me and have you ship 3,000 yourselves. Divide the two shipments equally; that is, I wish you to ship to Smith, Mackenzie & Co., at Mombasa, 8,000 cartridges, and have 8,000 which will go with me on the Hamburg steamer that I take from New York next March. Each lot should be composed as follows: 500 45-70 cartridges; 175 full jacketed and 825 soft nosed, 1,250 Government ammunition cartridges, 400 full jacketed and 850 soft nosed, and 1,250 405 cartridges, 400 full jacketed and 850 soft nosed.

Winchester had some ideas on packing the cartridges in assortments of each caliber. To this acting secretary Forster gave a prompt, affirmative reply on August 27: "The President has received your letter...and thinks it an excellent suggestion to have the cartridges proportionately divided up in cases, which should weigh sixty pounds each."

A misfire of a 45-70 round in TR's Model 1886 takedown rifle prompted Bennett to write Forster on the 29th:

Acknowledging receipt of your favor of August 26th and the misfire 45/70 cartridge which you call our attention to, would say we regret to note this accident and are sorry to say we are not in a position to explain the cause of the difficulty.... In view of this occurrence, which we are pleased to say is the first that has come to our attention in a good many years, we are firing and examining for defects a quantity equivalent to 10% of each item specified for in the President's order for ammunition which we are now preparing.

The chances for such a misfire were perhaps one in several million; what anguish this freak incident must have caused at the Winchester factory!

The President is "Very Anxious"

On August 30, Forster let Winchester know that President Roosevelt was "very anxious to get...the rifles he has ordered":

Your letter...has been received and handed to the President. He thanks you for what you are doing about the cartridges.

Will you be good enough to give the President the exact number of cartridges of each caliber, and also of full-jacketed and soft-nosed in each caliber, which are to be put up in sixty-pound packages? He is very anxious to get at the earliest practicable moment the rifles he has ordered, as he will want to test them, and he will only be here [Oyster Bay] three weeks longer. May I ask you to advise me, therefore, when he may expect them?

Forster received a reply for the President on the 2nd of September:

...in reference to packing of the cartridges for shipment to Mombasa, we enclose herewith memorandum which will show you just how we propose to pack each case. We have made the division in the various cases as nearly equal as the regular packing will permit. The goods are all put up twenty to the box.

You will note that we will put exactly 600 cartridges in each case, and these cases, when ready for shipment, will weigh from 55 to 60 lbs. We will mark on each case the number as shown on the memorandum and in addition we will mark the exact contents. Will you please advise if the President wishes the cartridges he is to take with him packed in the same manner and in the same size cases.

As regards the guns, as previously advised, we are still awaiting the recoil pads from abroad. We are expecting them daily, and just as soon as they arrive, we will get the guns ready and ship them.

We presume the President will want some ammunition to go with these guns. If so, will you please advise us the quantity he desires, and if this is to be in excess of the 6,000 which he has ordered for Africa.

Forster replied the same day; the President was showing signs of impatience:

Your letter of the 1st instant has been received, and the proposed method of distributing the cartridges in packing them for shipment is entirely satisfactory. The President will want the three thousand which he is to take with him packed in just the same way. He will want a small quantity of ammunition sent out with the guns for him to try this fall, and this will be extra....The President wants without fail to get those guns here before September 20th. Can you not cable and find out about the pads?

The Silver butt pads arrived late from London, causing a delay of the Model 1895's. On the 7th, Loeb wrote "In case the pads ordered from abroad should not arrive in time, would it not be possible to put on three-quarter-inch pads?" Lippencott assured him that the President:

may have an opportunity to test his rifles before he leaves Oyster Bay [for Washington on the 20th]...we will have the guns tomorrow put up with temporary stocks. These are not exactly the size as we will furnish when the guns are finished, and he may rest assured that with the regular stocks on, such as we are intending to equip the guns with, the fit and other particulars will be much more satisfactory.... After the President has tested the guns, will you kindly have them returned to New Haven, either direct or through our New York address and we will then put them up with the regular stocks and ship them to Washington as he may direct.

The President, not realizing the stocks and sights were only temporary, sent a sharply worded letter in return on September 16:

Gentlemen:

I am really annoyed at the shape in which you sent out those rifles. I return them to you, together with my Government rifle, so that you may have before you the stock and sights I use. I had already sent you, as you of course remember, rifles showing my sights; yet you sent out these rifles with a rear sight which does not pretend to be like that I use, and which have what taken with a front bead, I regard as the poorest rear sight ever used for game, the one with the sharp, narrow notch. It was entirely useless to send them out to me in such shape. Moreover, while the two 405's were sighted accurately, the 30 caliber shoots about twelve inches high and six inches to the left; and moreover, extraordinary to relate, its rear sight is actually different from the rear sight of the two 405's, and if possible, worse. I can not see what excuse there was, when I had already sent you the rifles as models, for you to send me rear sights such as there are on the three guns you sent me. Please be sure to copy exactly the rear sight of the Government weapon which I send you, and then have it sent on to Washington with your three rifles when they are ready.

There are two other matters to which I desire to call attention in connection with these rifles. By comparing the stocks you will find that at present the stocks of the Winchesters are shorter than the stock of my Government rifle. When you get the thick rubber pads put on, will this difference be equalized and will the stocks be of exactly the same length as my Government rifle? This you must surely see to, as I want them exactly and precisely in every respect like the stock of the Government rifle. Moreover, I find that the magazine mechanism is totally different in the two 405's from what it is in your 30 caliber. In the last, the 30 caliber, I can put all five cartridges into the magazine, and then by working the magazine the top one goes into the breech. But in the 405's I put only four cartridges in the magazine. If I try to put a fifth in it jams when I attempt to work the lever and get it into the breech. In other words. I can put four in the magazine and then one in the breech, whereas in the 30 caliber I put all five in the magazine and work the lever to get one of them into the breech. Now is this the proper and normal thing? I merely wish to be sure that everything is all right, as I am naturally a little unsettled by the extraordinary failure us the matter of the rear sights.

Now for something purely on my own responsibility. Would it be possible to substitute for the metal bead you have on the three front sights a small light pink ivory bead, in each case the color of the lightest pink billiard ball—that is, ivory stained so as just to have a pink tinge over the whiteness and still leave it light? If so, I would like to have this done. I would like, of course, spare sights, one for each rifle, and I think these spare sights should have the bead of gold. Moreover, I wish you to be sure to see that in the rifle barrel there is a little notch, or groove, or line, and a corresponding notch, or groove, or line in the sight itself so that I can see at a glance if the sight has been knocked to one side. Better still, can't the sights be screwed into the barrel, so that they *can't* be knocked to one side.

When will you have the rifles on to Washington for me to see and try them? I can not afford to take any chances, and this experience with the rear sight shows me that I must see them in ample time to have any changes that I desire made.

You have not yet sent me the four woven cartridge belts, the two for the 405 and the two for the 30 caliber. Please send these as soon as possible.

I also wish a half dozen cleaners for each type of rifle. Remember that your 30 caliber not only has the wrong type of rear sight, but is very badly sighted anyhow, shooting very high and somewhat to the left. Thanks for the clips; but I do not think I would care to use them in the field. [On the 15th Winchester had sent a newly designed clip device, TR was not interested.]

The company tactfully refused to express their own annoyance at the President's oversight of the temporary sights and stocks in their reply of September 21. Here again the detail tended to be of a technical nature; the letter is an important one, and well worth quoting in full:

We have yours of the 16th, and the rifles which you return are also at hand. We are very sorry about the sights and upon investigating the matter we find these sights were put on temporarily to be used while testing the special ammunition which we were making up to send to Africa. The rear sight, such as your 30-30 and Government rifles are equipped with, is a style which we do not now manufacture, and which we are obliged to make specially. These were not ready when the guns went to Oyster Bay last week, and we therefore sent along the sights which were on the guns and we should have

"Now for something purely on my own responsibility. Would it be possible to substitute for the metal bead you have on the three front sights a small light pink ivory bead, in each case the color of the lightest pink billiard ball—that is, ivory stained so as just to have a pink tinge over the whiteness and still leave it light? If so, I would like to have this done."

written you to this effect. When your guns are finished they will be put up with sights exactly the same as that on the 30 Government gun which we now have.

As regards the stocks, these, as we wrote you, are temporary and when the guns are furnished with extra thick pads, they will be of the exact dimensions which you wish. We are, however, a little in doubt as to how to proceed in the matter of the stocks. In your original order for the M'95 405 rifles, dated July 9th, you stated you were sending us the 30-30 as a model for the two 405s and that the sights were to be like those on that gun and the stocks, excepting, of course, the pistol grip. We have had your 30 caliber gun here while we have been making up the guns, and have followed carefully the dimensions, style of cheek piece, etc. of this rifle in making up the 405s. We [are] also following this gun as a pattern in making up the M'95 as you told us in your letter of July 23rd that you wished this exactly similar in style to the 405 which we were then making for you. You now say in your letter of the 16th instant in referring to the stocks that they must be exactly the same length as your Government rifle; that you want them exactly and precisely in every respect like the stock of the Government rifle. We find upon taking measurements that there is a difference between the stocks of the 30 Winchester, which we have been using here as a pattern, and the Springfield gun which you now send us. The measurements of the two guns are as follows:

30 Winchester [# 15659]
Pull or length of stock . 18 13/16 in.
Drop at comb................... 1 1/2 in.
Drop at heel.................... 1 7/8 in.

Springfield rifle [#6000]
Pull or length of stock ..... 14 1/8 in.
Drop at comb...................1 7/8 in.
Drop at heel...................2 3/16 in.

There is also a difference in the style of the combs and the cheek pieces of the two guns. Now, we have the stocks practically made up according to the dimensions of the 30-30 but if you desire, we will start all over again and copy the stocks on the Springfield gun.

In the matter of fastening the sights we will not only mark the barrels but on the front sights we will put a set screw which will enable you to screw the sight firmly in place so that it can not be knocked either way, and if for any reason, you desire to remove the sights the marks will enable you to put them back, exactly as they were before.

We will also endeavor to get you our ivory sights stained a light pink and if we are successful, will put these on the guns and will send along as extra sights the gold beads with which they are now equipped. If we are not successful in getting the pink sights, we will send an extra set of the gold beads unless you would prefer the plain ivory bead.

We are surprised at your report in regard to the sighting of the two 405s and the 30 caliber. These were shot by the same man and we got excellent results using ammunition of the same lot which we sent you. We will go into this matter again and will target the guns carefully with the special sights which we are making for you.

In regard to the difference in the capacity of the magazines in the 405 and 30 caliber, this is as it should be. The 30 caliber magazines are intended to take five cartridges but the 405 will only take four. This difference is due to the larger size of the 405 ammunition.

In regard to the belts, the manufacturers have not yet sent us the two smaller ones. We have the two of the larger waist measure and will hurry the manufacturers on the others.

We also note your instructions in regard to the half-dozen cleaners.

As to when we can send the guns to Washington to have them tried, this will depend upon whether you desire to take the stocks as we have now made them, corresponding to your 30-30, or whether we have got to start over again, making them to correspond to your Springfield rifle. If the stocks, as now made, will be satisfactory, we could probably get the guns to you in ten days after receipt of your reply. If we have got to make the stocks over, there will he a delay of about three weeks.

Awaiting your further instructions....

The next two letters from the White House ordered more accessories, asked more questions, and repeated the President's anxieties over "sights and stocks":

...Oyster Bay...September 21, 1908....The President wishes me to say that the Government rifle which he sent you shoots a little low so that he always has to put the sight up to the first notch, and he would like to know if you can not remedy this defect when you are sighting the other rifles....He also wishes me to ask you to send him, when you send the rifles, some of your red gun grease, red gun oil, red dust remover, and red crystal cleaner, all in cans suitable for carrying in Africa...

And on the 24th, from the White House:

The President has received your letter of the 21st instant. He is puzzled about the stocks. He sent you not only the 30-30 but the 45-70 which has a stock which he does not like. The stocks of the rifles you sent him are exactly like the 45-70 and he thinks you must have gotten mixed, and therefore he will ask you to have the stocks made just like the Government rifle which he sent you....Have you got the inch and a half pad now? If not, do not wait for it, but simply put on the type of pad you had on the rifles sent to Oyster Bay for trial, but be careful that, whichever pad is used, the stock when

fitted with it is exactly like that of the Government rifle.

Both queries were duly acknowledged, on the 23rd: "We have yours of the 21st. In the matter of sighting the President's guns and in reference to cleaning material put up in cans, all of which will have our attention." And on the 29th: guardedly expressing their own irritation at the President's change of mind on the pattern gun for the stocks, Lippencott of Winchester wrote to Loeb:

We have yours of the 24th inst., which refers to the matter of the stocks on the President's rifles. The stocks which we were making for his guns were exactly the same as on his 30-30 gun, which he first sent us and which he asked us to copy. As advised in our previous letter the stocks which we sent to Oyster Bay were only temporary ones and we had no idea of completing the rifles with these stocks attached.

We now understand that instead of copying the stock on the 30-30, the President wishes the stocks made exactly like those on the Government rifle which he sent us some time ago. The Special inch-and-a-half pads have been received, and we will fit them to these new stocks and will be very careful that the stocks which we are making are exactly like those on the Government gun in every respect, excepting, of course, the pistol grip which can not be supplied on the M' 1895 rifle.

Finally, on October 9, with an audible sigh of relief, Winchester dispatched one of the custom made Model 1895 rifles and the Springfield Sporter (#6000) to the White House. Bennett's letter expressed some reservations:

We are today expressing to you one of the Model 1895 405 Cal. rifles which we have been making for you, together with the sporting model Springfield of which you forwarded us sample.

The Model 1895 rifle we are forwarding you for inspection and criticism. We believe that we have carried out your instructions to the letter, and we have as far as possible copied the dimensions of the stock on the Springfield rifle, form of sight thereon, etc. We trust you will find the arm entirely satisfactory. If it is not we shall be pleased to have you return it to us with any criticisms which you may have to make.

Should you find, as we fear you may that the stock is rather too long to permit of the free operation of the finger lever from the shoulder, we shall be pleased to provide a stock as much shorter as you may desire. We trust you will give us an opportunity to do anything which we can to make the arm more satisfactory for your service....

Bennett's suspicions were immediately confirmed in a letter of October 14, though he must have been dismayed by complaints over both the stock and the sights:

The President is returning the two rifles. Somehow, the stock of the Winchester seems to come up as if it were a little longer than the stock of the Government rifle. It looks as if the lower point of the heel plate was a little longer. All the President wishes is to have the stock exactly like that of the Government rifle. Moreover, by looking thru the sights, those of the Winchester do not seem as distinct as those of the Springfield. It does not look to him as if the U of the rear sight of the Winchester was quite as large as the U of the rear sight of the Springfield, and there is not the small, light medium line down it.

Two more letters from Loeb followed the next day:

The President wishes me to ask how would it do for you to send the rifles to the President as soon as possible so that he can actually try them in shooting. The President wishes to be sure to have them all right, as he is going off on a trip for heavy game where there will be undoubtedly an interest aroused by a comparison between American repeaters and English rifles. The President is inclined to think that it would be a good thing for him to actually try them to see how the sights work, how the trigger pulls, and how the butt feels in actual practice. It seemed to the President as if the lower point of the butt or heel of the stock was a trifle too brought out. Perhaps he can tell this better after he has actually shot them.

The other letter of the 15th was quite brief "Enclosed I send you the President's check for $127.57, in payment of bill for cartridges shipped to Mombasa. Please be good enough to let the President know as soon as you learn that they have reached that place." Theodore Roosevelt was billed for his purchases of Winchester cartridges, rifles, and other items, but he received far more in terms of service than the company ever invoiced. By the same token Winchester could not have asked for more valuable or prestigious publicity than the coverage they would garner from the President's safari.

To the three White House enquiries of the 14th and 15th of October, Lippencott replied with both answers and advice:

We have yours of the 14th in reference to the President's two rifles which we sent to Washington and which have just been returned. We find by measuring the stocks that the new gun corresponds exactly with the Government rifle, but we note the President feels that the Winchester seems to come up as if it were a little longer than the stock of the Government rifle. This, we believe, is due to two causes, the first being that in operating the Winchester and the under lever requires a much longer reach than when operating the Government rifle, which has a top lever or bolt. Then, again, a gun fitted with a soft pad, such as the Winchester rifle is equipped with, naturally does not come up as smooth and clean as a rifle with a hard polished pad, and it is impossible to get a pad soft enough to do away with the recoil, which will present the smooth hard surface of a metal or hard rubber plate. We can reduce the length of the stock slightly if the President wishes, but, as stated above, the dimensions are now exactly the same as the Government rifle.

We have another suggestion to make and that is that we paste on the back of the rubber pads a leather patch made of material such as we enclose herewith. This gives a good smooth surface, and while we would not care to guarantee that these would not eventually come off, we have put them on a number of guns for customers and have never had any complaints. The greatest complaint of the soft rubber pads is the clinging or sticking to the clothing at times when quick shooting is required.

As regards the sights, while we find that the U is practically the same on both guns, we will open that on the Winchester, and will also make the light line below the notch heavier. We now await the President's instructions, and we will ask you to advise us immediately if we shall decrease the length of the stock and bow much, and if we shall put the smooth leather patch on the pads.

In regard to sending the guns to Washington after they are finished for actual test, would say we will be very glad to do this and will proceed to finish them at once upon receipt of reply to this letter.

We also acknowledge receipt of yours of the 15th enclos[ing] the President's check for $127.57 in payment for cartridges shipped to Mombasa, for which please accept our thanks. We have advised Smith, MacKenzie & Co. to cable us immediately upon arrival of the goods and as soon as we receive their reply will advise you.

TR welcomed Lippencott's suggestion on the buttpad. Loeb's reply, on October 18, was brief:

….The President approves of putting on the back of the rubber pads a leather patch made of the material of which you enclose a sample; and perhaps of making the Winchester stock just a quarter of an inch shorter by taking off just that much of the rubber if it can be done without much trouble. Otherwise leave it as it is.…As soon as the guns are finished send them on to Washington with some ammunition—not more than a hundred rounds all told.

Nearly a month later, on November 18, Loeb sent another brief note to Winchester: "Can you tell me when the rifles will be ready for the President to try? He would like to have some practice with them before the cold weather sets in." This query and a second letter were answered by Bennett on the 17th:

Your favor of November 15th, advising us concerning advices which you received from Messrs. Forbes and Lyman in regard to the behavior of the 405 caliber Model '95 rifle, at hand and contents noted.

We are very much surprised at this comment coming to us in such a manner, as we cannot find on our records complaint from either Mr. Forbes or Mr. Lyman of this difficulty, and we are at a loss to understand why they should not have brought such a serious matter directly to our attention.

The Model '95 arm 405 caliber is being used very generally and practically without complaint. It is possible, of course, that with ammunition manufactured by other parties, which possibly might not be adapted to it, difficulty might arise.

The arms which we have been making for you we would have shipped today, but in order to avoid any uncertainty, we will retain these for a day or two that we may make further tests.

The Three New Winchesters Are Shipped

Finally, after more than five months of correspondence, custom gun work and testing, the rifles were ready to ship. Winchester told the President his battery was en route to the White House:

We are sending you by express today [November 25] the three new guns and the two samples which you sent here for our guidance. We have made the three rifles in accordance with your instructions as near as possible to correspond to your Springfield rifle except that we have made the stocks of the guns 1/4 inch shorter, and have added a leather cover to the rubber pad, these changes in accordance with your instructions, dated October 18th. We trust, with the changes made according to your suggestions, you will find the rifles entirely satisfactory

Accompanying the guns we are sending, as requested, 100 cartridges out of the same lot which we are now preparing, and we hope you will find the shooting qualities of this ammunition satisfactory. In the box with the new guns, we are packing some wood rods and a small quantity of our various styles of cleaning material, also the slings for the guns and the four cartridge belts, two of each of the sizes ordered, one of each size for the 405 ammunition and one each for the 30 Govt.

In addition to this material, which we are now sending, we are preparing a lot of ammunition, the exact duplicate of that which we recently shipped for your account to Mombasa. We are also making up an assortment of spare parts, extra wood rods, jointed steel rods and Government or drop wipers for both guns and some of each of the four styles of cleaning material in bulk, packed in tin instead of

glass. This material we will hold here, subject to your instructions.

We would also suggest that before your departure for Africa you return the guns for repacking as we feel, that on account of the long journey, they should be packed in excelsior and that the case should be tin-lined. This style of packing will insure their delivery at destination in good order.

Hoping to receive your reply that the guns meet with your entire approval....

It must have drawn great sighs of relief when the President's reply was read by eager Winchester executives:

December 5, 1908

Gentlemen:

The rifles have come. They are beautiful weapons and I am confident will do well. After trying them this afternoon l am in doubt whether the 405's do not shoot too high. This fault could be met, however, by an alteration of the rear sight which will make the rifles shoot a little lower when the sight is slipt into the lowest notch of the bar. I shall first try them again.

Will you send me on another box of the 30 caliber, model 1908, and another box of the 405 cartridges?

The 405 Model 1895 Winchesters sent to the President on the 25th of November were serial #'s 68727 and 68786; the serial of the third rifle, a 30 caliber, is unknown. They had 24" round and matted barrels, flat top sporting rear sights, Lyman front sights with pink ivory beads, Silver's butt pads, fancy checkered oil-finished walnut stocks, crescent cheekpieces, shotgun style butts and were finished in blue and case-hardening. Except for the absence of custom engraving, the three rifles were about as fully deluxe as Winchester made in the Model of 1895. Each rifle underscored the tastes of Theodore Roosevelt as seen in his first custom Winchester of record—the Model 1878 and Model 1876 rifles shipped in July 1884 for hunting in the Badlands. Now, twenty-six years later, Roosevelt still favored the fancy checkered stocks with shotgun butt, the unusual (for a Winchester) crescent cheekpiece, the blue and case-hardened finish and special sights. His taste in sights had changed, however, to the so-called flat-top sporting rear sight, from the folding leaf and buckhorn rear sights he had preferred c. 1884—86.

Replying to Roosevelt's cordial and congratulatory letter of December 5, Winchester, on the 9th, shipped to the White House two more boxes each of 30 caliber and 405 caliber cartridges, with a suggestion: "....should you desire it, we should be pleased to send a representative to Washington at some time convenient to you, who could go out on the range with you and make necessary alterations to adjust the sighting of those arms to your complete satisfaction..."

The idea struck the President's fancy: "...December 11, 190....Your letter of the 9th instant has been received. The President thinks well of your suggestion and will be glad to have you send a man down here during the holidays. He will give you the exact day later. In that case he thinks you had better send on a few more boxes both of full metal patched and soft point 30 caliber model 1908, and 405 caliber WC.F cartridges."

On the 12th, Winchester Bennett confirmed the plans for a factory representative to shoot with Roosevelt, noting "we will see that [our man] brings with him a sufficient quantity of both full metal patched and soft point ammunition 30 Cal. M'03 and 405 W.C.F."

TR's next letter had more kind words for his gunmaker, and ordered a third Model 1895 in 405 caliber:

December 18, 1908

I can not say how much I like those two 405 rifles you sent me. Now, my belief is that in Africa those will be the two rifles my son and I will habitually carry in our own hands; the rifles upon which we will most depend. As this is so, I think I should like to have you make me a third rifle, a duplicate of these two. If you have any difficulty about the Silver pad of the full thickness for this you might make it a little thinner. Could you make me a duplicate of these two rifles in time for me to take it out to Africa next March? I would probably leave it at some central point, say Nairobi, where I made my preliminary hunts; but it would be a good thing to have it as a kind of insurance against accidents. If I cabled you from Nairobi how long would it take you to get me out extra cartridges for the rifle? Have you heard if those cartridges that you sent have arrived in Mombasa yet?

Bennett's response, on the 15th, noted with pleasure" that the "405 Cal. Model 1895 rifles which you have received are satisfactory and that you believe you will make use of them chiefly in your prospective work." He continued "we are pleased to advise that if the standard form of Silver's recoil pad (3/4" thick) would be satisfactory we could furnish you with an arm to be a duplicate of the two 405 Cal. Model 1895 rifle....in from two to three weeks from receipt of order. To use a 1 1/2" pad would mean an eight-to-ten week delivery. The last two [pads] which we procured had to be made especially for our order."

In answering the President's question on cartridges, Bennett inadvertently hinted at the primitive state of knowledge of Africa in 1908: "In regard to your inquiry [on] cartridges should you cable us from Nairobi, we regret to advise that we are unable to locate Nairobi [on the map]." Bennett estimated a six-to-ten week delivery time from New Haven to Mombasa. The cartridges already shipped were nearing Mombasa and were expected there soon.

It was fast becoming public knowledge that Winchesters would be Roosevelt's standard arms during the African safari. But the factory was in an awkward position, as explained to Loeb by Bennett in a letter of December 14:

We have been overwhelmed of late by requests from representatives of the press and individuals for descriptions of the Winchester rifles and ballistic data of the cartridges which it is understood that the President is to use on his coming African trip. Not knowing whether the President would care to have his equipment exploited, we have refrained from admitting that we have made any guns especially for his prospective African trip, the tenor of our reply to all inquiries being that President Roosevelt has used Winchester rifles to a certain extent for a good many years and that we presume some of them would be included in his complement of arms. Notwithstanding our reticence in the matter, considerable information more or less inaccurate has been published in different sections, which seems to have tended to whet the appetite of the press and sportsmen in general for accurate data, with the result that we are placed in a rather embarrassing position with many of our friends. Naturally we would like very much to be in a position to state frankly that the President is planning to use our product and, if agreeable to him, we would appreciate the courtesy deeply if we maybe permitted without objection upon his part to state in effect that the President will use Winchester Repeating Rifles and Winchester Ammunition on his forthcoming African Hunting and Collecting Trip and that the President's complement of arms includes the following:

Model 1895 rifle, 405 Caliber.
Model 1895 rifle, 30 Government Model 1903 Caliber.
Model 1886 rifle, 45/70 Caliber.
Model 1894 rifle, 30 W.C.F Caliber.

The above phraseology is purely a suggestion and we would be glad to change it to conform with the President's ideas.

Trusting that the President will be willing to grant this request, we remain....

Loeb's reply was immediate:

Persona....December 15, 1908...I am in receipt of your letter...in reference to the requests you are receiving as to the guns the President will take with him, and in reply would say that the President would not want the matter used in any way as an advertisement, but there is no objection whatever to your stating in answer to queries that the President will have your guns on the trip.

On the 18th, Bennett acknowledged Loeb's note and added. "We appreciate very much the privilege which the President grants us, and take pleasure in assuring you that we will take all pains to see that the privilege is not abused or made use of by us for advertising purposes." Some interesting developments were to take place on this matter later.

A Roosevelt letter of December 16 offered several queries; these were answered by Bennett the following day. After assuring the President there was no hollow point ammunition in his order, and that Winchester had not so advised a recent factory visitor, Bennett confirmed TR's order for the third 405 Model 1895 rifle, "to be equipped with *3/4* in. thick Silver's recoil pad, the wood of the stock to be lengthened out so that, recoil pad included, the over-all dimensions of the stock will be the same as in the case of the other two guns."

Bennett also confirmed that Winchester would investigate using Khartoum as a shipping point, "should you desire us to do so." The ammunition previously shipped was "already past London on its way to Mombasa," and in a letter of the 19th, Bennett was able to confirm the consignment's expected arrival there "about the middle of February...."

Finally, on the 26th of December, Loeb sent word to Winchester that: "The President will be

THE WHITE HOUSE
WASHINGTON

December 31, 1908.

Gentlemen:

Your representative and marksman, Mr. Laudensack, was on here to-day and I spent the morning with him. We thoroly tried out the rifles, and I am happy to say that I am extremely pleased with the results. The .405s shot high, but Mr. Laudensack had two spare rear sights with which he replaced the ones already on the tw~~~ *They are now all right.* all right. I shall send the rifles, includi~~ ~~ to you forthwith, and later on I shall prob~~ I desire that all of them, including the ne~~ that is, in all,

1 Springfield
1 Winchester taking the Springfi~~
3 .405 Winchesters *? Marlin*
1 little Stevens
1 45-70 Winchester T.~~

(I shall sent the latte~~
be put in leather cases and then in herme~~
before I sail on the 23d of March. Plea~~
size that I can place in my cabin on the~~
be separated from them. Also, please pu~~ ~o a~~
sights, perhaps spare parts, and the t~~
the rifles apart, this tool box being s~~
African trip.

189975

The 2 Cases for Mr Bishop

Be sure that the new .405 is sighted exactly like, and shoots exactly like, the two .405s I return.

You have made arrangements, as I understand, to ship 3000 cartridges with me. I should also want you to ship 1000 cartridges for the little 25 Marlin or Stevens, (whichever it is) I shall have with me. please also send out to Africa now 200 Government cartridges which I shall send you, and 1000 more .405 cartridges, 200 of them solid and 800 of them with soft points. I want these shipped to Mombasa as soon as possible in care of Smith, Mackenzie & Co., as in the case of your former shipment. I take this as a measure of precaution, as I do not want to run out of cartridges.

Sincerely yours,

Theodore Roosevelt

The Winchester Repeating Arms Company,
New Haven, Connecticut.

The President was determined there would be no ammunition shortage or misplacement of rifles: "Please put [the rifles and leather cases] in tin boxes of a size that I can place in my cabin on the steamer, as I do not desire to be separated from them."

very glad if you will send on your men so that he can be at the White House at nine o'clock Thursday morning, December 31st. Please advise me if he can come at that time." Bennett on the 28th confirmed that "we will have our Mr. Laudensack report at the White House at 9:00 o'clock Thursday morning, December 31st...." To President-elect Taft, TR commented in a letter on the 31st: "Ha! Ha! You are making up your Cabinet, I in a lighthearted way have spent the morning testing my rifles for my African trip. Life has its compensations!" On that day the President would write Winchester of the test results:

Your representative and marksman, Mr. Laudensack, was on here today and I spent the morning with him. We thoroly tried out the rifles, and I am happy to say that I am extremely pleased with the results. The 405s shot high, but Mr. Laudensack had two spare rear sights with which he replaced the ones already on the two 405s, and they then shot all right. They are now all right. I shall send the rifles, including the little Marlin, on to you forthwith, and later on I shall probably send you the 45-70. I desire that all of them, including the new one you are making for me, that is, in all,
1 Springfield [Sporter, #6000]
1 Winchester taking the Springfield cartridge [M1895, # unknown]
3 405 Winchesters [M1895, #'s 63727, 63786, 68180]
1 little Stevens [unknown]
1 45-70 Winchester [M1886, #125422]
(I shall sen[d] the latter to you)

be put in leather cases and then in hermetically sealed tin cases just before I sail on the 23rd of March. Please put them in tin boxes of a size that I can place in my cabin on the steamer, as I do not desire to be separated from them. Also, please put up a small tool box, with spare sights, perhaps spare parts, and the tools which

will enable me to take the rifles apart, this tool box being such that I can carry it on my African trip.

Be sure that the new 405 is sighted exactly like, and shoots exactly like, the two 405s I return.

You have made arrangements, as I understand, to ship 8,000 cartridges with me. I should also want you to ship 1,000 cartridges for the little 25 Marlin or Stevens (whichever it is), that I shall have with me. Please also send out to Africa now 200 Government cartridges which I shall send you, and 1,000 more 405 cartridges, 200 of them solid and 800 of them with soft points. I want these shipped to Mombasa as soon as possible in care of Smith, MacKenzie & Co., as in the case of your former shipment. I take this as a measure of precaution, as I do not want to run out of cartridges.

The President was determined there would be no ammunition shortage or misplacement of rifles: "Please put [the rifles and leather cases] in tin boxes of a size that I can place in my cabin on the steamer, as I do not desire to be separated from them."

Bennett, writing on January 2, 1909, confirmed TR's detailed letter of comments, questions and instructions, and noted the extra Model 1895 405 rifle, after having the sights adjusted by Laudensack, would be sent to the White House shortly. Bennett also noted the President's orders for 25, 30, and 405 caliber cartridges. Roosevelt's steamer, the *S.S. Hamburg* would sail on the 23rd of March, so that it was not too soon to finalize each detail.

The matter of ammunition had yet to be settled. Dated the 4th and 5th of January, two more letters from the White House cleared up some of the last details: The President decided not to take his 45-70 Model 1886 Winchester, so that changed the make-up, but not the quantity of cartridges (3,000) that would go with him on the steamer; 1,500 would be

30 caliber and 1,500 would be 405. He also wanted 1,000 405, 1,000 25, and 200 30 caliber cartridges to be sent "to Mombasa at once! It was also noted: "The President will be glad to have you send on to him the new 405 at your convenience."

Winchester promptly acknowledged both letters, but reminded the President that "there was a quantity of [45-70] ammunition included in the shipment which we made [in September] to Mombasa." Considering the logistics involved in the entire safari undertaking, the quantity of extra (and useless) ammunition was an error of minor consequence.

Final Details

By January 17, TR expressed not a little anxiety over his extra 405 Winchester Model 1895. That day he had Loeb send the factory a concise note: "The President directs me to ask you if you can send on to him the new 405 at once. He desires to try it forthwith. When will it be here?"

"This arm was ready for shipment," replied Bennett on the 18th, "shortly after Mr. Laudensack's return from Washington, but in refitting it with sights [to agree with the President's other M'95's] the finish on the receiver was injured and the gun has gone back to be refinished. We trust to be able to ship it by Wednesday...."

The new 405 reached the White House in good order, and the President evinced his satisfaction with it on January 29:

Gentlemen

I have tried the 405 rifle and it is satisfactory. I shall send it back in the course of two or three days. With it I shall send a double-barreled Holland which I am taking with me as a reserve gun for the heaviest game. Please have these thoroly oiled, just as you will with my other weapons, and as you will with the Mannlicher which I shall later have sent you. Then I shall ask you to have all these rifles hermetically sealed in whatever cases you think best-I suppose tin cases-each in addition, of course, having a leather case; and I will have you put them aboard the ship just prior to my sailing. I think I should like to carry them in my own cabin. They will include the three 405 Winchesters, the Winchester which carries the Springfield ammunition, the Springfield, the double-barreled Holland, and the Mannlicher which I shall send you later. You will at the same time put on the ship all ammunition in accordance with my previous letters. Have you sent out the additional shipment of ammunition, as I asked you to?

"We...are now awaiting the Holland and Mannlicher rifles," replied Lippencott on the 4th of February, [and] we should be very glad to have you give us a few days notice to get [your entire shipment] to New York so that there would be no difficulty in getting them on board the steamer." When the Holland and Mannlicher reached New Haven, special shipping cases for them would be made. Lippencott added that the "additional shipment of ammunition for Mombasa [had] left New York on the 23rd [of January]...." To this Loeb replied on the 5th.

....The President wishes you would keep him advised as to the arrival of the ammunition at Mombasa. All the President desires for the Holland and Mannlicher are the air-tight tin cases. He has the leather cases that belong to them. Of course you will provide leather or canvas cases for all the other rifles....Can you not have put on the cases of guns and on the cases of ammunition in large red letters the President's name....The President will sail on the Hamburg-American Line steamer *Hamburg* March 23rd.... [Handwritten note] Please keep date of sailing confidential.

Bennett's next letter to the White House regretfully announced one more mishap of many that

harassed both Winchester and TR in safari preparations. The note was sent on the 6th and advised.
"...the Holland gun has arrived....We have also received the last Winchester Model '95....and are
sorry to say that this comes to us in very bad condition. Included in the case with some other articles were 3 couple of bottles of our Crystal Cleaner
and the cork of one of these had come out, allowing the liquid to escape, which will require the gun
to be entirely refinished, both the metal work and
the stock." This was solely the fault of inept pack-
aging by White House workmen. Lippencott also
lamented "that the lock [on the Holland case] does
not work and we ask if we shall attempt to have it
repaired here." He added: "The cases of both the
guns and ammunition will be marked as requested
with the President's name in large red letters, and
we will put no other marks on the cases excepting
a number so that the contents of the several cases
may be identified according to the list which we
will deliver at the time shipment is made...."

Roosevelt was perturbed over the fate of his
extra 405; Loeb wrote Winchester accordingly on
February 7:

> The President has received your letter....He is
> much annoyed at what has happened about the
> 405, and of course wishes you to put it in prop-
> er condition before packing....Please repair
> the Holland guncase lock, and put up whatev-
> er oil and apparatus for gun-cleaning is need-
> ed, including cleaning rods, in proper form so
> that breakage will be avoided....The Mannli-
> cher will be sent to you in a day or two.

Four days later the Mannlicher, with scope, was
dispatched, as was the Fox double-barreled shotgun:

> Gentlemen:
>
> I am shipping you today the Mannlicher rifle,
> with telescope sight which is in separate small
> leather case. Please have this rifle and the sight

packed in an air-tight case exactly as with the
other rifles I have sent.

> I am also sending you a Fox double-bar-
> reled shotgun, which please have similarly
> packed in an air-tight case like the rifle cases.
> Will you see that both the rifle and gun have
> whatever oil is necessary put on them, and will
> you put into the gun case, for the gun, any ad-
> ditional oil or cleaning paraphernalia? Except-
> ing the gun, there is nothing but the cleaning
> rod in the case now. I have asked the Fox people
> to send you 50 ball and buck cartridges for ship-
> ment with the gun. Please advise me when they
> have come.
>
> Have you yet received news of the arrival
> at Mombasa of your first shipment of cartridg-
> es for me? Is the third 405 that you had to have
> recleaned in good shape? I want to be sure that
> there is no possible slip-up, and I shall make
> arrangements for you to have a representative
> sent aboard the ship on the 23rd of March with
> all these guns, to turn them over to me in per-
> son and to show me where the cartridges are
> which are put on board. The steamship people
> have told me that every possible facility will be
> given me.

TR was taking every precaution that there
would be no "slip-up." In a few more weeks, as an
ex-President, he would be off; Winchester would be
glad to see that steamer sail.

In a detailed letter of the 15th Lippencott confirmed that the factory now had on hand nine of
the President's guns, plus sundry cartridges, spare
parts, cleaning equipment, and several "tin-lined
air-tight cases." Winchester queried Roosevelt on
whether he wanted the guns packed in any special combination and on when to expect the buck
and ball cartridges for the Fox gun. The firm regretfully announced a delay in passage of the original shipment of ammunition for Mombasa and
reassured the worried Chief Executive both that
the shipment would arrive on time and that the

damaged extra Model '95 called simply for "re-finishing the frame and stock"; there had been "no damage...which would, in any way...affect its shooting qualities."

On the 16th Loeb wrote from the White House:

The President has received your letter...and directs me to state that it is very satisfactory. Do you think he is safe in assuming that he will find the ammunition which you have shipped to Mombasa on his arrival there? You are correct about all the rifles and it will be all right if you pack them separately or put two together. Do just as you think best about this. If you put two together the President wishes one of the 405's and the Springfield put in one case, with some special mark thereon, so that they may be identified, and he can take them out of their case as soon as he lands at Mombasa....The President will meet your man with everything on the ship, the exact time of sailing of which he will send you later.

There was still time for at least one more mishap, and it was presented to Winchester in a note from Loeb on the 16th of February: "The President has received from Mr. A. H. Fox, President of the A. H. Fox Gun Company, Philadelphia, a copy of Mr. Fox's letter to you concerning the shells to be packed with the Fox gun. The President agrees with the suggestions of Mr. Fox and requests that you govern yourselves accordingly."

Bennett's answer handled the situation forcefully, and his letter was directed to the President himself, bypassing Loeb:

We are today [16th] in receipt of advice from the A.H. Fox Gun Company, in matter of your Fox gun, which you forwarded us to be packed, and also in reference to matter of ammunition for this gun. We are advised by the Fox Gun Company to prepare the pack with the arm, *25 12 gauge shells, loaded with round ball, and 25*

12 gauge shells, loaded with buckshot. We note Mr. Fox's suggestion that we furnish you with paper shells, owing to what he supposes to be some difficulty in our turning out a brass shell, which will be sufficiently crimped, to properly hold charge in place. We have advised Mr. Fox that he is in error in believing that we cannot properly and firmly crimp brass shells. In fact we have put up brass shells for the Government and Express Companies for years, and are able to crimp them so that the shell makes a far more solid package than could by any possibility be obtained with the paper shell. Also, there is no possibility of its swelling when exposed to moisture and humid atmosphere, as is the case with any paper or paper lined brass shells. We would strongly suggest and recommend the use of a solid brass shell for your purposes in this instance. Undoubtedly Mr. Fox has never seen our product in this line.

We would also suggest that the amount of shot shell ammunition included with the gun, will probably be by no means sufficient for your use in Africa, and we should be pleased to furnish any material which you might order, and see that it goes with the other ammunition, which we will put aboard the steamer for you.

Awaiting your further valued orders, and directions in this matter....

Bennett's letter brought an immediate response from the White House on February 17: "...The President has received your letter...and is very much pleased to learn from you that Mr. Fox was in error about the brass shells and that you can furnish them. Please include 50 with ball, 50 with buck, 50 No.4, 50 No. 8, and 100 dust, all in brass shells." The President's selection demonstrated a shotgunner's knowledge of loads for African birds and small game.

On the 19th, Lippencott confirmed TR's order for shotgun shells, and on the 20th, he confirmed the company's plans for packing the arms, ammunition, and accessories. The case with the Springfield rifle

and one of the Model 1895 405's would "bear a star which will enable [the President] to locate this particular case without difficulty." Again Winchester assured Loeb that the two shipments of ammunition already dispatched would all be at Mombasa on the President's arrival there.

In a confidential letter of February 21, Loeb directed Winchester to have their "representative meet the President on the steamer *Hamburg*... at Hoboken, New Jersey, at 12:00, noon, Monday, March 22nd, with the guns and ammunition. The President will go to the steamer at that time especially for the purpose of seeing that all his things are put aboard." Winchester was leaving small margin for error, and Lippencott replied the next day: "We will send somebody from our New York office who is familiar with the piers and steamers so that there will be no possible chance of failure to meet the President." And on the 27th Lippencott let the President know everything was "ready for immediate shipment." He listed the contents and numbers of each case.

In cases #1-5 we have packed the 30 Govt. 1908 and 405 cartridges, putting an assortment of each style in each of the cases. In case #6 you will find the cartridges which you sent in with the Mannlicher and Holland guns and also the loaded brass shells which we made up for you for use in your Fox gun. Case #7 contains the M'95/405 and the Springfield rifle. You will remember that you asked us to pack these guns separately, and to enable you to identify this case, we have, in addition to the number, marked it with a star. Cases #8-11 contain the other guns, and, referring particularly to case #10, you will find packed with the Holland rifle all the extras which accompanied this when it was sent to New Haven. Case #13 contains a kit of tools, a number of extra parts and a quantity of cleaning material; also catalogue leaves covering instructions for dismounting our guns and with illustrations of the several parts and their numbers. All these parts are tagged separately so that there will be no difficulty in locating a particular piece.

The cases, in accordance with your instructions, are marked "Theodore Roosevelt" and bear no other marks except the numbers as indicated on the enclosed list. A duplicate copy of this will be handed you by our representative who delivers the goods to you on the steamship.

Trusting that we have handled this matter in accordance with your desires....

Cases #1 through #4 each held:
100 30 Govt. 1908 Rimless full metal patched cartridges.
200 30 Govt. 1903 Rimless soft point cartridges.
100 405 W.C.F. full metal patched cartridges.
200 405 W.C.F. soft point cartridges.

The remaining cases, as listed on Winchester's inventory of February *27,* showed that nothing had been left to chance. The Roosevelts were virtually assured that—at least in armaments—there would be no "slip-up."

CASE #5
80 30 Govt. 1903 Rimless full metal patched [cartridges].
220 30 Govt. 1903 Rimless soft point [cartridges].
100 405 W.C.F. full metal patched [cartridges].
200 405 W.C.E soft point [cartridges].

CASE #6
23 9 m/m cartridges.
15 500/450 metal patched soft point cartridges.
19 500/450 full metal patched cartridges.
50 loaded brass shells, 12 ga., 24 grains Infallible powder, single ball.
50 loaded brass shells, 12 ga., 26 grains Infallible powder, # 1 buck

50 loaded brass shells, 12 ga., 26 grains Infallible powder, 1 1/8 ounces #4 shot.
50 loaded brass shells, 12 ga., 24 grains Infallible powder, 1 1/8 ounces #8 shot.
100 loaded brass shells, 12 ga., 20 grains Infallible powder, 1 ounce dust shot.

CASE #7. Special mark
1 rifle, M'95/405 W.C.F.
1 leather case for above rifle.
1 Springfield rifle [serial #6000].
1 canvas cover for Springfield rifle.
1 leather case for Springfield rifle.

CASE #8.
2 M'95/405 W.C.F. rifles.
2 leather cases for above rifles.

CASE #9.
1 M'95/3O Govt. 1903 Rimless rifle.
1 leather case for above rifle.
1 Marlin rifle, 25-36 caliber.
1 leather case for Marlin rifle.

CASE #10.
1 Holland double barrel rifle [serial #19109].
1 leather compartment case for Holland rifle and parts.
1 canvas cover for above leather case.
1 funnel.
4 screw drivers.
1 ivory front sight in ivory case.
1 can of oil.
1 wood-and-brass jointed cleaning rod.
2 extra main springs.
1 lever lockpin.
1 special drop wiper.
3 tubes of Eley Rifleine Jelly.
1 leather muzzle protector.
8 sling straps.
1 bottle of sight black.
1 shell extractor.

2 dummy cartridges.
3 tubes of Cole's Rust Remover.
4 brushes for cleaner.

CASE #11.
1 Mannlicher rifle.
1 leather cover for Mannlicher rifle.
1 Goertz telescope in leather case.

CASE #12.
1 Fox double-barrel shotgun.
1 leather compartment case for Fox gun.
1 leather case for Fox gun.
1 jointed cleaning rod for Fox gun.

CASE #13.
2 barrel reflectors. 1 cartridge clip. 2 brass heads. 2 cans of Marble Boot Grease. 2 Marble jointed rods. 4 Marble rifle cleaners. 1 compartment tool box containing the following: 1 small hammer. 1 Bernard Combination pliers, 6". 1 hand file, #2. 6 steel drifts. 2 copper punches. 1 rat-tail file. 1 3-corner file. 1 combination screw driver. 1 large screw driver. [end of tool box contents] 3 Lyman front sights with pink beads, M'95/405. 1 [Lyman front sight with pink bead] M'95/30-1903 Rimless. 3 rear sights, M'95/405. 1 rear sight, M'95/30 Govt. 1903 Rimless. 3 main Springs, M'95. 2 hammers complete, M'95. 1 buttstock with metal buttplate, M'95. 1 magazine complete, M'95/405. 1 magazine complete, M'95/30 Govt. 1908 Rimless. 2 firing pins, M'95. 2 carrier springs. M'95. 1 sear, M'95. 1 trigger, M'95. 2 finger lever catches, M'95. 1 finger lever catchplunger, M'95. 1 [finger lever catch plunger] spring. M'95. 1 [finger lever] pin, M'95. 1 extractor, M'95/405 W.C.F. 1 [extractor] M'95/30 Govt. 1903 Rimless. 2 searsprings, M'95. Catalogue leaves showing instructions for dismounting etc., and illustrations of parts and their numbers. 4 wood rods, 405 caliber. 2 wood rods, 30 caliber. 2 Red

W Cleaning rods, 405 caliber. 6 Govt. Cleaners, 405. 3 Govt cleaners, 30 caliber. 1 Red W Cleaning rods, 30 caliber. 2 cans of Red W Gun Oil. 2 cans of Red W Gun grease. 2 cans of Red W Rust Remover. 2 Jars of Red W Crystal Cleaner.

On the 28th of February, Roosevelt sent to Winchester a letter expressing thorough satisfaction in his dealings with the company:

I thank you for your letter of the 27th. You have done exactly what I desire.

Now, let me further most cordially extend my thanks to you for the pains you have taken in making up my outfit. I very deeply appreciate it. I am sure that if the results are not all they should be the fault will be mine and not yours—and I am going to take mighty good care that the results *are* as they should be.

As soon as I return from Africa I will see you and tell you how everything has turned out, unless, indeed, I have already covered it all in *Scribner's Magazine.*

Thoroughly delighted, Winchester Bennett sent TR a cordial reply:

Your favor...is at hand and contents of the same noted with the greatest pleasure. It is this company's earnest endeavor to spare no pains to satisfy any and all of its customers, and we sincerely trust that the results obtained with the material which we have furnished you will be in every way satisfactory....It would indeed give us great pleasure to hear from you after your return and to receive any criticism which you might then have to make or suggestions for improvement on our product.

The cases were packed and ready to join TR on the steamer when the time came, but this would not prevent the President from a final brainstorm.

And so on the 27th of February Loeb let Winchester know they would be receiving "from General Crozier [US. Army Ordnance] a Springfield rifle and a 405 Winchester rifle, both fitted with Maxim's silencers, and one of them with an arrangement for shooting at night, together with 200 Springfield cartridges. Please add to these 100 cartridges for the 405 Winchester and the cleaning apparatus, with oil, and have them put in a case that will enable the President to use them on the steamer....." TR knew full well he could hardly spend some three weeks at sea and resist the temptation to open his tin-lined crates and shoot. The two rifles with silencers would solve that problem nicely.

In mid-March, letters from Winchester confirmed the handling of the silencer rifles, advised TR of the receipt in Mombasa of the first shipment of ammunition, and reassured him that the second shipment would arrive "in time for your requirements."

As of March 4th, Roosevelt was an ex-President of the United States, though he was still in the international limelight—and would remain so as long as he lived. His final two letters of March to Winchester were anti-climatic. On the 12th, he restated again his intention to be at the dock "at twelve o'clock Monday the twenty-second, to receive the rifles and so forth." He also reminded Winchester to expect the delivery of the two silencer-fitted rifles. On the 18th, TR's secretary wrote simply: "Reply to your letter [regarding 1000 9mm Mannlicher cartridges sent to Winchester by dealers Von Lengerke & Detmold], Mr. Roosevelt would like you to pack the goods in a tin-lined case and deliver them with the other goods."

Just three days before the *Hamburg* was to leave Hoboken, the two rifles fitted with Maxim silencers arrived in New Haven. The Springfield was a Model 1903, serial #352379, fitted with illuminated sights, and complete with a telescopic sight, leather case, and 200 rounds of 30 caliber cartridges. The Winchester Model 1895, serial number unknown, also had illuminated sights, a canvas case, and a spare

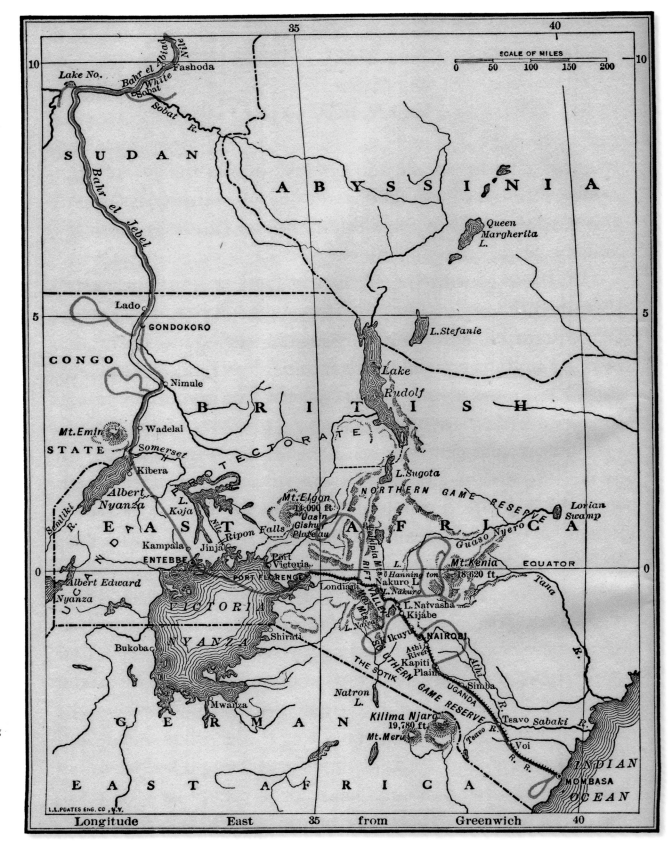

Map showing TR's route and hunting trips in Africa as printed in *African Game Trails*.

BOONE AND CROCKETT CLUB
PERMANENT COLLECTION

buttstock and forearm. The shipment also contained a small box with "9 spare lamps [flashlight bulbs] and 6 spare dry batteries, and 3 screwdrivers.

CASE #14.
800 cartridges, 9 m/m Mannlicher soft point.
200 cartridges, 9 m/m Mannlicher full metal patched.

CASE #15. (Special Mark)
60 cartridges, 405 W.C.F soft point.
40 cartridges, 405 full metal patched.
1 U.S. magazine rifle, M' 1908, #352379, fitted with illuminated sights.
1 telescopic sight for above.
1 Maxim silencer.
1 leather cover. (For above gun)
1 box containing 9 spare lamps, 6 spare dry batteries, 3 screw drivers and tools.
200 30 Govt. Cartridges, 1906.
1 M'95 405 rifle, fitted with illuminated sights.
1 Maxim silencer for same.
1 canvas cover, M'95.
1 butt stock for M'95.
1 forearm, M'95.
2 tubes of Red W Gun Grease
1 Govt. cleaner, 30 cal.
2 tubes of Red W Rust Remover
1 Govt. cleaner, 405 cal.
2 bottles of Red W Gun Oil
1 Wood Rod, 30 cal.
2 bottles of Red W Crystal Cleaner
Cleaning Waste

In the Winchester factory's Theodore Roosevelt file, the final document of this involved and often frustrating ten-month odyssey is a poignant one— a simple receipt for March 22, 1909, signed by the baggage department of the Hamburg-American Line Piers:

Received from the Winchester Repeating Arms Co, 15 cases, guns and ammunition for account of Theod. Roosevelt.

Roosevelt's "great adventure" had officially begun. Winchester's was over. ◉

The Cradle of Conservation

BY LOWELL E. BAIER
Originally appeared in the *Theodore Roosevelt Association Journal*, Volume XXVIII, Number 1, Winter 2007, pp. 12-24

The English word "icon" comes from the Greek word "eikón" which meant an image (picture, bust, statue, or emblem) considered holy or sacred, and adored and worshipped; or a revered and cherished belief (or superstition), such as eternal life after death. Icons therefore can be either tangible or intangible.

Because of America's short history of some 400 years since our European ancestors arrived on our eastern shores, coupled with an intense desire for rapid nation building, we have embraced a variety of icons, both tangible and intangible (i.e., people, places, values, and beliefs) while developing our unique national identity. The pilgrim, frontiersman, cowboy, industrial-capitalist, general, or astronaut—each archetype has a distinct place in our historical conscience of what this country stands for, and the type of people it took to wrestle and forge contemporary America from a wilderness initially inhabited by Indians. With each historic image or character-type goes a name, and today we celebrate a list of heroes who molded America into a great nation. Political leaders, moreover, enjoy a distinct place in our revered icons that represent nation building. George Washington, Thomas Jefferson, Abraham Lincoln, and Theodore Roosevelt: Each looms large in our American history and culture from atop Mt. Rushmore. To each we've attached a place: Washington is memorialized by Mt. Vernon and the Washington Monument; Jefferson by Monticello and the Jefferson Memorial on the Potomac; Lincoln by the log cabin in Kentucky and the Lincoln Memorial in Washington, D.C.

Ferris and Merrifield on the ruins of the first shack at the Elkhorn Ranch, from Hermann Hagedorn's *Roosevelt in the Badlands*.

THEODORE ROOSEVELT COLLECTION, HARVARD COLLEGE LIBRARY

Theodore Roosevelt has several "places" memorializing his legendary, restless place in our history: his birthplace in New York City, reminding us of his urban roots; his permanent home, Sagamore Hill, on Long Island; Roosevelt Island in the Potomac River in Washington, D.C., celebrating his presidency; and Theodore Roosevelt National Park in North Dakota memorializing his conservation legacy.

The tectonic plates—i.e., the core values—underlying our culture that give structural integrity and a distinctive identity to our nation are our deeply rooted beliefs, each an intangible icon: life, liberty, and the pursuit of happiness; a belief and trust in God; freedom of speech; tolerance for dissent and different ethnic groups and religions; a democratic form of government; capitalism and the encouragement of entrepreneurship and human initiative. Notable intangible iconic core values that secure our identity as a Nation and which we cherish deep in our national pride have been memorialized by linkages with geographic places or sites that symbolize and ensure their perpetuation. Examples of such significant historic sites include the following: the Statue of Liberty symbolizes our freedom; Ellis Island symbolizes a land of opportunity, hope, and promise made up of immigrants who forged it with their own hands; Valley Forge memorializes the cost of our independence; Gettysburg and Antietam symbolically define the price we paid to maintain a union of separate but indivisible states, united into one democratic nation; the domed Capitol Building in Washington, D.C., is the symbol of our democratic form of government. The churches and cathedrals across America are not just mere places of worship, but with their steeples and bell towers are distinct symbols memorializing the nation's trust in God. Most of these geographic places and sites are sacred and revered because they are the tangible symbols of our national identity and pride to which are linked the intangible core values of our national identity.

Nineteenth Century American Icons

While many of America's iconic core values come from our distinctive European ancestry, they were further embellished by the frontier spirit that conquered the wilderness continent. Some of these core values were defined in our Declaration of Independence (1776) and Constitution (1787), while others came later in our brief history. For example, the Bill of Rights amending the Constitution by adding ten additional "rights" was ratified in 1791, and the remaining seventeen amendments were added between 1798 and 1992. The abolition of slavery through the Emancipation Proclamation (1863) and the Thirteenth Amendment to the Constitution (1865) followed the Declaration of Independence by almost ninety years. America's core value of conservation—i.e., the ethic of husbanding our natural resources for both their aesthetic and material values—evolved at the national level roughly another 25-30 years thereafter, depending upon which benchmark is used. The early 1870s, however, appear to have been the seminal moment. Noted historian and author John F. Reiger, in his remarkable study on the origins of conservation in America, American Sportsmen and the Origins of Conservation, now in its third edition (2001), documents with original research the earliest conservation work in the nation of the anglers and fish culturists, followed by the foresters, wildlife naturalists, and bird watchers, beginning with game protection laws as early as 1708.[1] The very earliest nineteenth-century conservationist efforts were localized New England, site-specific, grass-roots efforts to protect a specific woodland, stream, pond, or species. Localized concerns about protecting and perpetuating a specific natural resource generally resulted in the organization of local sportsmen's clubs to address the issue. However, the big issues that faced the nation—the broad national landscape size challenges of the day—required broad national support to galvanize into action the political will needed to address the monumental threats to America's natural resource base. That resulted in the formation of national associations and organizations which flowed up from the well-spring of early localized groups focused on a single species or site, thus seeding the embryonic notions of conservation in America at the national level. In attempting to trace the origins of the notion or idea of conservation, one cannot ignore George Perkins Marsh's 1864 book *Man and Nature*, reissued in 1874 as The Earth as Modified by Human Action, which Lewis L. Mumford calls the "fountainhead of the conservation movement."[2] Marsh's first book was largely ignored because his attempts to check man's destruction of the country's forests belied America's optimistic belief that its resources were inexhaustible. However, in 1875, just one year after the reissuance of Marsh's book, there was formed the American Forestry Association, which in 1891 promoted, in unison with others, congressional approval for the President to establish forest reserves on public lands. Over the next sixteen years, 194 million acres were set aside by Presidents Bejamin Harrison, Grover Cleveland, and Theodore Roosevelt.[3] The American Fisheries Society was organized in 1870, and the U.S. Fish Commission was established in 1871. This was the first federal agency created to address the conservation of a specific natural resource; it was later merged into the U.S. Fish and Wildlife Service. In 1872, America's first national park, Yellowstone Park, was set aside by the Congress "as a pleasuring ground for the people." Sound management of the park, however, didn't occur until passage of the 1894 Park Protection Act and the National Park Act of 1916 establishing the National Park Service, which provided for managed public use "without improvement" of the parks. Lord Bryce said the national park idea developed during this era was the best idea America ever had.[4]

Naturalist writers of the day, in magazines and journals, led the way in focusing popular attention on the broad national landscape issues facing America. George Bird Grinnell and Charles Hallock popularized the word "conservation" in the magazine *Forest and Stream* beginning in 1873, and Grinnell thereafter started the Audubon Society in 1886 and *Audobon Magazine* in 1887, both of which promoted the protection of wildlife and birds. Theodore Roosevelt founded the Boone and Crockett Club in 1887, making it America's oldest wildlife conservation organization. John Muir followed by organizing the Sierra Club in 1892. As the noted writer, Western historian, and environmentalist Wallace Stegner observed: "Values, both those that we approve and those we don't, have roots as deep as creosote rings, and live as long, and grow as slowly. Every action is an idea before it is an action, and perhaps a feeling before it is an idea, and every idea rests upon other ideas that have preceded it in time…. The tracing of ideas—[in this case conservation]—is a guessing game. We can't tell who first had an idea; we can only tell who had it influentially, [and] who formulated it in a striking way…[so] that others could stumble upon it with the shock of recognition….Once they reached that stage, [the origin of an idea is] as easy to trace as a gopher in a spring lawn."[5] The seminal individual who influenced the formulation of the idea of conservation and institutionalized it during this period in the late nineteenth century, and then implemented many of its very cornerstones during his Presidency (1901-1909), was Theodore Roosevelt.[6] His name—then and now—became sacrosanct in and synonymous with conservation. America's public lands policy and its emerging natural resource policies thereafter forever changed from disposition to protection.[7]

Conservation: A Manifestation of the Vanishing Frontier

The notion of conservation which became a core value of America was cultivated during the same period in the late nineteenth century when the perceived demise of the Western frontier occurred, as characterized in the writing of Theodore Roosevelt's four-volume epic saga of westward expansion, The Winning of the West (1889-1896), along with his re-

Two philosophical schools of thought formed on how these precious resources should be utilized. One followed Theodore Roosevelt's wise or multiple use approach, and the other followed John Muir's environmental philosophy that emphasized aesthetic or recreational value to improve the quality of life. However, both had a common objective, i.e., the preservation of our natural resources in perpetuity.

This was why Theodore Roosevelt was such a champion of the National Park movement and setting aside other federal reservations for the protection of landscape and wildlife. He believed strongly that if the American character was forged in the wilderness, it also needed to be renewed from time to time in the wilderness.

lated books and articles, and by historian Frederick Jackson Turner, who alarmed the nation by declaring the frontier closed in 1893.[8]

Although the conservation movement was in large measure a movement to ensure sustainable production from our prairies, waters, and forests, it was, especially, a manifestation of America's desperate attempt psychologically to hold onto the wilderness of our vanishing frontiers from which we had forged a dynamic part of our national identity and character.[9] Our pioneer spirit symbolizing resilience, toughness, strong-willed rugged individualism, and self-reliance became the unique quintessential American character type forged by the frontier spirit during the conquest of the original thirteen states east of the Mississippi River prior to 1803. This frontier spirit was reinforced and embellished as successive frontiers followed the seven major political expansions of the country's boundaries over the eighteenth and nineteenth centuries. Settlers believed that with each "new frontier" came the mandate of manifest destiny to conquer and assert dominion over the wilderness biblically decreed to the Judeo-Christian world by Genesis and Isaiah. The rugged frontiers of the past were the geography of our mind in defining our identity as a nation. Regardless of how we reach out today and interface with our wilderness places, we embrace and hold onto our frontier spirit forged in the eighteenth and nineteenth centuries and thereby lay claim to our identity, the essence of the American being, born in the ethos of the perceived loss of the "final" frontier once we reached the Pacific and Alaska. Psychologically, we lose a part of our character and national identity without a mythical frontier mentality. The conservation of our lands—the idea, the act, and the places—became the symbolic manifestation of holding onto the vanishing frontier.[10]

In the late nineteenth and early twentieth centuries, conservation—the care and husbanding and wise multiple use of our natural resources to enhance the quality of life and provide material

value for our people—became institutionalized as one of America's cherished iconic core values. Two philosophical schools of thought formed on how these precious resources should be utilized. One followed Theodore Roosevelt's wise or multiple use approach, and the other followed John Muir's environmental philosophy that emphasized aesthetic or recreational value to improve the quality of life. However, both had a common objective, i.e., the preservation of our natural resources in perpetuity. Our forests, mountains, plains, prairies, and waterways provided wood to build our houses, energy to operate them, forage for our livestock, habitat for our wildlife, and recreational opportunities for our people, i.e., hiking, hunting, swimming, skiing, boating, and the scenic value thereof. These multiple uses came from conservation policies that limited extractive production and restored despoiled landscapes and polluted water and air, drawing upon the nation's resources for both their aesthetic and their material value: Use but don't abuse. Aldo Leopold elaborated on the concept of balancing conflicting approaches to the use of our natural resources: "The earth is...a community to which we belong, not a commodity it is our privilege to exploit."[11] The transition continues today from the notion that man is master of the earth separated from nature with the biblical authority of manifest destiny to conquer it to the notion that man is simply an important participant in the greater web of life.

The conservation movement continued throughout the twentieth century in reality and mythology, rooting itself deeper into America's consciousness and identity. In 1934 The Wilderness Society was organized by Aldo Leopold, Bob Marshall and others to take conservation to its next level of refinement—the designation of primitive areas as "wilderness" by congressional edict. Leopold's posthumous A Sand County Almanac published in 1949 became a manifesto igniting yet another revolution within the short history of the conservation movement in America. President

John F. Kennedy tapped into this theme in the 1960s when he called on the country to forge "new frontiers." From this period a new zeal was generated to protect public lands as wilderness, completely unimpaired by mankind, which Wallace Stegner calls the highest refinement of the national park idea since the turn of the century.[12] From this flowed the Wilderness Act of 1964 and the National Wilderness Preservation System, the National Trails System, National Wild and Scenic Rivers Systems, the Land and Water Conservation Act of 1964, the initial 1966 Endangered Species Act (later modified and expanded), and the National Environmental Policy Act of 1970. Rachel Carson's Silent Spring, published in 1962, made it clear that pollution was a principal conservation challenge of the future, and the Federal Water Quality Control Act of 1965 and Clean Water Restoration Act of 1966 promptly followed, together with a host of laws to protect the environment from toxic wastes and industrially polluted air and water. The era of preservationist environmentalism and a total revolution within America's conservationist consciousness had begun. The frontier mentality which President Kennedy exploited and from which the wilderness preservation concept flourished continues to define our national identity and conduct, a manifestation of our continuing attempt to recreate or reclaim the frontiers of our past.[13]

Today no other country in the world enjoys the unique legacy we cherish in our national parks, forests, wildlife and bird refuges, waters, and wilderness systems. These are nature's cathedrals where we reconnect with the universe and find peace and solitude, refuges for the redemption and repair of our souls. In these still places we find the vestigial heart of America's wilderness and the spirit of the frontier, long ago extinguished by the conquest of the West, yet coveted almost as a spiritual ideal or civic religion that gives strength to our very identity as an independent and free nation. This is why we embrace our national parks, forests, waterways, etc. with the passion and care and protection we harbor for these precious natural resources. In these wild places our subconscious mind finds America's now mythical frontier still alive and well and challenging—realized in both actuality and spirit. We can saddle up a horse and ride through virgin primeval forests and in wilderness areas uncut by highways, camp by azure blue jewel-like high mountain lakes and fish for our dinner, challenge our physical stamina with a backpack and walking stick climbing into high mountain valleys, watch eagles soar or bighorn sheep graze in lofty meadows amid brilliant wild flowers, hunt elk, deer, and turkey in quiet woodlands and valleys, run white water rapids on a wild and scenic river, or ski technical black diamond runs in national forests. Whatever the activity, we can test our resilience, toughness, individualism, and self-reliance in a natural setting not unlike the frontiers of the early nineteenth century. The spirit of the frontier is synonymous with these defining elements of our identity. In this interaction with nature, we embrace the elements of our unique national identity forged on the frontier.[14]

Author and historian Wallace Stegner eloquently synthesizes the connection between the forging of our national identity and the Western frontiers of an earlier century. "The remaining Western wilderness is the geography of hope.... [It] is hope's native home....The American character has been largely shaped by the experience of successive frontiers....Every time we go off into the wilderness, we are looking for that perfect primitive Eden....All human endeavor has to come back to the wilderness for its justification and its new beginnings....The result [is] the tendency to see the West in its mythic enlargement rather than as it is, and the corollary tendency [is] to take our clues from myths in an effort to enhance [our] lives."[15]

Dr. Robert J. Moore, Jr., a historian and Roosevelt scholar, characterizes the historical transition of Theodore Roosevelt's frontier to contemporary times very philosophically:

The verandah of the Elkhorn ranch house, photographed by Theodore Roosevelt, circa 1885.

An in-growing industrial frontier gradually replaced the outward-bound agricultural frontier of the 19th century, but the Western spirit of independence and freedom never changed. Cowboys still ride the range and drive cattle in the West, the railroads still move freight through mountain tunnels dug in 1869 for the Transcontinental System, many American Indian people still live in tribal groups on reservations, still hold religious ceremonies, dances and pow-wows. Plows continue to break the plains, and hikers and skiers now go where fur trappers and mountain men once explored. The West is alive and vibrant, and retains the flavor of, if not the population of, the best days of the frontier.

But the West as a construct, as a thing, as an entity as Frederick Jackson Turner and Theodore Roosevelt once described it, is disappearing. The essence of the West was as a place where anyone, immigrant, eastern businessman, rich, poor, could go to refresh themselves, to relax, to try to become one with nature and the landscape. To hunt, to fish, to ride over the plains, is a dream that could be realized in America like few other places on earth. So little of America's land was tied up with ownership by the wealthy, and so much of it was open, that personal refreshment was possible in the wild places of the continent. Certainly Theodore Roosevelt took advantage of this aspect of the West in 1884 when grief led him to ranch in western Dakota. But he was mightily aware of the swift changes coming over the West: diminished wildlife of all kinds but especially big game, more and more fenced off areas, thicker settlement, the use of technology for transportation and to extract goods from the earth. All of these things contributed to a projected future in which people would no longer be able to use the West for the purposes of refreshment and communion with nature. This was why Theodore Roosevelt was such a champion of the National Park movement and setting aside other federal reservations for the protection of landscape and wildlife. He believed strongly that if the American character was forged in the wilderness, it also needed to be renewed from time to time in the wilderness. These opinions were a direct outgrowth of having lived in the West and observed the swift changes that were taking place at first hand. TR was a historian, and he was able to project into the future the trends he saw happening in his lifetime. His creation of the Country Life Commission and calling of national conservation conferences in 1905 and 1908 while President, his concern with the loss of farmland and the agrarian lifestyle to urban modes of living, his urge to create national parks and monuments as well as large forest reserves, all attest to his thoughts and ruminations on this topic.[16]

In a recent article, Edward J. Renehan, Jr., an author and TR scholar, commented on Theodore Roosevelt who himself made this very connection between conservation and our national identity:

Roosevelt likewise saw good stewardship of wild lands and wildlife as exercises in preserving the national identity of the United States. As Roosevelt pointed out on more than one occasion, the United States lacked the long political and cultural history found in other nations located on other continents. For this reason, Roosevelt argued that Americans must rely on the natural landscape of North America to form the backbone of their culture. Natural history was, after all, an important ancient element in the country's otherwise brief past. In this spirit, Roosevelt insisted that Yosemite and other great natural monuments must be left untouched forever....[Roosevelt said] "they should be saved because of reasons unconnected with any return in dollars and cents. A grove of giant redwoods or sequoias should be kept just as we keep a great and beautiful cathedral. The extermination of the passenger pigeon meant that mankind was just so much poorer, exactly as in the case of the destruction of the cathedral at Rheims."[17]

The Cradle of Conservation

Theodore Roosevelt's name is synonymous with the word conservation. He is the acknowledged father of conservation in America. His commitment to conserving our natural resources was conceived and born during his 3½ years (1884-1887) of ranching and traveling in the Dakota and Montana Territories. His home ranch—the Elkhorn—was established and built on the banks of the Little Missouri River, twenty-two miles north of Medora, North Dakota, in what is today Billings County, ND. Theodore Roosevelt sought solitude and refuge in the remote Badlands of the Dakota Territory to repair his soul and heal from the emotional trauma of losing his wife and mother, who died of unrelated causes in the same house and on the same day, St. Valentine's Day, February 14, 1884, in New York City.

The Badlands where TR's Elkhorn Ranch is located are where the high plains in eastern Montana and those of North Dakota converge and literally erupt topographically with immense geologic diversity found nowhere else in America. It's North Dakota's best-kept secret. The Badlands are a biological oasis in the high plains, rich in diverse species of antelope, deer, elk, bighorn sheep, buffalo, birds, reptiles, and plant life. There exists no other such wildlife and ecological diversity for hundreds of miles in any direction. This oasis is further defined by its unique native archeology and history, both prehistoric and modern. During his time in the Badlands, Roosevelt traveled by horseback extensively through what is today Wyoming, Montana, Idaho, and the Dakotas. He came to recognize how vulnerable the Western lands were to the uncontrolled predation of man. He witnessed firsthand the destruction and pillaging of the West by rapacious logging and mining which polluted the rivers and despoiled the landscape; the decimation of game by commercial hunting for the purposes of feeding the laborers building the transcontinental railroads, the loggers, and the miners; the denuding of the prairies by stockmen overgrazing their sheep and cattle herds; and the pillaging of what was then its only national park— Yellowstone—set aside a mere decade earlier.[18] TR wrote extensively about his experiences and the realizations that led to his devotion to conservation in America in six books between 1885 and 1907.[19] Roosevelt's experiences in the Badlands and Montana Territory later resulted in his reputation as "the first conservation president," so characterized by his renowned contemporary and Pulitzer Prize winning biographer Edmund Morris:[20]

> TR once famously remarked, "If it had not been for my years in North Dakota, I would never have become President of the United States." In making this statement [Roosevelt] was alluding not only to the lessons in democracy he learned as a youthful rancher living on equal terms with pioneer settlers in the Badlands. He was also speaking of the dawning of his conservationist conscience, an attitude

of reverence for the western wilderness, which succored him both spiritually and physically even as he saw how threatened it was by the spread of interstate commerce. This conscience, born in North Dakota, made him our first great conservationist President.[21]

Morris has further characterized the dawning of Roosevelt's environmental conscience at the Elkhorn Ranch in the Badlands:

> As one of many guardians of Theodore Roosevelt's memory, [the Badlands are the] very sanctuary where his environmental conscience matured. It is true that he was a nature lover long before he built the Elkhorn Ranch here, but it was not until he settled in the Badlands and discovered the vulnerability of this fragile ecology to profit-seekers from outside, that he began to ponder the policies that culminated in his unsurpassed achievements as our first conservation President.
>
> To my mind, there is no memorial of marble or bronze anywhere in the country that evokes the conscience of Theodore Roosevelt as powerfully as the Elkhorn bottom and its surrounding hills. It is a crucible of calm, a refuge from the roar of worldly getting and spending. The very disappearance of the ranch TR built here—except for a few foundation stones—emphasizes the transitoriness of human achievement, and the eternal recuperative powers of nature....
>
> I fear in particular the most subtle and uncontrollable of all invasions of the wilderness, namely, noise....Theodore Roosevelt... was acutely responsive to the beauty of natural sounds, and indeed to that tapestry of almost inaudible rustlings and ripplings which we clumsily call "silence." The Elkhorn bottom is one of the few places I know where a pilgrim becomes aware of this tapestry, and bears it as background to the beatings of his own heart.[22]

The Elkhorn Ranch and
Theodore Roosevelt National Park

Theodore Roosevelt National Park was established in the Badlands of North Dakota in 1934 as a state park, which in 1947 became a national park, to symbolize and memorialize TR's conservation legacy. Topographically the park's 70,447 acres are divided into two units (each bisected by the Little Missouri River) which are separated by some thirty-five miles. Right in the center of the Badlands between the two units is a 218-acre third unit where Roosevelt's Elkhorn Ranch buildings were located, also on the banks of the Little Missouri River. Surrounding this 218-acre parcel are private ranches, state lands divided into state school and park tracts, national grasslands, Bureau of Land Management (BLM) lands, etc. The largest remnant of TR's Elkhorn Ranch still in private hands is a 5,200-acre ranch owned by the Eberts family, with grazing privileges on an adjacent 18,349-acre allotment in the Little Missouri National Grasslands. This ranch lies directly across the Little Missouri River from TR's Elkhorn cabin, and provides the viewshed TR wrote so eloquently about. In describing the Badlands around the Elkhorn Ranch, TR said:

> I grow very fond of this place, and it certainly has a desolate, grim beauty of its own, that has a curious fascination for me. The grassy, scantily wooded bottoms through which the winding river flows are bounded by bare, jagged buttes; their fantastic shapes and sharp, steep edges throw the most curious shadows, under the cloudless, glaring sky; and at evening I love to sit out in front of the hut and see their hard, gray outlines gradually grow soft and purple as the flaming sunset by degrees softens and dies away; while my days I spend generally alone, riding through the lonely rolling prairie and broken lands.[23]

TR's insights which led to his conservation philosophy were forged here at the Elkhorn, which in turn gave rise to the American conservation movement as we know it today. Later in life, TR stated, "Had it not been for the years spent in North Dakota and what I learned there, I would not have been President....Here, in the hills and plateaus, the romance of my life began."[24] Moore characterized Roosevelt's Badlands experience as follows:

> Certainly, if the genesis of TR's thoughts about wilderness and his conversion to the idea that resources (land, water, wildlife) are finite occurred anywhere, if his notion that the wilderness formed the collective character of Americans and America began at a specific location, if the idea that Americans need to periodically renew themselves in wilderness sprang from a location, it was from the prairie grasses and weird rock formations of the Badlands, the sites of TR's western ranches during the years 1883 to 1896. This period of time covers his relationship with the region from his earliest exposure until his last autumn hunt in the area before the press of national affairs took him away from his cyclical visits to North Dakota.[25]

The boundaries of Roosevelt's ranch are not known exactly since out of necessity he grazed his cattle over a wide area of the Badlands; but, Roosevelt wrote in 1888, "My home-ranch lies on both sides of the Little Missouri, the nearest ranchman above me being about twelve, and the nearest below me about ten, miles distant."[26] The Eberts Ranch, which lies directly across the Little Missouri River from Roosevelt's Elkhorn cabin, was once the central part of the Elkhorn Ranch.[27]

As Roosevelt grazed his cattle and hunted far and wide over the Badlands, he wrote profusely about his experiences on what is now the Eberts Ranch, which constituted TR's viewshed from his cabin:

> My home-ranch...derives its name, "The Elkhorn," from the fact that on the ground where we built it were found the skulls and interlocked antlers of two wapiti bulls who had perished from getting their antlers fastened in battle....The

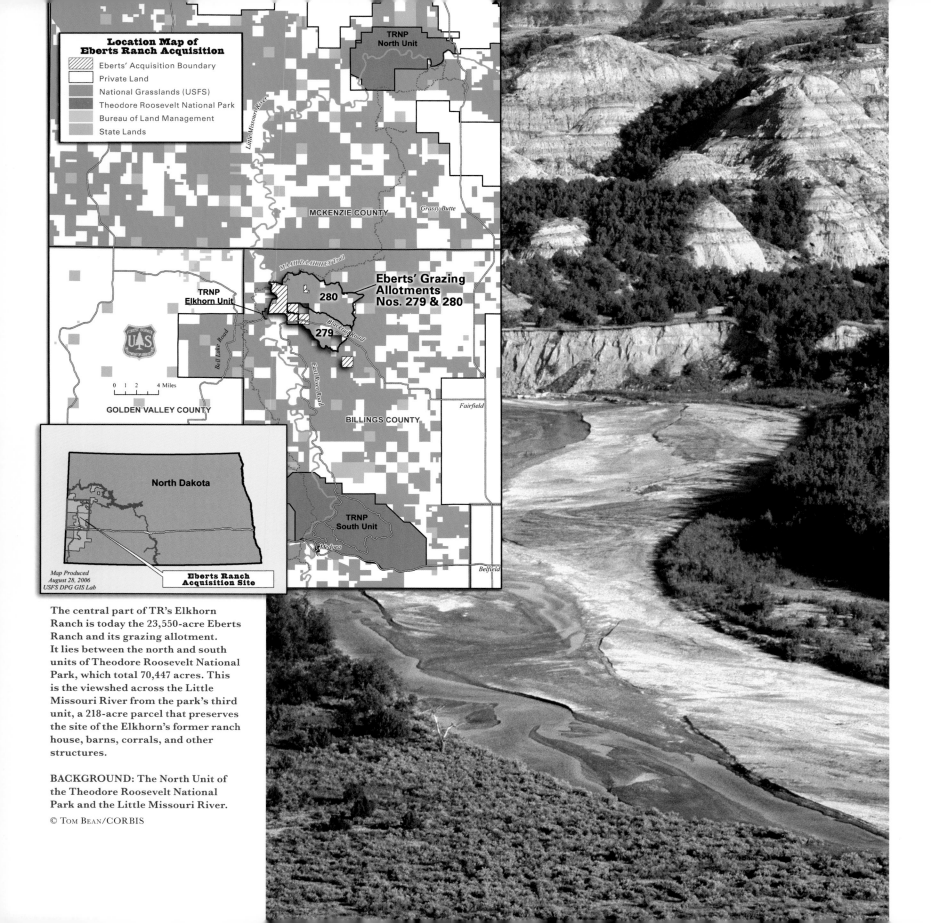

**Location Map of
Eberts Ranch Acquisition**

- Eberts' Acquisition Boundary
- Private Land
- National Grasslands (USFS)
- Theodore Roosevelt National Park
- Bureau of Land Management
- State Lands

Little Missouri River

MCKENZIE COUNTY

Grassy Butte

MAAH DAAH HEY Trail

TRNP
Elkhorn Unit

Eberts' Grazing
Allotments
Nos. 279 & 280

280

Blacktail Road

279

Bell Lake Road

East River Road

0 1 2 4 Miles

GOLDEN VALLEY COUNTY

BILLINGS COUNTY

Fairfield

North Dakota

TRNP
South Unit

Medora

Belfield

Map Produced
August 28, 2006
USFS DPG GIS Lab

**Eberts Ranch
Acquisition Site**

The central part of TR's Elkhorn
Ranch is today the 23,550-acre Eberts
Ranch and its grazing allotment.
It lies between the north and south
units of Theodore Roosevelt National
Park, which total 70,447 acres. This
is the viewshed across the Little
Missouri River from the park's third
unit, a 218-acre parcel that preserves
the site of the Elkhorn's former ranch
house, barns, corrals, and other
structures.

BACKGROUND: The North Unit of
the Theodore Roosevelt National
Park and the Little Missouri River.

© Tom Bean/CORBIS

ranch-house stood on the brink of a low bluff overlooking the broad shallow bed of the Little Missouri, through which at most seasons there ran only a trickle of water, while in times of freshet it was filled brimful with the boiling, foaming, muddy torrent….The river twisted down in long curves between narrow bottoms bordered by sheer cliff walls, for the Bad Lands, a chaos of peaks, plateaus, and ridges, rose abruptly from the edges of the level, tree-clad, or grassy, alluvial meadows. In front of the low, long ranch-house veranda was a row of cottonwood-trees with gray-green leaves which quivered all day long if there was a breath of air. From these trees came the far-away melancholy cooing of mourning-doves, and little owls perched in them and called tremulously at night. In the long summer afternoons we would sometimes sit on the piazza, when there was no work to be done, for an hour or two at a time, watching the cattle on the sandbars, and the sharply channeled and strangely carved amphitheatre of cliffs across the bottom opposite…a strip of meadowland, behind which rises a line of sheer cliffs and grass plateaus. This veranda is a pleasant place…gazing sleepily out at the weird looking buttes opposite, until their sharp outlines grow indistinct and purple in the after-glow of the sunset.[28]

TR's words are describing the very property and viewshed that are being purchased by the U.S. Forest Service (USDA).[29] Ironic as it may seem, this very viewshed Roosevelt looked at every day over the Little Missouri River as he sat on the veranda of his Elkhorn Ranch cabin has never been included in the national park or placed in public protection. Edmund Morris has reflected upon its significance:

Here one of our greatest Presidents repaired his soul, and acquainted himself with nature and the common man, after tragedies that might otherwise have struck him down. It is every bit as precious a public heirloom as Valley Forge

and Ford's Theater, and its fragile beauty makes it particularly vulnerable to private profiteering and temporary expediency. In fifty years, when the oil trucks stop rolling, they will have other sources of supply [sic]; but if [the] Elkhorn is slashed across with concrete now, it cannot hope to recover….You will honor his memory best by leaving the site undisturbed and undeveloped, so that its remoteness, tranquility, and silence…—its eloquent purity—…may speak for themselves, as they once spoke to him.[30]

The Elkhorn Ranch is where the very legacy of the American conservation movement started—in the Badlands of North Dakota. It is part of our cultural history and heritage. This is America's legacy to preserve, and North Dakota's to celebrate, because this is where our country's conservation movement was inspired, conceived, and born. One could call the Elkhorn Ranch the very cradle of conservation in America, the sacred ground of the conservation movement, a tangible arcadian icon of America's cultural identity, which has been called "the Walden Pond of the American West."[31] The U.S. Forest Service is purchasing the Eberts Ranch in two phases. In phase one, the back portion of the ranch was purchased in 2006, while in phase two, the remainder, which includes the most critical portion of the viewshed, will be acquired in 2007.[32] Once the Elkhorn Ranch viewshed is completely in federal ownership and protected in perpetuity, the Elkhorn can truly join the list of other treasured historic sites of national significance and reverence that symbolize and define our unique American culture and identity.[33] ❧

Endnotes for this article can be found on page 295.

The Omen of Death in the Moyowosi

At daybreak on the 12th of August, 1986, my wife Petra and I, professional hunter Bilu Dean, a gunbearer, a tracker, and a skinner pulled out of camp deep in Tanzania's Moyowosi Game Reserve.

As we ambled through the dark African morning, chilled and half asleep, I ruminated over the series of events that brought us there just three days before. We were blissfully unaware of the tumultuous and devastating calamity that awaited us only a few hours away.

A year before, the thought of going on an African big game hunting safari was the furthest from my mind. Early in 1985, I had purchased the largest group of Theodore Roosevelt firearms and related memorabilia in private hands, from the Richard Prosser Mellon Collection. Included were guns from Roosevelt's exploits in the Wild West, mementos from his White House years, and—most important to this narrative—a combination over-and-under rifle-shotgun, given to the President by renowned gunmaker Fred Adolph of Genoa, New York. The collection also included Kermit Roosevelt's Winchester Model 1895 .405 big game rifle, as well as his Parker shotgun, and the uniquely notable Holland & Holland 500/.450 Royal Grade Double Barrel Rifle, presented to TR by admiring British citizens for the historic 1909-10 East African safari.

Shortly after this acquisition, I was contacted by the author R.L. Wilson, who had been in

BY GREG MARTIN

The following text describes a harrowing event that took place in Tanzania, East Africa, during filming of the Theodore Roosevelt-inspired feature length film and video, *In the Blood*. Author Greg Martin, internationally known antique arms collector, dealer and auctioneer, has based his recollections on notes and photographs made at the time and on clear memories of an event forever fixed in his memory. Because the finished production deals with conservation and African safari themes, includes Roosevelt family members and TR and Kermit firearms, and shows footage from the 1909-10 expedition, this memoir has an important role in the saga of *Theodore Roosevelt, Hunter-Conservationist*.

After lunch Bilu Dean and party entered an area of fifteen-foot high grass, which enclosed them like a curtain. Greg Martin is pictured here standing in the rear of the overheated Land Cruiser, watching the fires merging in the distance. Minutes later, tragedy struck.

IMAGE COURTESY OF PETRA MARTIN

As the Land Cruiser pulled away from camp that morning of the 15th, my thoughts of past events receded with the darkness, and the great African landscape took precedence over all else. We passed a pride of lions lying in the distance, and farther out giraffes dotted the horizon.

communication with an East Coast filmmaker, interested in doing an African hunting movie, based on the Holland rifle, and the TR safari. The concept captured my imagination, and after several meetings at my home in San Francisco with Larry Wilson and the filmmaker, plans for the movie initially titled *Fine Guns* were put into motion. The documentary production would be shot on location in East Africa, retracing some of the hunting grounds originally traversed by the Roosevelts in 1909-10.

Participating in this project as modern day hunters revisiting the past would be a member of the Roosevelt family (Theodore Roosevelt IV), Larry Wilson, and myself. Accompanying the group as an observer was a New York lawyer writing a history of the African safari. Also accompanying the party, and to appear in the film, were Roosevelt's son TR V (nicknamed Bear), and the film director's son, Tyssen Butler.

The star of the film would be the Holland & Holland double rifle cased set. We would also use the Fred Adolph over-and-under, the Model 1895 Winchester and Kermit's Parker shotgun. The main contingent of hunting guns was arranged by Larry Wilson and included a Colt .45 and Uberti .44 Magnum single action revolvers, a .35 Whelen custom FN bolt action rifle by Alaskan guide and gunmaker Steve Berg, a Ruger Model 77 bolt action in 7 mm Remington Magnum, an Uberti replica Henry rifle (.44-40), Kermit Roosevelt's custom Springfield Sporter in .30-06 caliber, and an exquisite .375 and .458 double rifle by the renowned Liege gunmaker, LeBeau-Courally.

On recommendation of Larry Wilson's old friend David Mead, of Ker & Downey, Nairobi, safari operator Robin Hurt was selected to orchestrate the hunt at his vast concession in Tanzania. Petra and I left for Tanzania on August 7, 1986, flying with Larry Wilson and the battery of our guns and safari gear. Due to the extraordinary insurance premium quoted on the TR rifle, we did not bother to take out any special coverage.

Although any African safari has the potential of danger to the hunter, or possible loss of equipment, we figured our customary luck would be with us and that the exorbitant insurance premium would be unwarranted.

Connecting via an overnight layover in Amsterdam, we arrived in the wee morning hours at Arusha, Tanzania, on the 9th of August. We were met by a contingent of the Tanzania Game Tracker Safari staff, administered by Adam Hill, and taken to their headquarters for a brief rest.

From there a twin engine chartered plane transported us on a two-plus hour flight to our hunting camp deep in the Moyowosi. On arrival August 10th, no time was lost. We were greeted by Robin Hurt and introduced to the movie crew, which had already set up a field studio. Preparations were made for hunting and filming to begin the next day.

The filming would be with Hurt guiding Roosevelt. This left Larry Wilson and me free to hunt on our own; the filming of our hunting would come later, since TR IV was slated to be a featured player. Larry would be guided by Harry Muller, a seasoned veteran of the bush, and of the Mau Mau insurgency. I was introduced to my hunter, Bilu Dean, an experienced third generation scout and guide from the Sudan. Bilu, who appeared to be in his late thirties, was pleasant, soft spoken, sported a neatly trimmed mustache and wore short pants and a baseball cap slightly cocked to one side. He struck me as a slightly built, but agile, Errol Flynn type. My initial impression proved correct, for in the brief time that I knew him his cool veneer was shed to reveal a genuine swashbuckler.

Around the campfire and at dinner that evening, we were all regaled by tales of safari hunting, part of the traditional preparation of new clients for their forthcoming adventures in the African bush.

Next morning, August 11th, we were awakened by rifle fire not too far away from camp.

Roosevelt had shot a lion. This not only signaled that the hunt was on but was also the precursor to events that no one had counted on, or could have ever anticipated.

Even though Larry Wilson was along on that early morning hunt, he was unaware that the first cameraman had been so emotionally distraught at seeing the lion shot, that she broke down in tears and could not continue filming. Only the second cameraman took any usable footage thereafter, and he was at least another 35 yards further away from the lion than Hurt, Roosevelt, and the first camera crew.

While Larry, Robin, the filmmaker and trackers were enthusiastically congratulating Roosevelt, some of the members of the film crew reacted quite differently. They had not been prepared for the death of the lion being shot from a blind. The full extent of the first cameraman's tearful reaction in the blind was never revealed to us, and we never learned about her inability to complete the filming that morning until later on.

In any event, some of the crew were having misgivings about hunting. Shooting the lion, a regal old male with a fabulous mane, from a blind, just did not seem to them to be sporting. Robin Hurt was truly angry and said to Larry, "I've got half a mind to take them into the swamp and show them how tough hunting can be." Larry's reaction was an immediate "Do it!" The swamp hunt, which tested the resolve of the crew mightily, became one of the featured scenes in the final film released under the title *In the Blood*.

During the day, Bilu prepared for our departure from camp. We sighted in our rifles and the Toyota Land Cruiser was stocked with provisions. Bilu had decided we would go after the mighty Cape Buffalo in a remote and virtually untouched region, several hours drive away. This meant a full day's hunt, perhaps not returning to camp until nightfall. Accompanying us would be a tracker, a gunbearer, and a skinner.

Combination "Over and

"Teddy's" New Gun

Fred Adolph of Genoa, the maker of the finest guns in America, if not the world, returned Wednesday morning from Oyster Bay, Long Island, where he went to deliver the gun which he has been making during the last year for Colonel Theodore Roosevelt. Mr. Adolph visited Sagamore Hill, the home of Mr. Roosevelt, Tuesday.

The ex-President, in a khaki suit, waving a big Alpine stick, was just ready to start on a trip across the fields, accompanied by his son Archie, when Adolph drove up in an auto, and handed the gun to him. Roosevelt expressed his delight about the gun in very flattering terms, opened and closed the action several times, pointed it and admired the engraving and carving, regretting very much to be unable to do any hunting at this time. Evidently thinking that the gun was too beautiful to be put in his guncase, where nobody sees it, he suggested to the delighted maker, to exhibit it in a show-window and put a card on it: "Made for Colonel Roosevelt."

Most of the conversation was in German, which the Colonel speaks very well. The gun is now in one of the windows of the Abercrombie & Fitch Co., in New York, with mirrors placed behind and magnifying glasses to show the onlooker all the beauties of the work.

It is a single barrel shotgun 20 gauge, with .25 rifle barrel below, made of finest Krupp steel. The action is fine Swedish iron, the stock a beautiful piece of Circassian walnut. The action shows

in gold on the left side Hiawatha and Minnehaha, after a painting by Taylor; on the right side, Hiawatha with bow and arrow and a swan on his shoulder, and on the top the insignia of the Camp Fire Club of America in gold, surrounded by heavy relief engraving. Stock and fore end are beautifully carved with deer, fox and pheasant, and the gun is without the slightest doubt the most beautiful gun ever built in America, a work of art in the highest sense.—*Tribune.*

Lieut. Whelen, who ordered a similar gun, wrote in "*Field and Stream*," February, 1912:

"Many evenings were spent in pipe dreams on the subject, then I found a master workman who was capable of carrying out my ideas, and at last it is here, an all-around gun de luxe and good old American-made at that.

"To say that this gun was a surprise to me when I received it from its maker is putting it mildly. In my time I have seen many fine arms, but never such a dream as this. The work is such as to place its maker at once in the ranks of the best gun artisans in the world, for the arm is almost, it might be said, without an equal.

"On this masterpiece, when the action is closed, the fitting is so tight, that even with the aid of a magnifying glass the joints cannot be told from the lines of the engraving."

Guns of this type, plain finished with line engraving, in any gauge and caliber up to .30-30 and .22 high power, can be made for $175.00 up. More powerful cartridges cost extra, $10.00 to $25.00.

The guns are locked with double bolt on the lugs and cross-bolt through the extension rib.

Without cross-bolts, these guns can be made for $100.00 up.

Our guns, which included Fred Adolph's over-and-under, and Kermit's .405 (my intent was to use this collector's rarity to down a Cape Buffalo), were strapped upright in a specially built rack mounted on the back of the cab. I wore my favorite Colt Single Action revolver, with raised-carved Mexican eagle and snake grips.

Side view of the Fred Adolph's over-and-under.

GREG MARTIN COLLECTION

"'Teddy's' New Gun" from a Fred Adolph "Modern Guns" catalogue, circa 1914.

ALVIN A. WHITE COLLECTION

We were unable to take TR's double rifle, as it had not yet arrived from London, where it had been made ready for the hunt by Holland & Holland. It was delayed in customs at Dar es Salaam.

As the Land Cruiser pulled away from camp that morning of the 15th, my thoughts of past events receded with the darkness, and the great African landscape took precedence over all else. We passed a pride of lions lying in the distance, and farther out giraffes dotted the horizon. We made small talk with Bilu, and intermittently he would bark "Moto" to our crew in the back. They would dutifully drop matches, setting fires to the grass behind us. Bilu explained that this was common hunting practice, making it easier for our return and permitting fresh green shoots of grass to spring up on which the animals would feed.

Our attention was soon diverted to a herd of Cape Buffalo directly ahead. Suddenly, Bilu yelled "Hang on!" as he shifted gears and throttled directly towards the beasts. Crazed buffaloes swarmed around us, as our Land Cruiser became one with the herd, zig zagging, swaying, and bouncing crazily in a cloud of dust over the wild and rough terrain. While this experience was fully enjoyable, it did leave the nagging impression that something could have gone terribly wrong, especially since the vehicle had no doors on either side.

It was now noon, and after a brief respite to cool the engines and clean out the radiator clogged with grass and seeds, we took lunch under a large tree. As our crew laid out a tarp, and we brought out the soft drinks and sandwiches, the fires that we had set continued to burn in the distance, slowly moving towards us. Our conversation turned to fires, with Bilu commenting that fires were not dangerous, and were easy to get away from. Since I had some fire-fighting experience in my youth, I responded that fires are easy to get away from as long as the grass was low, and there is a diverse landscape with moisture-laden green vegetation, as in Africa. Suddenly the wind shifted, and in one capricious moment the fire in the distance was fast

approaching. We hurriedly threw our gear on the truck, and like a skilled matador sidestepping a charging bull, Bilu moved the vehicle to a verdant patch of ground, just as the fire rolled past us, devouring our picnic area.

At this point my uneasiness compounded, and I told Petra that if anything should go wrong, always head for the burned area. Without further comment, we calmly assessed our situation in the Land Cruiser, and took our position next to Bilu on the front seat. Heading into the afternoon sun, we proceeded to our destination. The terrain changed to a broad, flat expanse of an endless grass sea ("Moyowosi"), devoid of trees and areas of lush vegetation that had preceded us earlier. The animals had disappeared with the midday heat and were replaced by insects that seemed to ride the waves of the heat that shimmered in the distance.

We shed excess clothing, and I unstrapped the Colt Single Action from around my waist, placing it comfortably on the seat between us. Now our only excess appendages were the cameras that dangled around our necks.

As the Land Cruiser rolled over the catapulting dry grass, the drone of the engine was interrupted by Bilu, shouting "Moto, moto!" to our obedient crew in the rear, who continued to set fires behind us. Soon the parched grass rose higher than the truck and flowed around us like a curtain, obscuring all but the sky above. The Toyota's engine began to overheat, and after an abrupt stop, the gunbearers dismounted. In ritualistic fashion once again, they proceeded to extract the grass and seeds which had clogged the radiator.

I climbed to the back of the truck to view the landscape and, to my surprise, saw that the fires we had set began to merge in one sweeping line to our backs. Swinging back into the cab, I instructed Bilu to get out as fast as possible. Our men swarmed on board, as Bilu gunned the engine. Minutes later, the truck lurched to a convulsive stop—its engine whining, and wheels spinning helplessly. We had

TOP: **Old John standing motionless at left, as Greg Martin runs to the vehicle in a vain effort to save the guns. Bilu Dean had already fled.**

MIDDLE: **Greg Martin running from the truck as the ammunition begins to explode.**

BOTTOM: **The vehicle exploding in one rolling ball of fire.**

IMAGES COURTESY OF PETRA MARTIN

driven on top of a large anthill. Old John, the skinner, quickly unlatched a jack and began attaching it to the front bumper. I again mounted the rear of the truck. This time my heart stopped, as I saw solid sheets of flames branching out in all directions, being pushed our way by an afternoon wind.

Sensing the danger, our gunbearer and the trackers had vanished. There was no escape—I knew we had to go through the fire. I grabbed a shovel and raced to the rear of the hunting car, frantically hacking down the thick, dry grass. Each thrust ricocheted off the bone dry clods. Miraculously, the grass yielded an opening to a small barren patch of ground. This was our only possible escape. I ran back around the truck to get Petra who was still sitting next to Bilu, trying to rock the truck off the anthill. My eyes met Petra's as I clasped her hand and said, "Let's go!" She was instantly at my side, followed by old John crouching through the grass.

Bilu made no effort to move. Suddenly, a spout of flames shot through the air. Petra recoiled and choked, realizing the true horror that surrounded us. I yelled, "Run," but the grass was like a spider web that wrapped around our ankles, straining to hold us in place. Petra and John tripped over each other. In one desperate lunge, I picked her up, and we ran for the crudely cleared patch. We jumped through the flames as they swirled around us in one giant crescendo of wind, heat, and smoke.

In seconds, it was over. The fire was now at our back. We grappled with the burning embers that clung to our clothes and hair, twisting our feet into the ground, smothering our smoldering shoes. The three of us had escaped with only the clothes on our backs, a shovel, and the cameras around our necks.

I turned, only to see the Toyota's front end and cab immersed in flames. A vision of the guns mounted to the rear of the cab flashed before me as I raced to the back of the truck to save them from their certain fate. Too late. Vaulting over the side of the Land Cruiser, I was met head-on with a wall of flame as the whole cab became fully engulfed. The high-powered ammunition we had stored along the dashboard now began to explode in all directions. The extra gasoline tanks, taken for the long journey, would soon be next. I retreated to the cover of an anthill where I met Petra, John, and our tracker (who appeared out of nowhere).

In resolute helplessness, Petra and I photographed the final immolation to the Moyowosi, as the fuel tanks exploded in one rolling ball of fire that mushroomed to the sky. Gone were the guns, all our equipment, food, and water.

Chaos had turned to calm as we contemplated our situation. Out of the distance a bird call was heard. It was our gunbearer, Kafaka. He, too, had escaped the conflagration by using the same matches that caused our own havoc to burn himself a passage to safety. As was standard practice, Kafaka had taken Bilu's two guns when he left from the truck: a .22 caliber rifle, for which we had no ammunition, and a .375 Brno, loaded with three rounds. Things were now brighter as we had some protection and a means to get food. Kafaka, John, and the tracker, who had previously only been distant providers for our comfort, were now paramount to our survival.

What everyone wondered about

was whatever happened to Bilu. We walked over the charred ground, passing the smoldering Land Cruiser. I speculated aloud about whether Bilu's odd behavior during the day would lead to an even more bizarre confrontation when we met face to face. We stopped and looked over the vast, blackened landscape. A bright reflection from the sunlight appeared about a quarter mile from the truck. Petra immediately remarked that it was Bilu. "Impossible," I said.

The natives went on ahead. From afar, we could see them motioning for us to stay away. Right off, I joined them. It was Bilu. The reflection we saw in the distance was a metal back-brace, exposed by the fire. He lay in a crouched position, much like images I had seen of volcano victims from Pompeii.

His skin was orange and slick, like a china doll. He was wearing a pair of binoculars around his neck, its rubber cover had melted to the ground. He had been killed by the flames while trying to outrun them. I paused in stunned silence as the

gunbearer, displaying an equanimity between life and death, pulled a charred tree limb to Bilu's side and hung his hat on a branch. We turned away, hoping this primitive monument would ward off the predatory animals.

We rejoined Petra, and now a decision had to be made: whether to stay near the burned wreckage, or try to walk back to camp. We were six or seven hours from camp by truck, without food or water. We conferred with our three companions, whose knowledge of the bush far exceeded ours. In an exchange of sign language, fragmentary English and Swahili, we determined that it was best to press on. What Petra and I did not know was that their calculations were made without any concept of time or distance. Kafaka, in a grand gesture, resting his elbow on the palm of his left hand, lengthened his index finger somewhere into the distance, and uttered several times "Junction road. We go junction road," his compatriots keeping time to his incantations with their nodding heads.

"How far?" I asked.

"Not far," he replied, folding his arms across his chest. The question of how long, or how much time, met with the retort "not long," as he massaged his face in deep contemplation. It was now near two in the afternoon, the sun and heat of the day were at their zenith.

We left the .22 rifle behind. I placed the loaded .375 under my arm, and, guided by Kafaka's calculations, we marched onward towards the promised junction road.

As we left the burned area, the terrain changed to high grass and clumps of trees. Here, tsetse flies swarmed in profusion, with squadrons attacking our backs, their needlelike stings puncturing our clothing. We formed a human-chain, marching single file, with those behind sweeping the backs of those in front. Our tracker in the rear had found a dried buffalo tail on the ground, and kept double-time swatting his own back as well as the one in front. The tsetse flies eventually dissipated, and as the long afternoon wore on, I began to feel my lungs constricting and my tongue swelling.

After the fire, and back at the Moyowosi camp: from left, Greg Martin with Colt Single Action Army revolver, the ivory grips burnt off; Larry Wilson with the virtually destroyed Fred Adolph presentation rifle/shotgun combination, and Robin Hurt, holding the custom Winchester Model 1895 rifle of Kermit Roosevelt.

IMAGE COURTESY OF PETRA MARTIN

Although Petra and I were runners, the heat and lack of water began to take its toll. For the first time ever, I felt my life force waning.

At five in the afternoon, in a near state of exhaustion, we rested. At this point, our native guides were in no better shape than we were. I would have traded all I owned for a glass of water.

The natives wanted to make camp for the night, and continue in the morning. However, we felt that we must keep moving through the night, for the next day's sun would prove insurmountable. We gathered what strength we had left and continued through the bush. As dusk set in, we heard the intermittent crash of the underbrush around us. Our companions mumbled 'Simba, simba," in hushed tones. The hunters had now become the hunted.

A full moon illuminated the ground before us as we followed old animal tracks to no avail searching for water. Petra turned to Kafaka, motioning for him to draw his knife and pierce the bark of a tree she was patting, hoping for confined water. Our guides only shook their heads. Every hope disappeared like a mirage in the desert. I collapsed in exhaustion, no longer able to carry the Brno. Petra huddled at my side and asked if I thought we would make it, or if this was going to be the end. I replied, "We made it through the fire, so we will make it through this," although deep down I was not so sure. We made a contingency plan for the next morning, to kill a zebra and drink its blood, however improbable.

Meanwhile, back at the camp, Harry Muller gave further thought to having seen the tremendous smoke in the distance earlier in the afternoon, when he was out hunting. Becoming concerned when by nine o'clock we had not returned to camp, a truck was dispatched in our direction.

During the evening we set several signal fires, which also helped to keep animals at bay. At 9:45 p.m., Kafaka stopped abruptly and flung his arm across my chest, chanting, "Engine, engine!" I heard nothing. He pointed to the Brno, and I fired one of our three rounds into the air. Moments later, I saw a pinpoint of light pierce the darkness.

At first I thought we had come across another hunter's camp, but there were no other hunters or natives in the area. Slowly, the light grew larger, and we could see the outline of the rescue Land Cruiser, its spotlight on top of the cab pointing in the direction of the rifle shot. We had rendezvoused with the junction road.

We rushed towards the truck, and Ray Stanley, professional hunter and the driver, brought down the ice chest. We knelt before it as if we were at a sacred alter, devouring every form of liquid available. Once safely in the cab, still consuming our bottled elixirs, we sat numb from the day's trials, still 45 minutes by truck from camp.

Suddenly a large white owl flew across our headlights and landed on the road in front of us. Ray remarked that to the natives of the Moyowosi, this was the omen of death.

After Robin Hurt and Harry Muller recovered Bilu's body, a memorial service was held. After another day of recuperation, mourning and contemplation, filming resumed on the third day. A Tanzanian police investigation of the event confirmed my account of the incident.

It is now more than 20 years since this unfortunate disaster, the haunting memory of which remains unrelenting to this day. We were lucky not to have been killed such as Bilu, and that the historic presentation Holland & Holland double rifle cased set was not lashed to the gun rack in the Land Cruiser.

Who knows what might happen on a hunting safari in Africa. Such is the risk hunters have taken for centuries. Roosevelt luck remains with the Holland & Holland and was with us that fateful day of the omen of death in the Moyowosi. Ironically, some time later, we learned that the original Theodore Roosevelt safari had experienced their own conflagration in the Lado, Uganda, and the lighting of backfires saved the party from disaster. TR's experience was one of several adventures he reported in *African Game Trails*. Had TR seen the omen of the white owl? ☙

TR Recipient of the Congressional Medal of Honor, Posthumously

Awarded innumerable honors in his lifetime, one which Theodore Roosevelt fully deserved, but which was not given, was that of the Congressional Medal of Honor. Through the efforts of many, including particularly that of Boone and Crockett professional member Tweed Roosevelt, TR was finally so honored in a ceremony at the White House, on January 16, 2001. The special occasion was officiated by President William J. Clinton, whose statement is quoted (in abbreviated form) from information provided by the Theodore Roosevelt Association, web site, www.theodoreroosevelt.org):

Good morning, and please be seated. I would like to first thank Chaplain General Hicks for his invocation; and welcome the distinguished delegation from the Pentagon who are here—Secretary Cohen, General Shelton, Deputy Secretary DeLeon. I thank the members of Congress who are here—Senator Dorgan, Senator Durbin, Representatives King, Skelton, Weller, and Whitfield; former Representatives Lazio and McHale; members of the Smith and Roosevelt families.

In 1782, George Washington created the Badge of Military Merit. It was the first medal awarded by our nation's Armed Forces. But soon it fell into oblivion, and for decades no new medals were established. It was thought that a medal was too much like a European aristocratic title, while to fight for one's country in America was simply doing your democratic duty. So when the Medal of Honor was instituted during the Civil War it was agreed it would be given only for gallantry, at the risk of one's life above and beyond the call of duty. That's an extraordinarily high standard, one that precious few ever meet.

The Medal of Honor is our highest military decoration, and we are here today to honor two American heroes who met that mark.

After awarding the Congressional Medal of Honor to Andrew Jackson Smith, United States Army, who served as a part of the 55th Massachusetts Voluntary Infantry, a black regiment that fought in the Civil War, President Clinton continued...

The second Medal of Honor I award today is for the bravery of Lt. Colonel Theodore Roosevelt on July 1, 1898. That was the day he led his volunteer troops, the Rough Riders, in taking San Juan Hill, which changed the course of the battle and the Spanish-American War. We are greatly honored to be joined today by members of the Roosevelt family, including Tweed Roosevelt, here to accept the Medal of Honor on behalf of his great-grandfather.

This is the 37th Medal of Honor I have presented, but the first I presented in the recipient's old office—[laughter]—in front of a portrait of him in full battle gear. It is a tradition in the Roosevelt Room that when a Democrat is in the

Theodore Roosevelt with Rough Riders. From left to right: George Dann, Major Brodie, General Joseph Wheeler, Chaplain Brown, Col. Leonard Wood, and Lt. Col. Theodore Roosevelt.

© BETTMANN/CORBIS

> "Lieutenant Colonel Roosevelt's extraordinary heroism and devotion to duty are in keeping with the highest traditions of military service and reflect great credit upon himself, his unit, and the United States Army."

White House, a portrait of Franklin Roosevelt hangs above the mantle, and when a Republican is here, Teddy Roosevelt occupies the hallowed spot. I chose to break with the tradition these last eight years because I figured if we could have even half the luck and skill leading America into the 21st century that Theodore Roosevelt did in leading America into the 20th century, our nation would do just fine. TR was a larger-than-life figure who gave our nation a larger-than-life vision of our place in the world. Part of that vision was formed on San Juan Hill. His Rough Riders were made up of all kinds of Americans from all walks of life. They were considered unpolished and undisciplined, but they were true citizen soldiers. By taking San Juan Hill, eventually they forced the enemy fleet into the Battle of Santiago Bay, where it was routed. This led to the Spanish surrender and opened the era of America as a global power.

Twenty-two people won the Medal of Honor for actions that day. Two high-ranking military officers who had won the Medal of Honor in earlier wars and who saw Theodore Roosevelt's bravery recommended him for the medal, too. For some reason, the War Department never acted on the recommendation. Some say he didn't get it because of the bias the War Department had against volunteers. Others say it was because he ran afoul of the Secretary of War, who after the war was reluctant to allow the return of a number of American servicemen afflicted with Yellow Fever.

Roosevelt publicly called for America to bring its heroes home, where they had a far better chance to recover. The administration had to reverse course and it proved embarrassing to the Secretary. But while opinions about why he didn't receive the medal are mixed, opinion that he should have received it long ago is unanimous.

So here in this room will stand two great bookends to his wide-ranging life—the Medal of Honor, America's highest honor for warriors; and the Nobel Peace Prize, the world's highest honor for peacemakers, which he won for his role in settling the Russo-Japanese War of 1905.

This is a remarkable day, and I can't help but noting that for historical buffs, Theodore Roosevelt's son was the oldest man who landed on the beaches at Normandy on D-Day, where he also won the Medal of Honor. Tragically, he died shortly after that, in his uniform doing his duty.

We are profoundly grateful as Americans for this remarkable family. And I am honored that I had the chance before I left office to correct what I think is a significant historical error. I'd also like to thank all these people from New York who are in the Congress, and other people from other states who did their part to see that it was done. And I thank all of you, too.

Nearly a hundred years ago, standing in this place—I suppose I should also say this—the reason this was Theodore Roosevelt's office is that all the offices of the President were in the old White House, until Teddy Roosevelt became President. But the country was bustling and growing and so was his family. He had five kids, and no place to work over there. His children were rambunctious like him. They even let goats and other animals run through the White House during regular time.

And so they built the West Wing in 1902, believe it or not, as a temporary structure. But no one ever had the courage to go back to Congress again and ask for money to do it right. So it's held up pretty well for the last 99 years. And that's why this was President Theodore Roosevelt's office.

Here's what he said, way back then: "We know there are dangers ahead, as we know there are evils to fight and overcome. But stout of heart, we see across the dangers the great future that lies beyond, and we rejoice."

Let these words continue to guide as, as we go forth into a new century. May we continue to live up to the ideals for which both Andrew Jackson Smith and Theodore Roosevelt risked their lives. Major, please read the citation.

The following citation is read followed by applause.

Lieutenant Colonel Theodore Roosevelt distinguished himself by acts of bravery on 1 July, 1898, near Santiago de Cuba, Republic of Cuba, while leading a daring charge up San Juan Hill. Lieutenant Colonel Roosevelt, in total disregard for his personal safety, and accompanied by only four or five men, led a desperate and gallant charge up San Juan Hill, encouraging his troops to continue the assault through withering enemy fire over open countryside. Facing the enemy's heavy fire, he displayed extraordinary bravery throughout the charge, and was the first to reach the enemy trenches, where he quickly killed one of the enemy with his pistol, allowing his men to continue the assault. His leadership and valor turned the tide in the Battle for San Juan Hill. Lieutenant Colonel Roosevelt's extraordinary heroism and devotion to duty are in keeping with the highest traditions of military service and reflect great credit upon himself, his unit, and the United States Army.

THE PRESIDENT: Well, thank you all very much for being here today. This has been a very moving ceremony. Again, I want to thank the large delegation from the Congress, and former members who have come, and families and folks in the Pentagon who worked hard to get this done. This is a good day for America. I'll just leave you with this one thought. I said this yesterday, but I may say it every day in the last week of my presidency. In the case of a black soldier in the long-ago Civil War, it sometimes takes a long time to get things right.

But Theodore Roosevelt reminded us that the only way we do that is by constantly focusing on the future. And that's really what we're celebrating here today, two people who changed America in more ways than one by their personal courage, from very different vantage points. PBS has been showing Geoffrey Ward's magnificent series on jazz—I don't know if any of you have seen it. But there's a great section on Duke Ellington, who was a native of Washington, D.C. And he was asked what his favorite jazz tune was, and he said, "The one coming up." [Laughter.] There's always a new one coming up—that's why we're all still here after more than 200 years. Thank you and God bless you all. [Applause.]

U.S. President Bill Clinton presents Tweed Roosevelt (left), great grandson of Theodore Roosevelt, with a posthumous Medal of Honor for Lieutenant Colonel Theodore Roosevelt on January 16, 2001, in the Roosevelt Room of the White House.

"The Long, Long Trail"—cartoonist and Boone and Crockett Club member, Jay N. "Ding" Darling's poignant tribute to Theodore Roosevelt.

FROM THE *NEW YORK TRIBUNE*, JANUARY 8, 1919.

Selected Bibliography and Suggested Reading

Writings of Theodore Roosevelt or Members of His Family

Books by Theodore Roosevelt as author or co-author, with hunting subjects or with material pertaining to his use of firearms. Chronologically arranged by date of publication of first editions:

Roosevelt, Theodore and H. D. Minot *The Summer Birds of the Adirondacks in Franklin County,* N.Y. Salem: Naturalists' Agency, October 1877.

Roosevelt, Theodore *Notes on Some of the Birds of Oyster Bay,* Long Island. Privately printed, March 1879.

Hunting Trips of a Ranchman. New York and London: G. P. Putnam's Sons, 1886.

Ranch Life and the Hunting-Trail. New York: The Century Company, 1888.

The Winning of the West. 4 vols. New York: G. P. Putnam's Sons, 1889, 1894, 1896.

The Wilderness Hunter. New York: G. P. Putnam's Sons, 1898.

Some American Game. New York: G. P. Putnam's Sons, 1897.

The Rough Riders. New York: Charles Scribner's Sons, 1899.

The Strenuous Life New York: The Century Company, 1900.

et. al. The Deer Family New York: Grosset and Dunlap, 1902.

Outdoor Pastimes of an American Hunter, New York: Charles Scribner's Sons, 1905.

Hunting Tales of the West 4 vols. New York: Current Literature Publishing Company, 1907. vol.1: *Hunting Trips of a Ranchman,* vol. 2: *Hunting Trips on the Prairie*; vol. 3: *The Wilderness Hunter*; vol. 4: *Hunting the Grisly.* Volumes and 2 are a reissue of

Hunting Trips of a Ranchman, volumes 3 and 4 are a reissue of *The Wilderness Hunter.*

Good Hunting in Pursuit of Big Game in the West. New York and London: Harper & Brothers, 1907.

African Game Trails. 2 vols. New York: Charles Scribner's Sons, 1910.

Theodore Roosevelt - An Autobiography New York: The Macmillan Company, 1918.and Edmund Heller.

Life-Histories of African Game Animals. 2 vols. New York: Charles Scribner's Sons, 1914.

A Book-Lover's Holidays in the Open. New York: Charles Scribner's Sons, 1916.

Through the Brazilian Wilderness. New York: Charles Scribner's Sons, 1914.

Some of Theodore Roosevelt's hunting books were published in foreign language editions, among them: *Hunting Trips of a Ranchman* (French, German), *Ranch Life and the Hunting-Trail* (German, Polish), *The Wilderness Hunter* (German, Swedish), and *African Game Trails* (German, French. Swedish). Roosevelt's hunting books continue to be reprinted, in various editions.

Books edited or co-edited by Theodore Roosevelt, or to which he contributed written material pertaining to hunting and/or the use of firearms:

Roosevelt, Theodore, and George Bird Grinnell (ed).

American Big-Game Hunting - The Book of the Boone and Crockett Club, (vol. 1). New York: Forest and Stream Publishing Company, 1898.

Hunting in Many Lands - The Book of the Boone and Crockett Club [vol. 2]. New York: Forest and Stream Publishing Company, 1895.

Trail and Campfire - The Book of the Boone and Crockett Club [vol. 8]. New York: Forest and Stream Publishing Company, 1897.

Grinnell, George Bird (ed.). *American Big Game in Its Haunts - The Book of the Boone and Crockett Club* [vol. 4]. New York and London: Harper & Brothers, 1914. With contributions by Theodore Roosevelt and other writers.

Miles, Alfred H. *In the Lion's Mouth*. London: Stanley Paul, 1912. With contributions by Theodore Roosevelt and other writers.

Suffolk, Earl of, *et al. The Encyclopaedia of Sport*. London: Lawrence and Bullen, 1897-98. With contributions by Theodore Roosevelt [11 articles] and other writers.

Books on hunting, wildlife, or related subjects to which Theodore Roosevelt contributed foreword or introductory material:

Baynes, Ernest Harold. *Wild Bird Guests*. New York: E. P. Dutton and Company 1915. Preface by Theodore Roosevelt.

Beebe, William, and G. Inness Hartley and Paul G. Howes. *Tropical Wild Life in British Guiana*. New York: The New York Zoological Society, 1917. Intro, by Theodore Roosevelt.

Edward, of Norwich. 2d Duke of York. *The Master of Game*. London: Ballantyne, Hanson & Company, 1904. Foreword by Theodore Roosevelt.

Kearton, Cherry. *Wild Life Across the World*. London, New York and Toronto: Hodder & Stoughton, 1913. Intro, by Theodore Roosevelt.

Job, Herbert Keightley. *Wild Wings*. London: Archibald Constable and Company, Ltd.; Boston and New York: Houghton Muffin Company 190?. Introductory letter by Theodore Roosevelt.

Loring. J. Alden. *African Adventure Stories*. New York: Charles Scribner's Sons, 1914. Foreword by Theodore Roosevelt.

Pease, Albert Bigelow. *Captain Bill McDonald, Texas Ranger*. New York: J. J. Little and Ives Company, 1909. Introductory letter by Theodore Roosevelt.

Pease, Alfred E. *The Book of the Lion*. 2d ed. New York: Charles Scribner's Sons, 1914. Introductory letter by Theodore Roosevelt. Dedicated to TR.

Scull, Guy H. *Lassoing Wild Animals in Africa*. New York: Frederick A. Stokes Company, 1911. Intro. by Theodore Roosevelt.

Selous, Frederick Courteney. *African Nature Notes and Reminiscences*. London: Macmillan Company Ltd., 1908. Foreword by Theodore Roosevelt.

Stevenson-Hamilton, James. *Animal Life in Africa*. New York: E. P. Dutton Company; and London: Heinemann, 1912. Foreword by Theodore Roosevelt Stigand, Chauncy Hugh. *Hunting the Elephant in Africa*. New York: TheMacmillan Company, 1913. Intro. by Theodore Roosevelt.

Wallihan, A. G. *Hoofs, Claws and Antlers of the Rocky Mountains*. Denver: Frank S. Thayer, 1984. Intro. by Theodore Roosevelt.

Camera Shots at Big Game. New York: Doubleday, Page & Company 1901. Intro. by Theodore Roosevelt.

Selected articles by Theodore Roosevelt appearing in various periodicals. A great duplication appears in Roosevelt's hunting writings, since most of these articles later appeared collected in book form:

Roosevelt, Theodore. "A Zoological Trip through Africa," *Bulletin of the Throop Polytechnic Institute*, vol. XX, no. 51 (July 1911).

"Big Game Disappearing in the West," *The Forum*, vol. XV, no. 6 (August 1893).

"Frederick Courteney Selous," *The Outlook*, vol. 115, no. 10 (March 7, 1917).

"Harpooning Devilfish," *Scribner's Magazine;* vol. LXII, no. 3 (September 1917) .

"My Life as a Naturalist," *The American Museum Journal*, vol. XVIII, no. 5 (May 1918).

"Wild Man and Wild Beast in Africa," *National Geographic Magazine,* vol. XXII, no. 1 (January 1911).

Miscellaneous Manuscript and Other Sources:
Original Theodore Roosevelt Manuscript Material:
  A Jackal Hunt, 1878
  Game Book, 1883-1902
  Field Book for 1874, 1875 - Chiefly ornithology
  Field Book of Zoology [1876-79]
  Notes on the Fauna of' the Adirondack Mountains, 1871-77
  Ornithology of Egypt Between Cairo and Assonan, 1872
  Remarks on the Zoology of Oyster Bay, L. I. 1874-76
  Sporting Calendar, 1875
  Theodore Roosevelt Diaries, 1879-81, 1883-84
  Theodore Roosevelt Scrapbooks, 1881-91
  Sou'-sou'-southerly, 1881
  Winchester-Theodore Roosevelt Correspondence, 1908-09

Zoological Record, 1872-73
African Diary, 1910

Miscellaneous Unpublished Sources:
Elliott Roosevelt Diaries, 1875-81
Shipping ledgers of the Colt, Winchester, Savage, Smith
& Wesson, Remington, Marlin, and Holland & Holland
arms companies.
Hermann Hagedorn notes for *Roosevelt in the Badlands*.
Theodore Roosevelt collection, Harvard College Library.
*Inventory and Appraisal of...the Estate of...Theodore Roosevelt by
the American* Art Association, New York City, 1919.
Theodore Roosevelt as Police Commissioner of New York, by A.
D. Andrews, unpublished manuscript in the Theodore
Roosevelt Collection, Harvard College Library 1945.
Photographs in the Theodore Roosevelt Collection,
Harvard College Library Materials in the Theodore
Roosevelt Birthplace Museum (New York City),
Sagamore Hill National Historic Site (Oyster Bay Long
Island, New York), The Theodore Roosevelt Collection,
Harvard College Library (Cambridge, Massachusetts),
The Manuscript Division Library of Congress
(Washington, D.C.), Theodore Roosevelt National Park
(Medora, North Dakota).

**Books by Roosevelt relatives on hunting or with
firearms references, plus various collections of
Theodore Roosevelt letters:**
Abernathy, John R. *A Son of the Frontier*, Croton-on-Hudson,
New York News Press, 1935. Intro. by Kermit Roosevelt.
Anon. *Theodore Roosevelt's Diaries of Boyhood and Youth*. New
York and London: Charles Scribner's Sons, 1928.
Bishop, Joseph Bucklin (ed.). *Theodore Roosevelt's Letters to
His Children*. New York: Charles Scribner's Sons, 1929.
Cowles, Anna Roosevelt (ed.). *Letters from Theodore Roosevelt
to Anna Roosevelt Cowles 1870-1918*. New York and
London: Charles Scribner's Sons, 1924.
Irwin, Will (ed.). *Letters to Kermit from Theodore Roosevelt
1902-1908*. New York and London: Charles Scribner's
Sons, 1946.
Lodge, Henry Cabot, *Selections from the Correspondence of
Theodore Roosevelt and Henry Cabot Lodge 1884—1918*. vol. I.
New York and London: Charles Scribner's Sons, 1925.
Morison, Elting E. (ed.). *The Letters of Theodore Roosevelt*, 8
vols. Cambridge Harvard University Press, 1951-54.
Robinson, Corinne Roosevelt. *My Brother Theodore Roosevelt*.

New York: Charles Scribner's Sons, 1921.
Roosevelt, Anna Eleanor (ed.). *Hunting Big Game in the
Eighties - The Letters of Elliott Roosevelt, Sportsman*. New
York: Charles Scribner's Sons, 1933.
Roosevelt, Edith Carow [Mrs. Theodore Roosevelt], et. al.
Cleared for Strange Ports. New York and London: Charles
Scribner's Sons, 1927.
Roosevelt, Elliott, "A Hunting Trip to India," contribution
to *Hunting in Many Lands*. New York: Forest and Stream
Publishing Company, 1895.
Roosevelt, Kermit and Theodore Roosevelt. *East of the
Sun and West of the Moon*. New York: Charles Scribner's
Sons, 1926.
Roosevelt, Kermit and Theodore Roosevelt. *Trailing the
Giant Panda*. New York and London: Charles Scribner's
Sons, 1929.
Roosevelt, Kermit. *The Happy Hunting Grounds*. New York:
Charles Scribner's Sons, 1920.
Roosevelt, Kermit. *The Long Trail*. New York: The Review
of Reviews, 1921.
Roosevelt, Kermit, et al. (ed.). *Hunting Trails on Three
Continents*, 1933.
Roosevelt, Kermit. *A Sentimental Safari*. New York: Alfred
A. Knopf, 1963.
Roosevelt, Nicholas. *Theodore Roosevelt the Man as I Knew
Him*. New York: Dodd, Mead & Company, 1967.
Roosevelt, Robert Barnwell. *The Game-Birds of the Coasts
and Lakes of the Northern States of America*. New York:
Carleton, 1866.
Roosevelt, Robert Barnwell. *Florida and the Game Water-
Birds of the Atlantic Coast and the Lakes of the United States*.
New York: Orange Judd Company 1884.
Roosevelt, Theodore. *All in the Family*. New York and
London: G. P. Putnam's Sons, 1929.
Roosevelt, Theodore, and Harold J. Coolidge, Jr. *Three
Kingdoms of Indo China*. New York: Thomas Y Crowell
Company, 1933.
Waters, Robert S., et al. *Records of North American Big Game*
New York, Chicago, and San Francisco: Holt, Rinehart
and Winston, 1964. Article, "The Sagamore Hill
Medal,' by Archibald B. Roosevelt.

General Titles
Abbott, Lawrence F. *Impressions of Theodore Roosevelt*.
Garden City, New York: Doubleday, Page &
Company 1919.

Abbott, Lawrence F. (ed.). *The Letters of Archie Butt.* Garden City, New York:Doubleday, Page & Company 1924.

Abernathy John R. *In Camp with Theodore Roosevelt or the Life of John R. (Jack) Abernathy.* Oklahoma City: The Times-Journal Publishing Company 1933

Akeley Carl E. *In Brightest Africa.* Garden City, New York: Doubleday Page & Company, 1923.

Amos, James E. *Theodore Roosevelt: Hero to His Valet.* New York: The John Day Company, 1927.

Bade, William Frederic. *The Life and Letters of John Muir,* 2 vols. Boston and New York: Houghton Mifflin Company, 1924.

Bishop, Joseph Bucklin. *Theodore Roosevelt and His Time.* vol. II. New York: Charles Scribner's Sons, 1920.

Bronson, Edgar Beecher. *In Closed Territory.* Chicago: A. C. McClure and Company, 1910.

Bull, Bartle. *Safari: A Chronicle of Adventure.* New York: Viking Penguin, Inc., 1988.

Burroughs, John. *Camping & Tramping with Roosevelt.* Boston and New York:

Houghton Mifflin Company, 1907.

Burroughs, John, et al. *Theodore Roosevelt Memorial Addresses.* New York: The Century Company, 1919.

Bush, Noel. *T R., The Story of Theodore Roosevelt.* New York: Reynal and Company, 1963.

Caswell, John. *Sporting Rifles and Rifle Shooting.* New York and London: D. Appleton and Company, 1920.

Chapman, Frank M. *Autobiography of a Bird-Lover.* New York: D. Appleton Century Company, 1988.

Cherrie, George K. *Dark Trails - Adventures of a Naturalist.* New York: G. P. Putnam's Sons, 1930.

Clark, James L. *Good Hunting.* Norman, Oklahoma: University of Oklahoma Press, 1966.

Clark, James L. *Trails of the Hunted.* Boston: Little, Brown and Company, 1928. Cutright, Paul Russell. *Theodore Roosevelt the Naturalist.* New York: Harper & Brothers, 1956.

Dailey, Wallace Finley, ed. *Pocket Diary 1898 Theodore Roosevelt's Private Account of the War with Spain A Facsimile Edition of the Manuscript Accompanied by Extracts from His Published Recollections and Illustrated with Photographs,* foreword by Tweed Roosevelt, introduction by John Morton Blum. Cambridge: The Theodore Roosevelt Collection, Harvard College Library, The Houghton Library, Harvard University, 1998.

DeArment, Robert K. *Bat Masterson The Man and the Legend.* Norman: University of Oklahoma Press, 1979.

DeMattos, Jack. *Garrett and Roosevelt.* College Station, Texas: Creative Publishing Company, 1988.

Dresden, Donald. *The Marquis de Mores Emperor of the Bad Lands.* Norman: University of Oklahoma Press, 1970.

Ferleger, Herbert Ronald and Albert Bushnell Hart (eds.). *Theodore Roosevelt Cyclopedia.* New York: Roosevelt Memorial Association, 1941.

Fox, Stephen. *John Muir and His Legacy The American Conservation Movement.* Boston: Little, Brown and Company, 1981.

Grey Viscount, of Fallodon, K. G. *Twenty-five Years 1892-1916.* Vol. II. London Hodder and Stoughton. Ltd., 1925.

Hagedorn, Hermann. *Roosevelt in the Bad Lands.* Boston and New York: Houghton Mifflin Company, 1921.

Hermit Club of Cleveland. *The Hermits in Africa - A Musical Comedy in Two Acts.* Cleveland: The Brooks Company, 1909.

Higgers, Jim. *The Adventures of Theodore—A Humorous Extravaganza.* Chicago: H. J. Smith and T. H. Devereaux and Company, c. 1901.

Jinks, Roy G. and Robert J. Neal. *Smith and Wesson 1857-1945.* New York: A. S. Barnes and Company; London: Thomas Yoseloff, Ltd., 1966.

Lang, Lincoln A. *Ranching with Roosevelt.* Philadelphia and London: J. B. Lippincott Company, 1926.

Lorant, Stefan. *The Life and Times of Theodore Roosevelt.* Garden City, New York: Doubleday and Company, 1959.

Lutts, Ralph H. *The Nature Fakers Wildlife, Science & Sentiment.* Golden, Colorado: Fulcrum Publishing,1990.

McCullough, David. *Mornings on Horseback.* New York: Simon & Schuster, 1981.

Millard, Candice. *The River of Doubt Theodore Roosevelt's Darkest Journey,* New York: Doubleday, 2005.

Miller, Leo E. *In the Wilds of South America.* New York: Charles Scribner's Sons,1919.

Morris, Edmund. *The Rise of Theodore Roosevelt.* New York: Coward, McCann & Geoghegan, Inc. 1979. *Theodore Rex.* New York: Random House, Inc., 2001.

Morris, Sylvia Jukes. *Edith Kermit Roosevelt: Portrait of a First Lady.* .New York: Random House, Inc., 1980.

Osborn, Henry Fairfield. *Impressions of Great Naturalists.* New York and London: Charles Scribner's Sons, 1924.

O'Toole, Patricia. *When Trumpets Call: Theodore Roosevelt After the White House,* New York: Simon & Schuster, 2005.

Parker, John H. *History of the Gatling Gun Detachment.* Kansas

City, Missouri: Hudson-Kimberly Publishing Company 1898. Preface by Theodore Roosevelt.

Pringle, Henry F. *Theodore Roosevelt*. New York: Harcourt, Brace Company, 1931. Putnam, Carleton. *Theodore Roosevelt - The Formative Years 1858-1886*. New York: Charles Scribner's Sons, 1958.

Rattenbury, Richard C. *Hunting the American West: The Pursuit of Big Game for Life, Profit, and Sport 1800-1900*. Missoula, Montana: Boone and Crockett Club, 2008.

Read, Opie. *Adventures of a Vice-President - A Fable of Our Times*. Chicago: T. H. Devereaux and Company, 1904.

Riis, Jacob A. *Theodore Roosevelt the Citizen*. New York: The Outlook Company, 1904.

Riling, Ray *Guns and Shooting. A Selected Chronological Bibliography*. New York: Greenberg, 1951.

Selous, Frederick Courteney. *African Nature Notes and Reminiscences*. London: Macmillan Company Ltd., 1908.

Sewall, William Wingate. *Bill Sewall's Story of T.R.* New York and London: Harper & Brothers, 1919.

Shaw, Albert. A *Cartoon History of Roosevelt's Career*. New York: The Review of Reviews Company, 1910.

Sprague, Marshall. A *Gallery of Dudes*. Boston and Toronto: Little, Brown and Company, 1966.

Taylor, John. *African Rifles and Cartridges*. Georgetown, South Carolina: Small Arms Technical Publishing Company, 1948.

Trefethen, James B. and James E. Serven (eds.). *Americans and Their Guns*. Harrisburg: Stackpole Books, 1967.

Trefethen, James B. *Crusade for Wildlife*. Harrisburg: Stackpole Books, and Boone and Crockett Club, 1961.

Tweton, D. Jerome. *The Marquis de Mores Dakota Capitalist French Nationalist* Fargo: North Dakota Institute for Regional Studies, 1972.

Unger, Frederick William. *Roosevelt's African Trip*. W.E.. Scull, 1909. Site of publication not indicated.

Wagenknecht, Edward. *The Seven Worlds of Theodore Roosevelt* New York, London and Toronto: Longmans, Green and Company 1958.

Watrous, George R. *The History of Winchester Firearms 1866-1966*. Edited by Thomas E. Hall and Pete Kuhlhoff. 3d ed. New Work: Winchester Press, 1966.

White, G. Edward. *The Eastern Establishment and the Western Experience The West of Frederic Remington, Theodore Roosevelt and Owen Wister*. New Haven and London: Yale University Press, 1968.

Wilhelm, Donald. *Theodore Roosevelt as an Undergraduate*. Boston: John W Luce and Company, 1910.

Williamson, Harold F. *Winchester—The Gun That Won the West*. New York: A. S. Barnes; London: Thomas Yoseloff, 1952.

Willis, Jack. *Roosevelt in the Rough*. New York: Ives Washburn, 1931.

Wilson, R L. *L D. Nimschke. Firearms Engraver*. Teaneck, New Jersey: John J. Malloy, 1965.

Wister, Owen. *Roosevelt, The Story of a Friendship 1880-1919*. New York: The Macmillan Company, 1930.

Wood, Frederick S. *Roosevelt As We Knew Him*. Philadelphia and Chicago: The John C. Winston Company, 1927.

Miscellaneous monograph, introductory or periodical material pertaining to Theodore Roosevelt as a hunter and shooter.

Abernathy John R. "Catch 'Em - or Die!" *Boys' Life*. January 1938.

Abernathy John R. *A Son of the Frontier* Croton-on-Hudson, New York: News Press, 1935.

Anon. "Roosevelt's Best-Loved Guns," *All Outdoors*, vol. VII, no. 4 (January 1920). Armstrong, Orland Kay. "He Tracked Bear for Roosevelt," *New York Herald Tribune*. January 3, 1932.

Avis, William H. "Teddy' Roosevelt's Visit Here in 1915 History Making Event," *New Haven Register*, December 17, 1933.

Baier, Lowell E. "The Cradle of Conservation: Theodore Roosevelt's Elkhorn Ranch, an Icon of America's National Identity." *Theodore Roosevelt Association Journal*, volume xxviii, number I, winter 2007.

Barsotti, John. "Freund & Bro Gunmakers on the Frontier," appearing in the *Gun Digest Treasury*. Chicago: Follett Publishing Company 1961.

Anon. "African Trophies of Theodore Roosevelt," *Country Life*. May 1919.

Anon. "Fox-Hunting Near New York," *Harper's Weekly*, March 15, 1886.

Crimmins, Colonel M. L. "Elliott Roosevelt's Visit to Texas in 1876-1877," *The Southwestern Historical Quarterly*, vol. XLVIII, no. 2 (October 1944). Austin: The Texas State Historical Association.

Dantz, William T. "Theodore Roosevelt—Cowboy and Ranchman," *Harper's Weekly*, August 6, 1904.

Dawson, Warrington. "Hunting with Roosevelt in East Africa *Hampton's Magazine*. XXIII (November 1909).

Denison, Lindsay. "President Roosevelt's Mississippi Bear Hunt," *Outing*, February 1903.

Dickson, Harris. 'The Bear Slayer Holt Collier's Recollections of Man and Bear *Saturday Evening Post March* 13 and April 10, 1909.

Dunne, F. P. " 'Mr. Dooley' on Big Game Hunting," *The American Magazine.* September 1908.

Edwards, William B. "The Guns of Teddy Roosevelt," *Guns,* January 1956.

Ferris, Joseph A. "When Roosevelt Came to Dakota," *Wide World* March 1921

Foley William J., M.D. "A Bullet and a Bull Moose," *Journal of the American Medical Association,* vol. 209, no. 13 (September 29, 1969).

Foran, Captain W Robert. "With Roosevelt in Africa," *Field and Stream,* October 1912.

Gable, John A., Ph.D., "President Theodore Roosevelt's Record on Conservation *Theodore Roosevelt Association Journal,* vol. X no. 3, Fall 1984. Listings of National Forests, National Parks, National Game Reserves. National Monument Reclamation Projects, and Federal Bird Reservations, created by T.R 1909, and Conservation Commissions and Conferences during the Roosevelt administration.

Goff, Frederick R, "Theodore Roosevelt's Hunting Library" *The Quarterly Jour of the Library of Congress* vol. 21, no.3 (July 1964).

Gaff, John B. "The Roosevelt Lion Hunt," *Outdoor Life,* April and May 1901.

Grinnell, George Bird. "Roosevelt in Africa" *The American Review of Reviews,* October 1910.

Grinnell, George Bird. "Theodore Roosevelt As a Sportsman." *Country Calendar* November 1905.

Harbaugh, William H., 'The Theodore Roosevelts' Retreat in Southern Albemarle," *The Magazine of Albemarle County History,* vol. 51, 1993, published by the Albemarle County Historical Society, Charlottesville, Virginia.

Hornaday, William Temple. 'The Heads and Horns Museum," *Zoological Society Bulletin,* May 1922.

Johnston, Harry H. "Where Roosevelt Will Hunt," *National Geographic Magazine* March 1969.

Lambert, Alexander, M. D. "Roosevelt the Companion," introductory material vol. III, *Theodore Roosevelt Works,* Memorial Edition, 1924.

Laughlin, J. Laurence. 'Roosevelt at Harvard," *Review of Reviews,* October 1924 Mattison, Ray H. *Life at Roosevelt's Elkhorn Ranch—The Letters of William W. and Mary Sewall.* [Reprinted from] *North Dakota Historical Society Quarterly* vol. 27, nos. 3 and 4, 1960.

Mattison, Ray. H. *Roosevelt and the Stockmen's Association.* [Reprinted from] *North Dakota History,* vol. 17, no. 2 (April 1950), and no. 3 (July 1950). Theodore Roosevelt Nature and History Association, 1969.

Mattison, Ray H., and Chester L. Brooks. *Theodore Roosevelt and the Dakota Badlands.* Washington, D.C.: National Park Service, 1958.

McGuire, 1. A. "Governor Roosevelt's Colorado Lion Hunt," *Outdoor Life.* March 1901.

Naylor, Douglas Q "Col. Roosevelt as His Guide Remembers Him," *New York Times,* January 6, 1929.

Needham, Henry Beach. "Theodore Roosevelt As a Country Gentleman," *The Country Calendar,* vol. 1, no. 6 (October 1905).

Parker, John *M.* "Hunting with Colonel Roosevelt," *Outers' Book-Recreation,* September 1919.

Payne, George Henry. "Theodore Roosevelt, Fox Hunter," *Long Island Forum,* December 1939.

Rattenbury, Richard, 'The Roosevelt-Merrifield Connection," *Man at Arms,* vol. 4, no. 6, November/ December 1982.

Roosevelt, Kermit. "When T.R. Didn't Speak Softly to Winchester," *True.* vol. 47, no. 354 (November 1966).

Roosevelt, Tweed. "Theodore Roosevelt: The Mystery of the Unrecorded Environmentalist." *Theodore Roosevelt Association Journal,* volume 25, number 2, 2002.

Roosevelt, Tweed. 'Theodore Roosevelt's African Safari," paper delivered at the conference "Theodore Roosevelt and the Birth of Modern America," at Hofstra University, Hempstead, New York, April 12-21, 1990. Published in *Theodore Roosevelt Many-Sided American,* edited by Natalie A. Naylor, Douglas Brinkley and John Allen Gable, Ph.D., under the auspices of Hofstra University, Heart of the Lakes Publishing, Interlaken, New York. 1992.

Serven, James E. "Theodore Roosevelt," *American Rifleman.* August 1964.

Snow, Stanley "Theodore Roosevelt, Sportsman," *Outers' Book-Recreation,* February 1919.

Stefansson, V. *et al. Theodore Roosevelt Memorial Meeting at the Explorers Club.* Published eulogies and memoirs by selected members. March 1,1919.

Stewart, Kate. "The Theodore Roosevelt Centennial
    Exhibit," *The Library of Congress Quarterly Journal of Current
    Acquisitions,* vol. 15, no.3 (May 1958). Foreword by
    E. E. Morison.

Stewart, Kate. "Theodore Roosevelt Hunter-Naturalist on
    Safari," *The Quarterly Journal of the Library of Congress,* vol.
    27, no.3 (July 1970).

Vivian, James F. "Recollections of Theodore Roosevelt
    and the Badlands," *Theodore Roosevelt Association Journal,*
    vol. XVIII, nos. 2 and 3, Spring-Summer-Fall, 1992

Vollweiler, Albert Tangeman. *Roosevelt's Ranch Life
    in North Dakota.* [Reprinted from] *Quarterly Journal*
    of the University of North Dakota, vol. IX, no. 1
    (October 1918).

Wheelock, John Hall. *A Bibliography of Theodore Roosevelt.*
    New York: Charles Scribner's Sons, 1920.

White, Stewart Edward. "Roosevelt and the Pioneer
    Spirit," introductory material in vol. II, *Theodore Roosevelt
    Works,* Memorial Edition, 1923.

Williams, C. Arthur. "The President's Outing," *World To-
    Day,* June 1905.

Willis, John. "When I Hunted and Camped with
    Theodore Roosevelt," *Kansas City Star,* January
    22, 1922.

Willyoung, Arthur K. "Roosevelt the Greatest Outdoor
    Man," *Outing,* August, October, 1919.

Wilson, R. L. "Theodore Roosevelt's Revolver, Holster,
    and Spurs," privately printed by Herb Glass, Bullville,
    New York, April 1966.

An important up-to-date source of Roosevelt material is
the *Theodore Roosevelt Association Journal,* edited through
2004 by John A. Gable, Ph. D., Executive Director, and
currently edited by William Tilchin, Ph.D.

Acknowledgments

No book so dependent on a vast array of sources could be produced without the cooperation of many individuals and institutions. The author and publisher wish to express appreciation to those who helped to create *Theodore Roosevelt Hunter-Conservationist*.

To Archibald Roosevelt, for patience and insights in sharing his wealth of knowledge about his father's firearms and hunting interests, and for generously agreeing to write the Preface.

To John Milius, filmmaker, screenwriter, and sportsman, for his insightful Foreword based on his own extensive experience in Roosevelt history and lore, and expertise on firearms and the shooting sports.

To Mrs. Harold Kraft, formerly Curator of Sagamore Hill National Historic Site, and Miss Helen MacLachlan, formerly Curator of the Theodore Roosevelt Birthplace Museum, for many generous hours of assistance, and for answers and leads on every aspect of TR as outdoorsman, conservationist and hunter.

To Tweed Roosevelt (grandson of Archibald), for helpful suggestions and modifications. To Messrs. Kermit Roosevelt, Kermit Roosevelt, Jr., and J. Willard Roosevelt, for detailed information on specific TR firearms and other related matters.

To John A. Gable, Ph.D., Executive Director, Theodore Roosevelt Association, to Wallace Finley Dailey, Curator, Theodore Roosevelt Collection, Harvard College Library, and to Amy Verone, Curator, Sagamore Hill National Historic Site, National Park Service, for insights, information, images and suggestions.

To Thomas E. Hall, Curator of the Winchester Gun Museum for many years, and to his assistant, Mrs. Anita Sylvia, for research and documentary material from the Winchester and Olin company archives. And to R.H. Wagner, Martin S. Huber, Kathleen Hoyt, and Beverly Haynes, four generations of Colt Historians, for counsel on TR's relationship with the Colt company.

To Peter Tollis, and to Gregory C. Wilson, formerly Curator, Theodore Roosevelt Collection, Harvard College Library, for their editorial assistance.

To Messrs. Richard P. Mellon, Greg and Petra Martin, William B. Ruger, Sr., Peter Beard, Claude Blair, Leonard Brady (assistant to John Milius), G. Allan Brown, Colonel Robert Caulfield (White Hunters, Ltd., Nairobi), Robert M. Ferguson, Ward French, Tony Galazan and staff of Connecticut Shotgun Manufacturing Co., Inc., Vincent Gengarelly, Craddock R. Goins, Ralph Goodyear, John and Belinda Jones, Greg Lampe, Merrill K. Lindsay, R.L. Moore, Jr., Brig and Louise Pemberton, Charles F. Priore, Jr., Douglas Sandberg, Michael and Karen Salisbury, David Sewall, William M. Simmons, S.P. Stevens, James Supica, Greg Thomas, Thom Vallance, Alvin A. White, Lawrence C. Woods, Jr., M.C.A. Lyell of Holland & Holland, Ltd., Mark Keefe IV, Managing Editor, *American Rifleman* magazine, H. Wayne Sheets, Executive Director, NRA Foundation Endowment, John and Judy Woods of Woodsvalley Farm, Harold L. Peterson and James B. Thompson of the National Park Service, Edward C. Ezell, Ph.D., Harry Hunter and Sarah Rittgers of the Department of Military History, National Museum of American History, Smithsonian Institution, and Richard C. Rattenbury, Curator of History, National Cowboy Museum and Western Heritage Center.

To professional hunters Ian Manning, Heinz Pulon, and John Roxburgh who guided the writer on his first African safari, in Zambia (summer

1970), in an attempt to capture the feeling of a wilderness African adventure, with not a few of the trappings similar to what TR and Kermit experienced on their own great adventure of 1909-10.

Still another safari which was inspired by that of 1909-10 was the "In the Blood" feature-length documentary film adventure of August 1986, in Tanzania, including director George T. Butler, and Theodore Roosevelt IV, Greg Martin and the writer as hunting clients, accompanied by observers Petra Martin, Theodore Roosevelt V ("Bear"), Tyssen Butler, author and environmentalist Bartle Bull, and a professional film crew lead by 1st camera Diana Taylor and 2nd camera John Ward. Follow-up trips added 1st camera Robert Elfstrom. The writer wishes to express his appreciation to the participants in that complex project, including professional hunters Robin Hurt, Harry Muller, Calvin Cottar, Dougie Wright, Johnny Yakus, Webster Kapaliswa, Ray Stanley, and the late Bilu Deane, and to Issai Swai, Project Manager, Moyowosi/Kigosi, the Tanzanian Game Department.

With special appreciation to David Mead, Ker & Downey, Ltd., Nairobi, Kenya, who recommended Robin Hurt and his associates as the professional hunters for the "In the Blood" film.

To Alec and Jocelyne Wildenstein and family, for their hospitality at Ol Jogi, following the 1986 safari, as well as on several subsequent African trips.

To Roger Mitchell and David Winks of Holland & Holland, Ltd., for assistance with the .500/.450 Roosevelt presentation double barrel rifle cased set, in refitting for the 1986 Tanzanian film safari and in filming at the firm's London showrooms and factory.

To William C. Steinkraus, formerly President, Winchester Press, and to Ellen Enzler-Herring and Jim Herring, Trophy Room Books, for their enthusiastic support, encouragement and participation in the evolution of *Theodore Roosevelt Hunter-Conservationist*.

To Carla Peters Tiffany, whose peripheral connection to the Roosevelt legacy ultimately led to the research, which resulted in the author's fascination with the theme of this book. And to Herb Glass, who as far back as 1966 commissioned the author to provide extensive research on several Roosevelt firearms and equally rare memorabilia, objects which the legendary dealer acquired over several decades—including the Holland & Holland presentation .500/.450 double barrel rifle and TR's favorite Colt Single Action Army revolver.

The author is particularly indebted to past Boone and Crockett Club president, now Chairman, Robert Model, and current Club president Lowell E. Baier, and the officers, members, and staff of the Club, particularly Chief of Staff Tony Schoonen, Chairman of the Publications Committee Howard Monsour, and Julie T. Houk, Director of Publications, and the gifted producer and designer of this book. Founded in 1887 by Theodore Roosevelt, it is this historic organization which, under TR's bold and aggressive leadership, pioneered wildlife and habitat conservation not only in the United States but on an international scale. No organization has a longer or more comprehensive or exemplary record of achievement in this noble, and unending, undertaking than the Boone and Crockett Club.

R.L. Wilson
Telegraph Hill, San Francisco, California
October 9th 2009

Index

Aa

Abercrombie & Fitch 223
A Book-Lover's Holidays in the Open 90, 140, 205, 213, 281
Adirondacks 16–17, 23–26, 123, 281
Adolph, Fred 202–204, 271
Africa 5, 47, 90, 96–99, 103, 152, 163, 167–195 *passim*, 197, 205–208, 214, 216, 223, 226–246, 249, 253–269, 270, 272, 275, 282–286
African Game Trails 173–174, 176–180, 184–187, 192, 194, 216, 254, 275, 281
Agricultural Appropriations Bill 149
Akeley, Carl 168, 171
Akeley, Delia 192
All in the Family 87, 283
Alpha Delta Phi 30
America and the World War 217
American Big Game Hunting 95
American Expeditionary Force 217
American Museum of Natural History 10, 84, 205, 207, 213, 219
American Rifleman 286
American Trading Company 111
Amos, James 47, 131, 134, 219
An Autobiography 5, 35, 37, 87, 107–108, 214–216, 281, 284
Andrews, Avery D. 98
Atlantic Monthly 143
Audubon, John James 18

Bb

Badlands ix, 26, 30, 35–49, 52, 54, 56, 59–60, 64–66, 75, 79–80, 84, 91, 93, 95, 133, 141, 163, 165, 213, 243, 283, 286–287
Baier, Lowell E. 2, 85, 257, 289
Baker, Sir Samuel W. 214
Ballard rifles 24, 48, 103, 141
Barr, George F. 127
Barye, Antoine Louis 214
bayonets 75
Bell, John G. 18, 213
Bennett, T.G. 193
Bennett, Winchester 224, 243, 253
Benton, Thomas Hart 77
Beretta family and company, funding TR gallery 157
Bierstadt, Albert 81, 85, 214

Bighorn Mountains 44, 46, 49
Bismarck (Dakota Territory) *Tribune* 108
Boone and Crockett Club v, xiii, 2, 5, 26, 28, 30, 35, 37, 41, 49, 51, 64, 72, 75, 79–97, 121–122, 136, 149, 156, 161–163, 168, 173, 181, 185, 194, 205, 209, 211, 213–214, 216–217, 219, 228, 254, 280–282, 285, 296
Borah, Jake 161
Brewer, Henry 193
Brinkley, Douglas 2, 84
British Columbia 79, 91
Brooklyn Bridge 13
Browning Arms Co. 111, 157, 202
Bryan, William Jennings 119
Buffalo Bill Historical Center 223, 225, 228, 244, 295
Bullard rifles 47, 49, 63, 69, 141
Bulletin of the American Geographical Society 194
Bulloch, Anna 10
Bulloch, James Stephens 10
Bullock, Seth 87–88, 140
Bullock, Stanley 133
Bureau of Forestry 149
Burns, William I. 131
Burroughs, John 90, 136, 139–140, 143
Butler, Tyssen 270
Buxton, Edward North 168, 173

Cc

Camera Shots at Big Game 154, 282
Camp Fire Club of America 83, 205
Carepe, Colonel 211
Carnegie, Andrew 173
Carow, Edith C. 21, 77
Carroll, Royal 96
Carson, Kit 88, 216
    Hawken rifle of 216
Chanler, William 96
Chapman, Frank M. 205
cheekpieces, custom 26, 46, 63, 80, 140, 149, 177, 228, 242
Chemical Bank of New York 10
Cherrie, George 207
Children's Aid Society 10
Chimney Butte Ranch 65
Churchill, Winston 174

Civil Service Commissioner 91–95
Clark, Edward B. 143
Clark, James L. 213, 214
Clark, William 193
Class Committee 30
Cleveland, Grover 36, 86
coal strike 127
Cody Firearms Museum 48, 223
Collier, Holt 127, 130, 221
Collins, J.S. 54
Colt Firearms
    automatic pistols 111, 131, 133, 211
    derringer 132–133
    revolvers 38, 44, 61, 87–88, 100–111, 115–116, 130, 141, 207, 270
    Single Action 7, 45–46, 50, 52, 56, 65, 70, 88, 111, 113, 161, 271–272
Columbia University 35
Congressional Medal of Honor 277–279
conservation of wildlife 85
Cortelyou, George B. 131, 291
Cowles, W.S. 111
Crater Lake National Park 150
Cromwell, George 15
Crozier, General William 140
Cuninghame, R.J. 173
Cutler, Arthur 23, 25

Dd

Dantz, William 39
Dean, Bilu 269–270, 272
Debs, Eugene V. 126
Democratic National Committee 13
de Morès, Marquis 60
Derby, Richard 90
desert bighorn sheep 90
Dewey, Commodore George 108
D.K.E. 30
Dow, Wilmot 25–69
Dreicer & Company 164
Dresden Natural History Museum 15
dudedom xiii
duels, threats of 60–62, 100
Duke, Basil 111

Ee

Eastman, George 192
Edwards, Captain Frank 111

President Theodore Roosevelt sits at the head of the table with his cabinet members. Clockwise, from Roosevelt are: George B. Cortelyou, Secretary of State; Charles Joseph Bonaparte, Attorney General; Victor H. Metcalf, Secretary of the Navy; Oscar Straus, Secretary of Commerce; James Wilson, Secretary of Agriculture; James R. Garfield, Secretary of the Interior; George von Lengerke Meyer, Postmaster General; William H. Taft, Secretary of War; and Elihu Root, Secretary of State. 1907.

© GEORGE PRINCE/CORBIS

Egypt 11, 18–23, 32, 87, 194–195, 282
Eliot, Charles W. 130
Elkhorn ranch 41, 44, 57, 60–61, 262
Encyclopaedia of Sport 216, 282
Europe 5, 13, 15, 35, 90–91, 134, 177, 202, 214, 216, 219
Explorers Club 83

Ff

Ferguson, Robert Munro 87
Ferris, Joe 39, 41, 60, 103
Ferris, Sylvane 133
Fiala, Anthony 205
Finnegin, Mike 68
Fish and Game League 123
Fish Catching 13
Five Acres Too Much 13
Florida and the Game Water Birds 13
Forbes and Lyman 241
Forest and Stream 85, 101–102, 281, 283
Forster 235, 236
Fox, A.H. 177, 179
foxhunting 163
Fox shotguns 174, 177, 179, 184
Freund, F.W. 130, 142
Freund gun sights 24, 130
Frost, A.B. 35, 49, 51, 94, 214

Gg

Game Birds of the Coasts 13
Game Fish of the Northern States 13
Garland, Hamlin 96
Genest, Odilon 212
George V, King 219
Gerard, James W. 164
Gifford, R. Swain 214
Glacier National Park 83
Goff, John B. 121
Goodwin, Philip R. 185, 194, 286
Gorringe, H.H. 37
Gould, A.C. 97
Governors' conference on conservation 150
Grant, Franklin 99
Gregory, James R. 161
greyhounds, hunting with 163
Griffen, Hank 102
Grinnell, George Bird 2, 37, 39, 81, 95, 101, 216
gun powder 98

Hh

Hagedorn, Hermann 39
Harlem Record 36
Harper, Frank 207
Harper's Weekly 96, 285
Harrison, Benjamin 83, 86
Harvard Advocate 30
Harvard University 28–29, 130
Hasty Pudding Club 30
Hawken rifle 88, 216
Heller, Edmund 173, 183, 213, 216

Hepburn Act 146
Herrig, Fred 80
Hewitt, Marvin 89
Holland & Holland .500/450 presentation rifle, list of donors viii
Holland & Holland rifles ix, 141, 174–177, 183–184, 195, 205, 269–275 *passim*
hounds 64, 83, 93, 121, 123, 157, 161–164, 205, 208, 210, 214
hunting
    benefits of 76
    gear 49, 121
    with hounds 163
    with knife xvi, 164
Hunting in Many Lands 30, 96, 141, 216, 281, 283
hunting, joy of, Kermit Roosevelt 90
Hunting Trips of a Ranchman 35, 39–40, 47–52, 84, 88, 216, 281
hunts for
    African game 180–195
    antelope 42–43, 49, 71, 93, 96, 103
    birds 25, 30–33, 92
    black bear 92, 127, 129, 149, 157, 161–164
    bobcat 157
    buffalo 37–41, 103
    caribou 80, 92
    cougar 122
    coyote 123, 157, 163
    deer 24, 30, 80, 92, 93–95
    elk 52, 79, 92, 101–102
    fox 64–65, 163
    goat 73–75
    grizzly bear 50–51, 57, 92, 94–95, 120–121
    jaguar 208–209
    javelina 30, 56, 79, 163
    lynx 7, 122
    moose 80, 92, 211–212
    mountain goat 56, 71–74, 80, 102
    mountain lion 56, 66, 121
    sheep 80
    wild turkey 157, 164
    wolf 123, 145, 157, 163
Hurt, Robin 270, 271, 274–275

Ii

Indians 9–10, 63–64, 91, 108, 205
Interstate Commerce Commission 146
"In the Blood" 205, 269, 271

Jj

Jack Willis 75
jaguar 90, 208–209
Johnston, Sir Harry 150, 173

Kk

Kennedy shotgun 47–49
Kornbrath, R.J. 202–204
Krag rifles 110–111, 113, 118, 225

Ll

Lambert, Dr. Alexander 87, 121, 161, 211–212
Lang, Lincoln 42
Laudensack 246–247
L.C. Smith "ranch gun" 47, 56, 70
Lebo 49
Lee, Alice Hathaway 23, 35
Leeholm 43
Lefaucheux shotguns 9, 12, 17–19, 30–31, 88, 141
Levering, Albert 157, 159
Life-Histories of African Game Animals 173, 216, 281
Lincoln, Abraham 10
Lippencott, I.L. 229
Lirette, Arthur 211–212
Little Missouri 37
Little Missouri River 37, 44, 50, 66
Lodge, Henry Cabot 64, 84, 92, 105, 168, 192
Loeb, William 123, 125, 223, 232
Long, John D. 108
Long, William J. 143
Loring, J. Alden 213
Luffsey, Riley 60
Luger presentation pistols 199–201, 207
Lyon, Cecil 157

Mm

MacMonies, Frederick 214
Mahan, Alfred T. 128
Maine woods 7, 25–29, 33, 44, 73, 107–108, 111
Maltese Cross ranch 39, 41, 54
Manhattan Elevated Railway 36
Manitou, TR's favorite Badlands horse 59, 64
Mannlicher rifles 141, 192, 247, 248, 251–253, 255
Map of African safari 254
Marco Polo sheep 90
Martin, Greg and Petra 269
Matthews, James Brander 96
Maxim silencers 214, 253
McIlhenny Co. Archives xii, 220
McKinley, William 105, 118
Meadowbrook Country Club 64
Meadowbrook Hunt Club 66, 163
Mearns, Dr. Edgar 173
Merriam, Clinton Hart 2, 136
Merrifield, William 41, 46, 49, 51, 54, 71, 73, 91, 102
Merwin Hulbert & Co 54, 56
Mesa Verde National Park 150
Metcalf, Clive 129, 221
Metropolitan Museum of Art 10
Meyer, George 176
Milius, John xiii
Miller, Leo 207
Minot, Henry 29, 150
Mitchell, John 127
Modern American Rifles 97
Monroe Doctrine 134
Morris, Gouverneur 77
Muir, John 125, 136

Muller, Harry 270, 275
My African Journey 174

Nn

Naón, Romulo 205
National Bison Range 150
National Firearms Museum 116, 157, 202
National Firearms Museum, Beretta Gallery 157
National Geographic Magazine 194, 282, 286
National Parks 3, 150, 286
National Park Service 56, 88
National Rifle Association 155, 157, 217
Newlands Reclamation bill 149
Newland, Tarlton & Co. 176
New Nationalism 198–199
New York Evening Post 36
New York Fish and Game Commission 13
New York Herald 99, 127, 285
New York Nation 95
New York Sun 99, 217
New York Times 66, 105, 286
New York Zoological Society 83, 85, 282
Nimschke, Louis D. 130
Nobel Peace Prize 5, 146, 195, 278
Noble, John W. 83

Oo

OK Club 30
Orthopedic Hospital of New York 10
Osborn, Henry Fairfield 205
Outdoor Pastimes of an American Hunter 121, 126,
    142, 161–163, 214, 216, 281
Outing magazine 63
Owen, R.G. 140

Pp

Panama Canal 5, 133–134
Parker, Alton B. 145
Parker, Andrew 98–99
Pasha, Saltin 194
Patterson, Colonel John Henry 167
Pease, Sir Alfred 179, 183
Pershing, General John J. 217
Petty, Sergeant 100
Pinchot, Gifford 2, 149, 198
Platt National Park 150
Platt, Thomas 105
Porcellian Club 30
Price, Frank Julian 131
Proctor, Alexander Phimister 192, 214
Progressive National Convention iii
Progressive Party 198
Progressivism 145–146, 198
Protective War Claims Association 10
Puck magazine 157, 159
Pulitzer, Joseph 127
Pure Food and Drug Act 146

Rr

ranch brands 60
Ranch Life and the Hunting Trail 41, 52, 54, 64, 66,
    72, 75, 81, 216
Rattenbury, Richard 56
Reid, Mayne 13, 15
Remington firearms 131, 270
Remington, Frederic 37, 64, 72, 75, 109, 119, 171, 214
Rice, Cecil Arthur Spring 93
Rigby rifles 174, 176, 184
River of Doubt 199, 205, 207, 210, 284
Roberts, Charles G.D. 143
Rocky Mountains 71, 82, 92, 194, 282
Rondon, Colonel Candido 207, 211
Roosevelt, Alice Hathaway Lee (first wife) 35
    death of xiii, 42
Roosevelt, Alice Lee (daughter) 84, 89
Roosevelt, Archibald (son) xi, 86, 89–90, 205, 214, 217
Roosevelt, Corinne (sister) 10, 20, 24, 29–30, 33, 112,
    283
Roosevelt, Cornelius Van Schaack
    (grandfather) 9–10
Roosevelt (Cowles), Anna (sister) 10, 20, 23– 24, 32,
    43–44, 49–50, 213, 283
Roosevelt, Edith Kermit Carow (second wife) 21, 24,
    77, 84, 92, 132–133, 168, 171, 283, 284
    Colt deringer pistol of 132
Roosevelt, Elliott (brother) 10, 15, 23–24, 30–33, 42,
    81, 84, 214, 283, 285
Roosevelt, Ethel (daughter) 86, 89, 194
Roosevelt IV, Theodore 270
Roosevelt, James (great-grandfather) 9
Roosevelt, Kermit (son) ix, x, 5, 57, 77, 86,–91, 133,
    137, 140, 157, 164, 166–195 *passim*, 199–200, 207– 211,
    217, 219, 223–224, 231–234, 269–271, 283–284, 286
Roosevelt, Martha Bulloch (mother) 11
    death of xiii, 42
Roosevelt, Nicholas 89, 205
Roosevelt, Quentin (son) 86, 89–90, 205, 208, 217, 219
Roosevelt, Robert Barnwell (uncle) 9, 13, 17, 30, 84
Roosevelt, Sr., Theodore (father) 10–11, 20
Roosevelt, Theodore
    adult health problems 199, 210, 219
    African diary 184–185
    African hunting trip viii–ix, 90, 103, 140–142, 167–
        195, 223–255
    assassination attempt 199
    Assistant Secretary of the Navy 105–107
    asthmatic condition 9–10, 28, 37
    Badlands hunting trip 37–49 *passim*, 52, 59, 95
    bear hunting controversy 101
    Bighorn Expedition 49–55
    bird reservations, creating 150
    birth 10
    books by 35, 39–41, 47, 47–48, 52–53, 71, 77, 81, 87–
        88, 92–96, 128, 161–163, 174–180, 194
    Bronx Zoo 85
    buffalo, near destruction 154
    bullet performance, ballistics 97–99

campaign buttons 122, 206
capturing boat thieves 58–59, 66–68
cartoons of 86, 126–127, 129, 135, 152–153, 158, 169,
    170, 220, 280
charged by game 92, 180–192 *passim*, 211, 287
childhood hunting trips 15, 19–21
Civil Service Commissioner 86, 91–94
college hunting trips 25–26, 28–30, 33
Colorado bear and bobcat hunt 158–162
Colorado lion hunt 121–123
conservation activities 81–85, 136, 145–165 *passim*
dangerous game 191
death of 196, 219
death of wife and mother 42
debt to the West 76
double rifles 95–99
drag-hunting 163
early political career 35–37, 42
end of ranching career 77
expertise in firearms 96–99, 140–142
fair chase 29, 81–83, 150
family life x, 86–89
first marriage 35
forest reserves, creating 150
game reserves, creating 150
Governor of New York 118–120
greatness 77
gun collection 33, 44–48, 56, 87, 96–98, 129
handloading cartridges 98
harvesting of game 150–151
health, robust 75
in college 23–24, 26
interest in guns xi, 7, 9
interest in natural history 12, 13, 18, 19, 23, 29, 168
interest in wildlife conservation 29, 209
Inventory of shipment of arms, ammunition, etc., to
    Africa 251–255
Kaiser Wilhem II, presentation pistols 200–202
last hunt 211–213
last hunt, as President 165
library, big game hunting 214
Maine hunting 25, 28
manhood, qualities of 151
marksmanship 154, 187, 217
memorial, American Museum of Natural History 219
Midwest hunting 30
military preparedness 217–219
Mississippi bear hunt 127–128, 149, 220
National Bison Range, creation of 150
National Parks, creation of 150
"nature fakers" 2, 101–103, 143
naval gunnery 128
naval guns and marksmanship 107
Oklahoma wolf (coyote) hunt 157–163
on outdoor life 76–77, 95, 150–154
open sights 176
peep sight 176
pistols, carried as President 130, 134
Police Commissioner of New York 99, 105, 107
poor eyesight 17–18, 20, 26

presentation arms from River of Doubt expedition 211
Presentation arms from TR and wife 133
President of U.S. 52, 123, 125–165 *passim*
ranching ventures 41–42, 44, 71, 77
ranchman's life 54–56
return to politics in 1912 198–199
revolver selection for NYC Police 100
rifles for big game 96–98
rifle sights, preferences 130, 140, 142, 237
rifle training, national level 156–157
Rough Rider 104, 108–118, 135
second wife 21, 24, 77, 84, 92–93, 133, 168, 171, 283
self defense 130–131, 154–157
souvenirs 213
spurs 54, 57
Texas peccary hunt 93–95
"the great day of my life." 112
"the man behind the gun" 99
"the most beautiful gun I have ever seen" 179
"true sportsman" 151
Vice President 118–121
Walter Winans, gift of book xii
West Divide Creek Ranch house 148
Winchester Repeating Arms Co., relations with 47, 80, 129, 186, 193, 223–255 *passim*, 285
Yellowstone Park tours 3, 92, 134–140
Yosemite National Park tours 124, 134–135
Roosevelt, Tweed 277
Roosevelt, West 17, 84, 91
Root, Elihu 163, 291
Rough Riders 105, 109–119 *passim*, 158, 214, 216, 277–278, 281
Ruger, William B. 217
Rungius, Carl 214
Russell & Co., Green River Works 164
Russo-Japanese War 146, 278

Ss

Sagamore Hill 14, 18, 32–37, 39, 48, 57, 64, 80, 84–93, 111, 119, 123, 133, 140, 147, 157, 171, 199, 202, 213–217, 228–229, 283
   Gun Room 87, 214
   North Room 214
Sagamore Hill Medal 90–91, 283
Sandham, Henry 97, 214
San Francisco banquet, menu 141
San Juan Hill 88, 105, 109, 112–113, 277–279
Scharfenberg, Ambrose 155
Schuyler, Hartley and Graham 26
Scott, Sir Walter 15
Scribner's magazine 173, 179, 186
Selous, Frederick C. 122, 168, 173
Seton, Ernest T. 143
Sewall, William W. 25
Sharps rifles 7, 24, 26, 28, 33, 37, 39, 49–52, 80, 88, 98, 129–130, 133, 141
Sigg, Jacob 207
Simpson, John 70

Slatter, Captain Arthur 183
Smithsonian Institution 54, 123, 168, 173, 194, 213
Smith & Wesson revolvers 5, 111, 131, 134, 141
Soldiers Employment Bureau 10
South America 5, 90, 134, 173, 205–208, 284
Spanish-American War 111–115, 133, 277
Springfield rifles
   Model 1903 140–141, 244, 253
     Sporter 88, 137, 140, 161, 174, 183–184, 192, 239, 270
Square Deal 126
S.S. Hamburg 179, 223, 246, 251
S.S. Vandyct 207
Stanley, Ray 275
Steiff toys 128
Stevens, S.P. 56
Stewart, Philip B. 121, 123, 128, 161–162
Stickney, Dr. Victor Hugo 70
Stimson, H.L. 96
Stone, Melville E. 171
Strong, William 99
Sully Hill National Park 150
Superior Fishing 13

Tt

Taft, William Howard 142, 159, 179, 197
Tarlton, Leslie 173
taxidermy 18, 213
Teddy Bear 127–129
The Field 52
The Happy Hunting-Grounds 88
The Naval War of 1812 35, 128
Theodore Roosevelt National Park 56, 283
The Rough Riders 113, 216
The Union 36
The Wilderness Hunter 52, 88, 93, 94, 95, 97, 111, 163, 216, 281
The Wilderness Warrior 2, 84
The Winning of the West 81, 92, 281
Thomas, Jr., E. 32, 49
Through the Brazilian Wilderness 207, 216, 281
Tiffany & Co. iv, xvi, 56, 63, 217
   compass for Africa 172
   hunting knife xvi
Tourilli Club 211–212
Trail and Campfire 92, 103, 214, 216, 281
Trevelyan, Sir George Otto 168
trophies, big game
   at Sagamore Hill 213–214
   at the Smithsonian Institution 213
   in White House 126, 158
Trude, A.L. 101
Tweed Ring 13

Uu

Ulrich, John 48
Union League Club 10, 13
United Mine Workers 127
U.S. battleship *Maine* 107

U.S. Bureau of Corporations 126
U.S. Department of Agriculture 149
U.S. Department of Commerce and Labor 126
U.S. Department of Interior 149
U.S. Forest Service 149, 296
U.S. National Museum 168

Vv

Van Dyke, Mr. Theodore 96
van Roosevelt, Klaes Martensen 9

Ww

Walcott, Dr. Charles Doolittle 168
Washburn, John 133
Washington Evening Star 128, 129
Webley rifle 39, 49, 133, 141
Westbrook, Justice T.R. 35
Western Cartridge Company 137
White, Alvin A. 217
White, John Jay 174, 176
Whitney, Caspar 216
Wilhelm II, Kaiser 199–200
Willis, Jack 71–72, 100
Wilson, Woodrow 198
Winans, Walter xiii, 192
Winchester Repeating Arms Co., advertising and TR 193, 244
Winchester rifles
   Model 1873 46, 47, 69, 133, 141
   Model 1876 iv, 46–51, 56–57, 61–65, 68–70, 73, 80, 88, 103, 133, 141, 217, 243
   Model 1886 80
   Model 1894 88, 119, 121, 129, 133, 149, 214, 234, 244
   Model 1895 110–111, 116, 141, 157, 174, 183–184, 191, 193, 225, 228–247 *passim*, 253, 269–270
Winchester-The Gun That Won the West 193, 285
Wind Cave National Park 150
Wister, Owen 37, 84
Wood, Colonel Leonard 108, 112, 116, 157
Woody, Tazewell 102
World's Columbian Exposition xiii
World War I 90, 200, 213, 216–217
W.W. Greener 12

Yy

Yale University 131, 209, 285
Yellowstone Park 2, 3, 83, 92, 134, 139
Yosemite National Park 2, 125, 134, 136, 139
Young, Eugene and Oscar 111

Zz

Zahm, Father John 205

Endnotes – Cradle of Conservation (Page 257)

1 The ethics of sportsmanship and a code of conduct which provides an understanding of the earliest philosophical foundations underlying the conservation movement dating back to Izzak Walton's *The Compleat Angler* (1653) are best described by John F. Reiger in *American Sportsmen and the Origins of Conservation* (Corvallis: Oregon State University Press, 3rd edition, 2001), 42-50, 73-87.

2 Lewis L. Mumford, *The Brown Decades: A Study of the Arts in America*, 1865-1895 (Mineola, NY: Dover Publications, 1971), 78; Stephen C. Trombulak, ed., *So Great a Vision: The Conservation Writings of George Perkins Marsh* (Hanover, NH: University Press of New England, 2001).

3 President William McKinley refused to establish any forest reserves. Richard C. Davis, *Encyclopedia of American Forest and Conservation History* (New York: Macmillian Publishing Company, 1983), 246, 871.

4 Lord Bryce was formerly the Right Honorable James Bryce, O.M., British Ambassador to the United States from 1907 to 1913. James Bryce, "National Parks – The Need of the Future," *Outlook*, Vol. CII, December 14, 1912, 811-813. See also Wallace Stegner, "The Best Idea We Ever Had," in Page Stegner, ed., *Marking the Sparrow's Fall: The Making of the American West* (New York: Henry Holt and Company, 1998), 131, 137-142.

5 Wallace Stegner, *Where the Bluebird Sings to the Lemonade Springs: Living and Writing in the West* (New York: Random House, Inc., 1992), 117, 124-125.

6 Theodore Roosevelt's primary vehicle to implement the conservation movement was the brain trust of people he organized within the Boone and Crockett Club. They were his foot soldiers and lieutenants in creating and carrying out the implementation strategy of Congressional legislation, agencies, and departments, mobilizing public opinion, etc. One of Roosevelt's most stalwart colleagues was George Bird Grinnell, who said: "Roosevelt's services to science and conservation were many, but perhaps no single thing that he did for conservation had so far-reaching an effect as the establishment of the Boone and Crockett Club." *The Works of Theodore Roosevelt*, Memorial Edition, Vol. 1 (New York: Charles Scribner's Sons, 1923), xix; see also Paul Russell Cutright, *Theodore Roosevelt the Naturalist* (New York: Harper & Brothers, 1956), 68-79; Paul Russell Cutright, "I Must Have a B&C Dinner," in *Theodore Roosevelt: The Making of a Conservationist* (Urbana: University of Illinois Press, 1985), 167-187; Reiger, 146-174.

7 During Theodore Roosevelt's Presidency he established and set aside 151 million acres of forest reserves (as he created 150 national forests); four federal game preserves and fifty-one federal bird reservations in nineteen states and three territories, which today are known collectively as the National Wildlife Refuge System; five national parks; eighteen national monuments; and twenty-four federal reclamation (irrigation) projects in fourteen states. Roosevelt also established the U.S. Forest Service and convened four national conservation conferences. Roosevelt's total legacy was 230 million acres of lands protected in his 7½ years as President, or 84,000 acres for every day he was President, which covers approximately 12% of the contiguous forty-eight United States, or 10% of the fifty United States. John A. Gable, "President Theodore Roosevelt's Record on Conservation," *Theodore Roosevelt Association Journal*, Vol. 10, No. 3 (1984), 2-11; Tweed Roosevelt, "Theodore Roosevelt: The Mystery of the Unrecorded Environmentalist," *Theodore Roosevelt Association Journal*, Vol. 25, No. 2 (2002), 3-9.

8 Theodore Roosevelt, *The Winning of the West*, 4 volumes (New York: Putnam's, 1889-1896); Frederick Jackson Turner, "The Significance of the Frontier in American History," a paper delivered at the meeting of the American Historical Association in Chicago, Illinois, on July 12, 1893, *Report of the American Historical Association for 1893*, 99-227. See also Turner, *The Frontier in American History* (New York: Henry Holt and Company, 1921).

9 Char Miller, "Landmark Decisions: The Antiquities Act, Big-Stick Conservation and the Modern State," *Theodore Roosevelt Association Journal*, Vol. 27, No. 2 (2006), 8. Psychiatrists in their lexicon call the dynamic of holding onto a remnant or a piece of something perceived as lost or gone forever as "personification," i.e., a transference into themselves. In the ethos of loss to both individuals and a nation, the phenomenon of attempting to preserve and perpetuate anything perceived as lost is a normal human dynamic from which can flow dramatic consequences. For example, a remarkable parallel psychological phenomenon of national proportion was experienced in West Germany's gestalt in the 1980s when it was perceived that the treasured, mystical Black Forest, so much a defining part of the Republic's historic culture, was dying from acid rain. Clinical depression and suicide rates dramatically increased, and then returned to their original levels when the forest's decline was reversed and the national perception of imminent loss abated within the decade. "West Germany: Death of a Fairy Tale Forest," *Natural History*, April 1985, Vol. 94, Issue 4, 64.

10 Hal K. Rothman, *Preserving Different Pasts: The American National Monuments* (Urbana: University of Illinois Press, 1989), 15-16; Wallace Stegner, *Where the Bluebird Sings*, 199-200. Part of the national zeal to hold onto the vanishing frontier was expressed in our literature, art, and entertainment before and at the turn of the twentieth century. Ralph Waldo Emerson and Henry David Thoreau were the naturalist writers of the era celebrating "in wilderness is the preservation of the world," followed by novelists Owen Wister, Zane Grey, and much later Louis L'Amour. The nineteenth-century paintings of Carl Bodmer, Thomas Moran, and Albert Bierstadt portrayed the West writ large, idealized, romanticized, the stuff of enduring dreams of the nation. Frederic Remington and Charles Russell and other artists captured the West both on canvas and in bronze, freezing in perpetuity the cowboy astride a bucking horse, the pony express rider at full gallop, and the Indians hunting buffalo. Buffalo Bill Cody's Wild West Show, which toured the United States and Europe from 1883 to 1910, featured live cowboys and Indians, U.S. Army Cavalry, pony express riders, stage coaches and covered wagons, wild buffalo, and longhorn Texas steers depicting the passing of the Western frontier.

11 Page Stegner, ed., *Marking the Sparrow's Fall*, 183.

12 Wallace Stegner, *Where the Bluebird Sings*, 128. Stegner's greatest and most widely published work eloquently detailing the absolute necessity for a contemporary environmental ethic, and providing a "voice" for modern environmentalism reminiscent of biblical authority, is his essay "Coda: Wilderness Letter," in his *The Sound of Mountain Water* (New York: Doubleday & Company, Inc., 1969), 145-153.

13 The current chapter in this continuing dynamic to perpetuate wilderness areas began with the Roadless Area Conservation Rule published in the *Federal Register* on January 12, 2001, just eight days prior to the end of President Clinton's second term of office. This rule fundamentally changed the Forest Service's long-standing approach to the management of roadless areas. The rule established blanket, nationwide restrictions, generally limiting, with some exceptions, timber harvest and road construction and reconstruction within inventoried roadless areas in national forests and on grasslands across the country. This rule superseded earlier regulations through the development of individual land management plans that allowed for changes in the landscape caused by natural occurrences such as catastrophic wildfires. Since 2001, the roadless rule has been the subject of ten federal lawsuits, which continue, and its future implementation is uncertain. In 2005, the Bush administration proposed to replace the Clinton administration's roadless rule by establishing a process allowing governors with inventoried roadless areas within their states to review existing management requirements for their areas and petition the Forest Service to establish and develop state-specific management plans. On November 13, 2006, Governor Bill Owens petitioned on behalf of Colorado—following California, Virginia, North and South Carolina, New Mexico, Utah, and Idaho, which had earlier done the same for their inventoried roadless areas—thus perpetuating the wilderness preservation debate initiated by Aldo Leopold in the 1930s. (The idea of states determining management plans for the future of their roadless and wilderness areas echoes a similar outcry from the Sagebrush Rebellion era of the 1940s, an outcry that became heated in the 1970s and 1980s when a series of environmental laws affected grazing rights in the West.)

14 Perhaps one of the more demonstrable examples of an attempt to embrace the lost frontier of the past is a contemporary movement to recreate a wilderness anew. The American Prairie Foundation has raised $11 million and has assembled some 60,000 acres in central Montana, returned it to native prairie, and released genetically pure wild, free-ranging buffalo, with wolves and grizzly bear to follow. The foundation's intent is to raise $100 million, buy hundreds of thousands more acres, link up with federal lands, and create a reserve of about 3.5 million acres for tourism, bird-watching, and hunting. The foundation characterizes its plan as resurrecting the Serengeti of North America. This idea first surfaced in the 1980s as the buffalo commons of the great plains. Blaine Harden, "In the New West, Do They Want Buffalo to Roam?", *Washington Post*, July 30, 2006, A8-9.

15 Wallace Stegner, *Where the Bluebird Sings*, xv, 34, 68, 102, 131.

16 Letter to the author from Dr. Robert J. Moore, Jr., dated March 8, 2006.

17 Edward J. Renehan, Jr., "Visionary Teddy Roosevelt: Conservation President," *Veranda*, March/April 2006, 117, 237.

18 Cutright, *Theodore Roosevelt the Naturalist*, 38-52, 56-59; Cutright, *Theodore Roosevelt: The Making of a Conservationist*, 149-164. See also the first definitive work on Roosevelt's experiences in the Badlands: Hermann Hagedorn, *Theodore Roosevelt in the Bad Lands* (Boston: Houghton Mifflin Company, 1921).

19 Roosevelt, *Hunting Trips of a Ranchman* (New York: Putnam's, 1885); *Ranch Life and the Hunting Trail* (New York: Putnam's, 1888); *The Wilderness Hunter* (New York: Putnam's, 1893); *Big Game Hunting* (New York: Putnam's, 1899); *Outdoor Pastimes of an American Hunter* (New York: Scribner's, 1905); and *Good Hunting in Pursuit of Big Game in the West* (New York: Harper & Brothers Publishers, 1907).

20 Edmund Morris, *The Rise of Theodore Roosevelt* (New York: Coward, McCann & Geoghegan, Inc., 1979); *Theodore Rex* (New York: Random House, 2001).

21 Letter to the author from Edmund Morris dated March 3, 2006.

22 Letter from Edmund Morris to the National Park Service dated November 4, 1992. See also Morris, *The Rise of Theodore Roosevelt*, 270-295.

23 Anna Roosevelt Cowles, *Letters from Theodore Roosevelt to Anna Roosevelt Cowles 1870-1918* (New York: Charles Scribner's Sons, 1924), 63; Hagedorn, 197. See also Roosevelt, *Outdoor Pastimes of an American Hunter, Works of TR*, Vol. 3, 254-255; Henry Cabot Lodge, ed., *Selections from the Correspondence of Theodore Roosevelt and Henry Cabot Lodge, 1884-1918*, Vol. 1 (New York: Charles Scribner's Sons, 1925), 7.

24 James F. Vivian, *The Romance of My Life: Theodore Roosevelt's Speeches in Dakota* (Fargo, ND: Prairie House, Inc., 1989), ii, 30; Hagedorn, 466.

25 Letter to the author from Dr. Robert J. Moore, Jr., dated March 8, 2006. See also Vivian, 135-136. Prior to his establishment of the Elkhorn Ranch in 1884, TR purchased a controlling interest in the Chimney Butte Ranch, also known as the Maltese Cross for its cattle brand.

26 Roosevelt, *Ranch Life and the Hunting Trail*, Works of TR, Vol. 4, 390; Theodore Roosevelt: *An Autobiography* (1913; reprint, New York: Charles Scribner's Sons, 1926), 96. Here Roosevelt says the nearest neighbor is 10-15 miles distant. See also Roosevelt, *Game-Shooting in the West*, Works of TR, Vol. 1, 306-307.

27 While Roosevelt purchased the established Chimney Butte Ranch in 1883, he actually created the Elkhorn Ranch in 1884. He chose its location, gave it a name and distinctive cattle brand, brought in two Maine woodsmen to build and manage the new ranch, and had a house built based on plans he personally drew up. "It is clear from all that he wrote about his Dakota experiences that he regarded the Elkhorn as his true western home. It was there that he wrote his badlands prose.... It was there that he took Edith in 1890." Clay S. Jenkinson, *Theodore Roosevelt in the Dakota Badlands* (Dickinson, ND: Dickinson State University, 2006), 33-34, 42-43. See also Ray H. Mattison, "Roosevelt's Elkhorn Ranch," *North Dakota Historical Society Quarterly*, Vol. 27, No. 2, Spring 1960, 1-16. It is a common misconception that Roosevelt ever actually owned the Elkhorn Ranch lands. Back when the Badlands were part of the Dakota Territory, while technically one could claim a homestead of 160 acres from public lands, few ranchers did so until after the Dakota Territory was divided into states in 1889. The Badlands provided sparse forage for cattle, necessitating that a herd range far and wide. The opportunistic ranchers had little need to patent 160 acres, when the open lands were free to whomever claimed grazing rights. See Roosevelt, *Ranch Life and the Hunting Trail*, Works of TR, Vol. 4, 364-365; *Hunting Trips of a Ranchman*, Works of TR, Vol. 1, 6, 19. Order was maintained and disputes settled by the local grazing association, and Roosevelt was the organizer and first president of the Little Missouri Grazing Association. First users or "squatters" had first claim rights under the Pre-Emption Act of 1841, enacted to protect preemptive settlers and ranchers operating in frontier territories ahead of government surveyors. Under the 1862 Homestead Act, moreover, to claim 160 acres, one had to be a U.S. citizen of at least twenty-one years of age, file a legal preemptive claim, build a residence, raise crops, be the head of a family household, not maintain legal residence elsewhere, live on the land continuously for five years, and thereafter publish one's affidavit to close on the property. Eric Foner and John A. Garraty, eds., *The Reader's Companion to American History* (Boston: Houghton Mifflin Company, 1991), 509-510, 877-879. http://www.nps.gov/home/homestead_act.html. Roosevelt could qualify for only a few of these conditions. Only 60% of all homestead claims filed actually brought title to the lands, 70% of which occurred between 1900 and 1930. E. Wade Hone, Land and Property Research in the United States (Salt Lake City: Ancestry, Inc., 1997), 140; U.S. Department of the Interior, Bureau of Land Management, Homesteads (Washington: Government Printing Office, 1961), 13-20. What is important when looking at the Elkhorn Ranch and its broad grazing range is not who owned it, but what happened here and the effect it had upon Roosevelt, causing him to forge a conservation philosophy that became a unique part of America's cultural identity.

28 Roosevelt, *Outdoor Pastimes of an American Hunter*, Works of TR, Vol. 3, 254-255; *Hunting Trips of a Ranchman*, Works of TR, Vol. 1, 12; Theodore Roosevelt: *An Autobiography*, 96-97.

29 H.R. 5386, Section 428(a)-(e), 109th Congress (2006). See http://www.fs.fed.us/land/staff/LWCF/index.html.

30 Letters from Edmund Morris to the National Park Service dated July 4, 1990, and to the author dated March 3, 2006. Today there are seven active oil and gas rigs dotting the landscape on the 5,200 acre Eberts ranch (and fifteen abandoned wells), none visible from TR's Elkhorn cabin site. One day, when their supply is exhausted, the rigs will be removed, and the "visual" silence TR knew will be enjoyed in perpetuity by America's "unborn generations in the womb of time."

31 Bruce Kaye, Chief of Interpretation, Theodore Roosevelt National Park, Medora, ND, as quoted in Clay Jenkinson, "The Heart Leaps Best in the Beautiful Badlands," in *Bismarck Tribune*, February 19, 2006.

32 The desire to place the central portion of the Elkhorn ranch into public ownership started with the creation of what is today Theodore Roosevelt National Park in 1934. Repeated attempts to purchase the Eberts' portion of TR's original Elkhorn failed over the succeeding decades. In 2002-2003, the National Park Service attempted to purchase the ranch but met defeat by local political opposition. In 2004, the State of North Dakota attempted to purchase the Eberts Ranch but was likewise defeated by local opposition. In 2005, the Bush administration asked the Boone and Crockett Club to facilitate the acquisition. Representatives of the Club and the American Wildlife Conservation Partners organized a major campaign, enlisting some fifty national wildlife conservation organizations, the Theodore Roosevelt Association, Roosevelt family members, the Theodore Roosevelt Medora Foundation, prominent state and national citizens, and the five living former governors of North Dakota, who urged state and federal officials to support the acquisition by the federal government, which could then consolidate the ranch into the surrounding Little Missouri National Grasslands reserve managed by the Forest Service. After a vigorous and often contentious 18-month campaign, the entire property was placed under contract by the Rocky Mountain Elk Foundation, which then facilitated the legal acquisition by the U.S. Forest Service in two separate phases in 2006 and 2007. The critical viewshed will be managed jointly by the Forest Service and the National Park Service.

33 The protection, preservation, and enhancement of geographic places of historical, archeological, and/or cultural heritage and significance and of scenic vistas of merit, and the maintenance of rural and agricultural landscapes in expanding urban fringe areas, wilderness, wild and scenic rivers, watersheds, fragile coastal ecosystems, estuaries, and marshes, are part of America's traditional historic preservation legacy. The tools used to facilitate preservation efforts have included local zoning and land use regulations and ordinances, overlay zones on master plans, the public purchase of development rights and approval of transferable development rights, public and private partnerships and coalitions of multiple stakeholders, and a variety of public funding mechanisms, such as the Federal Land and Water Conservation Fund Act of 1964. In the last forty years, the 1964 act has been used to purchase over seven million acres with $9 billion in LWCF appropriations derived primarily from offshore oil and gas revenues. Every state in the union enjoys a multitude of such legacy projects. Some of America's more notable preservation projects have included the scenic Hudson River valley landscape in New York during the early part of the twentieth century and the Connecticut River valley in three states. Henry David Thoreau's iconic Walden Pond and surrounding viewshed was protected by the State of Massachusetts and local citizens. The viewshed of George Washington's Mount Vernon estate provides an interesting parallel to the Elkhorn. The entire viewshed across the Potomac River that George Washington enjoyed in the eighteenth century has been protected in perpetuity by the Mount Vernon Ladies Association, the State of Maryland, and The Conservation Fund, and the adjacent Virginia property by the National Park Service in cooperation with the Trust for Public Lands. The same holds true for Thomas Jefferson's Monticello, where 2,000 adjacent acres have been protected jointly by the Thomas Jefferson Foundation and the Trust for Public Lands. The Columbia River Gorge viewshed covers 16,000 acres. Lake Katahdin protects the viewshed from the top of Mt. Katahdin, the northern terminus of the Appalachian Trail. Our Revolutionary and Civil War battlefields enjoy a particular distinction in America's preservation heritage. Valley Forge, Gettysburg, Antietam, Manassas, Appomattox, Shiloh, Yorktown, and other sites are protected as National Parks, and many battlefields are protected as state parks or are owned by local or private non-profit organizations. Three notable "urban" viewsheds protected for over 200 years are Boston's Commons, New York's Central Park, and the Mall in Washington, D.C.

About the Boone and Crockett Club

Founded by Theodore Roosevelt in 1887, the Boone and Crockett Club promotes guardianship and visionary management of big game and associated wildlife in North America. The Club maintains the highest standards of fair-chase sportsmanship and habitat stewardship, and is the universally recognized keeper of the records of native North American big game. Member accomplishments include protecting Yellowstone and establishing Glacier and Denali national parks, founding the U.S. Forest Service, National Park Service and National Wildlife Refuge System, fostering the Pittman-Robertson and Lacey Acts, creating the Federal Duck Stamp program, and developing the cornerstones of modern game laws. The Boone and Crockett Club is headquartered in Missoula, Montana.
For more information about the Club visit www.booneandcrockettclub.com.

A Note About the Type

The text of this book was set in Baskerville, which is a transitional serif typeface designed in 1757 by John Baskerville (1706-1775) in Birmingham, England. Baskerville is classified as a transitional typeface, positioned between the old style typefaces of William Caslon, and the modern styles of Giambattista Bodoni and Firmin Didot. The refined feeling of Baskerville makes it an excellent choice to convey dignity and tradition, which is why it was chosen for this tome on Theodore Roosevelt.

The Baskerville typeface is the result of John Baskerville's intent to improve upon the types of William Caslon. He increased the contrast between thick and thin strokes, making the serifs sharper and more tapered, and shifted the axis of rounded letters to a more vertical position. The curved strokes are more circular in shape, and the characters became more regular. These changes created a greater consistency in size and form.

Baskerville's typeface was the culmination of a larger series of experiments to improve legibility, which also included papermaking and ink manufacturing. The result was a typeface that reflected Baskerville's ideals of perfection, where he chose simplicity and quiet refinement. His background as a writing master is evident in the distinctive swash tail on the uppercase Q and in the cursive serifs in the Baskerville Italic. In 1757, Baskerville published his first work, a collection of Virgil, which was followed by some fifty other classics. In 1758, he was appointed printer to the Cambridge University Press. It was there in 1763 he published his masterwork, a folio Bible, which was printed using his own typeface, ink, and paper.

After falling out of use with the onset of the modern typefaces such as Bodoni, Baskerville was revived in 1917 by Bruce Rogers, for the Harvard University Press and released by Deberny & Peignot. In 1923, the typeface was also revived in England by Stanley Morison for the British Monotype Company as part of its program of revivals. Most recently, the Baskerville typeface was used as the basis for the Mrs Eaves typeface in 1996, designed by Zuzana Licko.

Colophon

This edition of *Theodore Roosevelt Hunter-Conservationist* was printed and bound by Friesens in Altona, Manitoba, Canada. The book was designed by Julie T. Houk, Director of Publications for the Boone and Crockett Club headquartered in Missoula, Montana. Boone and Crockett Club president Lowell E. Baier, B&C vice president of communications Marc C. Mondavi, publications committee chairman Dr. Howard P. Monsour, Jr., and chief of staff Tony A. Schoonen provided oversight and direction for the project. Other Club staff intimately involved with this product included office manager Sandy Poston (OCR specialist) and assistant designer Karlie Slayer.